CONTENTS

WILD CHILD

WILD CHILD

———◆◆◆———

Life with Jim Morrison

Linda Ashcroft

Thunder's Mouth Press
New York

Published in the United States by

Thunder's Mouth Press
841 Broadway, Fourth Floor
New York, NY 10003

First published in Great Britain in 1997
by Hodder and Stoughton
A division of Hodder Headline PLC
338 Euston Road
London NW1 3BH

Library of Congress Cataloging–in–Publication Data

Ashcroft, Linda
Wild child : life with Jim Morrison / by Linda Ashcroft.
p.   cm.
Originally published : London : Hodder and Stoughton, 1997.
Includes index.
ISBN 1-56025-249-9
1. Morrison, Jim, 1943-1971. 2. Singers—United States—Biography.
I. Title.
ML420.M62A9 2000
782.42166'092—dc21
[B]   99-42132
CIP

Typeset by Palimpsest Book Production Limited,
Polmont, Stirlingshire

Distributed by Publishers Group West

Manufactured in the United States of America

For Jim,
My well of firsts

WILD CHILD

PART I: *1967*

1

A *Spy* in the House of Love

Music was my heartbeat the summer of '67. Midsummer, I had attended a music festival on Mt. Tamalpais, just north of San Francisco. The music had seeped into me. For the first time music wasn't something I only listened to, but carried within me.

Like most teenagers in the Central Valley of California, I plotted to escape home and the heat. That morning, I wangled an invitation and permission to go swimming with older friends from school. Going swimming meant heading for the big irrigation ditches that bordered Stockton. There was some dodging involved. The farmers who owned the land thought of us as trespassers. We considered use of the ditches compensation for the fine black peat dirt that rose from the asparagus beds and settled on everything else in our lives.

We piled into an old black Ford, gleaming with an excess of chrome, and streaked out the two-lane road that left houses and traffic behind. Big Brother, the Jefferson Airplane and The Doors screamed at us from the radio, and everyone in the car but me screamed back. I sat in the corner of the back seat, my feet up, my hair knotting in the wind, and said to myself, 'Yes, yes, yes.'

Cropland fanned out to the horizon. And we were the centre of the wheel. At the big ditch, we risked the car battery for the radio, stripped to our underwear, and jumped in. None of us had much skill or grace, but our enthusiasm was unlimited. Though I hung back by the landing, not having much trust of water, I felt so cool and free that the house I dreaded returning to seemed a thousand miles away.

The reprieve was never long enough. While the others struggled to pull on their jeans over their wet underthings, I dawdled as long as I dared. The drive back seemed too short. I closed the car door quietly and shoved my espadrilles into my Greek tote for the walk up the driveway. I opened the front door with the practised silence of a cat burglar. With luck, I could be in my room for hours before anyone noticed.

My father met me in the hall. I didn't need to see his face to know I was in trouble. Since I was small, I had been the barometer of my father's moods. I knew, not from a slammed door or raised voice, but by the very atmosphere, the intensity of the approaching storm. He was like an act of nature. It was as futile to reason with him as a summer squall. A second's warning came as the space above his upper lip flashed white like heat lightning.

It was the summer to run. I didn't look back until I reached the two-lane road I'd sped along a few minutes before. I walked in the opposite direction towards my best friend's house. The gravel on the shoulder crunched behind me. I stepped aside for a VW bus.

'Want a lift?' A young woman leaned out the window. I shook my head. 'We're going to San Francisco to see the Dead.'

I vacillated, but when she opened the back door, I climbed in and nested among the jumble of backpacks and sleeping bags. Putting some space between my father and me, without dragging my friend into the mess, appealed to me. And, well, offer me music . . .

'Where are they playing?' I asked.

'I don't know . . . somewhere.' Her hand swept the air.

Yeah. That was why we loved the Dead. They were our distant cousins who had made good. We experienced a sense of camaraderie with them. If the Grateful Dead were in the City, odds were they were playing somewhere. They loved music so much they couldn't help themselves. And we appreciated that.

We scored a parking space walking distance from the corner

4

of Haight and Ashbury where they, and half the Bay Area, were going to meet their friends. We strolled along a side-street, in and out of headshops, stopped to listen to street musicians. Distracted for a few minutes by a tray of silver rings, I was startled by the women's disappearance from my side. I squinted to try to separate the colour that was my temporary companions from the colourful mosaic of street. I'd lost them.

I wandered on my own. Although I thought of myself as biding time, I jotted down the number of a runaway hotline. In sharp focus close-up, the street was frightening. I nearly tripped over a young couple sharing a needle in a stairwell. Men pushed too close to me, saying, 'Hey, baby!' and clucking suggestively. 'Hey, baby!'

My head heavy, buzzing, I zigzagged away from the Haight and deeper into the city. I had as a hazy destination the area near the Art Institute, off Columbus, in the Italian section. It was a harder walk than I remembered. In the late afternoon, the sun had sunk behind the buildings and the sidewalks were in shadow. The temperature had dropped a few degrees, but the buildings radiated heat as if they were breathing on me. I pushed open a dark green door to escape their breath. Within stretched a café, long and narrow, wrapped in black and white tiles.

'Want something?' The sharp voice came from a stout, swarthy man behind the counter. He wore a spotless white apron tied high, European style.

'Tea, please.' I ignored his sneer.

He threw a tea-bag into a metal pot, splashed hot water into it, then slammed it on to the counter. The pot was rapidly followed by a cup and saucer which spun across the countertop and settled precariously close to the edge.

'Nice acoustics,' I smiled as the clatter echoed against the tiles of the room, empty but for us. He wasn't amused.

I dropped into the corner-most chair at a back table. Just sitting felt so good, I thought I might have a constructive thought at any moment. From my tote, I dragged the red bound sketchbook that served as my confessional, my Dutch uncle, and my place to write. I had filled half a bookshelf with these serious, self-conscious diaries since discovering Anaïs Nin's published diary the year before. This was the raw material from which novels sprang. Of course, she had been traipsing about Paris with Henry Miller in tow, and I was too tired to traipse anywhere even if I had someone to traipse with.

My pencil was poised above the blank newsprint, my head a little foggy about how to begin to describe the day, when the door slammed. I discreetly lifted my eyes towards the commotion. A handsome young man with dark windblown curls and a day's growth of beard was exchanging four-letter words with the brusque counterman. A dramatic gesture threw him off balance and landed him in the first chair in dishevelled elegance. He was drunk.

So not to meet his eyes, I dove back into my book. This was an effective trick. Writing in public made me invisible. I heard him approach, alternately hitting the counter and the tables lined up against the opposite wall. Were lined up. I imagined them randomly rearranged. The man leaned heavily on the chair next to mine. So much for being invisible. Not my day.

'Got any spare change?' he asked, each word soft and deliberate.

Setting my sketchbook aside, I searched the bottom of my tote. I produced eighty-five cents I couldn't spare. He held out his hand. His delicately shaped fingers ended in the ragged and dirty fingernails of a little boy. I dropped the change into his open palm. He closed his hand around mine. I pulled my hand back and his grip tightened. I looked up, caught in his slightly unfocused, overcast ocean-coloured eyes. Achieving the desired result, he released my hand.

'Thanks.' A grin, as slow as his speech, brightened his face. As he walked away, though he was unsteady side to side, he seemed to glide. I could hear his boots on the floor, but still craned to have a clear view of them.

My pencil scurried across the fresh page. Writing about the beautiful drunk was easier than facing the day's earlier events. I was so absorbed, I wasn't aware of his return until he placed his cup and saucer next to my hand. He had managed to get most of the coffee to the table, even if a lot of it was in the saucer. Settling into the adjacent chair, he made a show of pouring the spilled coffee from saucer to cup with great accuracy. We exchanged smiles at his success. Without warning, his hand darted towards my face. I automatically flinched and blocked him with my left.

'Great reflexes.' He let his hand hang there, inches from my face.

'Coulda been a contender,' I offered my best Brando, which wasn't very good.

He smiled and, revealing the innocence of his open hand, ran his fingers through my hair. 'It's as silky as it looks.'

I laughed at his charming *non sequitur*.

'Whatcha writing?' He grabbed my diary.

'Please!' I said with what I hoped sounded more like firmness than panic. He held it easily out of my reach, a big brother playing keep-away. I had more control than to jump for it, though I considered begging, 'Please.'

He held it open to where I had just been writing. 'If this is a sobriety test, I'm flunking,' he said, holding the book closer to his face. 'Your handwriting is beautiful, but, hell, you write small.'

'It keeps people from reading over my shoulder.'

He laughed. It was a ridiculous laugh punctuated with hees and snorts. If it were possible to die from embarrassment, I was on the verge with his reading about his drunken self, yet he had me laughing at his laugh. He finished the page and smiled. He met my eyes without hesitation. I might live. I put out my hand. 'Please.'

It still didn't work. He turned to the front and read at a leisurely pace. Without looking up, he reached into his coat pocket and extracted a small blue spiral notebook.

'Here,' he offered lightly. 'You can read mine.'

A man who kept a diary? I opened it. On the first page, in large round letters, was written, 'Jim Morrison'. Oh. I peered at him. Yes. He looked different from the photograph on his album cover. The hair was darker. The eyes brighter. Written in this little notebook, not a diary in the sense mine was, were what seemed more like poems than songs. Not that his songs were structured like other songs, but they did rhyme somewhere, and these did not. Some pages were given to single lines. A note. A thought. There were angular doodles in the margins. I thrilled at this glimpse of his raw words. His writing did not flow faultlessly. He had great bursts, but also allowed himself to reconsider. There were a few completed poems; whole pages with only a word or two crossed out. I strained to read beneath the heavy scratches. In each case, he had found the better word.

Jim closed my diary quietly and handed it to me with care. 'Keep writing.'

I hadn't expected a comment, let alone something I was anxious to claim as a compliment. I could have happily gone to teenage heaven. I laughed. I was prepared to die of embarrassment because he was reading my ramblings and then heaven looked good. What was this sudden preoccupation with my own demise? Laughing was not the expected response to his encouragement. I made an attempt to explain, and added, 'Thank you . . . and for letting me read your poems.'

'What did you think?' he asked.

I hesitated. In the silence that followed, I felt as if I were scooting along the narrowest part of the narrowest limb of a tree hanging over quicksand, and me, fifteen pounds overweight. He, in contrast, seemed comfortable with the silence.

I sighed. 'Your imagery is slightly askew.' Was this what he had asked? 'You put words together you don't usually see together so they have their own meaning.'

As he reached over, I made a concerted effort not to cringe. He lifted my chin gently. Affecting a subtle Southern accent, he said, 'Smile when you say that.'

I obliged.

'Are you from Virginia?'

I recognized the slaughtered quote from the classic Western, *The Virginian*. My speech was littered with quotes from books and movies, and it delighted me his was as well.

'Been there.' He smiled slowly.

'I was trying to say I liked your poetry.'

'Liking or not liking art is irrelevant.' He grew serious. 'You read it, not just looked at it.' He cocked an eyebrow and asked, 'Could I make a comment about your writing?'

'Sure.' I took in a slow, quiet breath to steel myself. I hated criticism.

'Be bolder. You can be shy in your life, but not in your work. You are at your best when you're barrelling through. I realize this is just your journal, but it's a good place to practise,' he smiled, 'when no one is looking over your shoulder.'

I let out my breath. 'Thanks.' Journal sounded good. He was right. I was too timid. I made a mental note: 'Barrel.' Encouragement and advice well worth eighty-five cents.

'I'm Jim, by the way. And you are?'

'Ginger,' I presented my hand and the childhood nickname I had intended to leave behind before my sophomore year began that fall.

'Ginger Baker? Ginger Rogers?' he prompted.

'You're on the wrong track. You're thinking rhythm, which doesn't apply to me. As a kid, I took the name, with great sincerity, in tribute to the tragic red horse in *Black Beauty*,' I laughed. 'That was more confession than necessary.' I stared into my cup of tea. 'Do they put truth serum in this stuff?'

'In San Francisco, it's more likely laced with acid.'

'Does acid make you tell the truth? I've never done . . .'

'Much of anything.' Jim finished my sentence matter-of-factly, and more accurately than I had intended. He smiled. 'Acid can make a meeting . . .'

'Seem more like a reunion.' My turn to finish his sentence.

'If you ever do want to drop acid, give me a call.' He ripped a sheet from his notebook and borrowed my pencil to write a number with a Los Angeles area code. 'Together, we might make the universe explode.'

'Maybe just a little star gone nova,' I suggested.

Jim smiled. 'You're gentler than I am.'

He was in no hurry. The Doors must not have been scheduled to play that night. Or they were playing as a trio. Jim got a refill. He settled in to talk about books, movies, art. His voice was low and soothing. I wished the café would stay open all night so that I could sit there listening to the slow cadence of his words.

'Where are you?'

The rise in his voice startled me. Where had I been? I had been looking at the narrow room reminiscent of a Van Gogh painting, and had mentally slipped away into it.

'Arles,' I told him, where Van Gogh had painted.

Jim laughed. 'Should have seen the family resemblance. That

9

hair! His eyes are blue, though. Yours are, what? Green and gold. Like a cornfield. Did he paint those fields for you? You never really know an artist's personal view. I didn't realize Vincent had a sister. All he talks of is Theo, Theo, Theo.'

So, he had read Van Gogh's letters to his brother Theo. I had never had anyone slip away with me like that.

Suddenly, Jim changed from his thoughtful, quiet self, to play the bigger and garrulous Gauguin. 'I think, sometimes,' he continued in character, 'I belittle your brother's work because his honesty scares me. My painting is dull by comparison.'

'Not dull,' I said to Jim's Gauguin, 'more cautious. Vincent throws himself at the canvas and you stand at the end of your brush.' The reverse, I thought, was true of Jim and me, as we talked as our other selves. We strolled the streets of the little town in the South of France that I had only read about in books.

'I lock the door in twenty minutes.' The counterman broke the spell.

We left Arles and returned to San Francisco. Jim was easily Jim again. He turned flirtatious. 'How many men are you?' I mused, unsure of how to handle this one, who pressed closer, unsettling me. He leaned over and kissed my lips lightly, parting them with his tongue. A slow and searching kiss. My first. I was glad for the chair beneath me. He sighed. We sat a few minutes. He took a bill out of his pocket and stuck it into my tote. I wondered why he had borrowed change when he had money. He certainly had better means of introducing himself.

'I owe you fifteen cents,' I said to say something.

He shrugged. 'Let it ride.'

I watched his sobered walk across the room. When he reached the door, he paused, but did not turn. Instead, he raised his right hand, knowing I would be watching. The counterman reluctantly collected the dishes. I, in mirrored reluctance, gathered my things. I grabbed the loose bill Jim had given me to put into my wallet. I stared at Ben Franklin. Ben graced hundred-dollar bills!

When I looked out the door, I saw Jim had reached the downhill corner. 'Excuse me,' I said as loudly as I could without yelling. He didn't hear me. I ran half the block. 'Excuse me,' I repeated.

Jim turned gracefully on his right boot heel. He flashed his wicked grin. 'Wanna fuck?'

'No, thank you,' I stammered. I felt reticent about closing the distance between us. He motioned for me to approach. I stiffened, but ran to him.

'You've made a mistake,' I said, blushing and breathless, waving the hundred-dollar bill. My ruffled state amused him. He laughed so hard he couldn't hear me. 'You've made a mistake.'

'Again?' he teased. 'Shit, I'm always screwing up.'

'This,' I held the bill in his line of vision, 'is a hundred-dollar bill.'

He looked. 'Is Abraham-Fucking-Lincoln your hero?'

'One of them,' I said under my breath.

Jim heard me and chuckled. 'Honey, I was never that drunk. I wanted you to have it.'

I was stunned. 'I can't take it. It's real nice of you, but I can't take it.' My mother's daughter does not take candy, even from fascinating strangers. I tucked it into the coat pocket that held his notebook to show I wasn't being coy.

'Do you have a place to stay?'

'Yeah, thanks,' I lied, 'in the Haight.' I charged off, calling over my shoulder, 'I enjoyed our talk.'

'Ah, Ginger.' I stopped, turned. Jim said, 'You're headed in the wrong direction. The Haight is that way.' He pointed in the opposite direction.

I had to walk back by him. 'I never claimed to have an interior compass.'

That grin. He grabbed my hand. 'It's like the wolf offering to watch the lamb while the shepherd takes a leak, but I'm not going to sleep tonight if I don't know you have a roof over your head.'

I laughed at the accuracy of his assessment. At that moment, I wasn't sure if I were more afraid of the street or of him. All that I was sure of was that I wasn't ready to go home. 'I appreciate your concern, Jim,' I liked saying his name for the first time, 'but I'm very self-reliant.'

He pulled me against him. 'God, we are in trouble! Now you're quoting Shirley Temple movies.'

'Nobody ever catches that,' I giggled, trying to imagine Jim even watching a Shirley Temple movie. 'Give me a minute and I'll think of someone over three feet tall to quote.'

'I'd feel more confident if you had stuck with Brando. Come on,' he urged, tugging my hand. I shivered. 'Cold or scared?' he asked.

'Both,' I said, my honesty returned and my teeth chattered.

'Take my jacket . . . I run warm,' he drifted into his Southern drawl. 'And my promise I'll be a Virginian gentleman. We take care of our womenfolk.'

'You keep that up,' I warned him, 'and the Southern voice of my youth will return.' He glanced sideways at me. The leather jacket on my shoulders made me ill at ease. I handed it back to him. 'Thanks. I'd be grateful for a place to sleep tonight.'

He slipped on his jacket, and with equal ease slipped his arm around me. 'My place isn't far. You can borrow some of my warmth.' A wave of excitement rushed through me.

After keeping a brisk pace for several blocks, I thought less about Twain saying the coldest winter he had ever spent was summer in San Francisco. Jim's stride outreached mine. His *not far* was taxing what remained of my reserves. Abruptly, he broke from me and danced into the middle of the street.

'Goldenhair, Goldenhair,' he taunted. Jim looked boyish, lit by the streetlight, his dark hair blown into his pale face. He owned the street. A car would not dare challenge him. He found his thought and, in an Irish accent very nearly as good as his Southern, yelled:

> *Lean out the window,*
> *Goldenhair,*
> *I heard you singing*
> *A merry air.*

A car edged on to Jim's street. He acquiesced a few inches without interrupting his poetry recital. When he finished his performance, he rejoined me casually.

'That wasn't mine,' he confessed.

I nodded. 'James Joyce's *Chamber Music*.' I would have preferred something of his own, but I loved the gesture. Jim Morrison spouting Joyce my first night in the City.

'Who even knows Joyce wrote poetry? You're a gem,' he tousled my hair, 'set in twenty-four-carat gold.'

Blarney. And I loved it. The only line I could remember from that collection of poems was, 'My breast shall be your bed.' Silence seemed the better choice.

In a town of hotels, Jim had found a motel. It was clean, but nothing fancy. I surveyed its contents from the doorway: a dresser, a lamp, a radio, a chair, a table, a bed. All in all, a singular room. Everything that was fabric was in a splashy blue and green floral. Anything wooden was painted white and well chipped. The only sign of Jim's having been there before was a small duffel on the dresser and an unopened bottle of black-and-white-labelled Irish whiskey beside it.

I took a tentative step inside so Jim could close the door. I was so weary, the double bed looked inviting, but the chair looked safe. I slumped into it. My stomach rumbled. Loudly.

'Hungry?' He smiled. 'I'll get us something at the deli. Like anything in particular?'

I shook my head and had to put my hand to my temple to steady the room. 'No . . . just cheese, maybe.'

'If you're up to it, why don't you take a shower?' Jim tossed me a black T-shirt from his bag. 'You can sleep in this.'

'Thanks,' I whispered. I studied the considerate offering. My Southern wolf, I smiled to myself. How could I trust this mercurial stranger? I considered a note and departure while he was out, but stood, instead, under the hot shower, crying. I had hit the lowest and highest points of my life in the span of a few hours. I wanted some time to think. I had always stood back, watched and weighed. I had been swept up in Jim's playfulness. For the first time that evening, I let myself look at the contradiction between what he chose to show of himself and his music. Throughout the day I had felt the sand shift under my feet. Let this not be a riptide. I wasn't much of a swimmer.

I thought I heard the radio. I turned off the water and listened. Big Brother and the Holding Company. Janis Joplin wailed. I couldn't remember if I had locked the door, and slid across the floor to check. I turned the lock as quietly as possible. If he tried the latch, I did not want him to interpret the unlocked door as an invitation.

'This is great,' I announced my entrance, half-wishing I'd stayed in the bathroom.

Jim sat cross-legged on the bed, an impromptu picnic spread before him. He had set out the meal as if we were old friends. There was one sandwich, divided, and one Coke to be shared. The deli must have been Italian. For mood, on the table by the bed, he had placed and lighted a candle. A Virgin Mary. She offered a beneficent glow.

'Next time, we'll do this on the beach, but tonight, between the fog and high tide ...' he trailed off in favour of chewing his food.

I made an attempt to look at ease sitting across from him on the bed. Scott McKensie's cloying 'If You Are Going to San Francisco' came on and Jim chuckled, snapped his fingers and said, 'Damn, you didn't stop for flowers.'

'I didn't stop for my toothbrush,' I said flatly.

He giggled. I'd never heard a man giggle before. 'You can borrow mine.'

'That's real Southern hospitality,' I smiled.

'Nah, I think sharing toothbrushes is definitely Western,' Jim, still giggling, sprayed a mouthful of Coke in my direction. He swiped here and there at me with his napkin. I was sorely tempted to remind him of yet another reason why the West was indeed the best, but he was taking another sip and I had to sleep in the T-shirt.

Usually, my remarks were met with blank stares. With someone to enjoy them and join in, I was in danger of lapsing into complete silliness. Jim felt no such constraints, feeding me his pickle, bite by bite, and asking for nibbles of my half of the sandwich. Even in pantomime, I was up to magenta in blushing. I was using my humour to keep my distance and he was using his to come closer. I felt the fog and high tide were in that room. And it was exciting.

When we had finished eating, Jim gathered the trash into a bag, made a hard ball of it, and threw a curve to the batter in the bathroom. He basked in his accomplishment for a moment, then grabbed my tote and upended it. He shook it to make sure all its contents had fallen on the bed between us.

'That's rude!'

He nodded and rummaged through my things; noted I had no family photographs in my wallet, asked if he could borrow my used copy of Anaïs Nin's novel, *A Spy in the House of Love*, and admired the drawings in my three-by-five-inch sketchbook.

The single drumbeat and wild organ of 'Light My Fire' erupted from the radio. Jim reached back and clicked it off, without comment.

'What do you call these?' He flipped through my little sketchbook again.

'Line drawings,' I told him. My current passion was for India ink and quill pen. No shading, just capturing the essence of things.

'So, you're an artist, too?'

'I think of myself as an artist who writes.'

He laughed, 'I think of myself as a writer who paints.'

'And occasionally sings,' I added.

I felt relieved when he seem pleased. 'I didn't think you knew who I was,' he smiled shyly.

'I knew when I saw your name what you did. I mean, who doesn't know Jim Morrison is one of The Doors? But I'm still trying to figure out who you are.'

Jim rolled his eyes as if considering a way to describe himself, but lunged for the novel instead. He reclined against the pillow and opened the book, 'What's it about?'

'Plot or theme?' I asked.

'Begin with plot.'

I thought a moment. 'It's about a woman who places these telephone calls at night. She dials at random to hear a voice, to find some stranger to talk with. One night, she reaches a man who is a lie detector.'

Jim reached for the phone. 'What's a San Francisco prefix?' I told him and he dialled, adding four numbers without deliberation.

'Hello,' his side of the conversation began, 'I just wanted, you know, to hear another voice. I'm Jim. No, you don't know me. It's easier that way, don't you think? No, I'm not going to say anything nasty. I thought maybe we could talk a while. Nobody gave me your number. It was just chance. What's your name?' He looked puzzled and hung up the receiver. 'So, what happens in the book?'

I laughed, 'Had you reached the lie detector, you would have been the one to hang up.'

'Would I have?' he considered, and linked his little finger with mine, as if we were sealing a childhood pact. 'But I invited you in,' he said simply, designating me his lie detector for the night.

Without releasing me, he seized the whiskey from the dresser. He broke the seal with his thumbnail, unwrapped two glasses, and filled one. I was impressed with his one-handed dexterity. Raising the drink, he asked, 'Like some?'

'No, thank you. But I could use a couple of these,' I said, taking two tablets from those scattered on the bedside table.

'If your head hurts, a couple hits of acid won't help.'

I studied them. They looked like aspirin. I returned them to the table. 'Pardon the fingerprints.'

'I'll get some ice for you.'

He scrambled from the bed and made a bootless exit. A few minutes later, there was a thump on the door. Jim's cupped hands brimmed with ice. He dropped the chips into the empty glass, warming his pink hands under his armpits before fluffing and stacking the pillows.

'Stretch out,' Jim ordered. 'The ice might make you feel better.'

He was making me feel better. Having someone take care of me was new. I felt both awkward and wonderful. Jim lazed beside me, his head on his fist, and held the glass so lightly against my cheek I felt it only because the cold stung.

I was curious about his knowledge of first-aid; the bit about using a glass as a substitute for an ice pack, its careful placement. 'Did you box?' I asked.

'Me?' he grinned. 'I've thrown a few punches, and caught a few, but that's it. It would embarrass me to get into a ring with somebody in my weight class. He'd be half a head shorter and beat the crap out of me.'

Jim was just under six feet, I guessed, and slender.

Jim explained his insight. 'Met a middle-aged dude in a bar. He was a corner man. That's the guy who takes care of the boxer

16

during a fight. He was convinced God had given him the power to heal and had wanted to be a doctor when he was young. But he was black and poor.'

'So he found a way to do what he wanted to do,' I deduced from Jim's voice.

'Yeah, yeah,' Jim nodded. 'That was his attitude. He was happy. He had just dropped in to have a cold one on the way home, and I was there to get blind. I like to talk to people in bars. I'm writing these bar stories. Have about six or seven of them, but he's my favourite.'

'I'd like to read them sometime.'

'Would you?' he looked surprised. 'I wish I'd brought them.' He paused. 'Want to talk about this?'

'It might help,' he coaxed.

'Who?' I asked defensively. 'Are you collecting café stories, too?'

He looked so wounded, I knew my tone was sharper than I had meant it to be. Jim set the glass on the table and replaced it with his chilled fingers.

'No, making friends,' he said very softly. 'I know the difference. I figure you're sweet sixteen and never been kissed.'

'Fifteen,' I corrected evasively.

'I'm sorry,' I said.

'Don't apologize.' He wiped a tear from my cheek with his thumb. 'I know you're not supposed to cry no matter how much it hurts. You'd think we all studied the same guerrilla handbook.'

Jim's voice sunk to a low rumble, a spoken lullaby, as he described the changing landscape of his childhood. His family, like mine, had crisscrossed the country. We were not so much what we had done, but where we had been.

He was born halfway down the Atlantic side of the coast of Florida and believed his earliest memory was of the white surf licking his toes. When he was not much more than a toddler, his family moved to Albuquerque. Up from the river bed, the widely scattered mesquite gave way to juniper where he lay watching lizards scurry between the tufts of the low, blue gamma grass. With his mother, he had hiked the golden rolling hills of Los Altos, with their live oaks. Their brittle limbs hung low. 'Widow makers. Child breakers,' he had taunted. From there, it was a difficult transition to a barren Washington DC. Then the wide streets and lonely palms of the suburbs near Los Angeles made him feel isolated. When they returned to New Mexico, he looked at the endless sky and vast horizon and wrote his first embarrassingly epic poem about the Pony Express. An impassioned 'And they rode' was echoed more times than he wanted to count. To leave the Southwest was wrenching for him, but Alameda meant a welcome proximity to San Francisco and the ocean. He could walk the city streets or disappear into the craggy hills. After the big sky of the West, the low skies and near-manicured green of Virginia seemed timid. He made a circle by attending college in Florida, where he cared less about his classes than hitchhiking.

'Let's get you comfortable,' he volunteered. My head felt like wet cement, so I offered no help or resistance when he unzipped my jeans and slipped them off. He lifted me just enough to pull the covers out from under me. The sheets were starched and cold. I slipped into a dreamless sleep.

I woke in darkness. Only a white ribbon of light flowed from a gap in the drapes and streamed across our thighs. If not his bed, my breast was his pillow. I listened to his steady breathing. He stirred and stretched his arm protectively across my body. His hand rested on my hip. I studied his form in the darkness. With so little light, he was without detail, himself a landscape. Artist Barbara Hepworth had said of her relationship to her work, 'I the sculptor am the landscape, the contours and hollows,' and I wondered, as I watched him sleep, if that were how Jim felt about his writing, that he and his words were indistinguishable.

Morning broke damp and cool. My face was buried in the pillow. In the night, I remembered, Jim had pulled the covers around us, but they had receded. His face was nestled in the small of my back. We shared warmth and heartbeat. My pensive mood lifted with the pleasure of this closeness. No wonder puppies look so content sleeping all over each other. I covered my mouth to stifle a rising giggle, which bubbled out, louder for having been suppressed.

'Good-morning,' I smiled into Jim's blinking eyes.

He drifted up to peel my borrowed T-shirt back to kiss my bare shoulder, 'Do you always wake up laughing?'

18

I tried to look serious, but laughed. He reclaimed his pillow and sprawled beside me. He hummed to himself a few slow and bluesy bars.

'Why were you so amused?' he asked with genuine, if sleepy, interest.

My puppies' delight theory sounded juvenile. He listened with a raised eyebrow, his grin widening, 'Your life is shit and you laugh about our cuddling.' He locked his arms around me and tumbled us across the bed. 'Fuck, I wanna be with you when the bomb drops. I want your laugh to be the last sound I hear.'

Jim had gone from our puppiness to Armageddon without missing a beat. The transition made me shake my head, but I wanted to thank him before I lost courage. 'When I woke up with you so close last night, I realized . . .' I searched for the words to describe how his tenderness had moved me, 'I had never felt so safe before. Thank you for being good to me.'

He looked uncomfortable and placed a sweet kiss on my cheek. 'Being good wasn't my intention,' he confided. 'I brought you back here because I wanted to get laid. You nearly woke up with me on top of you, trying to get into you.'

'But I didn't,' I giggled. 'And you didn't.' I thought aloud, 'Which is worse, having good intentions and not following through, or bad intentions and not following through?'

Jim laughed, 'Just what I need in my life, a fifteen-year-old philosopher.'

2

Bodies Confused

Jim leaned in the bathroom doorway, casual about his bare body. Each rib was delicately shadowed. His shoulder sloped to the casing. His arm hung loosely against his weight-bearing leg. The back of his left hand rested gracefully on his buttocks.

'You could lean professionally.' I looked directly into his eyes, too shy to look down.

'I *do*,' he smiled. 'But usually I am at least partially dressed and lean on a microphone stand. I'm very good at it. Want to join me in the shower?'

'No, thank you.' I returned his smile. 'After what you said about last night, I'd be more of an idiot than I feel if I did that. I'm not a tease.'

'I'm the one who's being a tease.' Jim took a step forward. I took a step back. He said, 'I had this idea that if I flaunted myself, you'd find my body irresistible.'

I blushed. 'Yeah, real good idea. I'm just not . . .'

'Ready,' he said. Was I going to say ready? Or sure? It didn't matter. Whichever I might have said, I wasn't going to budge. Jim pinched the front of the T-shirt he'd loaned me to hold me in place while he leaned down and kissed me gently. 'Anticipation can be sweet. I'm in no hurry.' He glanced down at

21

his erection. 'Well, my body is,' he smiled, 'but my head can wait.'

'I always thought,' well, at least for the last five minutes, 'the separation of body and mind was theological mumbo jumbo that people repeat without thinking.'

Jim shook his head slowly. 'Do you repeat anything without thinking?'

'Oh, only songs on the radio,' I said.

He laughed, 'Will you marry me?'

'Definitely keep you in mind when I'm looking for a husband. As it is, I'm still looking for my first slow dance.'

He left the bathroom door open. I was disappointed he didn't sing in the shower, but was tickled that he hummed when he shaved. His weekend plans hadn't included shaving and he'd run up the street for a few toiletries. So, at least he had pants on when he asked me to keep him company. He hummed a blues song I didn't recognize. I had just started to collect classic blues albums and tried to put a face and voice with the song. Only the few bars of Jim's voice on waking came to mind.

The haunting melody was one of those that makes you feel the composer knows every heartache in the world, and how to live with them. When he stopped, I sighed. He smiled at me in the mirror. I leaned in the doorway behind him with much less panache than he. I locked my thumbs in my jeans' pockets to have something to do with my hands.

'Can you draw on an empty stomach?' he asked.

'I suppose.'

'Would you show me how you draw?'

'It's not much of a performance.' I drew a line in the air.

'Very graceful. Could I hold your hand?'

'While I draw?' I was puzzled.

'Your drawing hand. So I can feel what it's like. I'd sell a corner of my soul to draw the way you do.'

'It's just eye-hand coordination. I could teach you everything I know in half an hour. The rest is practice.'

Jim wiped the odd bits of shaving cream from his face. He put on a fresh black shirt that was the negative of the last night's white one. His wet hair soaked his collar. He scurried around looking for something to draw on. The back of a flyer advertising a concert. Something smooth to put under it. The phone book. And something that would glide across the paper. His felt-tip pen. He wanted to draw his boots and spent fifteen minutes arranging them so they looked just as they had when he kicked them off earlier.

I concentrated on getting my hands to stop shaking. I didn't like anyone in the same room while I drew, let alone hanging on to me. I sat with the phone book on my lap. Jim sat with one leg stretched out behind me and one along my side. He rested his hand lightly on mine. I stopped shaking. It was a strange way to hold hands for the first time. Talking while drawing was awkward. I described the point on the first boot where I planned to begin my line. 'Watch the boot more than the paper,' I told him. I felt the slight weight of his hand without it dragging against me. We were dancers in precise synchronization. He anticipated each turn. Halfway through the drawing, without realizing it, I stopped guiding Jim verbally. When I lifted my hand, Jim's split leather boots were on the page.

'That's the best sex I ever had!' Jim shouted.

'Only sex I ever had,' I said under my breath. He winked.

Jim studied our work for a few minutes. 'It's like when the band is really on when we're improvising. Never felt it with anyone else. I thought it was something only music could do. You know, transcend. Whew!'

A rush of adrenaline surged through me. I couldn't sit still. Art had been a solitary experience. I'd never imagined a creative partnership. I wanted to draw with Jim all day.

Jim sighed. 'I gotta get rolling.' My heart tightened as I watched him stuff his dirty clothes, books, including the one he borrowed from me, and his little notebook into the duffel. 'I can have the drawing, right?' he asked. I nodded. He tucked it into a newspaper and set it on top of his things. While he was checking out, I added the neatly folded T-shirt I had been wearing, and sat on the edge of the bed with my tote bag in my lap.

When he returned from the office, Jim dropped the key in my hand. 'I really have to get back to LA. You're wonderful company. I can't remember better conversation. I know it's a difficult time for you. The room is covered for two more nights. That should give you a little time to decide what you want to do.'

'Thank you,' I teared up and swallowed hard. 'It's generous of you. I can use the time. If you tell me where to send the money for my share, I'll pay you back.'

'You were my guest, so it's not necessary.'

'It is.'

'Well, let's call it even. You bought us dinner last night.' He smiled. 'That's why it was a bit skimpy.'

'Oh,' I felt embarrassed for my warm presumption about the cosy meal, 'I thought you were being friendly.'

'That, too,' he said. 'But if you were a little more flush, I woulda had a beer. The deli didn't want to make change either, so I borrowed a five while you were in the shower. I didn't want to wipe you out.'

'Jim, isn't it a little . . .'

'Pretentious to only carry hundred-dollar bills?' He grinned. I'd miss his habit of finishing my sentences whenever I paused. 'Nah. Would be if I was flaunting them to be a rock asshole, which I admit I am sometimes, but I got these fair and square. I won a bet. I thought the other dude was a little pretentious to flash a wad of hundreds in a bar.'

'What was the bet?'

'Five hundred that I could walk the ledge of a three-storey building.'

I thought, 'You walked the ledge of a building? That's crazy! You really did that?' But I said calmly, 'Your life is worth more than five hundred dollars. More than any amount of money.'

'Aw, think so? Appreciate your concern, but I wasn't risking my life. It's fun to freak people out. I have this incredible sense of balance. If this rock 'n' roll thing doesn't work out, I can always join the circus. Be one of those drunk acts on a high wire.'

'You were drunk when you did this?' I pictured his entrance into the café the evening before and shuddered.

'Probably,' he said, pausing to consider. 'Probably wouldn't have done it sober. Wouldn't have been quite so much fun. I'll do almost anything when I'm drunk.'

'Then maybe you shouldn't drink,' I suggested shyly.

'Oh, but I like to drink.'

He didn't appear offended by my nosing into his business, so I took another step. I said, 'Then maybe you should have a bodyguard when you do.'

'Need a job?' he asked. He walked across the room boot heel to boot toe. He made a theatrical bow. 'Jesus, I should be in LA,' he said again. 'When I lived in Alameda, I used to play hooky and come hang out here. Guess I'm still doing it. I need to have some place where people won't think to track me down. I haven't written a decent line in weeks. Came up here to drop acid and write my fucking brains out. But I got sidetracked.' He kissed my cheek in brotherly fashion.

I felt a twinge of guilt. 'You can write on acid?'

'Yeah, it's easier, really. Songs come out whole, instead of in chunks.'

'The few people I know who have tried LSD seem to spout nonsense, and think it's great.'

'Well, you aren't going to find anything on acid that isn't already there.'

I laughed, 'Oh, it's like that saying about Zen.'

'What's that?'

I thought a minute, to make sure I got it straight, 'The only Zen you find on the mountain is what you bring with you.'

He snorted, 'John would love you.'

'John?'

'Our drummer. He's interested in all that.'

'Oh, well, I don't really understand Zen. I just like the humour. That wink at the universe.'

'Then you probably understand it better than people who *think* they do. When was the last time you flew a kite?'

'Is this a Zen joke?' I asked, not wanting not to get it.

'It's an invitation,' he smiled. 'But it's the same thing if we do it right. Hell, LA can wait.'

Jim grabbed his sunglasses and charged out the door. In the strong sunlight, I felt the worse for wear. I wanted to ask Jim if I could borrow his sunglasses, but was too shy. I sighed audibly.

'Big sigh,' Jim said.

'Just jealous. I could look cool, too, if I had sunglasses like that.'

He smiled, getting my hint, and shifted them from his face to mine. 'Nah. You look like Goldilocks incognito, but they're yours.'

First we found breakfast, then we found a barrel of Chinese kites outside the door of a Japanese store. People were doing childlike things that Summer of Love, but I was close enough to being a child that buying a kite embarrassed me. I picked out a blue bird, hoping it wouldn't show up against the sky. Jim bought a beautifully threatening red dragon. We had walked halfway across the city tracking down these perfect kites, and decided we may as well walk the rest of the way to Golden Gate Park. For the last of the journey, we followed the panhandle. Jim had a particular spot in mind deep in the park where he used to come daydream when he was my age.

Jim's personal niche was a wide gully edged with trees which stretched away from it. It was a quiet place to fly the kites, but there was no wind. We sat cross-legged, our kites in our laps. 'Well, it was a nice idea,' I comforted Jim. 'I can't remember not being windblown in San Francisco. Must be a moratorium on Chinese kites.'

Jim bit his lower lip while his eyes searched the sky. A slow grin broke across his face. 'This little cranny must be protected, but I can do something to help,' Jim pulled his knees up and wrapped his arms around them. 'Ever since I was little, I had this power. We lived in New Mexico, then. I must have been four or five, because I can remember, yet not quite remember. We were driving along – my parents and grandparents, I think my little sister – and me. The car stopped. There were these bundles of clothes along the road. Then it sunk in they were bodies. And the bodies were Navajo Indians. Covered in blood. It was eerie because it was like dreaming about death and not knowing what it was. I felt this thwack against my chest.' Jim struck his chest hard for emphasis. 'I was never the same. I had this other . . . presence in me. My inner music changed. My heartbeat was different. I could *know* things. *Will* things. I always wondered why the spirit chose me.'

Jim handed me his red-eyed dragon. He stood in one smooth

movement, his feet still crossed at the ankles. His dance began with the sweep of his left arm, letting his body follow it as if he were a bud opening up. His movements echoed an Indian Ring Dancer, I thought, still caught up in his allegory. Then he started to hum. The music, in contradiction, was all Southern blues. His body would lean so off centre, it seemed inevitable that he would fall, then he would right himself with a hand or foot in the air, an intricate series of counterbalances. This was a man who walked ledges. A wind dancer.

When he stopped, his face was rimmed in sweaty ringlets. He stretched out beside me. The air was still, but he seemed genuinely satisfied. He patted my hand, still breathless. 'Takes a while,' he assured me. 'Just as well. I couldn't run a kite yet.'

He lay flat on his back, his breath slowing some. The restlessness that engulfed him since the night before, lifted. His sense of play intrigued me. When he played, there was no self-consciousness. He didn't pretend to be Gauguin in the South of France. He was Gauguin. He didn't pretend to be possessed by an Indian spirit. He was. I wanted to learn from him how to be whatever I wanted to be. If I watched closely enough, I might see how he did it. A breeze touched my cheek. Jim half-opened his eyes, his smile radiant.

'Let's fly our kites.'

Jumping to his feet, Jim offered me his hand. I was afraid to take it. I believed he'd brought the wind up. I felt caught up in what he had said of himself as a child. Dreaming, this time of this man's power, and not knowing what it was. I felt I had jogged slightly out of reality. He reached down and pulled me to my feet.

I watched Jim lift his kite. He ran backwards, so he could watch it, too. It had been a long time since I had seen a kite in the air, let alone gotten one there. But if I were going to learn to play, I had to do it, and not just watch. We flew the kites in silence until our necks ached from craning to follow them and our arms tired of tugging against the wind. We reeled them in, and let them bob on our shoulders like umbrellas.

As we walked, I tried several times to ask what had happened. When I had given up, he leaned heavily into my shoulder. 'The wind always comes up this time of day,' he whispered. 'Sometimes, the magic is in the timing.'

We grinned at each other. We held hands across the open stretch of grass, heading more or less in the direction of Haight. At the edge of the park, Jim handed his kite over to a Chinese boy of about seven, buttoned into a bright blue jacket. 'Like kites?' Jim asked.

The boy smiled and nodded. I felt obligated to hand over mine to the boy's companion, a younger brother dressed in a smaller version of the royal silk jacket. The child exploded in high-pitched giggles which made it easier to let go of the kite. I wanted to keep the kite as proof when I told this story to my friends. Jim travelled lighter. Little lessons in living in the present.

'Your turn,' Jim said as we made our way along Haight.

'For what?'

'When I was four or five . . .'

'Oh, when I was four or five,' I began, not at ease with spontaneous storytelling, 'we lived in Tennessee. One day my mother took me into Memphis in my best yellow-dotted Swiss dress. She had done whatever errand had taken her there, and was looking at books on a rack outside this store, so I wandered a little. This big man stooped down and asked, "Whose little girl are you?" My mom heard this and came running. The man picked me up for her, shook her hand, and said, "Hello, Mam, I'm Elvis Presley."'

'You're kidding! You met Elvis Presley. What was he like?'

'I remember it more from the retelling than remembering. My real memory is of a parade. It must have been his fans or entourage. I remember he had big hands, a rough tweed coat, and smelled clean. You know, like soap, not cologne.'

'What else did he say?'

'I don't remember what he said. I just remember his chest vibrated when he talked. My mother said he was very polite. She was embarrassed that she had let go of me. My mom likes his music now, but back then she had just broken my sister's copy of "Ain't Nothin' But a Hound Dog" because she thought she'd go crazy if she heard it again.'

'That is great. You met Elvis!' he repeated.

'Guess it's my lot in life to make these brief appearances in the lives of rock singers every ten years or so. At least next time,' I said emphatically, 'I'll be old enough.'

'Honey, the way rock-stars think, you'll be too old. Better stick with me.' He dropped his wrist on my shoulder and every once in a while would say, 'Elvis,' and look skyward, shaking his head.

'Do you like silent movies?' Jim asked, stopping in front of a hand-lettered poster advertising a silent horror film, *The Cabinet of Dr Caligari.*

'Oh, yeah. I love Buster Keaton.'

'I was thinking about Artaud. He's . . .'

'A French actor. Anaïs Nin writes about him. I didn't know you could see his films.'

'Living in LA helps. His sense of theatre is close to mine. Mine's close to his,' he corrected himself. 'He wrote a good book about his theories. I'll send it to you when you know where you'll be.'

I hadn't done much thinking about just what I was going to do when Jim left. Without my saying anything, Jim rummaged through my purse and came up with the runaway hotline number I'd written down on the back of my sketchbook. He called the number for me. He set an appointment and we met with a sturdy woman in her twenties.

She guided us through a couple crash pads, large flats with mattresses covering the floors. She talked a steady line, accustomed to explaining to fifteen-year-olds how to survive in the city. I noticed one place had no door knob on the bathroom and another had no lock. I wondered about the lack of privacy, and asked Jim.

He bit his lower lip the way he did when he was uncomfortable. 'It's to discourage kids from shooting up in them,' he said softly.

One of the places had a bay window. It seemed clean enough. A couple of the young people seemed nice enough, and I felt I could start there. Buy some time.

When we were alone in the street again, Jim asked, 'Feel like a movie?'

Grabbing my hand, Jim led me through the open door of the building that matched the address on the poster that advertised the German silent film. The stairs and walls painted black made navigation tricky. A black light was mounted at the landing and, after stubbing my toes a few times, I figured out that the risers, not the steps, were edged in dayglo paint. Ahead of me, dressed in black, Jim was barely discernible.

The theatre was a large living-room-sized space, darkened by painted windows and lit by a chandelier that survived the '06 quake. Metal folding chairs, all empty, served as seating. The screen covered most of the far wall. An old upright piano soaked in purple paint was just to the right of the screen. The projector stood in the same room at the opposite end.

'Wonder when the show starts,' Jim said, sitting at the upright. 'Not many people I'd do this for. Or to.' He stretched his fingers over his knees. He straightened his back. Grinned broadly. He rested the fingers of his right hand lightly on the keys, then adjusted them, searching for the chord he wanted.

The first chord had to have been wrong. The next definitely was. As his performance continued, my cheeks were stiff from smiling. Jim's playing was loud and, while the rhythm seemed familiar, there was no recognizable melody. Then the rhythm wandered off. The stop was sudden. We looked at each other. He winked. I expected him to settle down and really play something, but apparently the recital was over.

'Did you study with John Cage?' I asked. I had once read a review of the avant-garde composer's masterpieces of cacophony that seemed to apply to what I had just heard. Cacophony, not masterpiece.

Jim laughed. 'There's a direction that might suit me.'

'You're not going to play one of your songs for me?'

'That was it. That's the best I can play, allowing for nerves. That was "Break on Through".'

'I guess you don't compose at the piano.' I tried to keep a straight face.

'No,' he put his arm around my waist and pulled me on to the bench next to him. 'Can't read much music. I took about three lessons when I was a kid. When I realized I was never going to sound like Jerry Lee Lewis, I quit. I should settle down and try again, but Ray's so good, I'm intimidated. It's easier to let him interpret my songs. The guy's incredible. He has this affinity for the keyboard nobody else comes close to. I never get tired of listening to him. Or the other guys either. I keep

30

waiting for one of 'em to tap me on the shoulder and say, "You, out!"'

'Wouldn't they miss your music?'

'I hold on to that hope in my darker moments,' Jim smiled.

A plump older man in overalls cleared his throat behind us. We gave him his bench. A few people had strayed in during Jim's stint at the piano. His cheeks were pink, 'Wonder how many people left when they thought I was the piano player.' He slumped as far down as possible on the folding chair. I sat on the chair next to him. He scooted the chair and me up against him with a piercing screech. The room darkened. The projector sounded like a jet until the piano drowned it.

Jim had seen the movie before. Just before every scare, he poked me. He gasped. He screamed. He was a great screamer. *The Cabinet of Dr Caligari* had the pace of a fevered dream from which you couldn't shake yourself. I had no idea what the impact could be of silent film on a large screen. I was relieved when the lights came up.

'Well?' Jim asked.

'I'm sleeping with the light on.'

'Great, wasn't it? Mind if we sit through it again? I'd like to catch something technical.'

'Promise not to poke and scream?'

'No.'

'Did you spend your entire school career in detention?'

'I spent most of it in solitary confinement.'

Yeah, I bet. After the second round of horror and harassment, the neon of the San Francisco night was welcome.

'What do you want to be when you grow up? An artist?' Jim asked.

'I'd like to be,' I hesitated, never having told anyone before, 'James Wong Howe.' I took a breath to explain who Howe was.

'You can't be,' Jim said matter-of-factly.

I bristled, 'Because I'm a girl?'

'No, 'cause I wanna be.' Jim laughed and tousled my hair. He let his arm settle around my shoulder. 'When I saw *Hud*, I left the theatre in a daze, turned around and bought another ticket. I realized I didn't even hear the dialogue. I just saw and felt it.

31

He's a genius with a camera. Especially in black and white. Don't know why they bother with colour just because they can do it.'

He was the only person I ever met for whom the cinematographer needed no introduction. I said, 'I've been trying to charm my parents out of their camera for about a year. I'll see something interesting and say to myself, "I'll put that in my movie," but people like me don't make movies.'

Jim lifted my chin, so I was looking into his eyes, and said softly, 'People like you can do anything.'

My feet didn't touch ground on the long walk back to the vicinity of the motel. For the first time in my life, someone had expressed belief in me. We stopped at a little corner café and ate spaghetti. Jim poured a little of his wine into my glass, 'Ever had good wine?'

'I took a sip of Mogen David Blackberry when I was baby-sitting once.' I made a face.

'Have you ever had good wine?' he asked as if I'd been silent.

I sipped the wine. It burned my tongue a little. It didn't sting my throat at all. The half-glass warmed me and, from my perspective, made Jim glow a little.

We held hands on the walk back to the motel. Jim hadn't mentioned Los Angeles again. I had his companionship for a little while longer. We just curled up together and talked. He seemed open and curious about everything.

In sleep, I had spliced the horror movie and my situation into a menacing nightmare. Jim shook me awake. I was grateful to see his face and the motel room.

'Thanks. I couldn't wake myself. I hate to go back to sleep after a nightmare.'

'I have something for that,' Jim said, setting his book of short stories aside and dropping his little notebook on the pillow. 'Works every time. You write a line. I write a line. We'll write a song.'

I smiled. 'How about you write a line, you write a line, you write a song. I'll watch.'

'Anybody can write a song. Let's do a simple melody.'

'Melody. Jeez, Jim.'

'That's how it goes. Music first. The words pretty much write

32

themselves.' He hummed a bit. 'That's a line's worth. I'll hum a verse. Then give you the line again. You just fill in the words.'

'Naturally,' I laughed. 'And I thought you woke me from a nightmare.'

'It's easier if you write the first two lines.'

'For whom?'

'Well, that way, I rhyme you.'

'You have a great technique for winning an argument. Striking terror.'

Jim hummed the melody again and kept time with his pen against the notebook. I tried to count syllables on my fingers. I felt flustered and blank. 'Couldn't we steal a Dylan song? I'd never tell.'

'Write anything. I never count syllables. I make my own meter, such as it is. None of my songs matches exactly. I just sing them like they do.'

We played this tic-tac-toe game of exchanging lines until the page was full and an hour had passed. Jim shuffled a few of the lines, added a chorus, and declared it a song. He sang it through and I felt thrilled. It wasn't very good, but it was a song.

'Fun, huh?' he asked.

'Terrifying . . . and fun.'

'How does the song really go?'

Jim thought a minute, closed his eyes and sang softly. Then he said, 'I wrote that a couple years ago.'

'Just that verse?'

'No, there's a whole song.' He started over and sang it through. '"Moonlight Drive" turned out to be my audition for the band,' he said when he finished.

'A classy version of "Patches"?' I smiled.

Jim's sides heaved but he didn't make a sound. He threw his notebook across the room where it landed like a dead bird by the door. 'When you grow up, I'll explain the metaphor.'

'Oh, try now.'

He blushed. 'Oh, let's just say that *drowning* and *going down* are sexual.'

'Oh,' my imagination was at a loss, 'I hope I get that straight when the time comes.'

Jim laughed. He had completely broken the nightmare's hold.

Alarms and Diversions, I thought. He held me in the crook of his arm and opened his book of short stories. 'We'll skip Poe's "The Telltale Heart" and move on to Chekhov. Chekhov should be safe.'

Chekhov put me to sleep. Morning was cool and sunny. Jim wasn't much of a morning person, grumbling with charm about how I had kept him up till all hours. By my memory, I'd fallen asleep while he was reading. We showered separately and quickly, then made a quest for a Mexican restaurant that opened early.

My shirt was beginning to smell a little ripe. I felt self-conscious until I could do something about it. Back at the motel, I borrowed his T-shirt again. Jim hopped on the gold-flecked Formica counter by the bathroom sink. He swung his legs, rapping his boot heels against the cabinet door, watching in rapt curiosity, while I squeezed suds through my paisley blouse. Soon bored with that, he made faces at himself in the rusty mirror.

'Do you think I should get braces?' he growled so I could see all his teeth.

He had a slight overbite, and his bottom teeth resembled the short uneven posts that Japanese gardeners use to border their gardens. I felt like kissing him.

'You'd risk offending the gods if you didn't have a flaw,' I warned him.

He laughed, 'I haven't spent this much time in the bathroom since I played in the bathtub when I was little.' Jim smiled, then something peculiar happened to his face. His jaw tightened. His eyes grew wide and alert. For a moment, he looked very young. He bolted from his perch and fled into the larger room. He paced a few feet and darted his fingers through his hair.

I followed him, my hands dripping. Jim couldn't stop moving, but went nowhere. Like a hamster on a wheel, he made a small circle on the floor. I reached for him and he pulled away. I wiped my hands on my jeans, and tried again, catching some of his shirt in my hand. Without quite touching him, I could feel him trembling.

'Are you claustrophobic?' As I eased my arms around him, there was so much fear in his body, I shivered. 'Want me to open the door?'

Jim shook his head. He rested his arms on my shoulders and laced his fingers behind my neck. His bowed forehead touched my bangs. Neither of us said anything for a few minutes.

'What's wrong, Jim?'

'Nothing,' he said, 'I'm just restless.'

That was a lie. I leaned back to see his eyes. He closed them to shut me out and kissed my cheek. He found my mouth and kissed it. I returned the kiss. He opened his eyes and smiled down at me.

'That's nice. This has been building between us,' he said, combing my hair with his fingers. I wondered if I had misinterpreted his fear. 'I didn't want to rush you,' he continued, 'I wanted you to come to me. Have you?'

I brushed his cheek with the back of my fingers, and caressed his ear. He shivered. I slid my hand down his throat. I kissed him. 'Yes,' I decided.

He pulled off his T-shirt, then mine. He traced the edge of my cotton bra with his finger. 'Suits you,' he smiled, unfastened it smoothly, and let it fall to the floor. Jim pulled me closer to his chest. He ran his hands down my back and cradled me in his arms, letting me grow comfortable about being so close to him that I could feel his heartbeat and his breath against my cheek. Unsure of how to hold him, I rested my hands on his slender waist. He kissed me. His mouth tasted of the beer and salsa he had with his huevos rancheros for breakfast. I laughed.

'What?'

'Your mouth is spicy. Never shared a meal like this.'

'It's been a long time since I thought about kissing as new. You taste new,' he said, kissing me and unzipping my jeans in a graceful unison I couldn't imagine of myself.

I concentrated on the intricacies of lowering the zipper of a man who shunned underwear. I eased my hand behind the zipper to protect him.

'Very thoughtful,' Jim sighed. He yanked off and dropped each boot, then extricated himself from his tight leathers.

He slid his hands down the back of my jeans to hold me while we kissed. The intensity of his kissing made me unsteady. He slipped an arm around my waist, the other at the back of my knees, lifted me easily, and rested me effortlessly on the unmade bed. Jim fluffed the pillows and piled one on the other. Instead of offering them to me, he laid back on them in invitation.

'Explore,' he offered.

I wasn't sure where to begin, so I started in familiar territory. My trembling finger outlined his lips. When I leaned over to kiss him, my hair slapped his face. Not seriously wounded, Jim smiled, and twisted the bulk of my hair into a knot at the nape of my neck. I followed the line of his neck and kissed its hollow. When I licked his left nipple, he sighed and released my hair, letting it cloak him.

My hand moving down his side felt as clumsy as if it were not attached to my arm. I sat back and studied his body. I played connect-the-dots with three small moles along the right side of his abdomen.

'Orion's belt,' I named them. The constellation of the hunter was one of the few I could always find in the sky.

Jim raised himself on his elbows to look. 'I always thought they were ugly,' he said, 'and you see them as stars.' I kissed each of them. When I wandered south with my kisses, he reached under my arms and pulled me up to his mouth. 'Which of the Pleiades are you?' he asked. I only knew one of the seven sisters, the daughters of Atlas and lovers of Orion, and didn't want to name myself Elektra. He bit my lower lip gently, then soothed it with a flurry of sweet little kisses. Were there seven?

'Your touch is so unrehearsed,' he said.

My hand stopped its journey along his hip. I flushed hot with embarrassment and retreated.

Jim laughed, 'Whoa! Come back. That wasn't a criticism. It was a compliment. It feels wonderful. No one has touched me this way in a long time.' His voice softened. His kisses became rougher. Deftly, he rolled me on to my back.

What I had attempted with awkward inexperience, Jim accomplished with grace. He traced my lips with his tongue, then lingered to explore every nook of my mouth. He kissed the length of my neck. He cupped each of my breasts in turn, pausing to circle the nipples with his tongue, kiss lightly, and suck rhythmically until fire swept through me. His tongue searched my navel and skirted the line of my thigh.

Kneeling between my thighs, he reached back to caress the arches of my feet. He moved his hands along the back of my calves and raised my knees slightly. Eyes closed, he folded his body as he kissed a path down my inner thigh. Jim placed a delicate kiss on my clitoris, and for the first time opened his eyes and looked into my face. He smiled the question, and not knowing precisely what I was consenting to, I nodded.

I started to sit up and Jim met me with a probing kiss. Excitement subsided, and my ragged breath became a pant as I felt panic sweeping through me. I leaned back. Slow down. 'Jim . . .'

He rested against me, breathing as hard as I was. Tiny beads of sweat glistened across the bridge of his nose. 'Hush, baby,' he murmured, 'I'm not going to do anything you don't want me to. Would you like me to stop?'

I shook my head. He smiled. Bearing his weight on his forearms, he raked his fingers through my hair. Slowly, he began to kiss me again. He rubbed my breasts with open palms, and kneeled again. I closed my eyes as he lifted my hips and rocked me gently.

'Hush,' his reprise. 'Hush.'

I laid my hands over his. He raised me to him, pressing against me. Panting over me, his breath filled my nostrils, and a shadow crossed my eyelids. I gasped, wrenching the strong hands from my hips.

Jim recoiled. He sat back on his heels. His hands drew into fists on his thighs. The veins in the back of his hands throbbed. His eyes darkened. Jim backed off the bed and flung his right fist against the wall. The impact sounded like a shot. I jumped.

His knuckles were bleeding. He studied them, then bit the torn skin absently. He crossed to the dresser, opened the bottle of whiskey, and poured a glass. He swirled the liquid. All the easy conversation of the last two days seemed a blur. I couldn't think of a quip to break the silence. I wished him in bed, beginning again, gently combing my hair with his fingers.

Standing with his back to me, Jim emptied the glass slowly. His reflection in the mirror was hard to read. His head was slightly bent and his pose a Donatello statue, lean and at rest, except for the still clenched left fist. He filled the glass again, left it, and returned to the bed. He sat on its very edge, one leg folded, one foot on the floor. He splayed his hand across my stomach, massaging me gently with his thumb.

Jim cleared his throat, 'Honey, were you raped?'

The question stunned me. I said, each word slow and distinct, 'You . . . have . . . a . . . foul . . . mouth.'

Jim nodded slightly in agreement. I replayed his question in my mind, heard the tenderness in his voice, and regretted the harshness of my own. I stroked his neck in apology. He crawled into bed behind me, holding the covers up for me to join him. When I hesitated, he gathered me into his arms. He adjusted the folds of the sheet with care and arranged my hair over my shoulders. I yielded to his deliberate kiss. He rested his cheek lightly on mine. His breath tickled my ear. We exchanged childhood secrets.

Graceless with the man, I instinctively pulled the boy into my arms until I could feel his ribs painfully against mine.

Jim buried his face in my hair. Pain radiated from him like the wavy air rising from an overheated engine, but was as solid as his hair, his shoulder, or his bloody knuckles.

'James Agee wrote about the uniqueness of each person, and how difficult it is to survive. I don't remember it all, but there's this line, "Wounded in every breath".'

'Sustaining, for a while, the enormous assaults of the universe,' Jim interrupted with the end of the quote. By sheer will, he contained his pain for a few minutes, then he buried his face in my hair and cried for a long time. When he quieted, he pulled back enough for me to see his face. He played with my hair. Jim said, 'Your hair is so red wet, so golden dry.' The door he had opened closed, but I felt we were on the same side of it.

I brought Jim a cool wet washcloth from the bathroom. I wiped his face gently. His red swollen eyes made his skin seem very pale. He took a few deep breaths and reached for his pants. 'Let's get out of here for a while.'

3

Strange Days Have Found Us

We dressed quickly. The atmosphere of the room had turned so dark that it startled me that it wasn't even midday. At the door, I slipped the sunglasses Jim had loaned me on his face. He grabbed my hand. We stood at the curb, not talking, trying to decide where to go, when a taxi pulled up. Jim shrugged and opened the door.

The driver asked, 'Where to?' before Jim had closed the door.

He didn't seem to have any idea, so I answered, 'The Museum of Modern Art, Van Ness.'

'Yeah, thanks,' Jim stroked my leg and took my hand again, rubbing it nervously.

Stopped at a light, windows down a few inches, we could hear the blast of the radio from the car next to us. Jim was singing, 'Light My Fire.'

'You winced,' Jim said softly, nuzzling me. 'Don't like the song?'

I smiled, 'I would be singing along if you weren't here.'

'Then what?'

'It's silly.'

'So? Be silly.'

'The grammar's wrong,' I said shyly, 'It's . . . "If I *were*".'

'Ah, bit of the school marm in you. We of the proletariat say *was*.'

39

'I'm sorry. Told you it was silly. My English is pretty casual, too. I'm fond of run-on sentences that end in prepositions. You know, it's just one of those things that jumps out at me.'

'No need to apologize. I didn't write it. I'll tell Robby his grammar sucks.' Jim's smile was wonderful.

'Don't you dare, Jim. I love the song. Beats anything on the radio.'

'I know, it's number one,' he laughed. 'Besides, when all is said and done, *If I was* sings better than *If I were*.' Jim sang from the first line until he felt he'd proven his point, then sang it with *were* at full volume. 'See?' he asked. The brakes screamed. I hit the back of the front seat and landed hard on Jim's boots. 'You okay?' he asked, retrieving me.

'You're The Doors!' the cab driver, a toothy young black man, yelled excitedly.

'One of 'em. Hey, man, it works better if you look out the front window.'

'Oh, yeah. Right,' the driver agreed, facing forward, but eyes on his rear-view mirror. 'Are you playing in town?'

'Not on stage. Just with my friend here. Wanna watch where you're going?'

'Oh, yeah,' he stared in the mirror. 'Would you sign my cab?'

'Sure. When we stop.' Jim turned to me, 'I must be a success. I'm being asked for graffiti. Used to get my ass kicked for it.'

'I had Johnny Mathis in my cab once,' the driver started again. 'That man is a real gentleman. And a couple of Jefferson Airplane.'

'Together? That's interesting. Probably going to do an album together. Broaden their audience.'

'No, not at the same time!' the young man said dramatically. 'Oh, you're pulling my leg. Did you know the Jefferson Airplane live in the city? I had the girl and the blond guy. They were drunk or stoned.'

'Hard to believe,' Jim shook his head in mock disbelief. When the driver insisted that she'd used rough language, Jim said, 'Really? Wouldn't think that of her.' Jim enjoyed playing along.

'Oh, yeah, kind of embarrassed me, I'll tell you.'

When the taxi pulled up in front of the museum, the driver

40

handed Jim a marker and Jim obliged with a large signature on the back of the seat. Jim ran up the steps and held the door for me. We paid our entry with loose change and rode alone in the elevator.

'I dream about living here,' I told him. 'Of course, my paintings are on the walls in that dream.'

Jim wouldn't let go of my hand. We mumbled comments in each other's ears about the photographs, etchings, drawings, and paintings. When we had walked through every room and hallway of every floor we were allowed, we sat on a bench in the middle of one of the high-ceilinged rooms. Jim held my hand in his coat pocket. We stared at the huge black and purple painting in front of us. A swash of red bled down the side of the canvas.

'What are we going to do about this?' Jim asked. He stroked the back of my hand with his thumb. Our hands were sweaty in the confines of the pocket. I assumed he meant the fiasco at the motel and that he didn't expect an answer.

'I want you to know sex is all right. I need . . .' he thought a few minutes before continuing, 'I can't remember ever being touched in a non-sexual way until this morning, when you held me. Nobody has ever really comforted me. I think that's why I fell apart. I'm sorry.' His voice drifted off.

I rested my head against his shoulder. 'When I was little, my mother used to come in at the end of my bath to wash my hair. She's a very reserved New England lady, not a demonstrative person. But when she would dry my hair with a big towel, she'd say, "Rapunzel, Rapunzel, let down your hair," and I was very sure she loved me.'

We left the museum. Van Ness was a jumble of late-afternoon traffic. Feet were faster than vehicles. We cruised through little shops. We browsed separately and met in the doorways laden with our purchases. A street vendor had a tray of silver Turkish puzzle rings. Tapkapi. The man called them friendship rings. Jim tried on several and bought a rough wide one. He shook it so the four intertwining rings separated. He put it together quickly. He held it out to me, three rings dangling from the fourth and watched me fuss with it for a few minutes. 'It's like worry beads,' Jim said, 'very calming to play with it.'

Personally, after a sincere attempt, I was ready to throw the ring across the street. Or accidentally dump it in the gutter, so I returned it to Jim. He solved its little puzzle, and put it on his left hand.

When we got back to the motel room, the bed was made and fresh towels were laid out. I stretched out on the bed to rest my legs. Jim took a giant step up on to the bed, then sat where he had stood and rustled around the contents of his shopping bag. His search produced a medium-sized box which was covered in an Escher-like Japanese print and tied with a large bow. In the middle of the bow nested a turquoise origami crane. He sat it in my lap. 'It's beautiful,' I declared.

'The present is inside,' he said patiently.

I admired the box for a while. I liked boxes.

'The woman at the shop asked me my favourite colour, then looked at me very intently and told me I needed a crane. She made it right in front of me. It was amazing to watch her turn a square piece of paper into this. She said this bird was a symbol of long life.'

'Do you know the story of the thousand cranes? Like to hear it?' I asked and Jim nodded. 'A Japanese friend told me this story last year. A little girl, who was in the hospital after the bombing of Hiroshima, saved the little papers from her medication to fold into cranes. She believed that if she folded a thousand cranes, she would get her wish. She wished that she would get well. As time went on, she watched the children around her die and realized that she had made the wrong wish. She then wished for peace so children would not die so horribly ever again. She did not live long enough to make the thousand cranes, but after she died, the other children finished folding them for her.' The story always made me cry.

Jim reached over and wiped a tear from my cheek. 'What say we fold a hundred thousand cranes and drop them on the White House? You fold 'em. I'll hire the bomber,' Jim offered. 'Hell, be worth learning to fly.'

I smiled and opened the box. It held a tie-dyed cotton T-shirt the colour of a tropical sky. White circles emanated from one side. I didn't think much of tie-dye. It seemed to lack artistry. But this was his favourite colour, the same dark turquoise of the origami crane. 'It's lovely, Jim. Thank you.' I strained across the bag and box to kiss him.

'It reminded me of you. How you look at things. You know, those strange days when there are rings around the sun.' It was the most interesting compliment I'd ever gotten. 'Why don't you put it on and we'll have an early dinner?'

I changed in the bathroom, ran a brush through my hair, and picked up my tote. Jim took his little notebook and put it in his pocket. We stopped at a neighbourhood park and watched old men playing bocci ball for a few minutes. Jim sat under a tree. He stretched his arm over his head and rubbed his shoulder.

'Need a kink massaged?'

'Huh?' his arm dropped. 'No, just a nervous thing. I catch myself doing it when I'm tense.' He pulled his notebook out of his pocket and sat it open in the grass, doodling, not writing. I sat beside him.

'Jim,' I interrupted, when our eyes met, 'may I write about this morning?'

'It's your journal. You can write about anything you want. This morning happened to both of us.'

I set down, without frills, as much as I could remember of what had happened between us and what Jim had said. At the closing word, I felt so emotionally spent, I couldn't keep my eyes open. Jim was watching the sunset. Its glow made his skin golden, and his dark hair highlighted crimson. His pen rested on the notebook, unmoving. I curled up against him and dozed for a few minutes.

'Trade?' Jim asked, holding out his notebook.

'Not a fair one,' I said, handing him mine nervously. I was anxious for him to feel I had been honest in my writing. I didn't want him to feel I had taken advantage of his vulnerability. His hands were trembling. I felt as if I were intruding by watching him read, so I dropped my eyes to his little notebook. During my brief nap, he had left the page of doodles, and on a fresh one had written seven lines about my unhappy sleep. The settting sun was the opposite of Hiroshima. The poem captured the feel of the day more intimately than my pages of writing.

When he finished reading mine, he kissed my cheek. 'If this was a deposition, I'd sign it. My God, how did you remember what I said so exactly?' Jim asked. 'Hold on to this, will you? By the time I write my first autobiographical novel, I hope the pain and detail will have dulled. This will remind me.'

Jim wrote 'Yes!' in the margin of my journal. An angry swipe of the pencil.

As evening fell, he spoke about his sister, Anne. 'I love her dearly,' he said. 'Sometimes, I miss her a lot. I'd like to be able to pull her hair and ask her what's going on. Nothing spectacular. Just be her big brother the way it should have been. It's really too late. She's outgrown that sort of thing.'

'Is that why you keep tugging my hair?'

'Do I? Maybe. And I don't even think Freud had his head on straight,' he laughed. 'I think with you, it's that I can't resist touching your hair. Rumpelstiltskin would have given up the straw theory in favour of your hair. Absolute gold. Something men would carry in lockets to the Crusades,' he said with a sharp jerk on my hair.

'Cut a lock,' I yelped. 'Don't pull it out.'

Jim laughed. 'Can you sit on it?' he asked, following a strand to its end past my waist.

'What about your brother?' I dragged him back to the real subject.

'Last I saw of him, his hair was short.'

'Jim . . .' I came as close as I wanted to whining.

'You'd like him. Andy's closer to your age. He's a lot nicer than me. If I wasn't a self-centred son of a bitch, I'd introduce you. He'd fall in love at first sight. You could go to movies, neck in the back seat of cars, and live happily ever after. But since I am, forget that.'

Dinner was Jim's retelling of the Greek myth of Orpheus, through a movie made in the late fifties called *Black Orpheus* set in Rio. His face lit up when he spoke of the film. He seemed more drawn by the art of the director, than by the mythological musician. I pushed my salad around and thought Jim could play Orpheus.

On the way back to our room, Jim shrugged, 'Most of my life, I've been a stranger talking to strangers. You know yourself, when you move around so much, you never belong. It's like the American obsession with the Old West. You become the stranger

44

riding into town, and everyone looks at you to change their lives. You are going to be the robber, the killer, or the saviour, but never one of them. I am the constant stranger. With a couple of exceptions. And you are one of those exceptions. That first time I made you really look at me when we met, I knew you. We *recognized* each other.'

We stood at the door to the room, saying nothing. I felt expectant. Jim leaned down and kissed me warmly.

'The key is in your bag,' Jim whispered. Oh. We searched together. It was his find and he unlocked the door. He lit the Virgin Mary instead of switching on the lights. He sat on the foot of the bed, and slid to the floor with a thump. He leaned against the bed, legs stretched out.

Morning seemed a long time ago. I brought a wet washcloth out to Jim. I squatted beside him, but instead of handing it to him, I wiped his brow lightly. From the inside of his left eyebrow, in a line up his forehead, was a deep furrow. I rubbed it gently until it softened, then moved down along his strong nose, across his cheek. When I found the shell of his ear, I knew I wanted to bathe him.

I unbuttoned his shirt. He smiled. I wondered if he were with me on my train of thought. I unwrapped the small bar of sandalwood soap I'd bought earlier, and placed it in his hand. He sniffed it. I filled the ice bucket with very warm water. I meant to bathe the little boy I'd had glimpses of since we met. Whenever I felt like lingering for a caress, or shadowing the washcloth with a kiss, I moved on. When I sat at his feet, I had removed each article of clothing and washed every inch of his body with tenderness, but no sense of foreplay. I let my hand rest on the toes of the left foot where I had stopped. We sat on the floor in silence. Tears caught in his short lower lashes. Some time passed before he rubbed my foot that was nearest him, then stood.

Jim turned down the bed, and lay face down, exhausted. I blew out the candle and watched him from the chair. At last, I changed into the black T-shirt I'd been sleeping in and tried not to disturb him getting into the bed. His breathing was so even, I thought him asleep until his hand closed around mine.

He woke me with a kiss on my cheek. The room was early-morning grey. Jim stroked the arc of my neck, 'I've never felt so close to anyone as I did to you last night. No one has ever been so . . . gentle with me in my whole life. I thought I came here to write, when I came here to have you wash the world away. It was a ceremonial cleansing. I can't explain how incredibly light I feel.'

My chest tightened. I had thought it a kind gesture, and was moved it meant so much more to Jim than I imagined.

'What scared you yesterday?' he asked bluntly.

'Everything,' I laughed.

Jim grinned, 'Oh, there were some sweet sighs along the way.'

'Yeah,' I smiled, remembering the beginning. 'It all escalated so quickly.'

Jim cleared his throat. He kissed me again. 'I want to make you feel what I did last night. To repay you in kind. Just let me please you. I'll respect your virginity. Remember, I'm the one you can trust.'

I had no way of knowing there were so many paths to the same destination. Jim gently introduced me to my own body. His touch had been expertly sensual the day before. That morning it was specifically mine. He eased me on to each new plateau of pleasure, sweet and unhurried. My heart pounded. My teeth tingled. As my excitement crested, Jim slowed, encouraging me to suspend my mind and relinquish control. And I trusted him. He held me in the moment.

'Like the flutter of birds' wings,' I said breathlessly.

He smiled. 'Flutter of birds' wings,' he repeated, enjoying my delight at the discovery. Then he fell silent. After a long pause, he inhaled slowly and sighed, 'I can't leave you here alone, Ginger.' He pulled me against him. 'Is it possible for you to go home?'

I intentionally hadn't mentally put myself alone in that flat. I didn't want to imagine what it would be like in San Francisco without Jim filling up my days. 'That place was okay. Just temporary. I'll meet people. Find a job.'

'The city is going to eat you alive.'

'I'm not stupid. I'm not fragile.' I was scared half to death, but that seemed better than going back. My protest sounded empty. I knew he was right. The city would swallow me.

'I know, baby.'

'And I'm not a baby,' I said defensively.

'It's an endearment. Not a judgment.' He kissed my cheek where he had wakened me earlier.

Jim shared my pillow and slept for a few hours. When he woke, he didn't mention our daybreak conversation. 'There's something I have to do,' he said sombrely. He got up and marched into the bathroom, turned on the shower. He stood in the doorway, and crooked his finger at me. When I reached him, he dragged me into the shower half-dressed. 'I want to wash your hair in the worst way.'

He was determined to give me a great last day of liberty. We had breakfast at a tiny café with linen tablecloths and gold-rimmed china. He took a white rosebud from the vase on the table, and tucked it behind my ear. When we were back on the street, Jim caught my waist, 'I know you are a woman of principle, but I can afford, and would be glad to buy you, a decent meal while we are together.'

'I enjoyed breakfast.'

'You always fill up on free sourdough and order the cheapest thing on the menu.'

I giggled, 'An observant writer. But you're no Sherlock Holmes. Your deduction is all wrong. I'm a vegetarian. Just happens that tends to be cheap.'

He stared a while, recounting my meals to himself. He looked at my woven bag, and cloth shoes. 'Do you find all this leather I wear offensive?' he asked at last.

Jim started hopping on one foot so he could pull off a boot. He dropped it on the sidewalk. Then he hopped on his bare foot, so he could drop the other boot. His feet were very white, edged in pink, and getting pinker. The cement was guaranteed to be cold in the morning shadows. He wormed out of his jacket, suspended it for a moment, and let it drop. We were nearly to the end of the block, looking back at his little trail of abandoned leather. He looked down at his pants. He shrugged, unzipped, and stepped out of them. 'The shirt,' he said twisting to look at his own label, and letting the half-dozen people on the street, including a uniformed policeman, know he wasn't fond of underwear, 'is cotton.' He turned back to me, 'I wouldn't offend you for the world.'

Jim hugged me warmly. There was some laughter and applause.

He righted himself a little, noticing for the first time we didn't have the street to ourselves.

'Young man,' an elderly woman's voice interrupted. She held a boot in her outstretched hand. Jim visibly cringed, expecting her to swing it at him for his risqué performance. 'Did you lose your boot?'

Jim smiled. Yep, he was just walking down the street and started losing his clothes. He was speechless, but took the boot. 'Thanks,' he said, an incredulous look on his face. He watched her retrace his steps and retrieve his clothing. Was she San Francisco's grandmother angel looking after all the young lost who were taking over her city? 'Thanks,' he repeated. He handed me the boots and jacket and pulled on his pants as she crossed the street.

He tore after her. 'Mam,' I heard him say. The rest was pantomime. He tried to get her to take a reward. She refused, and charged up the hill. On the next green, I took the rest of his recovered leather to him. 'Do you think if I ask real nice, she'd adopt me?' he asked. He leaned against the building to pull on his boots. 'She reminds me of my grandmother. She said, "Kindness is its own reward."'

'Well, you should know.'

He grinned, 'I slipped a bill into her coat pocket. Nice to be able to do that.'

Jim decided that I couldn't leave San Francisco without seeing City Lights Bookstore. For some the Golden Gate or Fisherman's Wharf defined San Francisco, but for Jim it was the bookstore that poet Lawrence Ferlinghetti had started in the fifties. As a teenager, Jim thought he caught a glimpse of him once, but had been too shy to speak with him. The store on Columbus wasn't far from us.

'Have you read *On the Road*?' Jim knocked the cover of the book with his knuckle.

'Last year. I thought I discovered it.'

'Me, too. That I discovered it, I mean.'

I told Jim, 'While I was reading it, I kept feeling I was Kerouac. I didn't even notice the first time around that the women were all pretty much overstuffed furniture.'

'Well, you read it as an artist. The women in this book aren't.'

'Dean Moriarty reminds me of my brother. I really didn't know him very well, and Dean seemed to fill in the blanks for me. Wildness bumping up against America. Reminds me of you, too.'

'Moriarty or your brother?'

I laughed, 'Both.'

'It's funny, because when I read *On the Road*, I saw myself as Moriarty. What was that? Wildness bumping up against America? Can I steal that? You said you *didn't* know your brother?'

'He died in Florida a couple years ago,' I sighed softly.

'Florida will do that to you,' he said, then bit his lip. 'I'm sorry, that was crude. I used to live there. I hate the place.'

'Me, too. Never been there, but hate it. Like I hate Dallas.'

Jim raised an eyebrow. 'Was your bother murdered?'

'No. That wasn't what I meant. Just illogical reasons for hating places.'

'How old was he?'

'Twenty-seven. Twenty-eight.'

'Young. A lot older than you, though.'

'Yeah, he was my mother's son from a previous marriage. He only lived with us when I was a baby.'

Jim cruised through the store pouncing on books. He picked up a small, square book with a black and white cover. 'Have you read *Howl*?'

I shook my head. Jim opened it to the title page and pointed to the lines 'Unscrew the locks from the doors! Unscrew the doors themselves from their jambs!'

'You've unhinged me,' he purred. I moaned. I had the feeling he only appreciated his own *door* puns. Serious again, he said, 'Allen Ginsberg made me realize I needed to be a poet. I found this book in a book trader's dive. I was standing by myself saying, "This is why I hear voices." Got some stares. Ginsberg is Carlo Marx in Kerouac's book. Started reading that stuff ten years ago. What were you reading?'

'See Spot. See Spot run.' My favourite character in *Fun with Dick and Jane*.

Jim looked sideways at me. 'Guess I'll have to spot you a few years.'

I moaned again, 'That's dreadful.'

'I *know*. Great, huh? Who influenced you?'

'Oh, real people? Helen Keller. Anne Frank. The maimed and the dead.'

His mouth hung open, 'That cynical remark came out of you?'

'Was that cynical? I thought it was accurate. Ah, fictional, Jo March. *Little Women*.'

'Skipped that classic. I think my little sister read it. Wasn't Katharine Hepburn in the movie? I'll read it if you'll read one of my early influences.' Jim handed me the copy of *Howl* as soon as we hit the bright street. 'For you. You hear voices, too. After Ginsberg screams at you, you will feel less crazy.'

'I've always felt comfortable with my voices.'

'Never thought you might be schizophrenic?' he asked.

'No. It always felt like my own voice. I did not hear God, or dogs speak.'

'Still haven't made peace with mine. Just know they are mine now. When I was younger, I'd be listening to them and wake up blocks away from my house or something. There'd be this time loss. You did it that first night. Toddling off to France.'

'Never had anyone come along before. That was great.'

We ravaged take-out Chinese in a little park. I peeked at *Howl*. Can you read it without thinking the man is screaming? He does yell at you. 'The rhythm reminds me of Dylan's "A Hard Rain's Gonna Fall",' I ventured.

'Bob had to have found this in some little bookstore in Minnesota. There can't be a writer today who doesn't owe some of his rhythm to Ginsberg and Kerouac. They not only made writers of us, they saved our lives. It's like they gave us permission to find our own voices. But when you lose yours, when you think you never will write a decent line again, you hear them,' Jim's voice dropped, 'and you pick up your notebook instead of a gun. Ginsberg, Kerouac, Joyce, my trinity of writers.'

'Ginsberg, Kerouac, Joyce,' I whispered to myself so I wouldn't forget.

We cruised into a used bookstore on Sutter. We sighed over a stack of art books printed in Europe. Jim found a dog-eared and crayon-filled copy of *Little Women* for a quarter. It seemed delightfully silly with the echo of his impassioned speech in my ears. We found a like-new copy of *Portrait of the Artist as a Young Man* for a dollar.

'I think we can tell up front which was the better loved,' I tapped *Little Women* the way he had Kerouac's book.

Jim laughed loudly. The woman clerk behind the register pursed her lips. I watched Jim take her countenance as a challenge. 'I like little women,' he began, 'short women, petites, midgets, munchkins. Do you know why?' he asked, and proceeded to tell her in graphic detail pornographers would envy.

'Sir, this is a children's book.' The clerk's lips were white, her cheeks bright red balls.

'Oh,' Jim leered, stepping over the line of any taste, 'little girls.'

The woman was nearly in tears and Jim showed no sign of relenting. The humour died and his monologue became nasty. I yanked on the back of his shirt. He creased his forehead, but stopped.

Outside, Jim handed me the Joyce book. 'Pull up a curb. I'll tell you why you liked *Little Women*, and you tell me why that hit home.' He smiled, loving the unfairness of the challenge. I did, too. I liked him, sitting on the curb dodging crayons. He read at an even clip, between large print and subject matter, he was turning three pages to my one. 'Marmee?' he asked. I had forgotten how questionable the writing of the children's version was. Maybe I was charmed by Katharine Hepburn's performance in the movie, and not the book. Due comeuppance to have Jim reading it.

Joyce's prose was not as accessible as his poetry. I kept enjoying the words, forgetting they were going anywhere, so I made more U-turns than progress. It was difficult to concentrate, literally on the street, with Jim turning pages noisily at my elbow. He spent an hour on the book and set it down.

'I'd give a lot more than twenty-five dollars for your hair.'

I shook my head of hair. 'Can't have it. Try again.'

'Jo March thinks she's Jack Kerouac instead of a Victorian chair,' Jim said confidently. 'Your turn. Why *Portrait of the Artist as a Young Man?*'

'I never raise my hand in class.'

'I won't flunk you.'

'There's the smell of burning wax about you,' I said honestly. The story of Icarus's father constructing wings of wax and feathers that took him too close to the sun so he fell back to earth leaped out of the book. All Jim. Me. Bright enough to find the answer, not wise enough to map out the consequences. The failed escape.

'You must scare the boys your age half to death.'

'No,' I blushed, 'mostly they scare me.' They would stare at me quizzically and ask me to do their homework, but I was embarrassed to tell Jim.

He looked at me quizzically. 'It would have taken me five minutes to explain. You've never read this before?'

'Smoke and mirrors.'

'Bet your IQ is more than I weigh.'

I imagined his was, too. 'You are kind of thin,' I ran the back of my hand along his ribs. 'What do you weigh?'

'146.'

'You could gain a little.'

'Fuck, you're a genius.'

'"Break on Through" is genius. This little trick is time with you.'

'Would you do that again? If I gave you a book, you tell me what it means to me.'

'Nope. I have no desire to be in your circus as a trained seal. Besides, I have to catch that bus.'

'We have to go back to the motel.'

I held up my bag, 'All packed.'

'There's something I want to give you. Please. Take the next bus. I'll call your folks and let them know.'

We walked back to the motel in silence, swinging hands, happy neither of us had watches to watch. At the room, Jim rustled through his bag, pulled out his notebook and read a few minutes. He bit his lower lip in thought. He nodded his head to some private rhythm, then flashed his slow wide smile.

'I'm gonna teach you to slow dance,' he said, only half as delighted with himself as I was with him. I was so tickled that he had seen the truth in my little joke, I felt like dancing.

'You'll have to show me what goes where.'

'Honey, I've been trying to do that for days,' he teased. 'Okay,

okay. I'll behave myself.' Jim took my left hand and set it down on his right shoulder. He took my right hand in his left. 'All set?'

'It would be easier with the radio.'

Jim nodded. 'I'm going to be your radio.'

To have him hold me a last time felt so good, I kept silent. I did not ask him if his feet were insured, which was the first line that came to me. I did not bring up Ginger, the poor horse. Jim hummed the slow, bluesy melody that he had sung off and on since the first morning, broken by occasional instructions geared to keep my feet off his. I missed the body language that we had while drawing together. I had no instinct to follow him. When his thigh pressed against mine, I would as often move into him as step back. Or, mesmerized by his soft hum, I would forget to move at all.

'Can you snap your fingers?' he asked.

I answered with a sharp snap of my fingers that splintered the spell for a few beats.

'Great. Snap on the downbeat.'

I blushed, 'Which is that?'

'Second, fourth,' he explained, and counted for me. 'I swear one day John is going to leap from behind his drums and wrestle my maracas away from me, because I am always meandering rhythmically. So, don't worry about it. Have fun. You gotta do this so I can give you your present.'

'Another present? I thought my first slow dance was the present.' But I obliged, self-consciously.

Jim held my waist and began to sing a song that began with the title of Anaïs Nin's novel. His voice deepened for the last line. He knew too much. The note surrounded us. I felt suspended in that moment. I wanted to tell him how beautiful the song was, how the music and words had touched me, but I couldn't speak.

'The melody is completely yours,' he said. 'Came to me dreaming about your walk. You have the most graceful walk I've ever seen. I woke up that first morning with the melody in my head. But the words are for both of us. I wrote them this morning, watching you sleep. San Francisco gave me a song after all. And it proves I can write straight.'

'Yeah, sure does,' was all that I could struggle out of my tight throat. Again, I wanted to tell him how beautiful the song was, and couldn't speak. 'Beautiful,' I mumbled. I rubbed my knuckles against the buttons of his shirt.

To reach the bus station, we had to cross downtown and more, but we didn't even debate a taxi. We walked. Jim slowed closer to my natural pace. We didn't talk much in an effort not to say goodbye. Jim walked me past pimps and sailors, mothers with crying children, and the plain weary, to my bus. There was what felt a last kiss. He removed the puzzle ring from his hand. It fell apart. He smiled, reassembled it, and slipped it on to my left ring finger. 'To hold my place,' he said softly. From his pocket, he took his notebook and tore out a page and gave it to me. The song. The music seemed in the words as I read it through. 'And I want you to take this.' He handed me the hundred-dollar bill from the first night. I pushed it back.

'Jim, you've given me all I want. If we are going to be friends, we need to feel equal. You can't keep giving me things like this. We need to have an understanding that you won't give me anything I can't afford to give you.'

'What does baby-sitting pay these days?' he smiled. 'You've given me so much,' his voice broke, 'I'll never be able to repay you.' Jim took out his pen and printed *FREEDOM* across the bill in block letters. 'That's all this is. That's all it means,' he said gently. 'If you get in trouble, use it to come to me.'

4

Show Me Some More

I liked buses the way Jim liked bars. A nagging illness kept me out of school off and on through the fall. I missed the din, the friends, and the ride, but at the end of my first day back, the bus was grating. The quiet block-long walk from the bus-stop to my house was a relief.

I turned directly from the hall into the kitchen to check the mail on the breakfast counter. Set to the side was a plump five-by-seven manila envelope. Jim's loose scrawl nearly covered the face of it. This was the second well-stuffed envelope I had received. The first arrived a few days after we had said goodbye in San Francisco. That one held the promised short story about the corner man he had met in the bar. The story had a telling description of the bar as an overturned shoe-box with a door cut in its side. Boys did that, too? Also included were a half-dozen poems and a two-page letter.

And there were calls.

I looked forward to his calls. As soon as Jim heard my voice on the phone, he would launch into whatever was on his mind without introduction, as if we had been momentarily interrupted in the middle of our conversation. The week after my return home, the phone rang very late. I ran to the phone and Jim began, 'Poor Ginger,' then read the entire chapter from *Black Beauty*, then hung up without editorializing. The tale of how I'd acquired my nickname was something I had repeated without much thought, and was uncertain how accurate my telling had been. I laughed alone that night in the cold kitchen. I pictured Jim sending yet another bookstore clerk into hysterics, this time over just what he liked to do to horses.

He called in August, bursting on the phone without preamble into a new song, 'People Are Strange', that he had written in only twenty minutes outside Robby Krieger's house. For two weeks, Jim had tried in vain to knock something out about being the *constant stranger* when the song came to him as if an unseen hand guided his. He was surprised the handwriting was his own. Jim laughed when I proclaimed it the perfect blending of words and melody.

When The Doors were to appear on the *Ed Sullivan Show*, Jim called the day of the show to make sure I was going to be watching. As if I'd miss my first chance for me to see Jim *leaning professionally*! He had thought of a way to say 'Hello' to me only I would understand. I wondered if I missed something during 'People Are Strange'. After the abbreviated break in 'Light My Fire', Jim sang, 'If I *were* to say to you.' He didn't even crack a smile.

Jim had wrapped and mailed his copy of *Finnegans Wake* in once plain brown paper which he had covered with instructions in wild printing. I was not, under any circumstances, to read the last page until he was present. A Hitchcockian ending? I was not to tell anyone I was reading it for fear they might give away the ending. I was not to use a handbook to get through it. The last note insisted I write down any questions I might have and ask him when he called. Jim was in danger of becoming my Auntie Mame.

'Ginger,' my mother called from the living-room, 'you have company.'

Standing in the archway between the kitchen and living-room, I could see my mother in her straight-backed rocker which gave some relief to her bad back. On the itchy brown settee to my right sat Jim. My little terrier, Joey, who never sat on anyone's lap but mine, was sitting on his having her ears scratched. My first thought was that I was dreaming. I had fallen asleep on the bus, and the envelope in my hand was the beginning of a very nice

56

dream. I enjoyed the calls and letters. His life seemed so frantic and separate from mine, I took Jim's saying we would see each other again as a pleasantry, not a promise.

'Hi,' Jim smiled. He had soft layers of hair around his face. His face looked tired. His eyes were bluer than I remembered. Maybe it was the teal sweater he wore pulled over brown cords. Based on everything in his duffel in San Francisco, I had pictured his wardrobe in black and white. 'Come sit with me.' He was right about my needing some stage direction. I had frozen on my entrance.

On the low coffee-table, Jim had an empty coffee-cup and cake crumbs on my mother's best china. We all smiled at each other. If I had been at my friend's house those few days last summer, where did I meet Jim? I knew he had spoken to my mother the night before. Jim had called, and for the first time I didn't dash to the phone. I couldn't drag myself out of bed knowing I had to face school in the morning.

When my mother carried the collected plates into the kitchen to give us some time alone, Jim took the maroon family album from the bottom shelf of the coffee-table. I was relieved to know he hadn't been there long enough for my mother to have pulled it out. Cake and small-talk. He opened the album and studied the small lacy-edged black and white photographs of my childhood. 'This is you?' he asked. Me bundled tightly, smiling in the hands of the fatima who insisted on carrying me everywhere.

I nodded. 'I was born in North Africa. Morocco. French Morocco, then.'

'You came from Africa?' He smiled, looking through a few pages of the pictures. 'Take me there,' he said. He went back to the beginning and turned each page slowly, wanting me to introduce him to each shadowy figure. Jim was fascinated with my brother Bill, an obviously red-haired and freckled kid even in black and white. The teenager had taken a few words of French, a quickness with Arabic, and his American slang and turned them into a thriving bartering business in the open street-markets.

I strained to remember the names of the places from family stories. My memories were from these pictures and our home movies. We left Morocco when I was still a toddler. When I had guided him through the markets, the Arab Medina, the flat-topped houses of Rabat, and the beaches at Casablanca, I continued with snatches of *Casablanca* and *Lawrence of Arabia*. Catching the shift from memories to movies, Jim joined in too. He was a great travelling companion. Through his imagination, I could feel the hot desert sand, hear the evening prayers, and see a flash of my brother considering charm a commodity.

'Ooh, I always hate to come back,' Jim sighed wistfully.

'Me, too. I envy the trips you share with other people,' I admitted. 'I think about it sometimes and feel left out. Where do you go with your other friends?'

'What? I don't do this with anyone else. That time in San Francisco was the first time anybody ever followed me on one of these . . . tangents. I get open mouths and confused silences. I get, "Jim, you are weird." I get, "Jim, what are you on?" Which makes me curious, want to try it on acid?'

Jim had mentioned acid a few times. I had managed not to answer. I was working on an uncomfortable silence. At last, I just went with the truth. I said, 'Drugs scare me. A brother of a friend of a friend wound up at Agnew's. The state hospital. I feel like my brains are all I have going for me. I'm afraid to mess with them.'

'Not even a close pal?' Jim chuckled. 'Amazing as they are, your brains aren't all you have going for you. But if you're scared, you shouldn't get into it. If you ever feel you want to, though, let me know. Until then, tempted as I am, I won't pester you about it. Brought you something,' Jim said, producing a neatly wrapped album.

I decided not to apologize for my old record-player all the way down the hall to my room. Jim might grant me some grace since it was the one on which my sister had played her Elvis records. My room was small and clean, but not neat. Piles of books, records, and art supplies were stacked anywhere there didn't need to be a footpath. I followed Jim's eyes as he glanced around the room.

A gold silk shawl from Morocco covered the small dresser which had been recently painted bright orange. Above it was an unframed round mirror. The old coral and white record-player stood on a table in the corner. The gingham curtains and matching bedspread on the twin bed under it were from a previous incarnation. On the wall was a single poster that quoted Camus, 'In the midst of winter, I found there was in me an invincible summer.'

'Yeah,' Jim smiled. 'Invincible.' He jerked my hair, 'Can we close the door?' I reached behind me and swung it closed. He caressed my neck and kissed my cheek. 'You're hot,' he informed me.

'Are you flirting with me?' I asked, even warmer from the kiss.

'Always,' he grinned, 'but I meant you have a fever. Should you be in bed?'

'Are you flirting with me?' I repeated, enjoying the play of conversation.

He laughed and hugged me tightly. 'I missed you. It's been too long. My life has been crazy, going from being unwanted to in demand in a year screwed up my personal life. I never seem to have enough time for what I want to do.' He felt my forehead with the back of his hand like a worried mother.

'What do you have?' he asked. 'Mono?'

I shrugged. 'No. The doctors can't seem to pin it down, so they just gave up on it. It's not catching, just something out of whack.'

'I think Navy doctors are only trained in the signal corps. Why don't you see a real doctor? Get this cleared up. You didn't feel well right after school started.'

'Probably allergic. I'm okay.'

'Your parents can't deny you medical care,' Jim said sharply.

'They aren't denying me anything, Jim. They do the best they can.'

'Honey, if it's a matter of money, just send me the bills.'

'Thank you. You are always so generous. But I'm on the mend. Back at school today.' He argued for a good doctor. I felt flushed and embarrassed. 'Jim, we made an agreement. You don't get anything for me that I can't get for you.'

'This doesn't count.'

'Everything counts,' I said.

I realized I was still clutching my books and envelope from Jim, and plopped them on the foot of the bed. Jim picked up the top book, 'You're reading Camus.' He opened it. 'In French!' He stared with a little awe at my copy of *L'Etranger* (*The Stranger*).

I giggled. 'You keep looking at me in ways no one else ever does.

I hate to lose that look of amazement – it feels wonderful, but we had to read a novel for French class. I chose *L'Etranger* because it was short.'

'How are you doing with *Finnegans Wake*?' Jim plucked it from the top of the stack of books near the head of the bed.

'Confidentially,' I sighed, 'a whole lot of it seemed like Irish jabberwocky.'

Jim laughed, 'Yeah, Joyce might have enjoyed that description. And the rest?'

'Drooled all over it.'

Pleased I'd neared the end, he wanted me to wrap it up right then. I didn't want to float in someone else's stream of consciousness with Jim's present, but he was excited about the prospect. He stretched out on my bed, and patted the small space next to him. Curled up in his arms, I could have read all night. I let him bear the weight of the book. He turned the pages on cue. When I reached the last page, the last incomplete sentence, I laughed. Jim's surprise! The book read in a circle. The river runs endlessly. I flipped back to the beginning. 'This is going to take a while,' I teased.

Then it hit me! I'd been given a 628-page hint that *The Doors* album sang in a circle. I turned to look into Jim's eyes to see if I were right. '"The End" is not The End because you "Break on Through to the Other Side".' I came as close as I ever would to squealing. Jim clapped his hands and hugged me.

'I knew you wouldn't let me down. Nobody, fucking nobody, got the damn point of the thing. Everybody is so damn preoccupied with the words that they don't get the meaning. The band doesn't get it. Pompous-assed reviewers didn't get it. So busy getting off wallowing in the dark, they refuse to see the light.'

'Jim, I think you might find a smaller hint,' I giggled and thought I could have read the first and last page and done as well. 'Hand out Joyce at your concerts, and your fans would sit on him. Know I would. More cushion than a programme.'

'Wonder if I could get a deal buying them in quantity. Be fun to enclose little response cards in them.'

'You are the tiniest bit impossible.'

'Thanks. I like that about myself,' he laughed softly.

'Why don't you just write an article that explains what you are trying to do as a band? As a poet?'

'The only band with *Cliff Notes*.' Jim slapped his thigh. 'Where's a pen? I'll start right now.'

'Maybe a comic book. I was busy reading something else when I was supposed to be reading *Les Miserables*, so a friend loaned me a comic-book version. My book report was concise and I passed the essay test. I think that's the way to go.'

'I'm tempted. I like to draw cartoons. A friend and I used to do these wild, slightly pornographic cartoons. See myself as one.'

'A wild and slightly pornographic cartoon?'

'Yep. Like my new haircut?' He shook his head. 'It got more reviews than my songs. It is *liontene*.'

'Oh, I thought this,' I ran my finger down his nose, 'was straight off the Serengeti.'

'Want to hear this?' he asked, bopping me on the head with the gift he had tossed at the foot of the bed. I apologizied for the ancient record-player, despite my pledge. 'This the one your sister played "Ain't Nothin' But a Hound Dog" on?'

I laughed and wanted to tell him I was just thinking of that. Instead, I unwrapped the album. 'Your circus!'

'Had to fight for that. Elektra wanted me staring malevolently on the cover.'

'I like the band as the poster. Where's the high-wire act?'

'Two storeys up.' He shot his thumb in the air. I reminded him it was three in San Francisco. 'But you strongly suggested I not do that any more.' He jumped from the bed and balanced on one foot for me.

I skimmed the contents and didn't see anything that seemed to reflect the song he wrote for us in San Francisco. I wanted that moment of hearing for the first time what the band created from Jim's haunting song. I wanted to hear it again. I had tried a few times to sing 'The Spy' myself and lost the melody.

'It's not there.' He must have caught the flicker of disappointment I tried to hide. 'You see, the way the band works is that I sing a song and they figure out what the notes are, fill in the bridges, and generally make musical sense of the thing. I had it in my head to, but I just couldn't sing it in front of them. It's too achingly personal.' And 'The End' wasn't? I thought. He seemed to sense my question. 'I need some distance before I can do that,' he explained. 'Besides, when you hear this, you'll see it doesn't fit musically. Are you terribly disappointed?'

Yeah, but I wasn't going to cry. 'Maybe you could sing for me sometime.'

'Sure,' Jim said. He put the album on the turntable very carefully and set the needle down on the precise beginning of 'Strange Days'. Jim had sung a couple of the songs to me over the phone, and I had heard Jim's 'People Are Strange' and 'Love Me Two Times', which Robby had written, on the radio. Being able to hear the whole thing with Jim was an exciting prospect.

He leaned against the dresser and surveyed the album cover as if he were inspecting the art for the first time. He turned the album over and stared at the back cover, then sat cross-legged on the floor, chose a felt pen from a jar on the floor, and obliterated the model from the doorway on the back cover. Between songs, I asked, 'Then who is the man holding out the tambourine to?'

'She's just inside the door.'

'That's a nice line.'

He smiled, 'Yeah, I'll make a note.' He sang, 'And she's just inside the door,' dropping his voice as if it were the last line of a song. From the record, Jim screamed, the first line of 'Horse Latitudes'.

I sat beside him on the floor. He started to recite the poem he told me he had written at my age. Lagging behind the record by a few words, speaking very softly, he became his own echo. He explained during one of our late-night phone calls that it was inspired by a painting depicting sailors throwing a cargo of horses overboard to lighten the load and save the ship in a storm. It was, as surely, Jim struggling, only to be swallowed by the emotionless sea.

I flipped the album over. 'Moonlight Drive'. The *going down* line I questioned in San Francisco was mumbled. When there were only two more songs on the record, Jim said, 'Show me your school,' suddenly on his feet and raising the needle from the turntable.

'It's across town.' I wanted to hear the rest of his album. I was dying to open the envelope on my bed that was fat enough to be another story. Poems. A long letter. All three.

'I have a car,' he held out his hand, 'I want to see where you spend your time so I can picture you there.'

'It's like any other school in California. Nondescript. Even after you see it, you won't remember it.' I didn't want to see school when I had to, let alone what little time I had left with him. Jim slid open my closet. Fortunately, nothing fell on him. He grabbed my pea coat. We were going for a ride.

'We're going for a drive, okay?' I half-asked my mother on the way out the door. I found it best to ask these things in motion. When she offered to hold dinner, I said, 'No, thanks,' imagining I'd rather starve than watch my father and Jim glare at each other across the table. 'We'll pick something up.'

Jim and my mother exchanged friendly 'Nice to meet yous'. Once outside, Jim smiled to himself, 'I didn't bring your address with me, but remembered the name of the street and that you lived in a yellow house. I stopped at the first one, and this small, red-headed woman, holding her place in *Anna Karenina* with her finger, opened the door. I thought, 'Whatever daughter she has, close enough.'

'Did you have cake and coffee there, too?' I enjoyed his laugh. He was my favourite audience. 'The thing about my mother I really like is that she's reading Tolstoy because he writes a good story.'

'Yeah. I liked your mom.' He had told her we met in San Francisco. 'I thought some part of our stories should match. She assumed it was at a concert.'

'Then she does know you're in a band.'

He smiled, 'I thought so, at first. But my name didn't mean anything to her. I thought it was good fun to be a poet, infatuated by her Rapunzel, but she was so nice in the end, I just didn't want to embarrass her. She thinks the world of you. She may not understand what you draw or write, but she understands your need to do it. My grandmother was like that.'

Jim's car, parked in front of the next house, was light green or blue, hard to distinguish in the fading light. Chunky and unattractive. He held the door for me. I slid over on the bench seat and fiddled unsuccessfully with the handle of his door. Jim opened it and climbed behind the wheel. He hesitated for an instant about where to insert the key. 'Not my car,' he explained.

63

'Oh, good. That,' I pointed at the pink and white 1957 Thunderbird in the drive across the street, 'is a car.'

'Aren't I supposed to say that?' He whistled. She was beautiful. 'What kind of car do you want when you get your licence?'

'Um . . . either a '56 or '57 Chevy . . . which has the smaller fins? Or a little Nash Rambler.'

Jim shook his head. 'Kinda different cars.' He thought a minute. 'I give up. I can't imagine what they have in common.'

'They come in turquoise and white. Did I mention that turquoise is my favourite colour?'

Jim smiled. He started the engine, then leaned over to kiss me. Just when I convinced myself that I wanted him to fill the void my older brother had left in my life, Jim touched me and I was all muddled again.

'May I turn on the radio?' I asked with my hand on the knob.

With Jim's 'Sure', I clicked it on. Jim sang 'People Are Strange' from the radio and he laughed next to me in the car. 'How did you do that?'

'I just turned on the radio. You wrote the song. How did you do *that*?'

'You know how I did that.' He tousled my hair. 'I didn't hear Doors' music once on the drive up from LA, not even goddamn "Light My Fire", and you turn on the radio to my song.'

'Must not have been on the right station at the right time. I hear you a lot.'

'You're being evasive.' He raised his left eyebrow. 'You're almost as good at that as I am.'

I was nervous about directing him to school. Accustomed to driving with people who knew the town, I kept forgetting to tell him the few turns there were. He was lucky I didn't give him the bus route. When we pulled up in front of the sprawling school, I had the same sinking feeling I had to shake off every time I looked at it.

'I wouldn't do this for anybody else.' I smiled to myself, thinking it sounded similar to what he had said in San Francisco about his piano playing. I said, 'I cut school as much as I come.'

Amos Alonzo Stagg High School, named for a famous football coach, consisted of long, low buildings with covered corridors arranged around the central sunken grassy quad where most of the students ate lunch and changed the world. I led him to the quad.

'You're right,' he laughed, swinging himself around a pole. 'Forgettable.' He let himself fall on the rough dry grass. 'I'm here and I can't remember what colour it is.'

I joined him on the grass. 'The Jefferson Airplane played here. Last year, I think, when my sister was going here. Somebody swiped their recorder.'

'Serves them right,' Jim grinned, 'playing high-schools.'

'They probably pay more than small clubs.' I stuck up for the Airplane.

He laughed, 'Even after figuring recorder losses?'

'And the audience listens.'

'Might be worth it at that.' He brushed my hair out of my face. 'Been on a date yet?'

'Does this count?'

'Besides this.' He poked me gently with his finger.

'No. Most of my friends haven't paired off.' Nobody had asked me out.

'Gotta be somebody you're interested in,' he prodded. 'Who are the cute guys here?'

'A friend's older brother is tall, brilliant, and mysterious,' I suggested, warming to the fun of Jim's game instead of feeling like the last surviving wallflower in California.

'Nah, that won't work. He'll only see you as his little sister's little friend,' Jim advised. 'Who else?'

I wondered how many of his little sister's little friends had vainly tried to get him to notice them. All those sweet things enamoured of the handsome, if peculiar, senior. 'Well, today, I was walking along the corridor and heard a beautiful voice. This boy in front of me was singing to himself. He looked like the young actor Kurt Russell. Light brown hair, streaked blond, blue eyes. I tried to catch up so I could make out the song. "Pretty woman, walking down the street. Pretty woman, the kind I like to meet." His voice had this hypnotic quality. I was following so close that when he stopped suddenly, I nearly gave him a flat.'

'Get his number?'

'No. I found out who he was, though,' feeling silly for admitting it. 'Nick Isaak. Nice name, don't you think?'

'Oh, yeah. Ought to call him up. Hey, Nick . . .'

'But he's a junior,' I sighed. 'I wouldn't call a junior. Besides, I don't know him. Why would I call him just because he's nice looking and sings?'

Jim fell back laughing, 'I don't know, Ginger, it works for me.'

I tickled his exposed side, 'I like *you* for your sense of humour.'

'Thank God, somebody does. I can't make anyone else laugh.' He held my hand away from him, 'You'd like me if I was a clerk at City Lights, wouldn't you?'

'Could you get me a discount?' I asked, and got a tickling in retaliation. Jim pinned me against the cool ground. In the twilight, I could make out the brightness of his eyes, and the white of his smile. The rest of his face was shadow.

'Does this kid Nick sing better than me?' he asked.

His kissing me wasn't going to make me cry uncle. 'Yeah, he does.'

'I don't have much of a voice,' he said, as if he were agreeing with me.

'Rock 'n' roll or the blues,' I said, recalling his being my radio while we slow-danced in that motel room in San Francisco, 'isn't about range or hitting all the notes right.'

'Is this supposed to make me feel better?' he giggled. 'I have no range and probably never once hit a note square on.'

'What? Are you kidding? You have an amazing voice. You have . . . magic.'

'Right,' Jim frowned. 'That's why I have to get a buzz-on to face an audience.'

'Do you? That's shyness, not lack of talent.'

'There's something Joan of Arc in you.'

I grinned. 'The voices I hear are my own. Didn't we clear that up?'

'But you'd lead armies to defend what you believed in.' Yeah, I thought. I would do anything for you, Jim. He asked, 'Have you ever driven all night?'

'Most of my life,' I said. 'When my dad traded in the family car, I felt like we lost Belle Rive.'

Jim laughed, shaking his head from side to side and his finger at me. 'Yeah, Belle Rive . . . Belle Rive. Tennessee Williams. The family estate Blanche lost in *A Streetcar Named Desire*. I know there is more to this. It was a Belair, wasn't it? A Chevy Belair?' He remembered the photograph of my brother and his friend in a traditional pose by our old car.

'You're fun to play with.' I rubbed his back.

'Does anybody else even know there's a game going on?'

'Not usually.'

'Let's go find a phone and tell your mother I'm dropping you at a friend's house for the night.' Jim was on his feet and extending a hand to me.

'I'll just ask her.'

'Honey, don't think your mom liked me *that* much. No teenage girl's mother ever liked a guy that much.'

We drove down Pacific Avenue. Jim eased into a gas station and up by the phone booths. He climbed out with me, and gleaned a handful of change from his pockets. He picked out a dime and deposited it. He started to dial the area code and had to start over. I liked his knowing my number by heart. Jim handed me the receiver. 'Lie,' he said firmly. When my mother answered the phone on the second ring, I closed the folding doors. I didn't need an audience.

We talked for a few minutes. I hung up the phone and leaned out of the booth. 'College boy?' I asked Jim.

Hands in pockets, he grinned. 'Now, I didn't out and out lie. Your mother asked me if I went to UOP?' He made a question of the initials.

'University of the Pacific,' I explained, nodding in the direction of the campus.

'So, I said, "No, I went to UCLA," which is true. I think I even have a degree somewhere. Can't say for sure. I majored in acid, minored in film.'

'So that's why you have an edge on being James Wong Howe! How,' I giggled at the repetition of sound, 'did that get you into rock 'n' roll?'

'Nobody wanted me to make dark and sensitive films. I always had music in my head, but thought it was for myself. I never took it very seriously. A friend from school, that's Ray, had a band. I wasn't doing anything. Gave me somebody to hang out with. Now, of course, everybody wants me to make dark and sensitive music. I discovered I have all this hidden ambition and am amused, or is it revolted?, that I want us to be bigger than the Rolling Stones. Well, do I drive you home?'

'No, we drive all night.'

'Your mother gave you permission to spend the night with me?' Jim was shocked.

'Yes. She'll cover for me. She'll tell my dad I'm with a friend if he asks. He'll assume it's one of my girlfriends.' I didn't know how to explain to Jim there were no spoken rules in my house. No curfew. No boundaries. Until that last summer, I had held a tighter rein on myself than my parents would have to avoid trouble. With Jim's protective nature, I didn't want to tell him if my dad found out, he'd probably kill me. 'My mother said there was nothing we could do at 2 a.m. that we couldn't have already done. She warned me, though, that college boys might expect more of girls. And was on the brink of telling me what boys and girls do when they are alone when her New England reserve got the better of her.'

Jim put his hand on my shoulder and leaned close to my ear to whisper, 'Well, as close as I can figure, they talk themselves hoarse.'

I smiled, 'I'm sorry, Jim. Rather take me home?'

'Not a chance. I have lots of people to fuck and nobody to talk to. When I was your age, all we did was make out. I still think it's really sexy. Especially with you,' he slipped his arm around my waist. 'For now, I know it's easier for me to remember what it was like to be that boy, than it is for you to pretend to be twenty. I'm not going to disappear if you need some time for your emotions to catch up with your brains. Truth is, you don't know what I'd give to be that kid Nick and be sixteen with you,' he smiled, then whispered, 'and I'd kill to have his voice.'

'I wish I had gone to school with you. Been there with you, instead of here alone.' I paused. 'Jim, I didn't mean to hurt your feelings about your singing. It never occurred to me that you didn't know how good you are. Can I tell you something about your voice?' I didn't look at him so he wouldn't wave me off. 'This summer I went to the music festival at Mt. Tam. The end of the second day, I was scorched from too much sun and just wanted to get home. My friend and I were waiting for the bus to take us down the hill, and "Crystal Ship" filled the air. I made her stop talking so I could hear the song. I don't know if it was the radio through the speakers or if The Doors were there,' I looked at Jim for the first time, hoping he would clear up that point, but he was staring at the ground. 'It was the first time I felt music was a part of me. I wasn't just enjoying listening to it. I was breathing it. That's the magic you have. It was the only spiritual experience I've ever had.'

'I dunno,' Jim looked up from the pavement, grinning, 'I think feeling Elvis's chest reverberate would fit into that category.'

'Kind of a distant second.'

'For a third, where are the best French fries in town?' he opened the car door.

'If you're with me, you can't have the best. You have to settle for ones that are not fried in beef fat or lard and . . .'

'Have a spiritual experience.'

'Could we pretend I didn't make that particular speech.'

'No. I love your speeches. You remind me of Shirley Temple saying "I'm very self-reliant." Your sincerity is a couple notches above that. You made me feel very good. I'm not very gracious about compliments. Thank you.'

'You're very welcome. Could I ask you something about the song?'

Jim pulled me up against his chest. 'Just ask. Don't ask if you can ask.'

'Is it gentle *rain* like a shower, or *reign* as in rule?'

He smiled and looked sideways in thought. 'I wrote it *rain* as in shower,' he explained, 'but the other is interesting. It is what you do in relationships. Give the one you love power over you and hope it is gentle.'

We shared French fries and sandwiches at a picnic table in front of the drive-in. When we were about to leave, Little Richard's 'Jenny, Jenny' blared from the loudspeaker. I took Jim's hand, and in my best effort to remember the *American Bandstand* dances, coaxed him into a brief bit of parking-lot rock 'n' roll.

69

I half-sang, 'Jimmy, Jimmy, ooh, Jimmy, Jimmy, won't you come along with me? Jimmy, Jimmy.' Jim ended the dance by giving me a gentle twirl.

He smiled, 'Cute. Clever. I'll dance with you anytime, but do you mind not ever seriously calling me Jimmy? Makes my stomach roll. *They* used to call me that when I was little.'

I couldn't seem to get my foot out of my mouth. But Jim was still speaking to me. As I was about to make another round of apologies, a girl I vaguely recognized from school pulled up.

'Hi,' she jumped out of her car and hurried over to us. 'Hi,' she gazed into Jim's eyes.

'Hi,' Jim said sweetly, mimicking her gaze to perfection.

I couldn't remember her name, so I introduced Jim. 'This is my friend, Jim.'

'Nice to meet you,' she said. 'Do you go to UOP?'

He rolled his eyes in my direction. 'No, I went to UCLA.' It worked once, and he enjoyed repeating it.

'They have a great football team, don't they?'

'Sure do.' He nodded politely. 'Rah, Bruins,' he said as soon as he got in the car. Jim threw his head back and shook his curls. 'Anytime I feel swamped by fame, I'll just hang out in Stockton.'

5

---·••·---

Free From Disguise

Jim turned the radio up so loud we couldn't hear the rough engine, and sang last year's 'Sunny Afternoon' with the Kinks that late-autumn evening. He made his way south to Five and hummed through the Beach Boys' 'Heroes and Villains'. Seventy miles, and a dozen songs later, he turned west. At eight o'clock, Hollister was asleep. Jim barely stopped for traffic lights. He peeled through town and on to the dark two-lane country road. When we lost the Stockton station, he tuned in Patsy Cline. He sang 'Walking After Midnight' with the same enthusiasm he sang with Ray Davies. I joined in on the last verse. I figured between Jim and Patsy, my little voice would disappear, and I very much wanted to get the sound of my own voice saying 'Jimmy, Jimmy' out of my head.

In Salinas, Jim stopped at a market and emerged with an open bottle of orange-juice. He swallowed a quarter of it in one gulp and handed it to me. I sniffed it and he laughed.

'It's unaltered in any way. No booze. No acid. Cross my heart.' He crossed his heart and looked like an alter boy who'd just nicked the gold candlesticks.

'Talk about an act of trust.' I took a sip.

We stopped at a little park. There was just enough moon to see the water's edge as we held hands and walked in step around its little pond. Startled geese honked at us. Jim laid out his suede jacket for us to sit on. He held me in silence for a long while. The geese whistled softly as they settled in again. Running a knuckle along my stocking, he said, 'Seems like there should be fireflies.'

'Maybe it's too late in the year,' I suggested, 'or maybe they're one of those things, like Tinkerbell, that only children can see. Come to think of it, I haven't seen them since I was little in Tennessee. There were great swarms of them by the gully near our house. Sometimes the next day, I'd go out and find dead ones. I'd look at them for the longest time trying to figure out how they worked from their dead iridescent bodies. Iridescence doesn't, on its own, translate into light, does it?'

'I think it may be more a matter of geography,' Jim assured me. 'I saw them in Virginia when I was older than you. Come,' Jim was on his feet again, 'I want to show you something.' So much for whistling with the geese. I groaned as I got to my feet . . . He asked, 'Are you tired? . . . It's not far. Promise.'

We didn't drive far, south on 101, not singing with the radio. We listened to the drone of the engine. He drove past whatever he had in mind, and had to pull off the highway and head north again. He guided the car off the road and rolled to a stop. Squinting in the darkness, all I could see was a big black field. Nothing. Was I supposed to see fireflies? Jim scooted across the seat and pushed open my door. Getting out, I stumbled on the slope. Jim caught my arm to steady me.

'You left the lights on.' They were the only light in the area.

'Yeah,' he said. 'Just be a few minutes.'

Jim held me by the waist and lifted me on to the hood of the car. The engine was warm under me. I could see my breath. The night was turning cold, but a few staunch moths were already gathering in the headlights.

Jim started walking down the side of the road. I wasn't invited. It wasn't long before I could hear his footsteps, but not see him, and not much longer still until I couldn't hear him. Sitting alone on the hood of the car, it seemed he was gone a long time.

As I was debating following him to see if he were all right, Jim walked back into the boundary of light, one foot nearly in front of the other, the grounded wire walker. He stopped in the headlights and caught a moth in his cupped hands. Pausing in front of me, he opened his hands under my chin so the moth brushed my cheek as it escaped.

'You didn't flinch.'

'It was a moth,' I said simply.

He walked around the car and turned off the headlights. He stood watching the road. An eighteen-wheeler passed so close, the car heaved in its wake. I was learning to comfortably ride out Jim's thoughtful silences. After some time, he came back to my side of the car. He slipped between my dangling legs and encircled me with his arms. 'This is where James Dean died,' nodding just ahead of us. 'A car accident in a silver Corvette. I've been working on a poem about him. You made me realize I've been trying to figure out how he worked from his dead iridescent body.' I shivered. Jim continued, 'He was twenty-four when he died. I'm going to be twenty-four next month. I wonder if anybody had the guts to tell him to slow down, tell him he was driving his life too fast.'

I was afraid to ask what he counted on me to ask. If I did, it would change what we could ever be together. 'Does anyone have the courage to tell you?' I asked softly, hoping he wouldn't hear. Jim shrugged and diverted his eyes. 'Want me to?' I rested my hands on his shoulders. I felt the tension through his jacket. He dropped his head. Half a nod. 'Slow down,' I whispered, running my fingers through his hair. 'Please, slow down.'

Jim was quiet for a few minutes. He drew in a long breath. He said, 'Thanks. I know I can't, but I wanted somebody to risk telling me.'

Risk. Yes. I knew it. 'I . . .' I couldn't say the word, 'care about you, Jim.'

'I know you love me,' he said the word softly. 'If I wasn't sure, I wouldn't have brought you here. I knew when you said that thing about *Portrait of the Artist* you were telling me then. I've never been so . . . accepted. People usually invent me. They fall in love with who they want me to be and then are disappointed I'm not that.'

'I think that's probably true of everyone, Jim. Part of it's not

73

being able to really know anyone for a long time. So you fill in with what you want to be there to make it seem safer.'

'Ah,' he smiled, 'you're one of the ancient ones.'

I laughed, 'Does that mean I'm old enough for you after all?'

'I'm an ancient one, too. Do you believe in reincarnation?'

'No . . . but I don't not believe in it.'

'I don't intellectually, but it wouldn't take long to convince me we've known each other forever. It's comforting, in a way, to think you'll be there next time around.'

I laughed nervously, 'I wish I could figure out what we are supposed to be in this life.'

'Oh, let's just make it up as we go along. We don't have to be anything anyone else has been. I love to improvise.'

'You have a talent for it. That's why I can't understand how you can believe Camus.'

Jim raised his eyebrows. 'Do I believe Camus? Why would that rub you the wrong way?'

'A third of the way through *The Stranger*, he has the protagonist proclaim that you can't change your life, then sets him up to prove it.'

'And you don't read French?' he grinned.

'I get a word here and there. I have trouble reconciling the writer of the book with the author of the line on my poster. Where is an *invincible summer* in his fatalist philosophy.'

'You are assuming that to have a destiny you can't interrupt is a negative thing. It also means if you are destined to be Buddha, you can't screw it up by making a bad decision today. I think Camus has his hero, if you can call him that, verbalize his philosophy at that point, because we spend the first third of our lives constructing a philosophy we spend the rest of our lives trying to prove.'

'You understand everything one step beyond my ability. It's frustrating to get close, and not quite get it.'

'Hell, I just thought of that because you told me where the heart of the book was. I don't think I saw it that clearly when I read it. Life helps.'

'Where is your life going, Jim? Where are you going to be two-thirds of your life down the line?'

'*We* will be walking along the beach in Algiers. A fifteen-year-old kid is going to run up to me and say, "Old man, that last book of yours was jive jabberwocky," and I'm gonna say, "Thanks, man."'

I laughed. He had us walking with Camus' protagonist in Joyce's tracks. 'That's a relief,' I said. 'At least you can see yourself older than James Dean.'

'The point was – how did you miss it? – I see myself with *you*.' Jim lifted me from my roost. 'Like a driving lesson?'

Fine time, talking about fatal traffic accidents. Inevitability. Who could resist? Even after moving the seat forward, Jim had to shove his coat behind my back so I could reach the pedals.

'Too bad this is an automatic. We could have some real fun.'

'This is enough fun. I've never driven at night. And I've only been behind the wheel a few times. The driver ed. instructor at school has a certain reputation. You kinda have to get your knees over by the door. You learn to drive side-saddle.'

Jim put the car into gear. He was a quiet teacher, not saying much, giving due warning of turns.

'Where are we going?'

'Big Sur,' he said.

The road that connected 101 to the coastal highway was black and winding. Jim said, 'On these little turns' – little turns? They snaked! – 'don't use the brake. Let up on the gas and when you are almost halfway through the turn, give it a little gas.' He went on about letting centrifugal force work for you. Not using the break was a terrifying thought. And a terrifying moment the first time I tried it. I was sure I would send the borrowed car into a tree. By the sixth curve, I thought, 'This is fun.' Using the brake was an act of cowardice. With Jim, I felt fearless.

When we reached Highway One, Jim took over. The moon's silver reflection played on the water and the surf glowed an eerie white. We stopped several times when there was room to pull off the highway. That stretch of the coast had rugged climbs down to narrow beaches, made even narrower by the rising tide.

We found a flat ledge a few steps down from the top of the cliffs and wrapped ourselves in a dirty sleeping bag Jim scavenged from the car's trunk. The padding helped against the wind and dampness. I was still a little feverish, but Jim shivered. I pulled him against me. 'Good use of a fever.' Jim settled in. 'I don't think I could ever live inland again. I was born by the water. Is Sagittarius a water sign?' Jim asked. 'When's your birthday?'

'January.'

'Really. A Capricorn? That's so odd. I swear I don't really believe in that shit, but everyone I'm close to is Sagittarius or Capricorn.'

'Coincidence,' I smiled. 'Like turning on the radio to your song. I could have turned on the radio and gotten Janis Joplin. I could have been born a couple weeks later and been an Aquarius.'

'Down-to-earth wild child.'

'Yeah,' I laughed. 'Only thing Capricorn about me. I do know it's an earth sign.'

'I feel like writing. Mind if I write for a while?' Jim asked softly.

'No. Have a flashlight?'

Jim was gone and back in a few minutes. We arranged ourselves as before. Jim laid his notebook on his knees. After a few attempts to make the propped flashlight hit the paper, I held it over his left shoulder. He spent half a page repeating the same line; then he drew a line of rocks, a jetty to divide the page.

'Would you rather I didn't watch?' I asked.

'No. You're fine. It's how I warm up. Let me know when your hand gets tired.'

Jim hummed something bluesy. On the second time through, I identified it as John Lee Hooker's 'Boom Boom'. And Jim was writing steadily. Each word captivated me. Mesmerized by his humming and the waves, I didn't realize my hand had begun to shake. Jim reached up to steady my hand.

'Your mother won't let you come out and play with me if I run you into a relapse. Let's drive up the coast and get a room.' I protested. Jim closed his notebook. 'Well, I'm cold.'

So was I. But I didn't want to be the one to give in. The hand holding the flashlight was frozen into a claw. I wasn't sure I could feel my nose. 'It's a good poem.' He had left behind the first line about the ocean's edge, and written about driving at night.

'It's a good start.' Jim handed me his notebook. This was a larger one than he had with him in San Francisco. The first third had the

76

fluffiness of used paper. He carried the bulky sleeping bag, but kept a firm grip on my hand until we were on safe ground.

The next town north was Carmel, an intentionally picturesque seaside town. I imagined our pulling into the drive of one of the charming cottages, but Jim had a magnet that drew him to the shabbiest motel in any given town. I waited in the car while he got a room in a little place with the painted pink vacancy sign. Neon was banned in Carmel.

'If anybody asks, you're my little sister.'

'Aren't I?'

When he switched on the light, Jim groaned. I laughed. The bulb was tired and dim. It illuminated a circle the size of a platter. I had good night vision. The room itself was about the size of my own bedroom. The curtains, original with the place, were bark cloth in a tropical leaf print. The bed had a decided slope towards the centre and was covered in a threadbare, yet somehow pristine, white chenille spread. If they threw in a bookcase, I would have moved in permanently.

'Let's turn the little light back off,' Jim said, spinning on his heel.

'I love it.' He stared at me and laid his hand on my forehead. 'It's not the fever,' I laughed. 'You absolutely can't love Elvis and hate this.'

Jim shook his head. 'Must be we are looking at the same painting and seeing different things.'

'This,' I whispered, 'is my childhood . . . bark cloth and chenille.'

He ruffled the drapes and dust flew. 'Bark cloth?'

'Refers to the texture.'

'Shit,' Jim laughed, 'let's see how bad the bathroom is. I'm chilled, I'd like to crank up the heat and take a bath.'

As soon as he hit the switch in the bathroom, there was a greenish glare and the buzz of a cicada. 'Now,' I said, 'that's annoying.' Two fluorescent tubes hung on either side of a cracked mirror over a rust-stained sink.

'I wonder how many people just climb into the tub and slit their wrists,' Jim mused.

'What's that stain over there?' Jim actually looked, then stuck out his tongue at me. I held out my hand. 'Give me the car key.'

'Are you going to sleep in the car?'

'No. You turn up the heat and run a hot bath. I'll be right back.'

When I returned, Jim was standing in just his corduroy pants, hands over his ears. The main room was cold, but I could smell the little bathroom heater at work.

I held my surprise behind my back. I reached in and turned off the cicada.

'How will I find the soap?' Jim asked pitifully. I clicked on the flashlight and set it upright on the back of the toilet. Jim laughed.

'Light and silence,' I said proudly. 'Enjoy your bath. Let me know if you want your back scrubbed.'

'Soap me and I'll soap you.'

'Jim . . .' I sighed.

'Just making out with water,' he pleaded. 'I don't like to bathe alone.'

I lifted my hair out of the way, and backed up to Jim for him to unzip my dress. He held it so I could step out of the dress easily. He kissed the back of my neck. As he peeled each layer, he folded everything in a tidy pile on the toilet seat. I unbuckled his belt and eased him out of his pants.

'Do you have a barrette?' he asked. 'I don't think you should get your hair wet.'

I collected my hair on top of my head and pawed through my tote for something to hold it. Jim slid down into the small tub and pulled his knees up to make room for me. We sat with our legs and arms around each other, noses nearly touching. His emotions ran across his face as if it were a movie screen. I wanted to see myself the way he saw me. He closed his eyes and kissed me. We soaped each other playfully, giggling and dropping the soap. When the water cooled, Jim reached around me for the hot-water tap.

'Gave you the bad end of the tub,' he apologized.

Handing me the little bar of motel soap, he waited patiently. 'How personal do you want me to get?' I asked, popping the soap out of my hand.

He hunted the soap down and closed my hand around it. 'Very. The advantage to playing here is that the bed stays dry.'

78

'Why does this remind me of your teaching me to take curves?'

Jim laughed, 'My guess is that you're scared and going to do it anyway.'

'Why do we bother to talk?'

'Yeah, got a Vulcan mind meld going. But we like the sound of our voices. I like the sound of yours. You like the sound of mine.' He wrapped a strand of my hair around his finger. 'Do you ever masturbate when we talk on the phone?'

I blushed. 'You already asked me this.'

'When?' he raised his eyebrow.

'You called from New York – 4 a.m.'

Jim crossed his eyes. 'Must have been drunk. I don't remember. Did you answer me or hang up?'

'I read *Little Women* to you.'

Jim cackled. 'Did you?'

'Wish I'd thought of it,' I smiled.

'What was your real answer?'

'Ah, what fun is that?' I asked, but answered anyway. 'I said it hadn't occurred to me, and you said . . .'

'What did I say?' Jim asked, caressing my neck.

'That you were, um, I forget the expression . . .'

'Jacking off?' he offered.

I laughed, 'That's it.'

'I'm an obnoxious drunk. Next time, hang up on me.'

'You weren't insulting. I didn't want to hang up. You sounded lonely and it was sort of sexy and romantic, in its way.' I slid the diminishing bar of soap down his chest.

Jim kissed me. 'Next time I call, read to me in French. Not Camus, though. Existential masturbation doesn't excite me.'

'My French accent is dreadful.'

He splashed me. 'I love you.'

In a husky voice, Jim gave me more guidance about touching him than he had on the road. I wasn't so much scared, as shy. I was concerned about embarrassing myself and disappointing him.

'You moan on key,' I said softly, kissing his open mouth.

'That's funny,' he whispered, 'because I usually sing flat.'

I put my finger on his lips. 'Don't.'

He licked my finger and sucked it into his mouth. 'Turn around and lean against me.'

The water lost its warmth. Jim lifted the plug with his toe. We towelled each other. Jim turned down the bed. No sheets. 'Maybe we should have slept in the back seat. Is it my turn to run out to the car for the sleeping bag?' he asked.

I suggested a run to the office for sheets. Jim dressed in his pants and jacket. I pulled on the sweater he left behind. There was a little television in the corner. I turned it on. Audrey Hepburn was breaking an egg for Humphrey Bogart. I wished my name were Sabrina. Or that I had Sabrina's newly acquired sophistication.

Jim entered with an arm full of sheets. 'The TV gives more light than the lamp.'

We made the bed together. Jim produced sharp military corners. 'Did you have to bounce a quarter off your bunk?' I asked him.

Jim laughed. 'And I hit the deck when ordered.' He pulled the corner loose. 'I like you in my clothes.'

I liked me in his clothes. Jim got under the covers before he gave up his pants. We watched the end of the movie. I volunteered to leave the warmth of the bed and turn off the television. A mission well worth it for the welcome back.

'Your fever is gone.' Jim pressed his cheek against mine. 'Would you like a little more attention than you got in the tub?'

'If you don't mind, I'd like it if you'd just hold me for a while.'

'That's fine, but I want to feel you, not my sweater,' Jim yanked the sweater unceremoniously over my head. He held it to his face. 'I like your fragrance. I slept with the T-shirt you borrowed under my pillow for a week.'

'You're sweet. I didn't sleep much that week. After sleeping with you, it was hard to sleep alone.'

'I don't like sleeping alone. The advantage to being an alley-cat is that I don't often have to.'

'Meow,' I whispered.

'Did that moment of truth cost my sweetness?' He cocked his head to read my face.

'No, there are lots of sweet alley-cats.'

Jim stroked my hair. 'I didn't mean that was how I felt about you. I need to talk to you about something,' he tightened his hold.

'There is someone I see regularly in LA, the girl I mentioned in San Francisco. We are going through a tough time. I guess I'm trying to get back to what we had. Just seems like we can't stop saying mean things to each other. On the road this fall, we got real drunk and for a joke took out a marriage licence. You don't do that sort of thing drunk.'

I pulled away. 'Then our playing around isn't quite right.'

'I'm trying to say that it is.' Jim pulled me back and locked his arms around me. 'We both have always seen other people. We don't do a lot of talking about it. She loves me, but loves to hurt me. Maybe I'm the same. I took a hard look at Pamela and me, and saw we were my parents in different regalia. That isn't what I want with a woman. I'll never marry her, but I love her. This is what the letter you got today is about. It's easier for me to write about my feelings. I didn't want you to find out, see a picture of us or something, and be more hurt because I wasn't honest.'

The girl in LA had a name. Hoping my voice didn't sound like my heart just cracked, I said, 'I hoped it was a flock of poems.'

'There are a few of those, too. Baby, I don't want to lose you.' Jim rubbed my shoulder. 'I used to look at Ray and his lady, Dorothy, in awe. I wondered how you found that kind of love. I always thought there was something missing in me, because I never felt like that about anyone. I'd like a girl, and be looking over her shoulder for someone who would make me feel more. I had all this emptiness. When I met you, all those empty places started to fill up. I don't know what the hell got into me in San Francisco. I never talk about myself like that. I thought I might never be able to face you again. But when I'm with you,' he paused, 'I feel . . . safe.'

In the morning, Jim's hand still rested on my shoulder. I felt awkward lying with him, and slipped out of his arms to take a quick shower. I exited the bathroom with my dress in one hand and the dead flashlight in the other. Jim was awake and reading Doris Lessing's *The Grass Is Singing*.

'We owe your friend batteries.' As proof, I clicked the dead flashlight on and off a few times.

'What are you doing dressed? Want to make the first bell?' He set the book aside. I might make lunch. 'Sexy slip,' Jim said. I looked down at my favourite bias-cut slip. 'Is it silk?' he asked, reaching so far to touch its hem, he nearly toppled from bed.

'Facsimile.' In yellow.

'Oh, yes. Is a silk-maker's lot a Dickensian one?'

I pretended seriousness, 'Slave labour.'

'The worm or the weaver?' he asked. 'Do you care about every last soul in the world?'

'I always liked that part of the doctor's oath. "First, do no harm." Seems a nice place to start. I am putting shoulder to the wheel to construct a philosophy, how did that go? If I'm going to spend the rest of my life proving it . . .'

'Come over here.' He pushed the covers aside and held out his arms. 'God, I'm afraid you're going to get broken.'

'I worry about you, too.' I was scared to death he was a firefly and one morning I would find his dead iridescent body. The thought made me tremble.

He took the flashlight and set it on the table. He threw my dress on the other side of the bed. He slid his hand up my thigh. 'Did I lose you last night?'

'No.'

'Then why up and dressed?'

'I don't know,' I shrugged. 'I don't know,' I repeated, hoping it would sound clearer. 'I want a boy who's doing everything for the first time, too. Someone I'd be enough for.'

Jim asked, 'Do you feel like I'm pressuring you to do things you aren't ready for?'

'I'm not sure. You don't push me physically, but I thought you were saying if we were lovers, you,' I smiled up at him, 'wouldn't be such an alley-cat.'

Jim played with my hair. 'If you lived in LA, I wouldn't be such a fuck-around. I'd happily divide myself between you and Pamela, and you are a hell of a lot easier to be with. But honey, I didn't mean you weren't enough just as you are. Let me know when I am being too pushy and I'll back off. You are the dearest lover I've ever had.'

'We aren't really lovers. We are friends.'

'Intimate friends. Spiritual orgasms,' he smiled, 'are the only real ones.' When he touched me, I lost my resolve. We caressed each

82

other until we were breathless, then snuggled in the blanket. He asked, 'Are you okay?'

'No. I don't think we should be doing this if you're in love with someone else. My body feels so good, and I feel so guilty. Stopping short of making love doesn't make it right. I can't be where you come when you and your girlfriend aren't getting along.'

Jim tangled his fingers in my hair and kissed my cheek. 'That isn't why I want to be with you. I want to be close to you because of how you make me feel. My feelings for you have nothing to do with her. I love you.'

Each time he said the word, I felt shy and confused. 'Does she know about me?'

Jim nodded. We dressed and made small-talk until our voices didn't sound so strained. We walked to a grocery and bought a sack of navel oranges. Holding hands, we ambled the few blocks to the white beach. Jim and I balanced on a hefty piece of driftwood. He peeled an orange and divided it between us.

The smell called up memories. 'When we moved out from Tennessee, there were oranges on the tree outside the motel. It was December. I thought it was a miracle.'

'Yeah, I lived for a while on stealing oranges out of backyards last year. No, year before.' Jim nodded in agreement about the miracle of oranges. 'You'd think I'd hate the sight of them. I lost weight and got sores in my mouth. But I smell an orange and I feel great. It's like you can always tell the SOB's to fuck off, because you can't quite starve in California.'

'Oh, look,' I pointed at the tracks in the sand smoothed by the tide. 'Crab cuneiform.'

'What?' Jim's eyes darted to where I pointed.

'Is crustacean cuneiform better?'

'I'd go with your first wave,' he said. 'But I want to see it in a poem by the end of the week.'

I laughed and tossed my hair. 'Two words doesn't make a poet.'

'You are a poet,' he said sternly.

'Poets know things. I don't know anything.'

'You know a lot. I hate didactic poets anyway. Question. Observe.'

I shrugged. 'I want to be an artist. Maybe make movies.'

'You have as much talent as a writer. Your journals should be full of these things you throw away in conversation. My God, you have your first orgasm and tell me it's like the fluttering of bird wings. You see ancient script in tracks. That makes you a poet. It's one of those things that chooses you. It's your obligation to pick up the pen.'

'Am I supposed to tell you when you are being too pushy out of bed, too?' I leaned on his arm.

Jim smiled, 'You're supposed to listen attentively and nod.'

'Poets are too naked. You can spill your guts all over a canvas and somebody will buy it because it matches their sofa. That seems safer than words.'

'I understand how you feel. I hide in the music. But do it. Write! That's why I let you read my notebook. I want you to see I write good things and lousy things and sometimes I'm not sure which is which. And I struggle most with the very personal things even though it's not important to me if people don't get my stuff on a personal level. I don't care if they like it 'cause it matches their sofa, or, you know, musically has a good beat, but I want them to get it in the larger sense. I want them to know what that trip is. I'd rather they get that first batch of songs sung in a circle than what any particular song means to me, because that's something they can use. They can't use my life.'

I stared into his eyes. 'I'm a better artist than writer.'

'You have a beautiful stubborn streak. You draw a line that could break my heart, but I want you to write, too.'

We walked back to the motel parking-lot. Jim took the two fives I gave him with a kiss instead of an argument. His new notebook was on the seat. I toyed with opening it while he was in the office but waited. Inviolate.

'Will you give me a birthday present?' Jim asked while he warmed up the car.

'December 8th. Already giving it some thought.'

'Oh, I know what I want,' he said.

'This is getting easy.'

'Come spend the day with me. I'm not sure where I'll be. I'll send you a ticket. The band is working. I'll do a great show for you.'

84

'Sure. I like this. Sounds more like a present for me. You don't know yet if it's LA or San Francisco?'

'Oh, it's back east. New York or Connecticut.' My heart sank. 'If it's going to be tough to get your mom's permission, you're going to have to learn to lie,' Jim smiled to ease the sternness of his voice. 'You aren't going to go to hell for saying you are staying at a girlfriend's house when you're with me.'

'It's not that. I lie all the time.'

'I'm sorry,' he bit his lower lip, 'I know. I remember when everything seemed like a lie. Christ, even breathing.'

'Even if I can work it out to go, Jim, I couldn't swing it without more notice.' I still had the hundred-dollar bill hidden away for emergencies, but I figured that was short of a round trip across the country.

'Hey, my invitation, my treat. Please, baby,' Jim touched my face lightly, 'if we're going to see each other, you are going to have to compromise. You can't let travel expenses be included in this foolish agreement about money or we'll never get to see each other. You can afford stamps. I can afford airline tickets. That makes them equal.'

Stubbornness was not my most charming trait. Not seeing Jim for months at a time was too high a price for maintaining the rule I made. I caved in. 'All right. Travel doesn't count.'

We shook on it. I picked up his notebook and read as we drove in easy silence up the coast. In Monterey, I called my mother to let her know I was fine and would go directly to school no matter how late. She hadn't slept all night. Relieved to hear my voice and second-guessing her approval, she wondered what let her put me into Jim's hands. I knew she had sensed that part of Jim that was like my brother, and she had trusted Jim as if he were her son, not a long-haired stranger she had talked with for an hour. Next time, I'd lie.

Beyond Monterey, I asked Jim to roll down the windows. Morning was cool and overcast, but I couldn't drive that part of the highway without letting in the eucalyptus groves. Jim tuned in the radio and did a duet with Tina Turner. They sang, 'River Deep, Mountain High', both of them at the top of their lungs. After the song, Jim turned down the radio. 'She's got one of the most incredible voices in rock. I wish she'd do some different material,' he laughed, 'like mine.' I never imagined anyone else singing Jim's music. His songs seemed completely his. I tried her voice in my mind singing 'Strange Days', then could really hear her singing "People Are Strange".' I'd never been able to hear anything so clearly in my imagination before.

I asked, 'Why don't you ask her to record one of your songs?'

'Doesn't work that way.'

'Why not?'

Jim rolled his shoulder. A startled crane darted up from the roadside. The volume went back up on the radio. We turned inland, holding hands in my lap most of the drive. A couple hours later, Jim pulled up where we had the evening before, by the flagpole at the front of my school. I looked out the back window at the levee, afraid to look at Jim. Saying goodbye in San Francisco was easier. He ran his fingers through my hair, and kissed me warmly.

Jim whispered, 'The real present is the next-to-the-last cut.'

That was where he had stopped the record on the second side. I studied his eyes and searched for a way to call him a liar in a nice way. 'Have you ever seen the movie *Pillow Talk* with Rock Hudson?'

'You just lost me.'

'He plays this womanizer.'

'Meow,' Jim, as an alley-cat, interrupted.

'Who writes Broadway musicals,' I continued, cracking a grin. 'Every time he talks to one of his girls on the phone, she asks him to play *their* song, and he sings, "You are my inspiration, so and so," changing the name of the girl depending on who's on the phone.'

'There are no names in my songs,' he smiled, then bit his lower lip. 'And I don't use my songs that way. Why do you feel this way? Are you upset with me?'

I shook my head, 'Something in your voice didn't ring true.'

'Well, the song should,' he said, then sang a line about looking for a lie.

A line from the song? The acoustics of the ugly car were endearing it to me. I said, 'You're doing pretty well. It seems convenient that you had another little song you never once mentioned, tucked away when you saw I was disappointed about "The Spy".'

'Ginger, I wrote this after we talked on the phone one night. There's a part about consuming the lines, who else would that be for? You were the one who taught me about line drawings. I was trying to draw you in my mind before I fell asleep and felt like I lost the real memory of you. I did change my mind about the photograph. The last line is about not wanting one.' From his jacket pocket he produced a school picture of me at six, copped from my family album.

'And a kleptomaniac. Stealing things you don't need is a sign.'

'Oh, I need this. You look like a wild animal caught in the headlights.' He smiled down at the picture of me with a windblown new haircut in a dress with a ridiculous bow.

'That's what happens when someone points a camera at me.'

'You won't look like that when I'm behind the camera.'

'You forget,' I tapped his arm, 'I'm the one behind the camera in my future. Even if you do have a head start.'

'We'll take turns. I'll teach you to use a movie camera so you can catch up, but you have to let me put you in my movies.'

'Fat chance.'

'Well, that's a chance.'

'If you aren't careful, people will think you can change your life.'

'Nah. Listen to the last song on the album. My reputation is intact.'

I kissed him lightly. 'See you on your birthday, Jim.'

Jim held my face and kissed me, 'Hate to let go of you.'

I left the car and stepped up on to the curb. Jim and I looked at each other through the dirty windshield for a few minutes. The car rocked as he put it in reverse. I stuck my hands in my pockets so he couldn't see them shake. I felt a piece of paper and played with it while I watched Jim back up. When the car curved out of my sight, I glanced at the scrap I had accordioned in my pocket. Jim had printed, 'Anything you need,' and signed '*JM*'.

6

Can't See Your Face in My Mind

The school day limped along with my singing the line Jim had
sung in the car over and over again the way I do when a tune gets
stuck in my head and I can't remember the rest of the words to the
song. Only I didn't know the rest of the words. The sweet bit of
melody kept replaying, but by the time I reached home, I thought
maybe Jim had sung, *I can't seem to find the right line*, because
he had said it was about drawing me in his mind.

My mother was nervous and silent when I got home. While I was
giving her an edited version of my escapades with Jim to smooth the
waters, my father arrived home from work. My mother hummed
a bar of 'I Walk Through the Garden Alone', then slipped into
silence. We worked side by side in the kitchen, our usual mother
and daughter dance.

After dinner, I sought the sanctuary of my room. Jim constructed
an entire album, but as much as I wanted to hear *Strange Days* from
the beginning for the whole effect, I turned on the record-player and
set the needle down on the next-to-the-last cut. The music puzzled
me, but I loved its dreamy mystery. When Jim sang the line about
insanity's horse, I knew he was referring to the Kandinsky painting
of a horse we had admired in the bookstore where Jim had brought
the stuffy clerk to tears over his passion for little women.

We had sat on the floor ogling the beautiful colour plates in the European publication. When she had insisted we purchase it or keep our hands off its shiny pages, I could see by the tension in Jim's hands that he considered tossing one of his hundred-dollar bills at her. *Little Women* was Jim's way of getting even.

St..nding by the wall phone in the kitchen, reading Salinger's *Franny and Zooey*, I waited for the call I knew Jim would make. I picked up the phone on half a ring. 'Okay,' I said, learning not to be bothered with a *Hello* either, 'you weren't just telling a nice fib.'

Jim heaved a victorious sigh and asked, 'What convinced you?'

'Kandinsky's horse.'

'Yeah, yeah! All right!' His applause stung my ear. 'That's my sweet girl.'

'It's a beautiful song, Jim.' I struggled to think what more to say. 'I love your odd little pauses and the song's brevity.'

'Glad you liked it. I was *so* nervous.' Nervous? I couldn't imagine my making *him* nervous. 'It was very important to me that you liked it.'

'Just the one line you sang stuck in my head all day. By the end of the day, I couldn't remember if it was, "*lie* or *line*".'

He chuckled. 'Couldn't find either one of 'em.'

'Why do you need to find a lie?'

Jim whispered secretively, 'To make you love me.'

'That doesn't take a lie. You talk about lies and tell me the truth.'

'Well, you are my lie detector.' His speech picked up pace. 'Did you like the melody? A sweet melody with a touch of loss. Like you. The best song on the album.'

I thought it had considerable competition, but there was something in his melody that caught the night. 'The melody reminds me of, you know, when you are really tired and have just gotten to sleep when something half wakes you? How you float for a few seconds? Like stopping at the top of a Ferris wheel, and when it moves again you feel afraid and pleased at the same time. That's how I feel when you touch me.'

'Whew!' Jim whistled. 'I'm trying to decide if I like that review better as a songwriter or a man. Either way, you can write that on my tombstone.'

'Write it yourself!' I hated his bringing up death even as a joke, so I veered back to the song. I confessed I couldn't distinguish the guitar from the organ.

'That's because they fucked with it in the studio,' he explained. 'Some of it's backwards. I hate anything we can't do live – we're a live band, not the fucking Beatles – but I didn't want to have another fight with Paul.'

I was confused and impressed. 'Paul McCartney?'

'Might be worth fighting with him. No. Paul Rothchild's our producer.'

'But it's your song . . .' I insisted.

'It's *your* song. I'll make a straight tape for you sometime.'

'Thank you for the song.' That afternoon, I so wanted to tell my friends about this other friend who writes me songs. Somehow, from my return from my brief San Francisco escape in July, Jim had been my secret. Out of a deep fear something terrible would happen should my father discover my friendship with Jim, I felt a growing strain not to let his name slip. My mother's hint and hush when my father entered the kitchen was confirmation.

'I can't tell you how much it meant that we had last night. I regret all the times I started up to see you and turned around. Most of my reluctance, like I said, was that I laid myself bare to you,' he chuckled softly, 'in every way possible. But part of it was, I was afraid that you were a perfect golden hallucination.'

'Some part of me must be. A hallucination, I mean. You think too much of me.' When he didn't say anything, I whispered, 'Maybe that's the lie.'

'Oh, no! Last night was wonderful. Writing. The bathtub. Sleeping with you. Oranges on the beach. All of it.'

'Thank you. And for the note. Thank you, Jim.'

'I meant it. Not just money. You know, if you need to talk. Even,' he paused and spoke more softly, 'even if you need me to back off some. If that's what you need. I know I threw some adult emotions at you, but I did mean it when I said that we can go at your pace.'

'Thank you for saying that.' For the first time, I remembered I had a letter about the girl he knew in Los Angeles, which I wasn't sure I wanted to read, and poems which I was sure I did, waiting on my bed.

Jim was quiet for a full minute, then asked, 'Are we okay, then?'

'Being with you is the only time I feel . . .'

'Real?' He returned to the reason for the call. 'What did you think of the rest of the album?'

'Oh, I hate pop quizzes! You know I think "People Are Strange" is perfect. How dare you think you can't sing! And I loved the music in "When the Music's Over".'

'Oh, you're full of compliments tonight. I'll be so disappointed if you don't ask me one of your *is it this or that* questions?'

I'd only heard the album once and was trying to come up with something to please him. I took a stab. 'Is it *Big Sleep* the book, or *Big Sleep* the movie with Bogart?' Philip Marlowe was always keeling over after being drugged, shot, or beaten, only to revive in a spider's web. How Jim courted that moment.

Jim laughed. 'Well, same thing. Raymond Chandler! Yeah! That dark hole opens up at your feet and you dive in. The experience Marlowe hated and I live for.' I held back a laugh. I was getting to know him pretty well. Jim sighed, 'Let's go for the movie because *The Scream of the Butterfly* is. Makes it tidier.'

I said, 'I never heard of that movie. Is it a Japanese film?'

'Do you like Kurosawa?'

The name rang a distant chime. 'The only Japanese movies I've seen are like *Godzilla* on television. I've never seen one of his films.'

'Well, this isn't one of his either. The reason *The Scream of the Butterfly* ties in,' Jim began to giggle and snort.

'Oh, no, Jim,' I caught on, 'it isn't a porno movie?' In *The Big Sleep*, Philip Marlowe, the hard-bitten, soft-hearted, LA detective, winds up in a subplot of porno photographs of General Sternwood's younger thumb-biting daughter.

Jim yelped. 'Oh, baby! You're great fun!'

'Was it good? The porno movie?' I thought maybe I could stand to sneak into a few for educational purposes.

'Well, actually, I just saw the title on a marquee. Can't remember why I didn't go in. Most of that song dates back a couple years ago when things were pretty lean. Maybe I didn't have any money in my pocket. Or wasn't *up* to it.'

'Jim . . .' I whined in good humour.

'I'm not much of a voyeur anyway. Rather be doing than watching. By God, I was taking myself so seriously then, I just had to make a little joke in the song to remind myself not to. But I also meant it in a genuine way. Sometimes, when you are thinking about dying, there is some little thing that makes you wait. Wanting to hear you just bellow, for example. You are so quiet. Do you ever raise your voice and just waller?'

'No. I'm too shy. Something happens when I try to yell. My voice disappears.'

'I'll give you screaming lessons next time I see you. I love to scream. Holler. I do it every chance I get. Guess it'll be a long life if I wait for your scream.'

'I'm not your butterfly. I do not flit, nor do I flaunt.'

'Sounds like a line from one of those old English poets, *She does not flit, nor does she flaunt . . . sweet promise . . . of the tide.*' He laughed, 'Well, they all can't be gems.'

'Guess not,' I giggled. 'But "When the Music's Over" is. Sometimes I wait hours to hear music that means something to me on the radio.'

'God, yeah!' Jim yelled. 'Bo Diddley saved my life! I was your age. I was a walking open sore. I would say these prayers constructed so tightly to tie up all the loopholes that a Harvard lawyer would have been proud. Nobody was listening.'

'The reason for "The Silence of God" is there is no God,' I ventured.

'Whoa! Where did you see Bergman?' Jim asked.

'Berkeley. Not the man, his movie.'

'You don't believe in God?' Jim was surprised. 'You're the most spiritual person I ever met.'

'Must be that hallucination. *Suffer the children* was a bit too literal in my house.'

'Yeah. Guess that's why I tried screaming this time around. *Jesus* . . . !' Jim screamed into my ear.

I prodded him back to his story about Bo Diddley. Jim rustled around, settling in to tell the story. 'I was lying in bed,' he began as if it were *Once upon a time*, 'wondering if I could just will myself dead without having to actively do anything about it. This feeling rose up and I started to feel like I could jump off a building or throw myself in front of a train pretty easily, when this song came on the radio. Bo Diddley doing "Crackin' Up"! I jumped out of bed and was dancing around my room. I felt so alive for three minutes! Not holding on. But alive! Then I *had* to hear that song again. And it had to be over the radio. I rushed home from school the next day, even though I couldn't get the black radio station from some little town in Texas – maybe it was Del Rio – until late at night. Every waking hour, I just kept thinking about that song. I waited three days to hear it again. By then, the need to die passed.'

'Thank the sacred radio-waves for Bo Diddley!' I hesitated, thinking of the poem he wrote during that period. 'Jim, the *consent* in "Horse Latitudes" worries me.'

'What else is giving up?' he asked simply.

'That's an incredible and terrible thing to know at fifteen.'

Jim took a deep breath. 'Maybe I was sixteen. Maybe I was a thousand and sixteen.' He shouted his demand for the world, laughing as he hung up.

'*Now?*' I asked the dial tone.

When I picked up the phone two nights later, Jim sang 'We Could Be So Good Together'. He sang a few lines and hung up. Thanks a lot. It is impossible to fall asleep and laugh at the same time. Three nights of that and Jim had sung a whole song. I didn't much like the tune, but how could I tell him that? At least it was funny. 'The Spy' had been so intense, and 'I Can't See Your Face' melancholy. My being a part of any wantonness wasn't likely and made me giggle every time I heard it. 'Not likely,' I told Jim.

'Didn't start out for you,' he confessed. 'Just ended up that way. I wrote it in Venice.'

Already spoiled, I was a little disappointed it wasn't really my song. The following day, just as I slammed my locker shut, I heard Jim's name. A couple other sophomore girls were head to head. One of them said, 'It's so sad about Jim Morrison.' My heart skipped a beat. I held my breath to listen intently. She said, 'His parents were killed in a car accident.'

I ran across the quad for the pay phone, nearly decking a sapling on the way. My fingers felt numb as I fumbled with the pages of my little phone book. Jim had given me a series of numbers to try should I need to reach him. No one answered the first two. At the third, a girl took a message. My voice shook. I tried a fourth number, a bar where Jim liked to hang out. The reluctant bartender let me hold while he went in search of Jim.

'This is Jim,' Jim said with a bit of a slur.

'Jim. Jim.' I hadn't thought of what to say.

'Ginger?' The slur disappeared. I heard the crash of what I assumed was a bar stool. 'Are you all right?'

'Are you?' I responded.

'Yeah. I'm sort of stunned. This is the first time you've called me. You sound scared. Sobered me right up. What's wrong? Do you need me to come get you?'

I hated his thinking my life was such I would only call in need of being rescued. 'No, I just heard about your folks. I know you've been . . . estranged, but I was worried about you. I'm so sorry.' No wonder he was drunk at noon.

'Oh, hell, Ginger. I never thought to tell you. Did someone tell you my folks were dead? I gave out that garbage about my family being dead, yeah, I think it was in my first bio. It shuts people up. As far as I know, my parents are fine and dandy. Hale and hearty.' He giggled impishly, 'Laurel and Hardy.'

Apologetic for tracking him down, I wondered why he was drunk before noon. I explained, 'I overheard someone say your parents had been killed. I thought it just happened. Guess it will teach me to eavesdrop.'

'Well, they are as good as dead as far as I'm concerned. I am an orphan in my *Soul*. Must be time to *drink a confusion*. Hell, what's that from? Oh, yeah. *Perry Mason*,' Jim snorted. 'The great American father figure. Interestingly, a bachelor.'

'Atticus gets my vote,' I said. Give me Gregory Peck in *To Kill a Mocking Bird*. The operator broke in to request a deposit. 'I'm out of change,' I explained quickly.

'I'll call you tonight. Thank you, honey. You're just who I'd want to talk to if something bad had happened. Promise you won't read any of the trash written about me.'

That night, I loitered around the phone waiting for Jim's call. When the phone rang, I said, 'Hello,' in case it wasn't Jim. There was no response. 'Hello? Hello? Hello? Is anybody there?' I asked under the voices of the television. 'Jim?'

Silence, then in a whimper what sounded like, 'I need you.'

'What's happened?' When he didn't respond, I asked, 'Where are you?'

'Not real sure.' His voice sounded a thousand miles away. He wasn't in Los Angeles. 'Not far from you. Pretty sure it starts with an M,' he hummed soft and low.

'Manteca?'

'Maybe,' he paused. 'No. Softer.'

Softer. A poet's clue. 'Modesto?'

'Yeah. Sounds right,' he said. I asked if he were drunk. 'No. I took something.'

'Do you need an ambulance?' I asked.

'I need *you*,' he pleaded.

'I'll come, too. But an ambulance can get to you faster. Did you take pills?'

'Oh, no. No. I'm having a hard trip. Will you come? I need you.'

I launched into a desperate series of questions. 'Is there someone there who can tell me exactly where you are?' He'd been dropped off. Questioning made me want to shake him. He finally managed to tell me he was in a phone booth at a gas station he couldn't name with a phone number he couldn't read. 'God, Jim, I hate to hang up. I need to call a friend to get a ride. It will take me a while to get to you. Can you wait? Sit tight. Believe I'll be there.' When Jim hung up, I felt such an adrenalin rush, I could barely get my finger into the holes to dial Pat's number.

'Hello,' a young male voice answered brightly.

'Hi, is Pat there?' I asked, trying to sound casual.

'Nope. Everybody's at the movies. Can I take a message?'

'Jesus,' I whispered, quoting Jim's song plea.

'Something I can do?' he asked.

I couldn't even steal the family car. The shiny new Volkswagen

96

with choke and gear shift was beyond me. Since my alternative was to enlist my mother's aid, I took a chance on the boy's young and friendly voice. 'A friend of mine is in trouble. He's taken something. Acid or something. He's in Modesto. I can't drive. I need to reach Pat.'

'Well, if you need to get to Modesto, I can drive you.'

My heart jumped. 'Who's this?'

'I'm a friend of Pat's boyfriend,' he answered cheerfully, nonplussed by my agitation. 'Where are you?'

That was that. I had a ride. I played out a scene for my mother about Pat needing my help with a term paper and how I'd just stay over and go to school from there the next morning. I was halfway down the walk, when my mother called me back to get a change of clothes. I grabbed the dress I hemmed earlier that evening and ran across the foggy street. I jumped into a strange car without a thought that it might not have belonged to the boy I had spoken with on the phone.

'Thank you. Thank you,' I said to him.

'Hey, we're all in this together,' he said as he pulled away from the curb. He seemed tall, even sitting, and fair enough that his hair was green in the dash light. He made me think of *The Boy With Green Hair*, an old anti-war movie with Dean Stockwell. The boy asked, 'Where in Modesto?'

'A phone booth. By a gas station. That's all I could get out of him. He wasn't very coherent.'

'How many gas stations can there be in Modesto?' He reached over and rubbed my knotted shoulder encouragingly. 'We'll find him. I've had a couple bad trips myself. Your friend will be okay.'

'He's done a lot of acid. It scared me that he sounded scared.'

Modesto was only a half-hour's drive, but the fog was tumbling in on us. We had rolled up close to a few phone booths, before it dawned, coming up from Los Angeles, Jim might be at the southern entrance to town. The boy agreed, and we drove to the far end of town and concentrated on the right side of the road.

At first, the lighted phone booth seemed empty. Then I saw Jim, huddled close to the ground, mostly hidden by the red paint along the bottom half of three sides of the glass. We pulled directly in front of the booth. His body was wedged against the booth's doors so I couldn't open them. He lay so still, I was terrified he was dead. A few seconds crawled by before his chest lifted slightly. Neither the Good Samaritan, whose name if he had given it to me I could not remember, nor I, could budge them. I squatted to be at Jim's height and rapped sharply on the glass, 'Jim.' Nothing about his countenance changed. 'If he's unconscious, we should call an ambulance.'

'If they take him to emergency, there's an automatic three-day commitment.'

'Commitment?' Jim locked up? The thought shocked me.

'No fun, speaking from experience. And it would probably be worse, you know, for him.' Jim's angelic white face ringed with curls made him recognizable even in a heap. 'Hey, hey, Jim!' The boy's yell made me jump. Jim half-opened his eyes, settling them on me. His blue-grey eyes looked metallic. His lips twitched in a brief half-smile.

'Jim, get away from the door,' the boy yelled.

'Back up,' I pleaded, motioning Jim back with my hand. There seemed a time lag before Jim heard the words. He stared, momentarily puzzled, then closed his eyes.

'Shit, stand up! Cops.' A police car cruised by slowly, made a U-turn, and eased up next to the parked car. I hoped the Ford and I blocked their view of Jim, and prayed to Bo Diddley to make them stay in their car. The boy walked over to them with a big grin, 'Isn't this tule fog the pits? I just had to take a break from behind the wheel. My sister wanted to call the folks to let them know we were running late.' His tall, sturdy body covered the window of the police car. I tried to look like his little sister. I had a talent for looking like anybody's little sister.

'We thought you might be having car trouble,' the officer said.

'Oh, no. Thanks, though.' The boy tapped the hood of the car. 'You have a safe night.'

'You take it easy.'

'Will do.' The boy backed a bit, hands in his back pockets. He said behind a stiff smile, 'Don't I do shit-kicker just great?' I was thinking of a promotion from Good Samaritan to Saint. 'We have about ten minutes before they figure I was too friendly to the pigs and they make another pass.' He yanked on the handle of the phone-booth door. 'Why don't these damn doors open out so you can't get stuck?' Their purpose, I suppose, was to conserve space and keep intruders out while you were using the phone. Between the two of us, we pried a two-inch opening.

'If you have a tyre iron, I could squeeze my hand through and break the glass out.'

The boy disagreed. 'No telling where the glass would fly. Could cut you both.'

'I could squeeze my jacket in to protect him. I'm not going to let him get busted.'

'Got that impression.' He patted me on the head. 'Can you move his boot?'

The aluminium frame scraped both sides of my wrist. The tips of my fingers just met the sole of his boot, but hadn't the strength to move his weight. Jim's hand fell against mine. His skin was cold. 'Jim.' The back of his hand lightly touched mine, then fell limp.

'Wanna use that tyre iron on his foot? Might get his attention.'

'Give me a tyre iron and a place to stand . . .'

'Are you a physics major?'

I'm a high-school sophomore in over her head. 'I'm an artist,' I said.

'Then you won't be offended if I tell you that if he gives suddenly, the damn iron will break the glass in your face.'

Against his better judgment, he fetched the tool, then moved around to the front of the car. Just in case, I protected myself with my jacket. I scraped off another couple layers of my wrist, steered the iron under the toe of his boot, and pulled. Jim's foot shifted just half an inch and the door opened with an anticlimactic *whoosh*.

The boy laughed, and ran to haul Jim to his feet. I opened the back door, and the boy backed in, dragging Jim behind him. I opened the far door to trade places with the Samaritan. The boy was behind the wheel, ignition on, when the police car made the corner. He pulled on the lights, honked, and waved.

'What did I tell you?' he asked through his smile. 'Ten minutes. We aced that! In this fucking – excuse me – fog, it's going to take a good year to find Stockton. What's our destination?'

'I hadn't thought of that. I just wanted to get to him,' I answered.

'By that, I assume, your house is out. Pat's parents are cool, but not *that* cool. I knew I should have done this week's dishes and made my bed,' he said, inviting us to crash at his place.

'Thank you,' I said with relief. 'Do you just go around doing good deeds?'

'Pretty much. That and taking fourteen units at Delta keeps me busy and out of the draft. To be a little more honest, I liked your voice on the phone. Thought I might get a date out of this. Didn't expect this kind of competition.' There went my first request for a date.

Delta, the junior college, was more descriptive of Stockton than the pricey University of the Pacific. Stockton was like the elephant-described-by-the-blind-man joke. The edge of town where new housing developments ate up agricultural land, it seemed rural. There were active docks. Its heart was working-class. There wasn't much acknowledgment that it was a university town with pockets of rich green lawns and sprawling houses.

In the back seat, I held Jim in my lap, feeling his pulse as if that would let me know where he was. The drive was slow and tense and quiet. The boy had turned off the radio to concentrate on staying on his side of the road. I couldn't get Jim to respond to questions. I felt guilty for aching to be standing in the line for a movie with this easy-going stranger, instead of holding an unreachable Jim in my arms.

The boy's apartment was the downstairs left of a converted Victorian house. Under the porch light, a sudden grin of recognition crossed Jim's face. Surprised and delighted to see me there, he kissed me so passionately, the boy and I blushed.

The boy said, 'I think recognizing female body parts is probably a good sign. He must have some sort of contact with the planet as we know it.'

Jim wanted to squeeze me up against the side of the house and kiss, but I coaxed him inside, tugging on his belt loops. We entered through the kitchen. Jim wasn't very steady on his feet, but made it all the way to the couch in the next room before he collapsed. Our rescuer was diving for dirty clothes and record albums and newspapers strewn across the floor. When I caught his eye, I asked, 'What do I do?'

'Somebody told me milk can help. Other than that, wait.'

I sat on the edge of the couch and ran my hand through Jim's hair to make contact. He smiled, which made him seem okay. I rested my hand on his chest, and he put his hand on top of mine. Inside the apartment was quiet. Outside, there were sirens wailing and dogs barking. The boy emptied the last of a carton of milk into a jelly glass. Jim pushed it away, then closed his eyes and seemed to sleep.

After a while the boy asked, 'Would you two like the bedroom? I could scare up some clean sheets.'

I stood up. 'This is fine, thank you. You've been wonderful.'

'I have an eight o'clock class, so I'm gonna hit the sack. Call me if you need anything.' He brought us a blanket. 'Make yourselves at home. There's not much in the fridge, but help yourself. Music won't bother me.' He seemed uneasy. He pulled at his sandy hair as if he hoped to make it longer. He patted my head again. 'Good-night.'

'Good-night. And thank you.' A thousand thanks wouldn't have seemed enough. When he closed the door to his bedroom, I flipped through the albums, and put on Segovia to fill the stillness with guitar. When I turned back to face Jim, his cheeks were wet with tears. He looked like a lost archangel who'd plummeted unexpectedly on to the coarse tweed sofa. I wanted to cross the room like a mad Spanish dancer to stir him from his painful reverie, but walked over and patted his cheeks with a wadded tissue from my jeans' pocket. 'Everything's going to be all right. I'm here.' For all the good I was doing.

Suddenly, Jim dug his nails into my wrists. I winced. 'Jim, you can let go of me. I'm going to be right here.' Even with his eyes fixed on my face, I couldn't tell if he understood what I said. He pulled me down and kissed me roughly. The power of the kiss was thrilling. After a few passionate kisses, he traded his grip on my wrists for one on my hips. He rolled over on top of me. When he couldn't unbutton my shirt, he tore it open. I laughed. 'Just ask,' I said. He dispensed with my only lacy little brassière in the same fashion. 'Jim,' I was miffed, 'I don't have that big a wardrobe.'

He pulled his own shirt off over his head, and rubbed his open hands from my waist to my breasts. He pushed low-slung leathers lower. I ran my hand down his stomach, shy about touching him. I stroked him once. He pushed my hand away.

Rebuffed, I didn't know where to put my hands. He settled the question by grabbing my wrists again. My raw wrist stung. He fell on me with playful nips and kisses, but was crying so hard, his tears were falling on my face. I tried to free a hand to lift his hair from his face, but he wouldn't release me. 'What's wrong?' I asked him. His only response was to bite my shoulder, then a nipple hard enough to make me yelp. He held my wrists with one hand, then lowered his free hand to unzip my jeans.

Jim's kisses slowed to match the slow and even rhythm of his hips. I felt him push against the crotch of my panties. He reached down and ripped them. 'Stop it, Jim,' I said firmly into his curls. Scared when I couldn't pull my hands free, I called, not loudly, 'Jim. Jim. Jim.' He let go of me and lay still, breathing in sobs against my chest. I reached between us to zip my jeans. I held him for half the night while he cried. I said every soothing word I could think of, and when I had repeated them all dozens of times, I made soothing sounds. He did not lift his eyes or speak a word. At last, his breathing grew steady and he slept.

The room was dark when the alarm went off in the bedroom, followed by music. Jim stirred against me, his mouth dry when he kissed me. He said a word I interpreted as 'Thanks' in a low, rusty voice. He pulled up his pants and sat at the end of the sofa.

When our host came out to make coffee, he diverted his eyes discreetly. Jim slipped his narrow frame between the back of the sofa and me. I buttoned the two buttons left on my shirt. Jim looked around the room as if he were about to ask, 'Where am I?'

'There's coffee. No milk. English muffins, no butter. Jam though. My mom made it. You're welcome to stay as long as you like. I have a break from ten till one. Maybe I'll see you then,' the boy said, backing out the kitchen door with books and coffee-cup in his hands and half a muffin in his mouth.

As soon as the door closed, Jim ran his finger down the front of my blouse. I sat up with a groan, stiff from a night of Jim's weight. I felt the need of a door between us, and hid in the bathroom. I heard Jim put *Strange Days* on the stereo. 'They sure are,' I said to myself. *Like those strange days with rings around the sun*, he had said in San Francisco about the tie-dyed shirt and me. Part of me stepped away from the experience of last night and was simply surprised how different the record sounded through decent speakers. The way he sang *down* revealed his drawl. Jim walked into the bathroom without knocking. I was glad I was only caught in the act of washing my face. He kissed my hair as if he missed my cheek, and whipped the toilet seat up.

'Never watched a man pee before,' I said before I realized I didn't have to watch him even if he stood between me and the door. I could have studied the dark circles under my eyes in the mirror over the sink.

'Should I go to school?' I asked Jim.

'Sure. I'll probably sleep. My head feels like hell.' He opened the medicine cabinet and settled for three aspirin, swallowed dry. Better. He could talk.

I studied his face. 'You'll be all right, then?'

'Yeah. Who's the handsome kid? Is that Nick?'

'Nick?' I laughed. Nick was the boy who sang so beautifully. I'd caught occasional glimpses of him on campus, but hadn't worked up the courage to nod or say 'Hello'. 'I don't know Nick. Remember, he's a junior. I don't know this guy. He's in college. He's the friend of a friend of an acquaintance.' Jim shook his head at my compulsive accuracy, then held it in his hands. I went on, 'But he had a car. He must have told me his name, but I was too much of a zombie to catch it.'

Jim took his record carefully off the turntable, slid it into the dust cover, and on into the sleeve. 'Have a pen?' I fished a green one out of my tote. He contemplated, then wrote and signed a thanks. He put it back next to his first album in the two-foot line of albums. 'Might be worth something someday.'

Out in the kitchen, Jim thumbed through the mail on the kitchen table. 'Occupant,' he read with a smile. When Jim looked up, I was transformed into a butterfly in my new yellow paisley dress with bell sleeves and a skirt that flared when I twirled, then folded my wings, vulnerable without underwear. 'You don't look much like winter,' Jim said. 'Can we meet after school?'

It sounded as if he were going to school, too, and I wished he were my age. 'Three-thirty by the flagpole. If you aren't there, I'll assume something better came up.'

'Nothing better could come up,' he assured me.

I struck out to find a bus-stop in a neighbourhood with no familiar street signs. I tossed the ruined shirt and underwear in the first public waste basket. How much I needed to talk to Jim about the violence and tears of the night before. Jim was a roller-coaster ride. I found it easier to face school with no sleep than a little, but by the time the last bell rang, I was so exhausted and strained, I felt like a cranky four-year-old.

Jim had acquired a shapeless grey pullover. With his shoulders hunched and hands thrust into pants' pockets, he appeared thin and brittle against the wind. His smile, when he saw me, made him look even more fragile. We fell into step. I said, 'I thought we could walk to the University.'

'May as well set foot on my beloved Alma Mater,' he said, deciding to claim it.

A bus would have been easier, but I needed to walk and struck out in its direction. 'Get some rest?' I asked. There were grey blotches under his still swollen eyes.

'Some,' he said softly, and took my books. No one had ever carried my books. Being at a loss about what to do with my empty hands reminded me of the night before when he didn't want me to touch him. I shivered. Jim shifted the books to his left side and wrapped his free hand around mine, taking a second look at James Baldwin's *Go Tell It on the Mountain* on top of the small stack of books. 'Are you reading this for English?'

'Just for me.'

'When I was a junior in high-school, I was sitting on some steps reading Baldwin's *Giovanni's Room*, and a teacher, not one of mine, came up to me in this rabid fury and said, "Don't bring that nigger's trash on campus again or you're suspended." I finished the book, but carried it around for a couple weeks. Daring him. The son of a bitch didn't have the courage of his warped convictions. I thought he was the kind of worm who would have found another excuse to suspend me. Wish now I'd confronted him.'

I was having trouble looking at Jim. I wanted to continue the conversation and make some comment about what you carry with you when you've lived in the South, but said, 'When I first saw you last night, I thought you were dead. I wanted to smash the glass to get to you.'

He put his free arm around my shoulder. 'I wasn't in danger, but I was relieved when you showed up.' I needed to know what he'd taken. Jim shrugged. 'I'd done some mushrooms earlier. After you called. They make me think of you. I mean that feeling. That bliss. So I decided instead of calling, I'd hitchhike up to see you. For the real bliss.' He yanked my hair for emphasis. 'The dude who gave me a lift asked if I wanted to trip. It didn't feel like acid. I can do a show on acid, even a lot of acid. Maybe it was a cousin to this experimental drug, an animal tranquillizer, 'cause it makes you feel like it's taking over your subconscious, not releasing it, like acid. But it wouldn't have lasted like that. Strange shit. I couldn't get my brain connected to my mouth. Sorry if it scared you.'

I met his eyes. 'Didn't it scare you?'

'A little. Before you came.'

I stopped. I felt my hand come up to rest on my hip. I'd never been so angry. 'Jim, this is no good. I care more about you than you care about yourself. You took some unknown drug from a total stranger. That's stupid. *Stupid!*'

He looked suitably guilty. 'Yeah, maybe, but it wasn't not caring. I was curious. I think there was too much of the mushrooms left in my system. They're poisonous.'

Jim's recklessness astounded me. 'That's reassuring.'

He grinned. 'If I knew what I'd taken, I'd promise not to do that again. And maybe even mean it. Don't be angry.'

'I'm not angry. I'm,' I laughed, 'angry.'

Jim tightened his arm around my shoulders. 'You can't really be angry with me,' he cajoled, ''cause it would hurt me. And you'd never hurt me. Don't worry. I never have bad trips.'

'What do you call being wedged in the bottom of a phone booth unable to speak?'

He smiled, slow and wide. 'Interesting.' He didn't seem to want to admit, if he knew, that he had been rough with me, and spent most of the night crying.

'Jim.' I hesitated. 'I want you to know if you come to me again, I'm not going to listen to you or anyone, I'm going to do what I think is best for you.'

At the University Book Store, Jim picked up a square blue composition book with a sewn binding. 'Now, losing my notebook,' he said, 'that was stupid. Maybe a couple dozen poems. And I think I was wearing a leather jacket when I left LA.' At the register, he looked heavenward. 'Could I borrow a dollar?' He turned out his pockets. 'I guess I got rolled.'

'Well, the idiot probably kept the leather jacket and money, and threw away the notebook.' I gave him a dollar.

'Could you send me copies of the things I've sent you recently? Might remind me what else was in the notebook.' I nodded. He pocketed the change. We walked out across the grass and looked back at the brick ivy-covered buildings that looked like they had been transported from New England.

'I forget,' he said, 'how far are we from the ocean?'

'About an hour and a half.'

'Let's thumb a ride.'

'Three hours.'

Jim bumped against me playfully. Unsure if I wanted to go through another night with him, I called my mother anyway. By the time I had finagled the weekend, Jim had scavenged a piece of cardboard, and enlisted me to letter the sign. Jim insisted on a wave drawn in the style of a Japanese woodcut to inspire a ride to the ocean instead of leap-frogging our way. A pale blue Valiant stopped in five minutes. The girl in the passenger seat hung over to unlock the back door, saying, 'Why not?'

As soon as we were in traffic, the driver offered Jim a joint, and Jim said, 'No, thanks, could I have a Marlboro instead?'

Both parts of his answer surprised me. I assumed Jim liked to get high on any available substance, but had never seen him smoke a cigarette in the six or seven days we had spent together. The girl lit Jim's cigarette. Jim whispered the confession, 'I only smoke when I'm nervous.' Van Morrison's 'Brown-Eyed Girl' came up on the radio, and Jim was singing along more than he was smoking. When I automatically waved the smoke away, Jim put the cigarette out.

After he and Van and the girl in the front seat finished the song, I asked, so only Jim could hear, 'Is Van a relative?'

'Nope. Wish I could claim him. He's Irish. I'm Scot.'

'Makes me wish I had brown eyes. Can't wait to hear more of him.'

'He was *Them*.' *Them* was a band that had had several hits.

'No. "Gloria"? No.' I couldn't quite believe it. 'No! "Here Comes the Night"?'

'Yep! I guess he decided he could sing the blues as a white boy.'

'Just as well if he is.' I laughed. 'What does he look like?'

'A fair-haired, don't-you-dare-fall-for-him leprechaun.'

There wasn't much conversation. We listened to the radio, the girl only changing stations periodically to elude static and commercials. Out of habit, I settled against the door to stare out the window. Jim startled me by grabbing my hips to hoist me over until I was almost in his lap. He held me against him. I felt good having the gentler Jim back and sharing a window.

7

Dance on Fire as It Intends

The Miracles were singing 'I Second That Emotion' when the Valiant dropped us south of Santa Cruz. The street that led to the beach was deserted. At the edge of the surf, difficult to distinguish in the moonless black, Jim discarded his boots a few feet above the tide line. He gave his pants' legs a couple turns to walk in the cold surf. Jim was miles away in thought. I trailed behind, humming, confident my voice was overpowered by the churning surf. I caught myself singing the last verse of Jim's 'The End'.

'It's *beautiful*,' Jim shouted over the ocean, without stopping or looking back.

Certainly not my voice. How could he have heard me above the ocean's roar? 'You have the hearing of a dog, Jim Morrison.'

'It's *beautiful friend*,' Jim corrected gently, turning to face me, but continuing to walk backwards. 'You sang *intrepid*.'

'It's not? It doesn't change at the end? It's not *beautiful* at the beginning and *intrepid* at the end?' I was so sure. My record-player had a negligible speaker, but I had listened to the album dozens of times before I met Jim, and a few times since.

'Nope. Not until now,' he laughed, stopping so I could catch up with him. 'You must have imagined *intrepid* because you are.' He leaned heavily against me. Unprepared, I lost my balance, and we both tumbled into the sand. He asked, 'Do you suppose we'd freeze our asses off if we went skinny-dipping?'

'No, I'd drown first,' I said, wiggling out from under his weight.

'You can't swim?' He sounded astonished.

'Not very well. I mean, I know how to swim, but I nearly drowned once. I'm kind of afraid of water,' I admitted.

'Oh, I'm part dolphin. I'll get you over that. When the weather warms. Not in November. At night. In the ocean.' The appropriate time for Jim to break into 'Moonlight Drive' passed. Being with Jim wasn't the same as being in an MGM musical. Jim did not burst into song on cue. We shook the sand out of my books, collected our footwear, and strolled down the beach.

'Do you remember the last night in San Francisco?' Jim asked.

'I remember it well. *You wore blue. The Germans wore grey.*'

Jim laughed. 'Always saw myself more Bogart than Bergman. The prospect interests me.' He grabbed my waist and whirled me off the ground. '*Casablanca*! When I was still trying to get used to this music thing being a job, I popped in to see *Casablanca* on the way to a show, and stayed for all three showings. Missed the gig. Everybody was so pissed. Especially Bill Graham. Do you know who he is?' Bill Graham was the guy who made it possible for me to hear all the bands I loved. 'I thought they would understand. I expected them to say, "Can see how you had to do that." Bogart has such truth. That scene . . .'

I finished his thought. 'At the bar. When he is drunk and close to tears.'

'Yeah. That's the best moment. Really doesn't matter that he says that classic line. You can tell his guts are churning from his face.'

'You have that.'

'I'm not particularly honest,' Jim confessed.

'I meant things play across your face.'

'They sure don't yours. I can never read you unless you're sleeping. He quoted the first line of the little poem he wrote at the park where the old men played bocci ball and he signed what he called a deposition in my diary.

I waited to see if he might recite the rest of the poem. He

110

didn't. I said, 'You could be a remarkable actor. Like Bogart. Or Montgomery Clift.'

'Thanks for the great company. I'm not sure I want to be a film actor, unless it's a way to become a filmmaker. I know I can act. Shit, I have everybody convinced I'm a rock singer.'

'What's going to convince you?' Jim didn't find the question worth answering. 'If I'd directed that scene, I would have tossed out the dialogue. I would have had Bogart wander over and play the first few notes himself. He wanted to hurt himself that night.'

Jim ignored my brilliant ploy to nudge him into talking about his self-destructive adventure the night before. He asked, 'Do you remember the last night in San Francisco?' I nodded silently, having forgotten there had once been a previous point to the conversation. He leaned down and kissed me. 'If I had asked you, when we were dancing, would you have come to Los Angeles with me?'

'I don't know.' I looked up into the eyes that were dark in the moonlight. 'No.'

The corners of Jim's lips turned up a little. He ran his hand through my hair and put his arm around my shoulder, holding me close to him. I put my arm around his waist to balance us. Down the beach, someone had built a fire. Closer, we could hear the hiss of driftwood. Lean bodies in ponchos seemed neither male nor female. 'Join us!' they called out in unanimous invitation. Jim and I hesitated.

'At least take the chill off!' insisted a girl, whose round glasses reflecting the fire made her Little Orphan Annie from the cartoon strip. She held out a bottle of tequila.

Jim walked up into the softer sand, squatted, and took the bottle. He took a swallow and handed the bottle back. 'Thanks,' he whispered hoarsely. He ran his hands down his thighs and stood to go.

'One's not going to do it tonight,' she thrust the bottle back at Jim. 'We've got food, too.'

Jim took another drink and sat in the space they scurried to make by the fire. He held out his hand to me, and I squeezed in beside him. The fire felt good against the damp night air. In the light, I could make out that there were two couples. One of the men, whose blond hair was in a ponytail, held a guitar. The girl with the blank-eyed Orphan Annie look had a flute across her knees.

No introductions went around. I couldn't tell if they recognized Jim and didn't want to make him uncomfortable, or if names weren't important around an autumn beach fire. The man strummed a pretty fair guitar, but the girl played the flute like an angel. Jim and I exchanged the same look. We sat incredulous when she dropped the silver flute back into her lap and returned to earth to take a bite out of a sandwich.

More than one bottle of tequila made the circle before the blond man kicked sand on the fire. 'Would you like to stay with us tonight? We have a house nearby.'

Jim accepted with thanks. He and Jim shook hands and exchanged first names. He was a stained-glass artist. He and Jim walked away together with Jim interviewing him. By the time we reached their house, Jim asked the artist to show off his studio.

The studio was the single-car garage. Huge sheets of glass were filed upright in two-by-four racks along the one windowless wall. A giant worktable ran down the centre with warehouse lights hanging above it as if it were a pool table. He held up a completed window to the light. The centre of the abstract design was dense, small opaque squares of glass radiating out with increasingly larger, erratically shaped translucent pieces of glass.

'It's beautiful, man,' Jim said.

He smiled. 'Thanks. My commissions are for whales in the ocean. Or poppies. People want craft, not art.'

'I want this,' Jim said, running his finger along a leaded line. He didn't make an offer. I knew his pockets held twelve cents.

At Jim's insistence, the artist demonstrated cutting a piece of rich cobalt-blue glass. When he scored the glass, it sounded like fingernails dragging across the blackboard. With fingers folded under and thumbs on top along each side of the barely discernible mark, he snapped the glass in two.

'Could I try?' Jim asked. Jim followed the same procedure with confidence. When he snapped the glass, he sliced the inside of his left thumb. He stuck the wound in his mouth without any concern, more interested in seeing if the piece fitted the pattern.

'That's what you get for cutting glass when you're running on tequila,' I chided.

Jim looked at me cross-eyed. 'You try.'

I never liked to try new things in front of people. 'Have a scrap?'

'Go for the real thing.' The artist pointed his stubby finger to a piece of green glass.

Though the glass-cutter wavered, I pushed hard enough for the fingernail-on-blackboard sound, picked up the piece of glass, and closed my eyes to snap it. Delighted I had a piece that fitted the pattern, I didn't notice I had cut my thumb in the same place Jim had cut his, until a big drop of blood hit the butcher-paper pattern. I blotted the blood with my sleeve.

Jim sucked my thumb. 'That's what you get for cutting glass sober.' He held our wounded thumbs together. 'Blood brothers, now and forever.'

Just what I always wanted. 'That settles that question. I've been wondering what we were.'

We were supplied with bandaids from a nearly empty can. 'The lessons in stained-glass are free,' he said to Jim. Then he looked at me and said, 'The lessons in karma are a thousand dollars. I accept monthly instalments.'

The cutter was working under a deadline. He cut an entire panel of the window with a concentration enthralling to witness. Jim nodded his head to the rhythm of screech and snap. When the final two pieces were laid down, there was a brief silence, broken by the low drone of a fog horn, followed by the calls of the seals settling in for the night on the cross-braces of the distant pier's pilings. Jim had a peaceful smile on his lips while being shown how to wrap the edges of the glass pieces in copper foil. We all sat on stools around the worktable, wrapping the glass, not caring much about our fingers being stiff from the damp cold. At last, he led us through the back door of his rectangular little house. There was a fire in the fireplace, fresh oatmeal cookies, and pots of tea and coffee.

Jim gravitated toward the collection of 45s in the corner. 'Who graduated from high-school the same year I did?' he asked the room over his shoulder.

'Must have been me,' the artist volunteered. 'They're my records.'

'Well,' Jim said, 'we gotta have a sock hop! *What'd I say?*' Jim screamed at the quiet group like Jerry Lee Lewis. He piled the record-player with a stack of choice songs.

The artist and the others moved the furniture back with an unspoken synchronicity that made it seem they often had strangers demanding a dancefloor. Jim's boots started the pile of footwear. He and the others were rolling up the musty Persian rug when Jerry Lee Lewis started screaming for himself.

'Got a date this time!' Jim grabbed me before I could get too shy to rock with Jim and Jerry Lee. 'The next one's for you,' Jim whispered, and laughed as Del Shannon began 'Runaway'. Giggling in Jim's arms, I forgot I was too shy to dance in front of people. Halfway through, Jim whined, 'Why the fuck can't I play guitar?' Then Fats Domino sang 'Fell in Love on a Monday' and Elvis Presley begged, 'Little Sister' to treat him right. The Ventures had me wanting to play guitar, too. We slowed for Roy Orbison's 'Running Scared', Sam Cooke's 'Cupid', 'My Empty Arms' by Jackie Wilson, and 'September in the Rain' with Dinah Washington, then picked up some with Duane Eddy's 'Ring of Fire'. Jim seemed to be the only one who could dance to the Dave Brubeck Quartet's 'Take Five'. 'Hey,' Jim murmured, 'you shoulda been a beatnik. Gotta close with a slow dance,' Jim said when Ben E. King's 'Stand By Me' began.

I told Jim, 'I feel that joy that school is over and fear we might lose touch over the summer.' Not bad for a cold November night. 'You can programme my jukebox anytime.'

'Where were you in sixty-one?' he asked.

'Just moved to Southern California. We landed in a blue motel with that orange tree outside. I felt like we were in Oz. Was that third grade? I went to three different schools that year. Never got the hang of spelling.'

'I noticed,' he said into my ear so it tickled. He had made some attempt to correct my spelling in my diary and letters, but had thrown his hands up in despair. When the song finished, he kissed me. I pulled away, shy in front of the others, who were too involved in their own kisses to notice us.

We were offered one of the bedrooms, but Jim said a sleeping bag would suit us. Our host brought two sleeping bags. We settled in front of the fireplace. Jim opened my Pee Chee folder and read every note from my friends. Their notes were filled with whether or not to go to a party where pot was going to be smoked, whether to sleep with boyfriends, not having boyfriends, favourite bits of songs. Quotes from Dylan, the Airplane, and The Doors. Recent poetry about love or war or confusion. Fear of not being the best. Fear of admitting wanting to be.

Jim said, 'I envy you your friends. I wish I had these friends when I was in school. I was such a freak. And you have this beautiful collection of freaks.' I wondered if that was what appealed to him in me. A chance to do fifteen better than he had the first time around.

Jim upended my tote, a deplorable habit. He pounced on the handful of coloured pencils tied up in a rubber band. We were going to colour. He and I stretched out facing each other with the handout between us so our hands wouldn't bump into each other while we worked. Engrossed in colouring the flyer, we stopped talking.

We both looked up for a delicate cough. One of the girls stared at us a moment, stunned to see us colouring. 'Excuse me. We neglected to tell you that we are on a septic tank here. It's strained enough with the four of us, so with company, we have to flush only for solids. Good-night. Oh, and it was really nice meeting you.'

Jim banked the fire. We sat and watched the blue and gold flames. Jim kissed my cheek. He held my hands in both of his. 'Did I hurt you last night? You've been so quiet. Every time I touched you, even when we were dancing, you jumped a little. I'm not clear about some of what happened. I wanted you so much. I promised I wouldn't rush you. Did I force myself on you?' I let him know he stopped when I asked. His chin dropped to his chest. When he looked back up at me he said, 'I'm deeply sorry. I'm sorry that I scared you.' He took my wrists gently. 'Did I do this?'

'The nail marks. I scraped my wrist myself.'

'I'm sorry. I didn't mean to. I remember thinking if I let go of you, I'd float away. I thought if I got as close to you as I could I'd be healed. Whole. I'm so sorry I hurt you. Tell me what I did.'

I inhaled slowly to steady myself. 'You wanted to make love.'

'Yeah, well, I always want to make love with you. Did I hurt you?'

There was a long silence while I debated that. He toyed with the hem of my sleeve and kissed the nail marks. 'I thought you were playing at first,' I said. 'Your rough kissing and touching was exciting. It felt passionate, not violent. But it was a brief prelude to your wanting to have sex whether or not I wanted to.'

He bit his lower lip. The gesture made him look very young. 'But I stopped when you asked me to?'

'Yes. If you hadn't, I wouldn't be with you now. I'm sorry, Jim, I'm just not ready for that step. If I were, it would be you.'

He rubbed my hands as if trying to warm them. 'That's the right thing.'

'Why the weeping?' He'd cried his heart out and it couldn't go unnoticed.

Jim took several minutes to answer. 'Belated mourning,' he said.

'It was my fault. Dredging up the loss of your parents.'

'You keep opening doors I've been afraid to open,' he said. I smiled a little at *doors*, which made him smile for a moment. 'With anyone else, I just shut down. I've never trusted anyone before, and it blows me away. I don't know how to do it, to be close to someone. I'd never have forgiven myself if I hurt you. Can I get back your trust?'

'I don't know. I don't know how much you lost. What happened last night can't happen again. Maybe it's asking too much of you to not treat me the way you do other women. Maybe we should just be . . . blood brothers.' I would know how to be that.

He smiled at his bandaid. 'I know I've told you I'd back off if that's what you wanted, but it's not what I want. I've always been a selfish lover. With you, I'm learning how much pleasure I get from your pleasure. When I was your age, I couldn't get much of anybody interested in my body. The last couple of years, since I've been with the band, suddenly I'm handsome. Women want to drive me wild so I'll remember them, and I forget them while we're fucking. You're the only one who treats my body with any respect. I would miss your body very much. I'd miss touching you. You calm the part of me that needs to be calmed. And excite the part of me that needs excitement. I've never found both in one woman. Can't we find a way to be together that would please us both?'

The sleeping bags were amenable to zipping together for a roomy envelope. We made separate trips to the bathroom. Jim crawled into the sleeping bag beside me. I sighed heavily. Jim laughed, 'Sleeping with me isn't *that* bad.'

'You weren't the mattress last night.'

Jim laughed. 'Fair is fair. I'll gladly be your pallet.' He patted his chest like he expected me to crawl up on to him. I curled up against him with my head on his chest. He rubbed my back. From the pile of my tote's former contents, Jim ferreted out Maugham's *The Razor's Edge* to read aloud by firelight. Its narrative style suited Jim's voice. His reading was punctuated with the fire's pops and crackles and hisses.

At daylight, I opened my eyes and caught a bit of a plaid shirt going through the kitchen door. Jim was awake and reading to himself. 'It's a selfish lover who finishes a book silently,' I teased, wondering if he had read all night.

'Oh, I'm just studying my lines.' He closed the book and kissed me. 'How you doin'?'

'Better, for the talk and sleep.'

Jim handed me my dress. 'Given up underwear?' he asked, smiling. I watched his eyes cloud as he realized he had a part in its absence. Rather than talk, we separated and rolled the sleeping bags, rolled the rug back, and tried to fit the sofa feet into the indentations in the rug. The room appeared, we decided, like it had before the sock hop.

'I need a bath,' I announced with a side-step in the direction of the bathroom. Jim moved with me. I felt uncomfortable. 'I feel like we are always starting over.' I took his hand in invitation. Jim divided my hair down the middle, then one side into thirds and started braiding. I braided the other half. 'You braid backwards,' Jim informed me.

When he finished his side, he undid my braid and re-braided it. 'So they match,' Jim explained, holding them out so I'd look like Pippi Longstocking. We splashed in the tub, more playfully than sensually, until our bandaids drifted away and the water was cold.

As we crossed the living-room, the television screamed with morning war news. We took refuge in the kitchen where music was on the radio. Jim, comfortable in the strangers' house, opened cupboards until he found glasses and made us fresh orange juice with an old-fashioned glass reamer, then served up delicately browned wholewheat toast.

The newspaper, open on the table, pictured two soldiers carrying what remained of a third between them. Jim turned the paper over. I couldn't swallow the piece of toast in my mouth. After I'd been chewing an inordinately long time, Jim held out his hand, offering a place for me to put my toast.

'I've been working on a song about the war,' Jim said. He wrote out a line over the newsprint about the end of the war. I teared up. How old was the boy on the other side of the folded newspaper?

We found the glass-cutter in his studio to say our goodbyes. I asked him directions to the beach. Jim drawled, 'I imagine it's west,' but our host was kind enough to tell us the best route. We walked the half-dozen blocks swinging hands. Across the street from the beach, Jim broke loose and ran across the street, the sand, and into the surf up to his knees. The surf fell back. Jim glowered at his wet boots.

We met at the edge of the damp sand. Jim dropped to his seat and dumped the ocean out of his boots. 'Sit!' he commanded. We watched the waves until I caught their restlessness. I walked the length of the beach that dead-ended at a wall of rocks. Sitting on one, rough with barnacles, I could see Jim fighting the wind for his new notebook.

When I returned to him, Jim held up a hand for me to pull him to his feet. I slipped my arms around him and said, 'You are *decidedly small in circumference*.'

Jim held out his arms and spun around for my approval. '*Oliver Twist*?' Jim asked, just to be sure, thereby proving an earlier boast that given a line from a book, he could name it.

'I'd rather talk with you than . . .' I fought for a comparison.

Jim interrupted, 'Make love with me?'

True. I blushed. 'Anyone.'

'Do you have enough money for a motel?' he asked.

We sat on a low wall and added up my dollars and change at

the bottom of my bag. 'I'm rich,' I announced. 'Twenty-seven seventeen.' The sudden burst of sevens made me wonder. 'Why seven?'

Jim grinned, following me back to 'The End'. *Seven miles.* 'Came out that way. Acid snake. Probably by way of biblical indoctrination. Seven-year locusts. We are supposed to renew our bodies every seven years. Could be my child brain recorded we were seven miles from town when I witnessed that accident. It doesn't matter which seven. It's a mythological number.'

'Seven sisters,' I suggested.

'*Seven Year Itch.*'

'*Seven Brides . . .*'

'*For Seven Brothers*,' Jim added, then bragged, 'I learned to jump a baseball bat like that guy did the axe handle.' He demonstrated flawlessly, with an invisible bat that on second thought may as well have been an invisible axe.

I applauded. 'I always wanted to walk over a sofa like in *Singing in the Rain.*'

'I do a real good impression of that woman who sings "I'm Just a Girl Who Can't Say No" from *Oklahoma.*'

'With a bonnet?' I asked.

'Not so far.' He pulled a pigtail. 'I'd rather talk with you than anything but make love with you. I wrote you a poem.' He sat cross-legged on the cement wall to read a seven-line poem about my shell collecting he called 'Small Change'. He rattled the broken bits of shell in my pocket as proof of the correctness of his metaphor.

I took the book from him so I could read it again myself. 'You wrote this while I watched?' I marvelled.

Jim rented us a room in a motel which was intensely white in the glare of bright, but sunless sky. The room was spartan in a near-the-beach way as opposed to monkish. There was a double bed, a dresser, and two stools under a narrow counter that separated the kitchenette. Sitting on the foot of the bed, Jim wrestled with his stiff, drying boots. He pulled off his sweater and shirt in one sweep.

'I'm gonna take a quick shower so we aren't sleeping on sand tonight. If you join me, we can take a slow shower.'

'I'm pretty clean. Probably still pink and puckered.'

Jim barely moved his hips in boyish and sexy invitation.

Considering briefly and slipping out of my dress, I stood on tiptoe to kiss him. When I stood flat again, he leaned down to give me a kiss as wild as the Santa Cruz roller-coaster I feared. 'Whew!' Jim shrieked. He skipped into the bathroom, then returned to retrieve me, standing dumbstruck in the middle of the room.

The toilet in the tiny bathroom was positioned so that you had to decide whether you wanted the door opened or closed before you sat down, but the bathtub was big, enclosed with a sliding glass door, and had a high tile-lined window.

Jim spent a long time unbraiding my hair inch by inch. Then kissing my face inch by inch. 'You are the most perfect pink in all the right places,' he said, caressing one of them, then stared into my eyes until I had to blink, but he did not. 'Peaking,' he smiled.

'Peeking?' I asked.

He held my hips against his. 'Acid. The summit. The best part.'

I felt uneasy. 'Your pockets were empty.'

'A bon voyage gift from the glass-cutter.'

'Back on the horse that threw you?' I asked casually. Jim grinned, then lifted me up on to the sink, which groaned, but held. 'I wonder why,' I said, when Jim stopped kissing me, 'everybody isn't always kissing everybody else if it feels this good.'

'It isn't always this good.' He winked. 'We kiss like we draw boots.'

I felt momentarily forlorn. 'I wish we danced like we draw boots.'

Jim preferred his shower cooler than I did mine, but I couldn't complain about the sensual way he washed my hair. I had to reach up to wash his. When I questioned getting soap in his wide eyes, he promptly sank to his knees. As I rinsed his hair, he began kissing my navel. He embraced my hips. 'I won't let you fall,' he assured me, but I clung to the window-sill with one hand and the top of the shower door with the other.

When he stood up, he took my head and his hands and kissed me. He ran his hands down my arms and laced our fingers. He kissed me playfully, biting my lips gently, and grabbing my tongue with his teeth, laughing when he let it go. 'Your hair is on fire,' he whispered. 'The gold in the red.' He put my arms around his neck and flattened me against the tile with his body. He warned me. 'This time. Hold on.'

'What am I supposed to do?' I asked. He sang softly about snake riding. 'I'm gonna have to listen to that song again.'

He sang a bit of 'The End' and laughed warmly. How did he get away with that? Simple rhyme moved so deeply sung. 'I'll sing it for you. But not now. Don't worry, baby. I'm a fifteen-year-old kid in love with a fifteen-year-old kid. I'll just slither between your thighs until we both feel real good. Feel real good,' he sang to 'The End's' melody.

My own words failed me. 'I never dreamed,' I said in stolen dialogue with honest breathlessness, 'any mere physical experience . . .'

Jim rested his forehead against mine until he could stop giggling. 'After I'm with you, I go back to LA with this grin on my face, and people ask me for days, "What are you on, Jim? Give me some." You are my favourite drug.' Not that he was willing to stop with me.

Jim took forever to dry me, enjoying my being perfectly pink in all the right places. That part of Jim on acid seemed boring, until I dried his body with the same intricate pleasure. Jim took my dress from my hands and backed up to the bed. He pulled me on top of him and rolled us into its middle, stopping us on our sides facing each other. 'I was noticing in the shower, a cunt is a mysterious and exciting creation.'

The mood snapped. I sat up. '*Cunt* is an insult.'

'Oh, no! It's a better sound than vagina. Like cock sounds better than penis. Cunt and cock go together.' Jim giggled and snorted, letting his head loll back. 'In a poetic way, like us, not just physiologically, like the rest of the unlucky world. Did I say I was going to sing something? Where the hell am I in this concert?' He drew snakes on my thigh with his finger. 'Oh, yeah. I don't want to sing that. Something I wrote for you.' I rather hoped he would sing 'I Can't See Your Face', because somehow it didn't seem quite like *my* song with the band's music. He'd never just sung it for me. 'The Spy' was mine. He stroked my neck, taking

121

an incredibly long time to choose between the two. At last, he pulled me down to share his pillow. Was it not so long in his acid time? His hand rested at my waist. He didn't take much of a breath before he slipped into the first line of 'Crystal Ship'.

I had to put both hands over my giggle. I lost a line of the song wondering if he thought I were someone else, or if he remembered what I had said about hearing the song that late afternoon at Mt. Tamalpais. Then my always busy mind quieted and there was only the sweet thrill of hearing him really sing for the first time since our slow dance in San Francisco. Though he insisted his slow singing was no more than a whining croon, he had a way of meeting a note just so and making the word he hung it on matter.

When he finished, he tapped my skull, 'I know your mind. You're thinking, Jim's on some weird trip and he thinks I'm somebody else. He wrote that song *years* before we met. Weren't you listening? Didn't *you* get it?' he asked me. 'This is the first time I sang that song with *reign* as in rule, not *rain* as in shower. Whole new song, don't you think?' Jim fell back on the pillows with an infectious peal of giggles. I sat up on my heels to watch. 'You have a violet aura,' he said. 'It would clash with your hair, but it has a gold lining. Last night, it was all gold, like a painting of the Virgin Mary.'

I giggled until I snorted like Jim had. 'The only thing Mary and I have in common is our dubious virginity. I'll assume she deserved the halo.'

He wanted my opinion on his aura, but I wasn't on acid. 'Oh,' he said, 'I thought you could see auras without help.'

'Why would you think that?'

'You come in and out of this world.'

I shook my head. 'I'm firmly fixed in this one.'

'No, you're not,' he argued sweetly.

'Are we having our first fight?'

'Didn't we have that yesterday afternoon when you scolded me for taking drugs from strangers? Right now, I think I'm going to come just looking at you.'

I giggled. He did have an erection. I was entranced by the workings of his male body. 'You do shimmer. I think it has more to do with sex than auras.'

Jim crawled over to me on his knees. 'I want to see if we share the same aura when we are close.' He straddled my thighs, wrapped his arms around me, and rested his cheek against mine.

'Do we?' I asked.

'Haven't opened my eyes yet.' He nuzzled my cheek. He raised up on his knees and sat back humming. He ran his hands down my back and under me. He raised me with him. 'Close your eyes,' he said. 'Hum with me.' How could I hum a song I didn't know? He insisted, 'Hum with me.'

Jim guided my body in a precise dance on our knees. He'd read that, in India, lovers achieved orgasm without touching and wanted to prove we were as in sync. We moved slightly up and down, back and forth, his hum vibrating on my skin. As he repeated the melody, I could hum more closely with him. The humming grew into a chant. He lifted me with music. The chant grew more intense. My body felt light. Jim moaned, and fell into soft gasping. I opened my eyes on his smiling face, his eyes still closed. He lifted his lids slightly to peer at me. 'What happened?' he asked.

I smiled back. 'I think I levitated.'

Jim grinned. 'I took you to the top of the Ferris wheel.' He kissed me delicately, then broke the spell by trotting off to the bathroom for a damp towel to mop me. 'Let's have a picnic. Know a nice spot?' he asked with his hand between my legs in one of his endless *double entendres*.

'Were you weaned on Mae West movies?'

'My problem is I was probably never breast-fed. It was out of vogue in the forties.'

How odd to think he was born in a whole different decade than me. 'There's a ledge near Natural Bridges where it looks as if the waves will engulf you, but they break just short.'

'Clothes, then!' Jim announced.

Our coffers allowed for bread and cheese with something left to front dinner. Natural Bridges, just north of Santa Cruz, was a long walk or a short hitchhike, so we walked with Jim's thumb out. We got a quick Volkswagen ride. Getting in and out of the back seat took more time than the ride itself, but Jim thought it was well worth it because the driver gave us half a bottle of wine.

For my benefit, Jim asked, 'Anything in this besides wine?' The driver shook his head, frowning, 'Sorry.'

Jim stood on the edge of the ledge to face the breaking wave. He spun back to me with a brilliantly happy smile on his face. 'Perfect!' he screamed. It wasn't a place for conversation, but it was an amazing niche in which to get drunk for the first time. Half of half a bottle of wine and I had a grin fixed on my face. Jim kept a strong grip on my waist as if he were as afraid as I was that I'd slip into the ocean.

There was a problem climbing back up because my feet weren't quite where I expected them to be, but I felt fuzzy and full and wonderful. Instead of heading back to town, we walked north along the highway for a while. The sun came out and turned the sky and ocean cerulean blue. I sighed.

'Tired?' Jim asked.

'No.' The problem was clear. 'The ocean isn't the colour of your eyes any more.'

'Yeah, that's worth a pretty big sigh.' He wrapped his arms around me and whirled me off the ground. When he set me down, he held me until the world stopped spinning. 'I'm sorry. I forgot one of us was drunk.'

'Reminds me of spinning as a kid, to fall back and watch the sky spin.'

'One of my favourite things to do when I was seven,' Jim said. That didn't surprise me at all.

We laughed for a couple miles, then hiked a narrow path down to a flat stretch of beach. We danced barefooted in the cold surf. Then raced until we were breathless. A terrible stench hit us, and we gave a wide circle to the decaying body of a Black Labrador tangled in seaweed. Circling gulls' cruel screams drowned Jim's comment.

Beaches along that part of the coast were a row of scallops ringed with rocks. We climbed out on to a bed of rocks to look at the anemones in tide pools. Jim stretched out on his stomach with his chin on the edge of one of the pools.

'What do you see on acid that I'm not seeing?'

'Considering your eyes, probably nothing,' he answered. 'The acid is lifting.' He turned on his back and shaded his eyes with his hand. 'Mild stuff, but nice.'

124

We hiked up to the highway and beat the sunset into town. We wandered through a grocery store. Between us, our cooking skills covered spaghetti. I charmed him into Marinara sauce, with my 'Isn't it interesting that every culture has its vegetarian cuisine?'

In the little motel room, Jim perched on a stool marvelling at how thinly I could slice carrots with a dull paring knife, so he wouldn't have to make the attempt. If he hadn't been thumping his pen on the notebook balanced on his knees, I would have asked him to be our radio, since the room didn't have one.

'No radio, no clock, no time,' I said to myself, slicing the carrots.

'Nice beat,' Jim said.

'I'm sorry,' I apologized for interrupting his work. 'Do you have radar?'

'Mm.' Jim patted my bottom gently with his boot. When I tried to read what he had written upside down, he opened his arm and beckoned me into it. I leaned against him on the stool, and he rested his head on my shoulder. He had written:

> *Dog carcass on the beach*
> *We hold our breath*
> *and look back*

'You write the next line,' he said, handing me his pen. 'Write the first thing that comes to your mind. Go!'

Shakily, I wrote, *Crab ridden.*'

'Yeah! Wasn't that eerie? Movement over the corpse.'

He wrote under my line, *Seaweed.*

I reached for the pen, which Jim relinquished without comment, and wrote beside it, *wreath*, so the poem ended:

> *Crab ridden*
> *Seaweed wreath*

Jim wasn't nearly as surprised as I was that the spaghetti was good. We had gotten tiny jars of oregano and basil and Jim had been finicky about the precise proportions, insisting basil dominate. Jim grimaced at the glasses of water. Our budget hadn't extended to even a cheap bottle of wine. 'If I hadn't gone and gotten drunk this afternoon, you could have had wine with dinner.'

'Baby, you were smashed on less than a glass, which I would have drunk if you hadn't. Do you have an itty-bitty hangover to go with your itty-bitty binge?'

'No, but I feel like I hiked ten miles.'

'We did.' Jim took off his shirt rather than roll up his sleeves, and insisted I stay on the stool while he washed the dishes and handed them to me to dry.

'Is this what it's like at home with Pamela?' I asked, dreaming how good it would be to be grown-up, wishing he had asked me to LA that summer and I had said yes.

'Nope! We usually throw dishes at each other. Duck!' he yelled, spun the plate into the air and caught it himself. He handed it to me with a kiss that lasted long enough for the plate to dry on its own.

'It's been nice having this time with you,' I said.

'We have tonight and tomorrow. Don't start saying goodbye.'

We strolled to the beach arm in arm, mostly so we could keep our hands in our pockets. The summery day had chilled back to November. To our left lay the deserted boardwalk and roller-coaster. We turned right and crossed the street. Palms cast threatening shadows across the Coconut Grove. We dropped our footwear at the edge of the sand, and walked separately, hands jammed back into our pockets.

Jim freed his hand from his tight pocket and held it out for me. We ran on the hard wet sand until our lungs stung, then Jim veered into the ocean. I tried to brake in the sand, but Jim held me tight. He stopped when the water was past his hips. Grabbing my waist, he lifted me above the incoming wave. The clouds sailed away from the moon and the black water was suddenly silvery blue. He lifted me for another wave. We shivered through a kiss and ran back on to the beach. Jim wrung out the bottom foot of my hair while I twisted my dress. We ran all the way back to the motel.

'What happened to "Not November. Not night. Not the ocean?"' I asked, my teeth chattering from excitement as much as the cold.

'This wasn't a swimming lesson,' he said patiently. 'This was proving you could trust me again.'

We shed our soaking clothes and towelled each other wildly. We huddled under the blankets. 'Looks like we sleep with the beach,' I said.

'I don't mind. Your Pacific isn't my Pacific. Jesus!'

'Our surfers, you may have noticed, wear wet suits, not baggies. I've heard the stretch of ocean from here to San Francisco called Shark Alley.'

Jim shivered. 'Might have mentioned that before we made bait of ourselves.'

'We? Would it have stopped you?'

'No,' he said, 'but knowing would have been more exciting.'

In darkness, Jim wanted to explore me all over again. He licked my toes. 'Aren't they sandy?' I queried.

'Like scallops.'

Jim woke me with a kiss on my cheek while it was still dark. The neon light that filtered in through the curtain made Jim as silvery blue as the ocean. 'Will you kiss me?' he asked. I answered with a sleepy kiss. Jim's kiss back roused me. 'Let's dance on our knees. I want to see if we can do what we did this afternoon when I'm straight.'

In the grey morning, Jim lay crosswise across the bed with me as pillow humming to himself. 'What's that?' I asked, not recognizing the tune.

He sang a few lines. 'It's a *morning song*. You know how babies sing to themselves in their cribs?' I had to take his word for it. As the youngest, I hadn't much experience with babies. 'I remember doing it when I was very young. I just never stopped like most people do. When I am in a good mood, I always wake with a new song in my head. Often words and music now, instead of sounds and music. They are the basis for all my songs and a good deal of my poetry.'

8

Not to Touch the Earth

After everyone had gone to bed, I would huddle by the wall phone in the kitchen waiting for Jim to call. I went through equal amounts of corn chips and book pages. I developed a routine. Around ten o'clock, I turned off the ringer on my sister's bedroom phone, and lowered the one in the kitchen. That way, if I went to bed early or stayed at a friend's Jim's always late-night calls wouldn't disturb my family. Two or three times a week, he called from Los Angeles. Less often, he would call while on tour, barely able to speak racked with the *Road Lonelies*. He claimed that he plotted to deface phone booths coast to coast with *Jim Loves Ginger*.

'Whatcha reading?' one of Jim's favourite phone hellos.

'*I did not read books that first summer. I hoed beans*,' I answered.

'*Walden*!' he exclaimed. 'I just sent you a philosophy book. Do you know anything about Nietzsche?'

'Enough to know I wouldn't invite him to Walden Pond.'

He juggled the phone, then returned laughing. 'Might have kept him out of the looney bin. I'll write a new verse to that old song . . . what is it? You know, he says one thing and she says another. You say *Thoreau* and I say *Nietzsche*.'

'Got the wrong Ginger again,' I teased, picturing Fred Astaire and Ginger Rogers arguing their duet on roller-skates, a nifty visual metaphor for their precarious relationship in *Shall We Dance*.

'Do me a favour,' Jim said in a near laugh, 'and stay away from *Civil Disobedience*.'

'Too late. I read it a couple years ago when lying down in front of troop trucks seemed like a good idea.'

I'd been to a couple peace marches where the fringe was lunatic. Right, not left wing. At last Jim whispered, 'Be careful then.' After another silence, he said, 'Anyway, baby, read the book I sent and you'll be able to read my mind even better than you do now. Shouldn't that scare me?' Jim sounded less introspective than eager. 'I tucked your airline ticket somewhere in the middle. I'll meet you in New York and we'll go up with the band. We're playing a college upstate. Dress real warm. I'm so excited and nervous about singing for you.'

'Feels like Christmas morning when I was little. Only, I know I'm getting *exactly* what I want. Doesn't seem fair to you that I'm getting what *I* want for *your* birthday.'

When the expected package arrived, I studied the return address. Jim had spent time creating illuminated letters which, no matter how I turned them, looked like an L and a K, not his familiar JM. 'Who's LK?' I asked when he called.

'Me. Well, me and not me. My stage persona. I created him because I didn't want to be up there. He does occasionally seem to have a life of his own. The Lizard King.'

When we met he had told me about his fascination with desert dwellers in Albuquerque. 'Something from your childhood?' I asked, having the inside track.

'Oh, no. The Lizard King is half this Australian lizard I saw a picture of once. He has these wing-like structures he can flare out to look big when he rushes at his enemies. I found that works real well on stage. That rush at people.'

'What's the other half?'

'I'll let you guess. From the movies. Who does the same thing?'

I ran snippets of film through my mind, eliminating everyone who appeared. 'Don't tell me. I'll find the right image,' I assured him. Jim hummed. 'Is that a clue?' I asked, not recognizing the tune.

'No, it's a new song. Take your time.'

The melody kept pulling me away from the black and white images running through my head. Jim did not hurry me or bring up that it was a long-distance call. When I hit film noir, I had him. 'Robert Mitchum,' I said confidently.

Jim laughed. 'No wonder I'm bored when I play with anyone else.'

'Does the song have words?'

'It's your part of an *epic* poem entitled *Celebration of the Lizard*,' he pronounced pompously.

I didn't believe him. 'I dare you,' I challenged him to prove it.

'Let me get my notebook.' Never challenge Jim. He'd write an epic on the spot to win a dare. He riffled pages. 'Let me find your part.'

I got a part? 'Is this like *Spoon River*?'

'Just fucking intimidate me,' he said playfully. 'I don't have the piece arranged the way I want.' He groaned. He slipped away to take a drink, infinitely more shy about reading his poetry than humming a new tune. There was what I thought might evolve into a chorus . . . *Not to Touch the Earth*.

Jim read unfinished stanzas, asked for words. Tried out rhyme. My hand grew stiff. My ear ached. We stayed connected by the phone until I heard my mother's five o'clock alarm.

The night of December 7th, I didn't go to bed with any intention of sleeping. I peeked at the clock every few minutes. At 4 a.m., I gave up and dressed. A friend guaranteed a ride to the airport. I needed to make the earliest plane to meet up with The Doors' flight up to upstate New York. Dressed as warm as my California wardrobe allowed, I searched for the ticket nestled in Nietzsche. The ticket was gone. No need to search. I knew I hadn't misplaced it. On the way out the front door, my father peered over his coffee-cup in the dark kitchen to ask, 'Who do you know in New York?'

I answered, 'Nobody,' without breaking my stride out the door. By the time I reached Pat's car, I was in tears. I wouldn't see Jim on his birthday. She drove us to a phone booth where I emptied both our purses of change leaving messages for Jim from Los Angeles to his hotel in New York. Pat only knew I had a wild heart with no place to go. We sat in her room the whole bleak day listening to records by the quiet phone.

'Are you all right?' Jim's voice was anxious on the staticfilled line.

How I hated a life where that was his first thought. I felt raw. 'I'm just so disappointed. I'm glad you got my message. I left them everywhere. Both coasts. Which one reached you?'

'I didn't get any message. When you didn't show up, I waited for the next plane, then called your house. Your mother gave me this number. Why didn't you come?' Jim yelled. 'You promised!'

My heart became a knot. 'The ticket disappeared,' I said softly.

'Shit! What do you mean, it disappeared?' Jim's voice was anxious.

'I kept it in the book you gave me. When I packed up to come over here, it was gone. On the way out the door, my father asked who I knew that lived in New York. I decided to stay at my friend's house, like it was what I was really going to do all along. I'm sorry. I'm a coward. I couldn't stand up to him and ask for the ticket back.'

'Of course not. That makes you sane, not a coward. I'm pretty damn pissed no one gave me your message. How much trouble are you in? If you need me, I'll catch the next plane to San Francisco. Fuck the concert. No problem.'

I wished Jim knew nothing about me. I wanted to be able to slip in and out of his life less painfully. 'I'm not in trouble. My dad probably thought I was running away. He seemed satisfied that he stopped me. Can you get your money back?'

'I don't give a fuck about that. I want you safe. I want you here!' he shouted. The line went dead.

The phone rang again. I didn't answer the phone even though my hand was on it. My friend picked it up with a cheery, 'Hello,' then handed me the receiver.

'I killed the damn phone,' Jim laughed. 'You'd think they could take a good bang against the wall.'

'I thought you hung up on me.'

'Baby, I wouldn't do that. I'm not mad at you. I wanted to sing for you tonight. And sleep with you. I hate my birthdays. I never had a good one.'

'I'm a lousy camp follower.'

'Another thing to love about you,' Jim soothed me.

I wanted to cheer him. 'I'll have to give you your present the next time I see you.'

'I thought you were my present.'

'Oh, you have to have something in ribbons. I want to surprise you.'

He moaned, 'Well, I have to go if I'm going to make this gig. I missed the band's plane. Gonna see if I can charter something.'

My hands turned to ice. They were so cold I couldn't move my fingers. 'Not one of those little planes. Jim, no! You can't do that!'

Laughing, he asked, 'Ordering me around, now?'

'Jim, please.'

'Baby, you're being . . .'

'Buddy Holly. Patsy Cline. Don't get on a small plane!' I begged.

'I have to. The band hates me enough without my not showing up at all. I mean, if you needed me, I'd put up with their being mad at me, but just because you have a funny feeling . . .'

'You're going to die if you get on that plane,' I said with absolute certainty.

There was a full minute's silence before Jim asked, 'Is this like the way you can turn the radio on when my music's playing?'

'Yes. When you said *charter* my hands turned to ice, as if I were touching you and you were cold. I know this sounds crazy. Let me be crazy this once.' I felt crazy. I pleaded with all my heart, 'I'll never ask for anything else. Don't get on a little plane.'

'You never ask for anything anyway. All right. I trust you more than anyone else on God's earth. I'll see if I can rent a limo. How does that sound?'

'Fine. Fine. Thank you, Jim. I wish I could give you your birthday bath.'

He laughed softly, 'You wish . . . Aw, honey.' I wished him a happy birthday. He said, 'Well, if you're right, you just gave me a *real* birthday. I'll do the show for you. But I'm not gonna surprise the band with an a cappella on "The Spy".'

Two days later, I heard on the radio news that Jim had been

arrested for obscenity the day after his birthday in New Haven, Connecticut. There wasn't much detail, except to announce that he had been released. After the lack of success trying to reach him on his birthday, I tried to wait for Jim to call, but was on my way out the door to find a pay phone, when the phone rang. Jim's first words were, 'Don't worry.' He tried to make light of the arrest, but his voice trembled a little over a joke about police brutality.

When he got back to California, we arranged a meeting in San Francisco because he was pressed for time. He'd gotten a room in a fancy hotel where the bellman stared at my beads and jeans, and followed me up on the elevator so I wouldn't steal the doorknobs and hide them in the birthday package I carried. He followed a few steps behind, obviously trying to be obvious, like a cat following a mouse in a cartoon. When I knocked on his door, Jim flung it open and kissed me in the doorway.

'Did he show you up?' Jim asked, looking at my shadow.

'No, he *followed* me up.'

'No tip in that. Fuck off,' Jim said sweetly, before pulling me into the room. The private kiss was nicer. I handed him his birthday present. The anticipation on his face tickled me. When he saw it was a shirt, he stripped off the one he wore. Bare from his hiphugging leathers up, Jim held the new shirt out for me to unbutton. I stared. Bruises ringed his wrists and mottled his arms purple and green. There were bruises on his chest, and when I walked around him, above his right kidney.

'Jim, they beat you!'

Jim stroked my sleeve. 'I took a tumble down some stairs.'

'I know the difference between a punch and a fall!'

Jim's smile was counterfeit. 'They didn't like my act.' I wanted him to sue. He said, 'I've been told to lay low.' He reached for the shirt and unbuttoned it himself. How could the people he did business with care so little about Jim?

'It's my fault, isn't it? If I had been there, this wouldn't have happened.' I started to cry. 'I'm so sorry, Jim.'

'Ginger, please don't cry.' He tried to wipe my face with his hands, but it was too much of a downpour. 'You have to stop taking the blame for my screw-ups. It started because a cop maced

134

me backstage. If you'd been there, I still would have gotten maced.' He laughed. 'I take that back. You would have thrown yourself on the grenade.'

Despite my worry, I smiled. 'Why did they mace you? Are you okay? Have you seen a doctor?'

'In order, I was, you know I'm an alley-cat,' he bit his lower lip, and rolled his eyes, that charming ploy that probably got him out of trouble as a child. 'Making out with a girl, and a cop, who didn't know I was the star of the shindig, swore at me and I swore back. So, he maced me. I was too damn stubborn not to do the show anyway, and too damn mad not to say something about it. I was doing a pretty good improvisation to "Backdoor Man". If the show had been here, the cop would have come on-stage to take a bow. I'm fine. I saw somebody. That's all we need to say about it.'

He gave me his best bad-boy look and slipped into the shirt. He grinned at the reflection of the white-on-white embroidered lizards marching up the left sleeve, across the shoulder, and disappearing into the pocket. 'This is wonderful! Where did you find it? I want a dozen.'

'One-of-a-kind Happy Birthday lizards!'

'You sewed this?'

I took a moment to consider whether I felt flattered or insulted by the wonder in his voice. I chose to be flattered. 'I thought a Lizard King deserved minions.'

He took the shirt off carefully. Then his leathers less carefully. Jim undressed so easily, but I still didn't know what to take off after my beads. Jim reached for my blouse. We splashed in the beautiful bathtub. We soaped and laughed and came with mutual pleasure. Jim screeched, 'Jesus!'

When I whispered, 'Save us,' Jim initiated a splashing war. Jim had a plane to catch. I had a bus back to Stockton. We'd never had so little time. We shared a cab as far as the bus station, holding hands in silence.

When I hopped out of the cab, Jim leaned over the door to kiss me goodbye and ask, 'Do you want to try again? We are playing in San Francisco for the three days after Christmas. Pick one. Or all three.'

'That's wonderful!' I brightened considerably. I'd seen the posters for The Doors and Chuck Berry at the Winterland. 'I'll ask for tickets as a Christmas present.'

'I can, very likely, get you in. I have a certain influence with the talent. I'll just leave your name at the door.'

'Well, my only friend with a car couldn't keep a secret if her or *my* life depended on it. She thinks my friend in the band plays frat houses. Simpler to buy tickets.'

The next day, I asked my mother the big question over the ironing board. She still sprinkled sheets with a corked Coke bottle, storing them in plastic bags in the fridge so they wouldn't mildew before she got to them. 'There's a concert I'd really like to see the day after Christmas. The Doors and Chuck Berry are going to be at the Winterland in San Francisco. Could I go?' There was a mad mash of people at every Winterland show. I had in mind to go up first thing and hang around until tickets went on sale.

'Chuck Berry sounds familiar,' my mother said, resting the iron on its heel.

'Oh, he was on the radio a lot.' I sang a little of 'Mabelline' terribly. 'He's one of the original rock 'n' roll people. He influenced Elvis Presley and the Beatles.' My mother had long since forgiven Elvis for 'Hound Dog' and liked the Beatles. 'The Beatles do his song "Roll Over Beethoven".' I did that one slightly better, though my mother showed no great flash of recognition. I didn't sound much like John Lennon.

'Is it one of these daytime concerts?'

'Evening,' I explained. Evening sounded safer than night. 'But Pat could take me. Probably be a car of us.' My mother believed in the safety of numbers. I was attempting to work in all the good selling points. 'It *is* vacation.'

'Ask your father.'

How I hated that answer. 'Couldn't you ask him?'

'If you're old enough to go to these concerts out of town, you're old enough to take the responsibility for arranging it.'

'He'll say *no*.' *Mama, please.*

'He let you go to all those concerts this summer. Can't hurt to ask.'

My father was engrossed in his current woodworking project

when I peeked into the garage. I watched him work, handing him an occasional tool or nail. When I was small, I used to tottle around behind him. I knew the difference between a rabbit and a rabbet before I went to school. 'What I'd really like for Christmas this year,' I said after a suitable silence, 'is to see a concert the day after Christmas in San Francisco. A ticket only costs four dollars. You wouldn't even have to wrap it.' He hated wrapping presents.

He smiled, but as much as he hated wrapping presents, my father wasn't going to let me rock 'n' roll in the big city at night.

The next time Jim called, I wished I had practised something clever to say. 'Jim, about coming to hear The Doors . . .'

'Your folks won't let you come?' It wasn't much of a question.

'I shouldn't have asked.' I should have lied. 'Now, I've blown it. I'm sorry.'

Jim was amused. 'Do you suppose you're the only teenage girl in California who hasn't seen The Doors?'

'Most likely.'

'Most likely,' Jim, the mimic, repeated in my voice. 'It's wonderfully absurd. I'll just have to think of something else to give you for Christmas.'

On Christmas Eve, the knock at the door was a long-haired young man with a white rose in one hand and a turquoise box in the other. I beamed and the young man beamed back. 'Let me get my purse,' I said, knowing from movies, my source for worldliness, a tip was in order.

'Oh, no. Mr Morrison took care of that. Merry Christmas!' he said. He climbed into a regular car at the curb, not a delivery van.

I stood at the door with the white rose in one hand and the box in the other. My mother came up behind me. 'A Christmas present from Jim,' I explained.

I made a commotion about finding a vase for the rose, then whisked the box off to my room. Even though I knew she followed me, not out of nosiness, but delight, I resented having to open the box in front of her. The lid announced in silver letters that the box was from Tiffany's. Inside was a typed poem: the first stanza told of why he came to me. The second what he got from me. Ending

137

with our being together always, it spoke of what we think we need from people, how what they naturally give may be worth more. No other gift mattered.

My mother read the poem upside down. 'Your Jim has a way of saying things. The afternoon we met, he told me he wrote poetry.' She smiled, remembering her visit with Jim. I smiled because she called him *my* Jim.

Beneath the poem rested a rectangular box wrapped in white with the little gold stars teachers put on papers in grade school glued in a pattern that even at a glance I was sure was the Pleiades. The box held a tiny bottle of Chanel No. 5. I opened it and sniffed. I put a tiny dab of the elegant fragrance on my wrist.

'He has classic taste in perfume,' my mother said.

Another turquoise box lay in tissue at the bottom. I closed the larger box and put it on the bed.

'I haven't wanted to pry,' Mama began, 'I know you are a private person and tell me things in your own time, but I don't want you to get hurt. This boy is a lot older than you. From the sound of the poem, I need to ask, are you two getting serious?'

'That doesn't really apply to us. We're friends. We care a lot about each other.'

'He's the one who calls you late?'

'Yeah,' I hesitated, so much for my great deceit. 'Could you not tell . . . anyone.'

I loved her for the nod. And for closing the door behind her as she left. In the last little box was a note in Jim's writing: 'This reminded me of the moon on the water in Santa Cruz.' *This* was a diamond pendant. A friend's mother had a two-carat diamond engagement ring and the single square stone at the end of the gold chain seemed larger.

Jim called after I had been sitting by the kitchen phone for an hour. 'Merry Christmas,' I whispered, since it was just barely.

'Merry Christmas, darlin'! Thank you for the little book. At first, I thought it was printed, but couldn't find the copyright, then I realized there was a drawing from every time we've been together. I'm overwhelmed you did all those drawings for me. I've never seen you draw in pencil. You seem to write in pencil and draw in ink. Why is that?'

138

'I'm more confident drawing,' I answered honestly.

'Well, you do both well. The drawings must have taken days of work.'

'Nights.' More accurately.

'I wish you lived in LA. We could use our mutual insomnia to create a book together.'

'That would be better than a cure for it. Be real nice to do that sometime.' I thrilled that he gave me status in his creative world, like we were just in different places on the same road. 'Thank you for the poem. The things you write go right to the centre of me.'

'Well, a poet couldn't ask for a better review. And a friend couldn't know a truer heart,' he said, sounding very formal. 'Sometimes I think we don't have much choice in who we love, but we do in who we like. I've never felt both for a woman before.'

Now you expect me to talk? I coughed to get my voice back. 'Thank you for the perfume, too. It's my first grown-up fragrance, which made me feel about ten.'

'Please, don't get any younger!' We giggled together.

'Jim . . .' I hated to tell him. 'I've never cared about diamonds. I'm not someone who is going to have an epiphany at Tiffany's, but this one, Jim, this one *is* the most beautiful bit of moon on the water. Like that night you held me in the waves in Santa Cruz. For that, I want it very much.'

'*Epiphany at Tiffany's?*' Jim laughed. 'If I was Noël Coward, I'd have a musical comedy by morning!'

'You smoke when you're nervous. I . . . um . . .'

'Alliterate.'

'Thanks. What would I do without you to finish my sentences?'

'Probably be more mysterious than you are.'

I wish I were mysterious instead of fifteen. Somehow, the two seemed contradictory. 'Jim, the diamond is beautiful, but I can't keep it.'

'Hey, I'm a pretty smart guy. You can't tell me it doesn't fit.'

I didn't want to spoil our first Christmas, but he had broken our agreement to not buy me anything I couldn't buy him. 'It doesn't fit *us*.'

The silence became a lengthening shadow between us. 'I'm sorry

139

the diamond made you nervous. I saw it right after Santa Cruz. When I got my first royalty check, I bought it for you. It will never belong to anyone else.'

'Maybe you could find some moon on the water made of glass,' I suggested.

Three days later, a little box was waiting for me in the mailbox. Inside lay a heart-shaped pendant made of rows of glass *diamonds* set in silver that caught blue and gold light. The accompanying note read, 'Sun on the water close enough?'

Jim called. 'I'm in town,' he said. 'Want to come to San Francisco with me to see a Kurosawa film?'

I was in my best mini and at the corner in half an hour. Jim sat in a rip-roaring red Mustang which pretty much had to find its own way to San Francisco because Jim and I were busy singing 'Like a Rolling Stone' at the top of our lungs. I'd given up being shy about singing with Jim in the car because it was so much fun. We sang every song that came on whether we knew the words or not. Did anyone other than Sam the Sham and assorted Pharaohs really know the lyrics to 'Wooly Bully'?

We sat in the old theatre, dangerously south of Market, transfixed, transported to feudal Japan. The film revealed the characters' varied interpretations of the same event. What is truth?

Afterwards, we didn't discuss the film, we walked at my top speed, at the pace of Jim's mind, until he abruptly braked for a drugstore that was all that green glaring fluorescent lighting. He picked up a canary-yellow legal tablet, scissors, glue. A pink capped bottle of baby oil. Then made two other unannounced stops: one at a Chinese take-out place where Jim had to have a quart of Kung Pao chicken and ordered me vegetarian fried rice. The second stop was for beer and Coke at a corner store. While the take-out was still hot, we checked into a hotel that was at our elbow, The Californian.

The room had two double beds, a TV, a dresser and a view of the air shaft. Jim plopped on the first bed. I was probably the only kid who grew up with Japanese friends in Stockton and couldn't master chopsticks. The friend who had recounted the story of the thousand cranes and enlightened me about Japanese internment camps had put her hands on her hips and informed me I would always eat like a peasant. Jim's remarkable patience with me wore thin when his Kung Pao was cold, and he let me trade chopsticks for the plastic fork.

I cringed when Jim wiped his hands on the bedspread. He caught the motion out of the corner of his eye. 'You don't want to go on the road with a rock-star. It ain't pretty.' Then he tore the garish tablet in half along its binding and thrust the one without the cardboard at me. *Not fair*, I thought. Like getting the faucet end of the bathtub. Jim demanded, 'You write about tonight. I write about tonight. Our own *Rashomon*.'

I asked, 'Do we write on both sides of the paper? How long should it be?'

Jim waved me off. 'No rules. Go!'

Jim sat with his back to me so I couldn't cheat. We wrote for an hour. Jim took my pages and cut it along the ruled lines, then his, until both our stories were fettuccine between us. Jim spread glue over a fresh page and stuck the paper noodles on without reading them. He put me to work, too. When we finished, Jim set them out in single file to dry. Visually interesting. I would have hung them in a gallery. His odd half-printed, half-cursive hand in racy black felt pen, and my silly curlycues in faint pencil created a graphic energy.

While I admired their beauty, Jim swooped up the first page to read aloud. He had written in second person, the observer. I had written in first, as if I were writing a letter to Jim. The story read like a fever, where a thought would appear, only to vanish just as it was recognized. There was no order. Jim said. 'Eerie and beautiful. I love random. Chaos! Let's type this up and send it someplace. It's time I was published. Who are we?'

I stretched out on the opposite bed to consider. Ginger James sounded like an exotic dancer. I drifted back to thinking how remarkable the pages looked. What if we used different colours and textures of paper? Different languages. Wrote with twigs dipped in ink. Dipped in mud. What if I had a movie camera?

The bed was lumpy. I felt under my back and pulled out the bottle of baby oil.

'So much for being the Princess and the Pea,' Jim teased.

'What's this for?' I tossed it on to his bed.

'I want a message.' Jim had stayed dressed for a record length of time.

Oh, dear. 'I don't know where to begin.'

'Where you begin isn't as important as where you end.' He reached up under my mini for my tights. 'I see I'm going to have to choreograph this.' Jim picked up his felt-tip pen. I helpfully offered a tablet. He took it and tossed it. His back to the mirror, Jim looked over his shoulder, and lifted his hair to write a *one* on his neck. The *two* came out backwards on his left shoulder. He nimbly twisted this way and that until he was tattooed with numbers, head to foot, back to front. The last number he made of little dots on the shaft of his penis. 'Tickles,' he commented.

He started to flick the pen at me, then dropped it, saying, 'I don't need a diagram.' Jim belly-flopped on the bed. The advantage to Jim's soluble map was that I could tell where I had been as the numbers vanished under the oil. So often Jim was the disembodied voice over the phone, there was pleasure feeling the man so solid in my hands. Two weeks had passed, but the bruises over his kidney still had a sharp outline.

PART II: *1968*

———◆·❮◆❯·◆———

9

Saviour of the Human Race

The birch tree scratched against the screen of my bedroom window. The familiar sound was comforting while I lay in bed, not sleeping, trying to get a San Francisco station to come in on my plastic radio. A sharp rap on the window made me jump. I didn't want to peek for fear someone would peek back at me. I turned down my radio so I could listen. My dog cocked her head. Growled low. The tap had a definite rhythm. 'Break on Through'! I pulled the curtain aside. Jim's nose was flattened against the window. I opened the window to the winter air.

Jim removed the white rose he had clenched in his teeth and sang a verse of the Tune Weavers' old song, 'Happy, Happy, Birthday Baby', reminding me he was a teenager in the fifties and that I was on the brink of sixteen.

'I never had a surprise party before. I don't know what to say.'

'"Come in" would be a nice start,' Jim suggested.

I pressed my nose against the screen. Its rusty metal smell brought back Tennessee summer nights when I would sit by the window waiting for something to happen. 'Come in,' I said.

The screen was in Jim's hands before it crossed my mind what might happen if we got caught. Jim presented the single rose quite formally, then tossed me a wrapped and bowed paperback-book shape. After an initial grunt that heaved him on to the window-sill, he dropped stealthily on to the bed. Jim kissed my cheek, picked up my dog, and collapsed cross-legged. 'Gonna open your present?'

Suddenly, I was far more concerned about being caught by Jim in my ratty flannel nightgown than the book. I stood on the corner of my bed and unwrapped the present. From the streetlight, I could make out it was a collection of poems by William Carlos Williams. I recognized his name from the foreword he had written in Ginsberg's *Howl*. 'Thank you, Jim. Thank you.'

'Always welcome. Could you sit down or something?' Jim, looking up at me, seemed angelic. The wispy layers of a couple months ago were growing out. His hair moved past his shoulders, no bangs to hide his eyes. I stopped staring long enough to cross my legs and plop down. I opened the book, but couldn't make anything out in the dim light.

'I think you'll like Williams' poems. Whenever I feel like my writing is stilted, I go back to Williams.'

I smiled. 'This is your gentle way of telling me the poems I sent you weren't very good. I told you I wasn't a poet. There is no "Horse Latitudes" hiding in me.'

I leaned back to switch on the lamp so Jim could read his favourite parts. He took the book and turned its pages, smiling and nodding, warm recognition on his face, as if looking at pictures of old friends. He read in a whisper, my dog licking his knuckles.

'That is so beautifully simple,' he said after reading a few lines. 'I can't do that very often.' He rested the book in his lap. 'I don't want you to copy my stuff. I don't want you to write "Horse Latitudes". I want you to write *your* soul. Your poems aren't as good as your letters. Your letters flow. I could take one of your letters and make it a better poem than what you sent. Do that with your poetry. Let it flow and edit later.'

'Is that how you write?' I asked.

'That's how I write the good pieces. Williams wrote some long poems like *Patterson* which are excellent, but the gems are the brief ones. Williams was a doctor. Sometimes he would write poems on prescription pads. He challenged himself to say all he needed to on that little piece of paper. I think that's why I like my *morning songs* more than some of my longer pieces. They are usually very clear thoughts. Nothing grand. No . . . artifice,' Jim laughed. 'That's one of Anaïs . . . how do you say her name?' I told him how the dots over the *i* note a new syllable and he shook his head. 'Miss Nin's words. I think some of her stuff is full of it, but she tells you, "This is the mask, look beneath it," so gently, you forgive her.

'Now to totally contradict myself, your second present. I wrote a poem for you. It began as one of those morning songs. Originally, it was just the first verse which seemed like one of those perfect little gems, but I keep thinking of things I want to say about you, us.'

From the pocket of his leather jacket, he took a piece of typing paper that was carefully creased in half lengthwise, but rumpled from its stint in his pocket. He refolded it, suddenly shy. He reached over and switched the radio on low. Mobey Grapes' 'Omaha' was just beginning, the accompaniment to my birthday poem, 'Wild Child'.

After Jim read a few lines, my throat constricted until it hurt nearly as much as his making fun of me did. I sat taller and asked, 'Like *enfant terrible?*'

'Oh, yeah. Like the genius you are. Also, it's a reference to a movie by Artaud. I'll invite you to LA if it pops up again. I just wanted to somehow set down how great your mind and soul are.'

I stuck my tongue out. I swept through most of the poem to ask about the closing line, 'Africa as in Leakey or Africa as in our fantasy trip through my family album?'

Jim peered over the paper in his hand, smiled, 'Our little trip. Didn't think of Leakey. Yeah. *The Cradle of Mankind.*'

I backed up a little. I asked, '*Ancient lunatic?*'

'Here,' he said, waving his hand. 'That's no historical reference. That's me.' Jim lay the paper on his thigh, turned each top corner in turn to meet the centre, pressed the creases, and continued to fold his poem into an airplane. 'Close as I can come to a crane. At least it flies.' He made a grumbling sound at take-off. When the paper airplane landed on the dresser, it tipped over a little glass dog with a ping.

I retrieved the airplaned poem and sat on the edge of the bed. 'Why is it,' I tapped my finger on his chest, 'that you get to be the ancient lunatic, the pirate prince, *and* the hollow idol, and I get stuck being the child?'

He laughed, 'My poem, my ego.' He proclaimed himself the *Lizard King*. 'I can be anything.' For the first time, I noticed he was wearing the shirt I had embroidered for his birthday.

'I thought lizards shed their tails, not their skins.'

'You are so damn logical. You mean I'm going to have to go dig up a book on reptiles and check this out? Don't they shed their skins like snakes? That's what I get for having this uncontrollable attraction to Capricorns. It's about magic. Calling up forces.'

I know, I thought. 'And do you?'

'Every time I get on stage.'

'Do you believe in magic?'

He repeated the line in a decent Lovin' Spoonful imitation. 'I don't believe in God. Christ. Or the devil. Except as folktales. Most of the time. Every once in a while, I believe that there must be a God, but what the fuck is He doing? It's like, your parents tell you about Santa Claus, and you grow up and find out it's this agreed-upon lie. And you hold on to God a while longer, because it makes you feel so alone not to believe when everybody else is sharing this agreed-upon lie. Well, happy birthday! I hope you didn't still believe in Santa Claus. Where was I? Oh, I believe in magic. Humanly produced. Aren't you ever going to unwrap me?'

'Do you have a car?'

'Yeah. Rather go for a drive? *It's your party. You can ride if you want to!'*

Jim blinked in innocence while I laughed at his pun on Leslie Gore's song. I felt shy even deciding what to wear in front of him, let alone doing something about it with his eyes on me. After I stared blankly at my open closet for a few minutes, Jim pulled a green sweater off a hanger and held it up to me. I did as much dressing as I could underneath, before trading my nightgown for the sweater.

Jim retreated through the window easily, then lifted my dog and me down from the sill. He sniffed the air and sighed. 'Is that you that smells so sweet?'

'Hyacinths.' I pointed to their shadowy forms under the birches.

Purple in daylight, they appeared pewter by streetlight. A night without a moon.

Jim, Joey and I piled silently into another strange car Jim had dug up. I guided him out to Thornton Road, out from the suburbs into the country, past where a friend of my mother's raised gargantuan red pigs, then cut across to where they filmed the Paul Newman movie *Cool Hand Luke*. I pointed both sites out to Jim. 'Met Newman once,' he said, giving the film location only slightly more interest than the pig farm. James Brown was hollering at a frantic pace and Jim drove at the same speed.

'Do you have any new songs with you?' I ventured.

'Nothing much. Anywhere. My notebook's in back.'

He had a new unlined tablet. There was a little poem he had sent in the first batch of writing he ever sent me. He had added some repetitions, buried the earlier poem in the song. 'What's the difference between a poem and a song?'

'Music!' he screamed, then glanced sideways. 'Okay, that was a cheap shot.'

'I thought, at first, you know, when I looked at your notebook in San Francisco, that your songs rhymed and your poems didn't. But you have some rhyme in your poems. And parts of songs that don't rhyme. So, it's not that simple.'

'Before, the difference was that I heard the music first and put words to the melody to remember it. They were always songs, expressing the music as much as anything. But now, I'm trying to do the reverse. I'm finding it next to impossible. I stare at words and hear no music.'

'It must be like . . . well, there are a couple basic techniques in sculpting. One, you start with a piece of stone, or wood, whatever, and like the cliché goes, take away everything that isn't Michelangelo's *David*. And the other way, you start with something, like clay, or found things, and build something. Totally different creative processes.'

'Yeah. Yeah. Which do you do?'

'Never did either. But I think I'd start with the music.'

'I meant in art.'

'Oh, that was a metaphor. Slipped a metaphor by the metaphor lizard.'

149

He enjoyed that. 'You'd start from nothing, and build something.'

'So, you aren't hearing music?' I asked.

'Not songs. I always have music in my head. No tunes I can pull out, though.'

He did have a song he could record. ' "The Spy" isn't here.'

'Not going to be. That's nobody's business but ours.'

'It's a beautiful song, though.' 'We Could Be So Good Together' was there with some changes. I didn't like that it was a second-hand song he started from someone else, or no one else, but liked its flirtation. He was playing with the line about the end of the war he'd written over the front page of the newspaper in Santa Cruz. Several different versions of the first verse were bracketed with question marks. *Celebration of the Lizard* remained the collection of loosely jointed poems he had read over the phone that night in late December. 'You had a good melody for this,' I reminded him.

'I lost it.' *Where?* '*In my head, he said,*' he said. He sang the line a few times with different melodies and rhythms. Frowned. Hard to please. '*In my head, he said.*'

'Since you can't write music, why don't you hum into a tape-recorder so you won't misplace things up there.' I swept his brow with my hand.

'Too much like work.'

Something titled 'Orange Country Suite' was a series of unconnected lines. About Pamela. There wasn't much else in the notebook. The Doors were to record right away, and there was no album in my hands. 'Robby will contribute some songs, won't he?'

'He better.' Jim drove with one hand on the wheel and one hand on my knee. I never wanted to stop riding when I was with Jim. 'You make up a song,' he ordered as in, *If it's so easy, you do it.* We could only see as far as the headlights.

'*Ridin' in the country,*' I wavered softly. While I was waiting for a second line to show up, Jim whistled the tune back to me.

'I like that. Can I steal it?' Jim winked.

No second line ever showed up. I rested my head against Jim's arm. 'More is going on than lack of tunes,' I said after a long silence.

'I thought you were sleeping.'

'I was thinking.'

'Don't you ever give that thing a rest?' Jim stroked my head. 'You're right,' he began thoughtfully, 'when the band first got together, we used to practise in a circle. Playing around LA in the beginning, I didn't have much confidence. I was too shy to face the audience, so we played in a circle the way we rehearsed. These tiny stages. I'd be singing with my eyes closed, and look up and be able to see the guys.

'Obviously, it looked a little odd. What I was afraid to acknowledge, but knew, was that when I turned around, it would be the beginning of the end of The Doors. When I turned to face the audience, I broke the circle. It's taken a while for the magic to spill out, but it's almost gone. I'm mourning the loss and trying to make something new that has no magic. I dread going to the studio.'

'I'm sorry, Jim,' I said, rubbing his shoulder as if it were some physical pain I could soothe. 'Other bands survive the lead singer getting more attention.' I was thinking of Mick Jagger and the Rolling Stones.

'We aren't other bands,' he said without rancour. 'I keep reminding people it isn't *Jim Morrison and The Doors*. *We* are The Doors. I get offers all the time to go out on my own for more money, which means the music business doesn't understand anything about me. If I'm not one of The Doors, I'm not in the music business. I'll write or make movies.'

'You said before, joking about your alter ego, that you could call up forces. I know it was part serious, and part playful, but can't you do that in the studio?'

'No. Sorta sneaked in the door with us when we recorded "The End" on the first album. It was as close to a good live performance as we've done. And oddly, I like the singing more than the spoken part. I usually like the spoken part. The music was wonderful on that. We're a live band. Every performance is different. I like to juxtapose songs. Make an audience listen. Records are so static. The producer wants to completely control my performance, so I

151

get to the point where I don't sound like myself. Like when you repeat a word over and over until it's nonsense.'

Jim drove towards the Sierras until we were informed we had to have chains or turn back. We celebrated my birthday with a snowball fight and breathless wrestle in the snow before making the U-turn.

January ended. The sky hung heavily over February. Stockton was too far inland to enjoy the ocean breezes in the still, hot summers, but suffered its influence with days of fog and overcast through the winter months. Jim woke me late one Friday, 'Do you like camping? I've rented camping gear. We'll conjure up Jack Kerouac's ghost in Big Sur.'

'Jim, Kerouac isn't dead.'

'From what I hear, he isn't writing. Same difference.' For Jim, writing was breathing.

'There's a big difference,' I argued. 'Alive, we can invite him.'

By nine in the morning, I'd hustled everyone out of the house and was rushing to clean the place, my trade for getting to go camping for the weekend. When I wanted to go somewhere with Jim, I'd casually talk about some plans another friend had and how I wished I could go along. Then when the conversation veered off, I'd suddenly ask if I could hang out with my friend. My friend, in my mind, being Jim, not the one I'd previously mentioned. I probably should have just crossed my fingers.

Jim breezed through the doorway at nine-thirty without a knock. When he squatted to her level, Joey flew into Jim's arms, wagging every inch of herself, licking his unshaven face wildly. My parents' German Shepherd, Tanya, hung back and wagged her tail more sedately. I felt somewhere closer to Joey's excitement, but feigned Tanya's. Jim looked relaxed in his navy-blue sweater and jeans. I'd never seen him in jeans.

Jim stood and gave me a slow, back-rubbing hug. I didn't know how to make coffee, so I offered him tea, and made hopefully melt-in-your-mouth blueberry muffins from my mother's Maine recipe. While they baked, Jim fetched records from my room. With the Stones on the stereo, the volume cranked up higher than it had ever been, Jim snatched the dustcloth out of my hands. He gently lifted each knick-knack, ran the cloth over it, dusted the spot vacated, and returned each rather precisely.

We ate muffins to Dylan and packed lunch to Bo Diddley. After Jim told me how Bo had saved his life, I thought a power like that belonged in my limited record collection. I'd lost heart, not finding any older Bo Diddley albums in the music stores, then I found this album tucked in a pile of tatting and old lace at the Salvation Army. Twenty-five cents. The Salvation Army immediately became my favourite record store.

Wow! Jim's car was a two-tone car like they drove in *Route 66*! I ran my hand over the low roof. 'You're a real hep cat,' I told Jim as if I were George Maharis. A good thing I said that before we got into the car. Oh, he got the car humming, but couldn't find reverse to get out of the driveway. I was going to suggest neutral and roll, but he was squirming, so I slipped my hand under his and pushed down and back.

Where the radio should have been was a dark hole with a tangle of wires, so Jim obliged. Can't very well drive without music. Jim sang 'Break on Through', so he could stop squirming and tear out of town, down the dull straight Five that ran the entire San Joaquin Valley. He streaked a comfortable eighty-five until he had to talk a Highway Patrolman out of a ticket with an autograph.

We cut sideways and eventually found Big Sur. We hiked until the sun was suddenly everywhere. 'I brought a camera,' Jim announced and my heart jumped. My first lesson in being James Wong Howe! I loved Jim remembering to help me catch up!

He placed the camera in my hands. My heart clunked. A still camera. Heavy, with shiny metal lens, and numbers all over it, beautiful, but not a movie camera. 'Don't cry,' Jim said sweetly. 'I think it's the best way to learn composition.'

My heart was up and running again. My sister got a Brownie one Christmas, but I was never allowed to touch it. I'd never even held a camera. Jim patiently demonstrated focus and the light meter. I accidentally clicked the shutter searching for the light meter and the camera made a rushing sound that made me jump as if it were a rattlesnake.

Jim, through the lens, was fascinating. To give me something to shoot, Jim drifted from talking about the flute in the distance that

153

sounded like a bird calling his mate into Hamlet's soliloquy. He spoke the familiar words as if they had just come to him, placing the startling pauses and leaps in his speech that were in his music. My tears fogged the viewfinder when Hamlet considered death. I had more respect, I realized, for someone who had looked hard at death, and made the choice to live, than someone who let life sweep them along unchallenged.

He played subtly to the camera or me. Flirting with both of us. He rubbed his chest under his sweater and stretched with feline grace to tempt. He slowly unbuttoned each button of his jeans. 'Your focus is a little low. You just chopped off my head.'

'I knew exactly what was in frame,' I assured him, an expert in composition after an hour's practice. 'Too bad there's no film in the camera to prove it.'

He took the camera from me. 'Who said there's no film in the camera?'

'I just became a child pornographer,' I said, embarrassed and pleased.

Jim laughed and rewound the film. 'With you behind the camera, it was art.'

Not only could Jim dust knick-knacks, he could put up a pup tent. 'I was a boy scout,' he confessed, 'until I was drummed out of the corps.' He grinned mischievously. 'I think swearing was the offence.'

The day was short and darkening. Jim took my hand and we walked across the meadow. 'Let's play!' he invited, breaking into a run. We ran until our legs wouldn't move and lay in the damp grass, amazed there were low evening stars so close to the ocean. The moon rose, bright and lopsided.

Jim settled against me. 'Let's really play. Not take a trip with our minds, but our bodies. He lifted his head, like a dog catching a scent on the wind. Then I heard what he had, the plaintive flute in the distance. 'I'll be Pan. And you can be the Wood Nymph I happen upon.'

Protests bubbled out of me. I was too shy. I was no actress. It was too dark. Jim was Pan and wouldn't listen. He pulled at my dress. Wove leaves in my hair. He played with movements until his boots sounded like hoof beats. 'Leave your mind. Lead from

154

your soul.' His kisses frayed my mind just enough to let me give up control.

The game closed wordlessly when we ran back across the meadow. Jim tossed a couple logs on the fire and threw off his sweater. 'Dance with me.' Instead of letting my objections spew out, Jim held up an index finger, so I could begin to list them to my logical mind's delight. To the waist, Jim was golden from the firelight. From above, silver from the light reflected off the fog that closed in around the white high moon. We danced. Close to the fire. Close to each other.

Our first night together in so long kept us both awake. We retired to the warmth of a fire and shared sleeping bag. I held a flashlight while Jim wrote. Hours later, Jim flexed his hand, stiff from writing. I took his between mine. A caress became a massage. We fell asleep near dawn for a nap broken by laughter and voices. We cuddled closer. I asked, 'Is there frost on my nose?' Jim yawned so his hot exhale would warm me.

One of the passers-by practically stood on his head to stick his head in our tent with an invitation to lunch. He gestured beyond Pan's meadow. 'A good half-hour hike,' he told us. The happy band of campers gave us chunks of bread and cheese and large cups of sparkling fruit juice with slices of oranges I ate contentedly.

When I lifted my cup for a refill, Jim covered its lip with his hand. 'That's probably enough,' he warned me. I looked forlornly at my cup. Nobody bothered to tell me Sangria was made with wine. I felt warm, though the clouds had sucked up the sun. All I wanted to do was kiss Jim, even if we weren't alone.

By the time the sky broke open with a downpour, I had vowed never to drink again. My head ached and my ears rang. Closer to where we parked, we took refuge in the cramped car for a few hours. The rain of the roof was determined to split my head open.

'I'm sorry, baby,' Jim said. I was trying not to look too pathetic. 'I forgot you didn't know about these things.'

I asked morosely, 'If you know you're going to feel like this, how can you drink?'

'How did you feel to be a little more aggressive making out with me?'

155

The man could make a point. I would have felt more Wood Nymph the night before with help from the Sangria. 'Did you like me better?'

'Nope. Being with you is terrific however you are.'

I held his hand. I'd never known anyone like Jim. He held firm and fast when he felt something was right for me, but applied no pressure on decisions he felt should be entirely mine. I couldn't even name what I felt for him. There had to be a bigger word than I knew to hold the expanse of emotion he filled me with.

If the rain didn't let up soon, I thought we would have to share a bucket seat. My head throbbing wildly didn't diminish my desire to be closer to Jim. We were both charged by the time we hiked back to the tent, but Jim slowed for an enticing inch-by-inch search of me. A winter's sleeping bag was not the most promising place for the exploration, but we were both supple and silly.

When the rain started again, we had to give up and protect our shoulders with sweaters, but refused to budge from the sleeping bag. He opened a bottle of Cognac for a drink or two. We stared at each other until what light there was, left. A snap of twigs outside brought us to and a young man peeked into our cave.

Jim grumbled, but couldn't send him off into the elements. A tent for two heaved with two lovers and a stranger and his guitar. He retreated to the far point, silent until he took out his guitar. Jim made a soft, 'Tsk,' in my ear. I wondered how the man found his strings in the blackness. I had to watch my hands to play. Tuned, he started to play in earnest. His style was strident and almost harsh, but I thought it was the truest guitar I ever heard.

When the young man wandered off into better weather with a mumble and nod, I asked Jim if he hadn't felt as I did about his talent. Jim affirmed my opinion. 'Then why didn't you offer to help him?'

'I did help,' Jim said. 'I told him to teach and play for himself. The music business would chew him up. He'd be dead in a year.'

As we started to pack up to leave, Jim became quiet. By the time the car was loaded, he mood was dark. 'Have I done something wrong?' I asked his back, because he hadn't looked at me for half an hour.

Jim shook his lowered head. 'I'm sorry. It's me. I don't want to leave you. I don't want to go back.'

'Do you have to?' I thought, *You're grown up. Why do you have to do so much that you don't really want to do?*

Jim shrugged, 'Yeah. Yeah.' Before we left the camping area, Jim tossed his notebook into a metal trash-can and had to drag me into the car to keep me from retrieving it.

We drove north on Highway One until the turn-off for Gilroy, taking the quicker, less scenic route. In the dark, it mattered less, but also meant we would have less time together. Jim stopped for his favourite take-out tacos and picked up a burrito for me in Gilroy. At a little corner store, he bought a beer for himself. I bought a soft drink from Mexico made of tamarind pods. Jim took a sip and made a face at the taste of the sweet raisiny liquid. I indulged about once a year in what tasted like hot Los Angeles summers when I was ten.

Just south of Modesto, a big Pontiac changed lanes right into us, only grazing the side of the car because of Jim's adept swerving. 'Fucking nigger!' Jim shouted.

My stomach turned. The close call had scared me. Jim's profanity scared me. I was afraid to say anything. Jim lifted the hair gently from my face, 'Are you okay?'

I held on to the door handle. 'I think I'm going to be sick.'

Jim eased the car into the pullout for a boarded-up fruit and vegetable stand. When I sat unmoving, he reached over to open my door for me, then came around to offer me a hand. *Don't be your considerate Southern gentleman, now.* I walked past his open hand, waving Jim off, and stopped behind the roughly built stand. Leaning against the building, I breathed deeply so I wouldn't vomit. Jim paced in the gravel. He gave me a few minutes of privacy before he came to check on me.

'How you doin'?' he asked in his low, soothing voice.

'Why don't you head back to LA, Jim? I can hitch a ride from here easily.'

'Don't be ridiculous. There's no rush. I'm not going to leave you on this highway at night.' He tried to take my hand, but I kept both of mine glued to my jeans. 'Honey, that wasn't my fault. I'm not drunk. I only had a beer.'

'It's not that.'

'Then what?' he asked, his voice very young and apologetic.

I spoke at him, not able to face him. 'What you said, Jim. I can't pretend you didn't say it.'

'I swear all the time. Sorry. I do try to watch my mouth around you.'

'It's more than swearing.'

'I'm sorry. I don't even remember what I said. You're so sensitive. Please accept my apology. Come on.' He tugged at my wrist when I wouldn't take his hand. 'Get back in the car.'

'You called him a . . .' I couldn't say the word.

'*Fucking son of a bitch!*' Jim finished the sentence with exuberance.

'That wasn't what you said.'

'What's the big deal?' Jim had his fists on his hips, looking amused. 'What did I say?'

'You called him . . .' My voice dropped. I'd never said the word before. 'Nigger.'

'Jesus! Did I? I'm sorry. It was just a foul thing to say to the bastard that nearly killed us. He nearly killed us! It's not like I thought about it. My goddamn life was flashing before me. I heard that a lot growing up. I didn't even see the driver. It wasn't a racial epithet. It's like saying *son of a bitch*. It's part of the Southern vocabulary that you have to unlearn. It just came out under the stress of the moment.'

'I learned to talk in the South, Jim. I didn't talk for a year when we moved to California, because kids laughed at my *y'alls*. I never used *that* word.'

He kept shaking his head, smiling. 'You're more upset about a damn word that almost being killed. It's just a foul word. You're making too big a deal out of this.'

'It's not just another foul word. This isn't easy. It's not too big a deal. I know you find my politics amusing.'

'I find your politics charming,' he said sweetly, bobbing for a kiss.

'That's patronizing, Jim. Like "Wild Child". I know I'm sixteen. I can't vote.' Doing my best not to cry, I paced away from him, then steeled myself to look at him. 'Shortly after we moved to

Tennessee, I got thirsty in a Woolworth's.' Jim leaned against the spot I had vacated, making me feel the story was already too long, but I couldn't shut up. 'The clerk showed Mama and me the drinking fountains in the back of the store. She pointed to one as *White* and another as *Colored*. With visions of Koolaid, I made a beeline to the *Colored*. The clerk nearly tore my arm off pulling me away from it. Mama was in tears trying to explain to me what *Colored* meant.

Time in the South has given Jim and me a lilt to our speech and writing, but had also encumbered us. Winding down my story about my childhood in Tennessee during the budding civil rights movement, I said, 'I got it in my head, there's a price you pay every time you don't put your body where your heart is. If I don't speak up to you, we can never really be friends.'

Jim slumped back against the wall and slid into a crouch. He pitched forward, balancing himself with his elegant fingers spread on the ground. He rocked back and forth. 'When I wrote your birthday poem, I had this wonderfully light feeling.' He lifted his right hand to his chest. 'The way I read it to you on your birthday was how I heard it in my head. It had a sweet lilt. Never had music. You know I haven't had a tune in my head in weeks. Listening to you just now, I heard this lament. Jim drew the music in the air between us as he sang the first few lines. 'Most people, the more I know them, the less I like them. The less respect I have for them. I always believed *familiarity breeds contempt*. I've always kept apart. I've never given myself to anyone before you. Do you have any idea how much I love you?'

The intensity of emotion in his words made me lose hold. 'Immeasurably. More than anyone. Better than anyone.'

Jim covered the distance between us in a few quick strides. He left his hands at his sides, afraid to touch me. 'May I?' he asked. He combed my hair with his fingers. 'I thought you just didn't think it was much of a poem. Why didn't you tell me "Wild Child" hurt your feelings?'

I tried a little laugh, 'I didn't want to hurt yours. I love your sense of humour, but it stung to have it directed at me.' I touched his chest. 'I liked the poem very much, particularly . . .'

He smiled. 'The line about Africa. I know. I wasn't making fun of anything, but your being the quietest person I've ever known. That screaming wild mind of yours hidden from everyone but me.'

'And what was that about saving the human race?'

'You're its best chance,' Jim smiled, taking my hands in his. 'You're brilliant enough to have designed the bomb, but cosmically wild enough to have known better. Einstein got that too late.'

I shook my head. What Jim thought of me! 'Jim, I was flunking Intermediate Algebra last semester.'

'Einstein flunked grade-school math. That's irrelevant.'

'The only scientific bent I have is to discover how much Nestlé's Quick can be suspended in a glass of milk.'

Jim sang a couple lines of what was becoming the song 'Wild Child'.

I laughed flatly, 'I'm not going to save anyone.'

He moaned, 'Sometimes, I'm afraid, not even yourself.' He sang the little lament, improvising a new rhyming line.

'Why are you having trouble with the new album when you can do that so effortlessly?'

'Don't change the subject.'

'Your music is important. Why can't you write new songs when you can improvise like that?'

'You're not going to tell me, are you?' He provided a long silence I was supposed to fill in. At last, Jim gave up. 'For starters, this is more sober than I've been in a month. With you was the first time I actually slept in weeks. I don't sleep any more, I pass out.'

He made it sound so matter-of-fact. I thought he was drunk when we spoke on the phone a couple times, but I hadn't seen him drunk since he stumbled into the café the night we met. The obvious question. 'Why?'

Jim raised an eyebrow. The sky was opening and the moon cast hard shadows on his face. 'Why what? Why do I drink? Why don't I sleep?'

'Are they different answers?' I thought of what he said about my kissing him when I was filled with Sangria.

'Up to a point. I like to drink. I like the way it tastes. I like feeling warm and high. It quiets the lions that roar in my ears. I have this piece of music I can't get out of my head. I've timed it.

160

It's twenty-six minutes. I don't know enough about music to say what it is. Maybe a concerto. Suite?'

'That's exciting. Is it classical?'

'In scope, not content or structure. Gershwin meets rock 'n' roll. I'd like to have it as one side of the album and *Celebration of the Lizard* on the other.'

'And the band disagrees?' I asked.

'Well, they're cool about the poem if I can pull it off. I haven't mentioned the music to them.'

'Why not?'

'We aren't exactly communicating.'

'Aren't they all struggling, too? Wouldn't they be excited to hear about this? I am.' I held my arm out so he could see my goose bumps in the sudden moonlight. 'I thought *Strange Days* could have worked without your words.'

Jim laughed, 'Thanks, baby.'

'You know what I meant.'

'I love what you meant. But this is one of God's – *that Merry Prankster's* – jokes. I hear music that goes beyond my ability to express it. My voice is limited. I have no facility for instruments. So this music plays over and over and over. I can't sleep. After about three days, I start to hallucinate.' When I nodded, he said, 'Oh, yeah, you're a raving insomniac yourself. What do you do?'

'Yoga.'

Jim sang, '*You say Thoreau and I say Nietzsche.* That works, huh?'

'No,' I giggled. 'But it makes you feel calmer when the lions come. I stretched my tense muscles. 'Couldn't Ray help here? Didn't you say he was classically trained? There's music on both your albums that goes beyond what you could sing ... Well, nobody could sing it.'

Jim shook his head, grinning. 'Except Nick.' There was a real kick to the 'k' when he said the name.

'You remember that?' I was so pleased he recalled the boy I followed down the hallway at school.

'I remember everything.' Jim sang a few watchful lines from 'The Spy'.

'For somebody with no songs in his head, you seem to be doing a nice medley.'

'Did I apologize for what I said in the car?' I admired his chancing damaging the changed mood. 'I *am* sorry. It concerns me I may be saying that and you're the only one who has called me on it. It bothers me not knowing if it's because they think that way, or are afraid of me. I use it as a political tool in writing.'

'Keeps it in your vocabulary, Jim. Even *Huck Finn* makes me uncomfortable. And I'm disappointed . . .' I paused, 'that you are Tom Sawyer and not Huck.'

'God, I've never felt so insulted,' Jim laughed and snorted. 'And I'm not sure why. Give me a clue. Are you studying Twain in English?'

'No. I read Mark Twain the summer I was twelve.' I used to pick an author and try to read every book he or she had written before the next school year began. My race with summer.

This time he just snorted. 'So what was your twelve-year-old insight – or insult?'

He charmed me so easily. 'It just seemed to me that for Huck,' I hesitated, because I'd never put my feeling about the fictional boys into words, 'that was what you called Negroes, for Tom the word was a judgment.'

'Jeez! I'm not Tom. Cross my heart.' He pounded his heart, but did not cross it. He leaned down and kissed me. 'Let's run away to Yucatán.'

'I wish we could.'

'Yeah. I'm going to get you home late as it is.' Jim stood, brushing the dirt from his hands. We walked back to the deserted car, both doors still open like a dead insect on a window-sill. My knees buckled. Jim caught me from behind. 'It's okay, baby. I've got you. I think it just hit you that we almost died.' It'd just hit me that he was twenty-four like James Dean and we'd been driving in a sports car on the same highway. He gently rearranged my hair and coaxed me into the car.

Jim stopped the car the block before mine. I reached for the door handle. 'Don't leave without a kiss,' he said softly, but just brushed my cheek with his moist lips. 'Do you have a piece of paper?' I rummaged a little envelope from my purse. 'Pen?' he

162

asked. I handed him my Scripto pencil. He groused, 'I hate writing in pencil.'

'Good-night, Jim,' I said, upset he'd discarded a notebook's work for an envelope.

He hit the lock on the door. 'Wait. Please,' he pleaded, his voice even softer. He stared at the envelope a few minutes.

'As good as a prescription pad,' I said aloud, thinking of what he said of William Carlos Williams the night he climbed through my bedroom window. 'Can you make your thoughts fit?'

'Out!' he ordered playfully. 'Watch your mailbox.'

On Tuesday, the envelope arrived within an envelope postmarked Stockton. The faster Jim wrote, the choppier his handwriting. The words were broken every few letters and all the words crammed together. I deciphered the lines which perfectly filled the three-and-a-half-by-five-inch envelope. He used how I said he loved me, *immeasurably*, to describe how deeply my eyes disturbed him.

10

Five to One, One in Five

'**B**rian Wilson!' I said into the receiver like 'Eureka!'

'Ahuh,' Jim responded patiently, then sang 'Surf City' in its entirety to prove he could sing a Beach Boys song without their prompting from the car radio. 'The Beach Boys made me want to come back to California.' I decided not to tell him that was a Jan and Dean song. Wilson may have co-written and sung back-up, but it was not a Beach Boys' song!

Talking on the phone didn't seem good enough that night. We hadn't seen each other since I'd gotten on my high horse on the roadside. When I tried to bring up the incident and apologize, Jim would stop me. Finally, he cautioned me, 'Never apologize for being right.'

'I had this thought,' I bubbled excitedly. 'You were saying how you had this piece of music – Gershwin gone rock 'n' roll. I just heard *Pet Sounds* at a friend's house. Now, I know you aren't interested in all the lush sound, but if you listen to the backbone, it sounds to me like Wilson was breaking the rules to great effect. Maybe you don't need somebody classically trained to get your music out of your head,' building to my great discovery, 'so much as another genius rule-breaker!' When Jim didn't say anything, I asked, 'Why don't you call Brian Wilson up?'

'You have a good ear. Why can't you tune your guitar?' Jim laughed and snorted at my expense, then added kindly, 'Honey, that's a brilliant idea, but there's no way Brian Wilson would take my call. We aren't on the same level of the music business.'

'It's worth trying, isn't it?' I cajoled, wishing he were close enough to poke and prod physically.

Jim devoted a week to trying to contact Brian Wilson, then he told me, 'The guy has a wall of people around him. I can't reach him. The great pang in my heart is, you know, I bet he would understand what I want to do. We might have made music history.'

'You've done that already,' I comforted him. A day still didn't pass without 'Light My Fire' on the radio, but I ached with Jim I'd never hear what a Wilson/Morrison collaborative concerto would sound like.

Jim's response was, 'I appreciate your faith, baby, but nobody's going to remember The Doors in five years.'

Jim settled in to try to write songs. He'd call to sing fragments. Call just to ask, 'What rhymes with . . .' believing it more interesting if I didn't know the context, then hang up when I hit a word that appealed to him. He called himself a *word man*, like a *sax man*, rather than a songwriter. Words were his instrument.

One night, Jim appeared to pull me out of my bedroom window, disheartened the hyacinths had gone, and to drive me into the country toward Lodi where he could sing the portion of *The Celebration of the Lizard* for me months before: 'Not to Touch the Earth'. The beat had a building intensity that stunned me. There was no resemblance to its initial melody. He swore the shadows were the witnesses, but I loved that witness moon.

A girl at school was carrying on about having seen The Doors, even before they were famous. She had seen them six times and had even gotten close enough to look into Jim Morrison's beautiful brown eyes.

'I thought they were blue,' I said. She challenged me. 'Have you ever seen The Doors in concert?' I had to admit I hadn't. 'Well?' leered the expert on The Doors.

When I relayed the story to Jim, he was generous. 'Maybe I was so stoned, my eyes looked dark.' Well, when he was moody, they leaned towards grey.

Home from school on a brilliant Thursday afternoon, I found one of Jim's five-by-seven-inch manila envelopes on the breakfast bar, his handwriting winging edge to edge. There were more polished versions of songs I had seen in his notebook in January, and completed versions of songs I had heard in those bits over the phone. One I hadn't heard before was titled 'Five to One'. After reading a verse, I ran to a phone booth and started my search for Jim at the bar where I had reached him when I thought he'd lost his parents.

'Ginger,' he slurred a little, 'what wretched thing have you overheard this time?'

I didn't answer. I could only ask, 'Do you have a gun?'

'Who do you want me to shoot?' Jim bleated. 'Oh, I can figure that out.' He paused, then spoke more clearly. The guy could sober fast when motivated. 'Are you in trouble? Do you need me?'

'No. I'm worried about you.' All my emotion seemed in my shaking hands. I couldn't feel my heart.

'You only call when you're worried about me. You've only called me twice in all this time. Almost nine months.' He sucked in a slow breath, 'Why don't you call me?'

Despite my concern, I felt pleased he kept track of how long we had known each other. It seemed poor sport to bring up not being able to reach him when I couldn't make the flight to New York in December. 'I can't make a long-distance call from home. And, really, it seems like most times when I really need to talk to you, you call.'

'I'd call you every day, but sometimes I don't have much to say. Be so nice if you lived down here. I could just put my head in your lap and read. That would feel so good.'

Jim seemed more maudlin than depressed. I tried to calm down and feel cradled in his sentimentality. 'You sound lonesome.'

'I guess I am most of the time,' he confessed.

I returned to the reason for my calling him. 'Jim, honestly now, I need to know if you have a gun.'

'Nope, but I know how to use one. Truth be told, I probably

167

couldn't shoot anybody, though. I thought you were a pacifist. What's this about?'

'I got your songs in the mail today. "Five to One" scared me half to death.'

Jim chuckled. 'Wanna get out of my head?'

'You invited me in,' I insisted quietly.

'True. You're always welcome. People come up with the strangest interpretations of that song. Some creep let *me* know that *he* knew that was how they cut street heroin. News to me. Doesn't anybody read the Russian classics any more?'

According to Jim's creep's interpretation, what would *one in five* be? A better high? A deadlier high? 'You're cheating. That's not how you play Russian roulette. Changing the odds to one in five means you don't spin the barrel the second time.'

'Nobody digs that. That I changed the odds. What better time to cheat than when you really want to lose? Where's a pen? I should write that down. You bring out the philosopher in me.' He repeated slowly, '*What better time to cheat than when you really want to lose?*'

'Jim,' I hated saying the words aloud, 'are you thinking about suicide?'

'Not at this minute,' Jim's voice was silky. 'Right now, I'm thinking about you.'

I wanted to give myself the out he was offering, but found the courage to ask, 'Have you since that time you told me about when you were a teenager?'

'Occasionally, but not too seriously. I occasionally say I want to die for effect. But nope, not since Bo Diddley saved my life.'

'This song scares me,' I admitted.

'Don't be scared, baby. "Five to One" is just a song.' His voice was so soothing.

But I pushed on, 'The first verse reads like a murder/suicide.'

'Well, that's Pamela's scene, not mine. She yelled that at me in a fight when I threatened to leave her. Though, I think it was, "You'll get yours, you son of a bitch, and I'll get mine." I thought *baby* sang better. I like to sing *baby*.' He sang an ironic chorus of Buddy Holly's 'Maybe Baby', then said, 'Pamela's terrified of growing old. I'm looking forward to it. Funny, it's the first time she helped me write a song and she didn't get it. Guess she was too wasted to remember. I wonder if between our memory lapses we've even had the same relationship.'

I wondered if my remembering every second of ours was the blessing I imagined. 'Should I be asking if Pamela has a gun?' Maybe I'd stop keeping a diary.

'Nah. She just has a quick red-headed temper, you know. She plays her games.' He hesitated. 'She's swung at me a few times. I slapped her once when I thought she was hysterical. You see that in movies. Snapped her out of it like it was supposed to, but I felt like a heel, because part of hitting her was anger. So, now, I take a walk. I'd never hit her again. Our fights are drama. That's all. It's the only time we talk any more.'

I couldn't shake my uneasiness. 'She wouldn't hurt you?'

There was a pause. 'She loves me. The gun thing was just a touch of fun. Fiction. A song is just a song. What was that song John Lennon did? Freaked me. There's this catchy little tune and he's singing about how it's curtains if he catches his girl with somebody else. I swear, if I sang that, the cops would have floodlights and a backhoe digging for the dead body before I got off stage. And my songs are scary?'

'Little Girl': I'd sung along with that song without any panic. Just a song about jealousy. People feel all kinds of things they don't act on. 'You're all right, then?'

'Well, hearing your voice has me jumping out of my pants. Mind if I give your erection to somebody else?'

Our relationship was more sensual than sexy. Jim hadn't pressed to go all the way since he told me we could go at my pace. And my pace was tortoise. I still skipped the sexy parts of books to get to what I considered the good parts. 'It's yours to do with as you please.'

'I want you to be jealous,' Jim whined. 'Not so jealous you want to kill me, just enough to ask me not to screw around so much. Why don't you tell me not to hole up in motels with women I don't know and don't want to know?'

'It hurts me that you don't seem to have much respect for yourself or the girls you make love to,' I said self-consciously.

'That's real true, except I only make love with you. The rest is

169

just fucking. I like fucking, but it's not the same thing. God, I miss you. If I wasn't so drunk, I'd haul my ass up to see you.' I asked him to promise not to drive drunk. He said, 'That way, I wouldn't hardly drive at all. I promise I won't drive tonight. I'll check into the first motel I see, maybe even alone. How's that? Is it a school night?' Jim came back around to wishful thinking. 'I wished you lived here. I could put my head in your lap and read. That would feel *so* good.'

'Yeah. Especially if we could trade places sometimes.'

He giggled as ridiculously as I could. 'Sure. I'd love your head in my lap.'

'Do me another favour?' I asked.

'What's that?'

'Don't write a song about me when you're angry.'

He snorted, 'Can't imagine being angry at you, but I promise.'

'You sure shredded Pamela in that song. The "Ten Cents a Dance" reference was pretty cruel.'

'It was just a little joke. She danced for a while, but it was more a dime-bag reference. See, now, there was a real drug reference. She danced for drugs. She danced for men who would buy them for her. She has crummy taste in men. I look good next to most of them.'

'You look good next to most anybody.'

Jim laughed. 'Thanks. I meant as a man.'

'So did I.'

The following night, Jim called with no *hello*, just read poetry to me for a couple hours. The rhythm wasn't his. A couple days later, he called, 'That was *A Coney Island of the Mind*. Thought it was time you met Lawrence Ferlinghetti. When I was a kid in Alameda, I'd cut school and thumb into San Francisco. I'd hang out at City Lights hoping to catch a glimpse of Ferlinghetti. When I finally did, I was too shy to speak to him.'

He'd mentioned the event when he took me to the bookstore, but then he'd said he *thought* he'd seen the poet-owner. My mother had recently given me Homer's *Iliad*, so I produced an inaccurate quote I thought appropriate, then said, 'I could understand your being intimidated. It would be like meeting the Big Kahuna.'

Jim chuckled, 'I admire an intellect that can embrace Homer and

Gidget in the same sentence.' I admired his ability to catch them both. That was why we got along so well. He didn't succumb to intellectual snobbery.

That night, Jim started pestering me about finishing the story I had started the summer before in my journal. I made excuses.

At last, Jim sent a postcard depicting the La Brea Tar Pits, where my third-grade class had taken a field trip when I lived in Los Angeles. On the back, he had written in block letters: TO WRITE, WRITE.

He had me. I couldn't argue with the best advice anyone had ever given me and finished the story on the notebook paper I was so tired of with the mechanical pencil that Jim teased was an extention of my hand.

Waiting for the friend I usually rode the bus with, I was attempting progress in the latest book Jim had sent me. A Russian novel, by chance or design. He had a certain perverse pleasure in presenting me with long books in fine print. I was still in the first chapter and there had been no Russian roulette. Still, the thought of 'Five to One' caused me to shudder in the hot afternoon sun.

A tap on my shoulder made me turn. 'Surprise,' Jim said softly. A flat-topped black-leather hat sat squarely on his head. His eyes were hidden behind sunglasses. 'Want to go for a drive?'

For days, I had longed to see him, but something in his stance scared me. Out of the corner of my eye, I caught a glimpse of older boys, Nick Isaak among them, heading off with baseball gear. I hadn't noticed Nick on campus in weeks. Each glimpse made my heart jump. I turned my attention back wholly to Jim. He lowered his sunglasses. One look into his troubled eyes and I wanted to run after the boys. Not much chance of them letting a girl play. I missed the ease of days when I was the first girl picked for street ball.

'You're distracted.' Jim turned to survey the boys.

'I can't field, but I'm a hell of a hitter.' I felt wicked saying *hell* out loud. I reached for the door handle of the flashy red Mustang. Everyone around us paid more attention to the car than to Jim.

Jim asked over its roof, 'Which one's Nick?'

I climbed in. Jim joined me. 'Why does one of them have to be Nick?' I asked.

'The one in the middle,' Jim said definitely, staring into the rear-view mirror. He was right. Jim studied Nick until he was out of view. 'Not only does he sing better than I do, he's better looking than I was at his age. Ever show you a high-school picture of me?'

While Jim gassed up the car, I made my excuses to my mother. The roar of the engine was getting on my nerves, so I clicked on the radio. 'Strange Days' . . . Jim turned himself off and managed a half-hearted grin. 'Do you still have that T-shirt I gave you? Like the circles round the sun? Like you?' I nodded. 'You tell people that song's about us?' he asked, and I shook my head. Our bodies were sure confused. And our memories . . . I found the song painful to listen to. I had never even told anyone I met Jim.

He whipped in and out of lanes, driving carelessly toward San Francisco. I dug my nails into the black bucket seat. 'What do I do?' he asked. 'I need to talk to someone about Pamela, and you're my best friend.'

I said, 'You talk to your best friend.' Out of discretion, Jim didn't often speak of Pamela Courson, though when he did, he was most often disgruntled. He'd stare off over his shoulder and mumble slurs. I kept feeling I should stick up for her, since I imagined she had to have her good points or they wouldn't still be involved.

The speedometer bounced around eighty. Jim slowed a little. He reached over and popped the button on the glove compartment. He gave up trying to dig and drive. 'There's a poem in there.'

I collected the maps and odd bits of paper in my hands, then found a half-sheet of notebook paper with Jim's writing; a few lines of pain and love. Pamela losing her humanity through her descent into drugs, soon to vanish, a final scream for her return. In the poem, she was his *Wild Love*. Jim had sung pieces of a near-chant that was going to be on the new album, but while the song was fantasy, this little poem was heart-gripping reality.

I sighed, 'I'm sorry, Jim. What's happening to Pamela?'

'It's hard to find a place to start. Everything is so wrong.'

'You can tell me anything,' I assured him, rubbing his arm with my knuckles.

Jim lifted his sunglasses. His eyes made my assurance evaporate.

'Thank you, baby.' He shoved his glasses back down and drove silently. 'Pamela OD'd.'

My throat constricted. 'Jim, no! She's dead?'

'No. She does this periodically to get my attention. She has her drugs and I have mine. The only one we have in common these days is alcohol.' He was quiet for a few miles. 'She likes heroin. She has a little circle of friends she does it with. I don't hang around. She says she can take it or leave it, like she's the only person in the world who can use the stuff without becoming addicted. She says it's a great high without a hangover. I'm not interested. I tried opium in college and spat up blood. I decided I'm allergic to opiates. Have to live without a pipe dream.' He smiled briefly. 'She balances her world by using meth, that's speed, and the animal tranquillizer, that's the dangerous shit I told you about. The combination makes her, I swear, schizophrenic. I never know who I'm going to find when I walk through her door.'

'I'm sorry, Jim,' I said again, because I was, and didn't know what else to say. Any remaining envy I had of the time they spent together dissipated.

Tears fogged his sunglasses so he had to take them off. 'There's nothing left of the woman I loved. I look at this body I used to love. She's just bone. And no one is inside. She can act like Pamela, but it's like an actress playing the part. She fools me now and then. I fall in love again. Or whatever it is. Maybe it isn't love.'

He had to pull out of traffic to collect himself. I handed him crumpled tissues from my tote bag and rubbed his back. 'This weekend, she hunted me down at my motel . . .' He couldn't go on. When traffic let up, he pulled back on to the freeway, turned the radio up high, and didn't say a word even when we reached the City.

We got stuck behind a cable-car in heavy late-afternoon traffic and followed it in increments down to the wharf. We bought sour-dough bread and wine and found a bench. Every time Jim built up to speak, someone would pass by so closely, Jim would clam up.

I asked him, 'Why don't we get a room?'

'Thought I'd give you a head start if you want to run when you hear what I have to say. We do this here. I just don't know how to tell you.'

173

'Pretend it's a movie,' I suggested.

He caressed my cheek with his thumb. 'Flashback,' Jim announced. He rested his arms across the back of the bench, his outstretched legs crossed at the ankle, unintentionally Christlike. 'Maybe a couple years before, he saw a girl dancing in a club. She was the first girl to show any interest in him as a writer, so he fell head over heels. He thought she understood his writing. It took him months to figure out that she was just parroting back things he said. So much for our hero's insight. He had genuinely liked the girls he dated before. He's still in touch with them. But he'd never been that in love.

'They did a lot of acid. A lot. They wanted to see how much they could take and how far they could take it. Really, it took the place of sex. She didn't even like him sleeping in bed with her. When he was around, he would crash in the living-room. One night, he was passed out on the floor, and she woke him up. She was sitting on top of him with a knife at his throat. She asked, "What would you do to keep me from cutting you?"'

Jim looked at me squarely, pulling his arms in to his chest. 'Pretending to attack him, they had the kind of sex they had never had. Then she handed him the knife and said, "Your turn." He thought, *What an interesting game.*'

With effort, I remained motionless, a real test of the *cool face* he claimed I had.

'A few nights later. He scared her. Not using a weapon or anything. They both let the game escalate,' Jim paused. 'Want to walk out of the theatre?'

Yes. 'Obviously, you knew me well enough not to cast me in this movie,' I giggled nervously. 'Wood Nymph and Pan was enough of a challenge for me.' And, I thought selfishly, *I hope we play again sometime.* No wonder he needed more than one playmate.

'One night, she really scared me.' Without realizing it, Jim had dropped the movie pretext. 'It started out like the first time, only after we had sex, she said, "Not good enough," and cut me.' Jim automatically rubbed his scalp behind his right ear. I'd felt the ridge of the scar when I had washed his hair. 'I really had to fight her for the knife.'

'I told her, "That's it." Part of the fun had been that it was like playing outside at night when you're children. You get scared, but feel it's really safe, because only your friends are out there in the dark. Who needs a shrink when you have acid?' He held his arms tightly against his chest. 'You still there?'

I nodded. 'But the game had to stop.'

'Yeah. And I broke up with her. She followed me everywhere. Stood outside my motel room screaming at me. I thought she'd give up, but eventually it just seemed easier to go back to what we had. I loved her, but couldn't trust her. It broke my heart. I didn't know how to let go either. We went back to having a relationship in front of people that both of us occasionally believed, but I started staying away more and more.'

Reluctantly, I asked, 'What happened this weekend?'

'Let's walk,' Jim suggested. 'Hold my hand?'

We clasped hands and headed in the direction of Aquatic Park. The crowd thinned. 'Where I spend my nights has been my business. Especially since I met you. I keep my own place. This weekend, Pamela came to my motel . . .'

The fog swallowed the sun and we stood in a shadowless silence. Jim sat on the grass facing the ocean. He pocketed his sunglasses, laid back, pulled his hat over his eyes.

'Who did what?' I encouraged him.

'If I tell you, I'll never be able to look at you again.'

I brushed his side with the back of my hand. 'We've told each other some tough truths and our friendship survived. You drove all the way up from Los Angeles to tell me, Jim. Was this a suicide attempt?'

'The first time you put a needle in your arm, you start committing suicide.'

'I don't know about that.'

From under his hat, 'Thought you had a pretty strong stance against drugs.'

'Seems like you're the one who will try anything once, wants to test boundaries. Maybe that was where Pamela started. Just with, "I wonder what's it's like." Not down the road she's on. That's all. You said she wanted to get your attention. She has your attention. Now, you have to decide where the two of you go from here.'

What I said sounded much more grown-up than my voice, which was unnaturally high and shaky.

'Why do the two of us have to go anywhere?'

'Because it's impossible for you to let go of anyone.' We lay quietly in the grass. Then I said, 'Your relationship with Pamela is like a fine gold chain tangled at the bottom of a jewellery box.'

'What?' He lifted his hat and deposited it on his chest.

'That was just the image that came to mind. You remember how beautiful it was, so you take the chain out and work at the knots until you are too tense and tired. You can't throw it away, because you care about it and hope you can fix it. So, you put it back in the box, and take it out every once in a while to fumble with the knots again.'

He squinted, a little irritated with me. 'Great metaphor, but it's just a prettier way to say we're fucked up.'

I sat up. 'I was trying to say that maybe what you need to do is keep at those tough knots. And if it's beyond the two of you – take it to a jeweller!'

Jim's pained face softened with a wide smile. 'If I ever criticize your metaphors, feel free to kick me. My bright new gold chain.'

He toyed with the ends of my hair. 'We have our own knots,' I said. But we weren't going to talk about them. Or what had happened between him and Pamela that weekend. His story unsettled me. That cynical line of "Five to One" ran through my mind as we walked back to the car. I made a last attempt to elicit the story he was afraid to tell.

He was walking so fast, I fell behind a little. I knew he wanted to drop the subject, but I had one more thing I needed to say. 'Jim, you told me why you played this game, but have you thought about why Pamela did? It was her game. She's the one who doesn't think it's over.'

Jim stopped abruptly. He looked over his shoulder at me, his mouth slightly open. When I caught up to him he settled his arm around my shoulder. We reclaimed the car. He asked me to take the wheel as we headed out of the city.

The Mustang had a lot more energy than the other car Jim had let me drive. We turned off in Capitola, a small town just below

Santa Cruz. The main street had a few closed shops and galleries. The sand beyond was dark and uninviting.

Jim had in mind a night at the elegantly shabby hotel that faced the beach. Instead of waiting in the car, Jim let me hang on his arm while he signed us in as Mr and Mrs, rather than brother and sister. Since he paid extra for a view, I stared at the ocean until fog obscured it. Jim leaned with his back against the window, staring at me.

'I'm not doing you much of a favour by staying in your life,' Jim said softly, fingering my hair.

'You're the best part. The summit. The best part of the trip,' I said in a whispery imitation of Jim high on acid.

'Do I sound that spacy?' Jim grinned. 'I deserved that. Don't feel like I deserve you, though.'

I shook my head; he wouldn't let me just be a nice kid from Stockton. I reached up on tiptoe to kiss him. 'If you don't let me off this darn pedestal, I'll jump. Break my neck. You'll spend the rest of your life riddled with guilt.'

'Having known you,' he said, returning the kiss, 'I'd just be riddled.'

Jim confiscated an envelope he found in my bag. 'Let's play I write a line, you write a line,' he said matter-of-factly. 'I have a melody in my head.'

Trying not to giggle, I said, 'There's a certain problem with my trying to write lyrics to a melody in your head.'

'What's that?' he made the most bewildered face he could, then eased into his best smile. 'Trouble in my mind,' he sang, motioning me toward him. He wrote the line on the envelope.

I whisper-sang, shy singing on my own, 'Trouble in the wind.'

He handed me the pencil for me to take a turn at writing. Then he took it, singing as he wrote, 'Lose it all to fire . . .'

I wrote, 'Start over again,' pleased that *wind* and *again* didn't exactly rhyme.

'You know, sweet one, I didn't sing the melody for you. You caught it.'

Looking into his eyes, heavy-lidded from a day's drive on no sleep, I saw that magic I'd felt in Golden Gate Park, when I wondered if he could really call up the wind.

'It's a simple little melody,' I said to make it seem rational.

'Mmm,' Jim agreed, stopping to add a line at the beginning and one at the end.

Once conscious of what we were doing, the song seemed more like work. We laughed when our efforts fell short. Jim had convinced me that it was best to go for a big leap and fall on my face, than take a tentative step. By the time we called it quits, the envelope was a jumble of our combined handwriting, his bold and mine not, arrows and strike-outs. But my last waking thought was that Jim and I had written a song together.

Jim nudged me. 'Wake up, baby,' his breath tickled my ear. 'Shake the troubled dreams from your hair.'

Trouble in my mind. 'It's still dark,' I said sleepily, half remembering the tune. *Trouble in the wind*.

'But it's a long drive to Stockton,' he shook my whole body. 'Don't you want to make your first class?'

'What's this repulsive fit of responsibility?' I complained, but in due time, Jim deposited me back into my high-school life, where I pretended to do my homework in the cafeteria before my first class and hummed Jim's new and simple tune to myself.

Only a few days later, the scene on the black and white television my parents had bought to follow the news when President Kennedy was assassinated turned eerie. Black men pointed from the balcony of the Lorraine Hotel in Memphis. The Reverend Dr Martin Luther King lay at their feet. I stood with my hand on the phone waiting for the rumble of the quieted ring.

Jim said, 'You probably think I have no right to say this, but I feel like America just lost her conscience. The country will never be the same. Just like people can't live without a conscience, neither can a country.'

11

Under Television Skies

Suddenly, it was May. Stockton was in the mood for summer. Days were long and hot. The horizon was dark with peat dirt from the surrounding fields. Jim's May Day call opened with, 'I had the most fun today! I caused this major pandemonium.'

'What did you do? Strip on the Strip?'

'Nobody would notice that. I cut my hair.'

I missed his lustrous hair even from a distance. 'Do you have a 1956 Elvis pompadour?'

'There's an idea. But I think it's too short on top. I caught my reflection in a window and found myself humming "Ferry 'Cross the Mersey".'

I pictured Gerry of Gerry and the Pacemakers and felt momentary despair. 'That's pretty short. What brought this on?'

'Oh, the band was ragging on me, implying I was looking feminine.'

'Ought to ask us women about that. I thought you looked very appealing.'

'Well, thank you, baby, but I'm trying to save my fights with the band for music. At first I just cut it the way I usually do. Whacked it off at my collar. Then today, I thought, you know, if I cut it real short, I could swing up your way and meet your father.

179

Look presentable. Look collegiant. I could borrow a school sweater with a letter in some acceptable sport. Do you think he would be impressed my father is an admiral?'

'Admiral?' I asked, thinking, 'Don't call me *baby*.' 'Do you feel the need to promote him? What happened to commander?'

'I didn't promote him. Heard the Navy did last summer.'

I laughed. 'Well, Jim, for an admiral's son, my dad would probably grovel to your face and swear behind your back.'

'I'm serious. I think it's time. That way I could call for you at the front door. I will be very polite and charming. Your mother likes me. I'll make your dad like me.'

'That's not possible. It's very sweet of you to want to do this, but please, no,' I hated the sound of the plea, so added, 'Tired of being my "Backdoor Man"?'

Jim chuckled and snickered. 'That isn't what the song means, honey. It's sexual. You know, a *double entendre*.'

'I thought it was about being a secret boyfriend. Sneaking around.' I flushed hot and mumbled, 'Remind me young white girls shouldn't go around quoting the blues.'

'You love me,' Jim said seriously. 'Let me tell people I love you.'

'If my father knew about you, that would be the end of our being able to see each other.' I felt panicky. Jim could be so insistent when he felt he was right. 'I can't even invite boys from school over.'

'I think it would be good for your dad to know somebody is looking out for you.'

'Knowing about you would make things worse.' There was silence on Jim's end. I had been too blunt. 'You really cut off your hair! I'm trying to imagine what you look like . . . "Ferry 'Cross the Mersey"? If anybody knew you did it for me, I'd get hate mail. People would call me Delilah. Lost any prowess?'

'Not noticeably.' There was a long pause. He wasn't going to be side-tracked. 'If charm isn't the way to go. I could scare him.'

'Who could you scare?' I laughed wildly.

'Oh, I scare lots of people,' he paused, giving up the fight. 'Myself mostly.'

Without warning, my father announced that he was retiring from

180

the Navy, and as soon as school was out we were moving to Florida. My parents had land there. Probably swamp with the family luck. I'd looked up the location on a map and it wasn't all that far from where Jim was born. Yet I couldn't imagine pulling up my fragile roots, which were entwined as much in my friendship with Jim as in Stockton.

Jim called three times that week, but I couldn't tell him. I was busy making deals with God to do great deeds if my father would just let me stay in Stockton. As a backup, though, I made plans to attend a two day Folk-Rock Festival at the Santa Clara County Fairgrounds in San Jose, where a group of friends could say farewell. Three girlfriends, a writer friend, who at sixteen was rewriting the history of the world, and that tall and mysterious older brother of one of my friends. All of us were crammed in the back of the family station-wagon with guitar, tambourine, blanket.

We all felt the stress of my leaving. My friends and I couldn't seem to talk. Eventually, it fell to my having the longest conversation ever with Tall and Mysterious – the high point of which was when he confided, straight dark hair in his eyes, that algebra was like a waterfall. He was brilliant in a way I would never comprehend.

When we arrived at the fairgrounds, a young woman handed me a yellow and orange programme. I couldn't believe what I read. I shivered. I had wanted to attend the Saturday concert when the Grateful Dead and Big Brother were playing – the real way to say goodbye to California, I thought. But Sunday was the day everyone could make it, so we were set to hear the Youngbloods and Country Joe and the Fish. There at the bottom of the flyer, I read that The Doors were scheduled to play. Last. Jim told me he always insisted on that. About to leave California I was going to see Jim's band for the first time accidentally. The irony suited us.

The grounds were a patchwork of picnics. My friends and I were very far back and to the left of centre stage. We walked around most of the day. Everyone wanted a last piece of me. I happily split myself into a suitable number of pieces. Time for everyone and music, too. A black vendor gave me an Apache tear.

181

Taj Mahal was the best of the early part of the day, dedicating 'I Am the Walrus' to appreciative cops on duty.

The overcast skies leaked. When Bill Graham announced The Doors, I edged away from my friends. I stopped centre stage and all the way back. My first glimpse of Jim on stage made me timid. His newly cropped hair made him appear very young and vulnerable, even in his high-buttoned white shirt tucked into low-slung brown leather. Fascinated with watching Jim, I couldn't hear him. Huge banks of amplifiers were stacked behind the band, but for me there was just Jim dancing to some rhythm in his head.

I zigzagged my way up through the sprawling crowd. Halfway up, I stopped. Jim opened his eyes on me. His face froze. Then disaster struck. Jim either tripped on the microphone stand or the slippery flooring and he hit the stage hard. My hearing restored, I heard the thump when he landed. He'd demonstrated his stage-fall for me and that wasn't it. The band kept playing. Jim struggled up and sat on the raised drum stand. I tried to catch his eye to see if he were embarrassed or hurt, but he wouldn't look at me. After a considerable rest, he swaggered out to finish the song.

Bill Graham interrupted the show to hold up a lost child, and handed the lucky kid to Jim – big grins on both their faces. Jim said something to Graham when he passed the child back. Graham frowned. Despite the smile for the kid, Jim didn't seem thrilled to have his momentum stalled. The crowd was wet and tired and probably had nearly as much drugs and liquor in their bodies as had Jim.

Jim dug down and did a hot 'Light My Fire' which he had told me he never wanted to sing again. Yep! He came back after the instrumental break with *If I were*. The moment pleased me to a wonderful degree. A huge man came up behind me. I tried to hedge away. I manoeuvred politely through the denser up-front crowd to put some distance between the imposing stranger and me. Finally, he grabbed my shirt. My first instinct was to yell for help. I feared if Jim saw this brute, he'd fly off the stage at him. Fortunately, Jim was singing with his eyes closed. I said a terse, 'Hands off!' then added a feminine, 'Please,' neither of which was audible against the amplified music.

'Jim Morrison,' he spat into my ear, 'wants you backstage.'

I gathered, then, that Jim had asked Bill Graham to have someone escort me backstage. 'Tell him, "Another time."'

'Jim Morrison, *himself*, asked you to come backstage,' he yelled in my face as if he thought I might have been too stoned to have understood.

When the persistent giant dragged me what was actually sidestage, there was a clamorous commotion, at the centre of which was Bill Graham yelling at Jim. Jim's eyes were downcast, either listening to or tuning out Graham. When Jim looked up, he beamed in my direction.

'*Now is the winter of our discontent*,' I whispered, figuring with his ears he could hear me ten feet away.

Jim's grin widened. He glanced at his wrist, where he never wore a watch. 'My watch must be fast. Could have sworn it was spring.'

Because Bill Graham was still talking, I mouthed the question, 'Are you all right?'

He nodded, but made a small circle in an increasingly exaggerated limp. As Richard the Third, Jim plunged into the soliloquy, '*Now is the winter of our discontent.*' He knew the speech as well as Hamlet's, but paused to introduce the band racing by.

Everyone was in motion. Only Robby stopped for a moment. As he reached out to shake my hand, his long guitar-plucking thumbnail sliced my hand. I winced as I said, 'I love your mysterious guitar.' What an absurd thing to say! He thanked me anyway. There wasn't time for me to explain why that comment popped out. I wished I had known I was going to meet him, so I could have thought of something eloquent to say.

Jim took my hand and swiped at the blood with his cuff. 'Stigmata?' he asked before returning to his speech from Richard the Third, pausing to answer questions, sign an autograph and sulk about the lousy audience. Bill Graham shook his head impatiently, realizing if he ever had Jim's attention, he had lost it.

Graham glared at me for a second, then switched to Jim. His voice boomed, 'And I'm not your pimp.'

My face flashed hot and my ears rang. I wished the San Andreas Fault would open right where I stood.

183

'Aw, Bill,' Jim drawled, 'that's no way to talk. This is my little sister.'

'Excuse me,' Bill said roughly, 'I'm sorry. Please accept my apology.'

'Sure,' I whispered, all the more embarrassed to have an adult apologize, especially when I knew that he didn't believe for a moment I was Jim's sister. To the rest of the world, Jim's family was dead.

Jim hobbled in a small circle. When we were alone for a second, he said, 'Gonna come with me?'

'I can't. I shouldn't be here now, but I thought that guy might throw me over his shoulder and carry me backstage.'

'Yeah, that's how I get most of my girls. Hey, honey, you look so sweet, wanna show me a good time?' He sucked in a breath seductively.

After Mr Graham's comment, I wasn't in the mood to play. I said, 'See ya,' with a more winning smile than I felt.

Jim borrowed a pen and wrote his number on a scrap of paper. 'Call me up and we can get it on.' He handed the paper to me and I let it fall. He picked it up and put it in my pocket. I fished it out and stuck it in his belt. 'Ooh,' he said, 'now I know you can make me feel fine.' I turned to go and felt a painful tug of my hair. When I looked back at Jim, he held his hands up in innocence.

For a few nights, I didn't sit by the phone. I couldn't seem to shake the humiliation of what must have been less than five minutes stage-side. My mother tapped on my door. 'Phone,' she said simply. I glanced at the clock radio – a little past ten, early for a call from Jim, late for anyone else to call.

My suspicious 'hello' was answered rapidly. 'I appreciate your taking my call,' a man said. 'I hope it isn't too late.'

'No . . .' I said, trying to place the sharp and confident voice.

'I wanted to make a better job of an apology. My behaviour last week was way out of line.'

'Mr Graham?'

'It's Bill. Nobody calls me Mr Graham. I was upset with Jim and, really, I don't say things like that to young girls. It had been a long day, but that's no excuse. I was wrong to take out my bad mood on you.'

'That's okay,' I said.

'Well, no, it's not, but I hope you will accept my sincere apology. Anytime you want to see a band, just give me a call. Even if it isn't one of my shows, I have enough pull to get you tickets. Jim explained who you were.' He took a pause and laughed, 'Or tried to. He was rambling some, but he did get across that you were a close friend. He said there was something very cosmic between you. Then he said something about you being blood brothers.'

I cringed. 'He was rambling.'

'Mind if I ask how old you are, Ginger?'

When I told him, he sounded disappointed. 'Only sixteen? I was hoping you looked younger than you were. Probably unfair to ask, but since Jim said you were so close, I feel like I need to. Do you know about Jim's problem?'

My mind was instantly cluttered. I asked shyly, 'Which one?'

Bill Graham laughed. 'You are close. His drinking problem, honey.'

I'd never spoken with anybody who knew Jim. How many times I had wanted to when I felt overwhelmed. The chance was there and I felt tongue-tied. 'Mr Graham, I don't want to breach a trust.'

'Anything you say remains between us. Honestly, whatever you tell me is in confidence.'

I said finally, 'I would have to talk with Jim before I say anything to anyone.'

'Well, could you do that? This is important enough to take a chance. I think a lot of Jim and hate to see this going on. I'm not sure he doesn't think he's just cutting loose. But I think there's something different in the way Jim drinks. I know he's not comfortable with this whole sex symbol thing. I tried to talk to him up in San Francisco last year. We spent a day off together, talking about when we were young, but when I brought up his drinking, he pretty much told me to, excuse me, f-off.'

Sometimes, I felt Jim was being eaten alive from the inside, but as much as I had needed to talk with someone about Jim, I knew there was a line I couldn't cross.

While I was still trying to reach Jim, he called me. 'What got into you, baby? Since when can't you take a joke?'

185

'Mr Graham didn't think it was a joke,' I answered defensively. Since Mr Graham's repeated apology, I felt even more embarrassed.

'Well, *we* knew it was. I called him up and explained. I didn't mean to hurt you. You sure can't believe I think of you like that. You know that I love you. I was embarrassed I fell. I was shocked to see you. I'd rather you'd told me you were coming, but I really sang my heart out as soon as I saw you. And I bet you were the only one who gave a shit. That's it for these outdoor daytime gigs.'

'You surprised *me*. I was just going to hear some music, I didn't know until I got there you were going to sing.'

'You looked like you were going to cry all through the show. And backstage even before Bill offended you.'

I blurted out the truth. 'My father is retiring and we are moving to Florida right after school gets out. I couldn't say goodbye backstage like that.'

Jim asked, 'You're really going to leave me?'

'I'm not leaving you, Jim.' How could he believe that? 'I don't want to go. What choice do I have?'

'I feel like I've wasted so much time. Let me tell a few lies and get two or three days off. We'll have that anyway. Well, we aren't going to say goodbye,' he told me. 'We can still talk on the phone. Write. Planes go to Florida. So, no goodbyes. We'll just have a good time. I thought Big Sur. Our Eden. Anything special you'd like to do?'

'Yeah,' I knew at once. 'I'd like to try peyote.'

Jim considered, 'I haven't done that in a while. I'll bring some.'

How like Jim to show up at school as if we had a set date. 'Can I sign your yearbook?' Jim asked shyly.

Our yearbooks had been delivered – hulking things suitable for pressing flowers and use as doorstops. 'Sure,' I said, touched he wanted to.

'I need to think about what I want to say,' he said, explaining why he was staring at the cover. 'I didn't sign many yearbooks when I was at school. Let's see. He's a junior, isn't he? He thumbed to the section. 'What was his last name?'

186

'Whose?' I asked.

Jim did his eye-roll to imply impatience and sang the little alphabet song we all learn in kindergarten as he turned the pages to the 'I's'. He laughed when he hit Nick's picture. I had to agree, it didn't flatter Nick. Jim said, 'Looks worse than my mug shot.'

'You have a mug shot?'

'New Haven last year. Front. Side.' He demonstrated. Front. Side. Handsome at both angles.

'You didn't smile either.'

'One doesn't for mug shots,' Jim said, then added, 'traditionally.'

'And you are so traditional.' I played with his short hair.

'That's me.'

'You don't seem to smile for your publicity shots either.'

'It's frowned upon,' he snickered. 'Photographers want me to look sinister and I pretend I am so I don't have to show them my crooked bottom teeth.'

'You have a beautiful smile.' He also had a sinister smile, though he rarely brought it out except for amusement.

'So do you, but you are always covering it up like a geisha.' He mimicked me in laugh and gesture with embarrassing perfection.

'You can just laugh for me from now on. People say I resemble Alice from *Wonderland*, but I see the white rabbit looking back at me in the mirror.'

'I think your overbite is sexy.' He gave me a juicy kiss, then opened the heavy yearbook to search for a desirable page. Obscuring my view with this cupped hand he wrote carefully. When he closed the book, he said, 'I need a white shirt.'

We were off to the best department store I knew in town: *Weinstocks* where some of my friends shopped, way out of my budget. We took the escalator up. 'I heard the Beach Boys' "Good Vibrations" for the first time on this escalator,' I said.

'Where did you hear me for the first time?'

I didn't even have to think about it. 'In the car.'

'Where were you going?'

'Away from school,' I said happily. 'My favourite direction.'

Jim fell off the escalator backwards and I had to leapfrog over him to avoid doing him serious damage. We were asked to leave.

'Oh, this isn't the men's floor. I'm used to daydreaming for myself. I haven't been here since I used to visit my dress.'

I helped Jim off the floor. 'You *visited* a dress?'

My girlish confession. Once I started in on describing the white dress I loved and could not afford when I was fourteen, I could not stop. I delineated the square neck, the cloth, the zipper hidden under the arm, just where the hem fell on my thigh.

At last, I connected with Jim's eyes. He had said he could walk out of a burning building with just his signed copy of *On the Road* and his current notebook and not look back. And I'd gone on for a good ten minutes about a dress I didn't even own.

Jim blinked in the fluorescent lights and asked, 'What's piqué?' He'd listened to every word. How deeply I would miss this friend.

He let me choose the shirt with the tucked bib and no collar like a grandfather's from the turn of the century and changed in the car while he drove. When I offered to button him up, he declined. The sun was a glare against the windshield. The car was hot. When it was obvious Jim was headed towards San Francisco, not Big Sur, I was disappointed he'd forgotten about tall trees and peyote.

In Golden Gate Park, Jim found parking near the Heard Museum. He held my hand and ran his other along the glass display cases that contained the jade collection in the Asian Museum. We made a solemn parade. He offered and invited no comment about the intricate carvings, the colours, the subjects. He simply let his hand rest over the ones he admired as if touching their cool stone surface.

At the museum door, Jim, gripping my hand tightly, broke into a dead run dodging traffic to reach the stone bandstand. The seats and trees that faced the stage were laid out formally. Plane trees, low, with knurled fists aimed at the sky in winter, became leafy umbrellas in spring.

In fluid contrast, a small group of older Chinese men were engaging in T'ai Chi. Jim studied them intently for a few minutes. His eyes wandered over their movements the way his hand had caressed the glass in the museum. With an abrupt turn on his heel, he ran and leaped on to the high stage.

Off to the left, he became Ray Manzarek's organ. A dive to the back, John's drum. To the right, Robby's guitar. Then settled for being himself. The whole concert sincerely sung. My eyes never left him. At the end, he sat on the edge of the stage and slid to the ground. Soaking wet from the performance, he sat beside me.

'With my apologies for the show you saw,' Jim said between deep breaths.

'Thank you, Jim.' I took his hand. While he caught his breath, I thought about the Christmas poem he had given me that said he had come to me for certain things, and come away with others. Every moment with Jim was that for me. How could I be disappointed about my expectations, when the unexpected was so rich?

'Very, very fascinating,' a gentle voice said. One of the men who had been doing T'ai Chi seated himself behind me. He rested his hand on Jim's damp shoulder.

Jim looked over that shoulder, 'Thanks.'

The man was small and solid. He gestured toward the stage. 'Do you do this sort of thing professionally? It was not the performance of an amateur.'

'Neither was yours,' Jim said.

'You could possibly learn something from the practice. You are not in balance. Although,' the man said with a twinkle, 'you have great balance.'

Jim liked the careful play of words. He laughed warmly. Jim asked questions about T'ai Chi and the man answered unhurriedly. He demonstrated a few movements, nodding Jim into following him. At ease on stage, Jim was self-conscious as a student.

'May I say, Miss, you have too much yang and your friend too much yin,' the old gentleman said as he started to leave. He said yang as if it rhymed with song, not sang, the way I had always said it.

As we walked to where Jim had parked his car I said, 'Not only did I say yin and yang wrong, I had them mixed up. I thought yin was feminine, and yang, masculine.'

'You just pronounced yang wrong,' Jim said. 'You had which is which straight.'

'He thinks I'm masculine?' I was offended. 'What's so dang

yang,' I asked, accentuating the mispronunciation to make it rhyme, 'about me?'

Laughing, Jim patted my head. 'Now, don't pout. He doesn't know you can hit a baseball like a guy. He sensed you have ambition and creative drive. According to his culture, those things are male.'

Jim shivered, damp in the evening air, and switched to his older, drier shirt. In Monterey, we stopped for beads. Jim wanted me to string beads for him as a goodbye gift. He held up the shop's closing, the girl behind the counter in shock while he studied the glass vials of tiny seed beads. He admired their delicacy. Held them up to the light, lined possibilities up by the register.

'Is he who I think he is?' she asked me, her blue eyes wide.

Big Sur was bathed in fog-diffused moonlight. The arches of the bridge rose out of low fog. With the fog above us in the mountains and below us on the beach, we sat in the car unsure of what direction to chance.

'We could wait for the sun,' Jim suggested.

'You've already written those lyrics.'

I should have known better than to tease Jim, because he threw the car into gear and roared across the road into the mountains. We parked when he felt we had driven as far as we could and carried the single sleeping bag and rucksack into the interior of the park. The air was so damp with fog, our faces were wet when we kissed.

'There's something in the Bible about young men having visions,' Jim said.

He'd brought the peyote. But not for that night. We shared the sleeping bag under an arching tree, not talking, just being physically close. We slept more than we usually did. We were damp with dew. Jim's body clock had no ties to the sun. He did not stir, as I did, at first light. The fog was still low, so the change in light was gradual. When Jim finally roused, it was mid-morning, and he was ready for a sleepy run to the beach. The sand was alternately hot and cold, depending on whether the sun had broken through. I wouldn't stray beyond the surf up to my thighs, but Jim swam out into the ocean until he was small enough to make me hold my breath until he headed back towards shore.

We survived the day on a jug of water. Jim had warned that anything eaten would come up when we ate peyote. The rite of purifying oneself fell into common sense. The sun was low when Jim placed a peyote button in my mouth. The nub was so dry it soaked up moisture from my tongue and tasted like a clump of dirt.

'Spit it out,' Jim ordered.

I spat the button into the hand he held out for me. I wondered what I had done wrong when we had just started.

'A shaman would have a vision for the tribe,' he said softly. He laughed and popped the peyote button into his mouth. 'Rock writers are the shamans of contemporary society. The difficulty is, shamans are prepared, we are not.'

Disappointment rose and fell. Jim knew me better, often, than I knew myself. I wouldn't know what to do if I were on a path I did not want to take. Jim was more able to relinquish control. I needed a firm grip.

We walked by the moon, barefoot in a cold stream we used as a path, moving upstream, so the water pushed gently against us, and the air against our lungs. When we reached a clump of three boulders, Jim gave me a hand up on to them. The sleeping bag was laid out. Jim disrobed in the cool evening and sat on the hard bed.

He waved his right hand in front of his face. 'Are you old enough to remember how mothers used to wash windows with wax?'

Seemed a strange question. I was old enough. The stuff came in cans. We used it at Christmas to make tree shapes from stencils we held up to the windows.

'That is how it begins, sometimes. A veil of hard white. Not like this fog. Very thin and hard. You have to ask your mind to wipe that away.'

For a time, the veil seemed between us. Jim bobbed his head gently, taking in what he could see and I could not. His body was alabaster in the subdued white light of the fog-draped moon. He struggled into his shirt, left it unbuttoned, and described the images that lingered long enough for him to define. He saw a small pool in the distance which he felt someone warned him not to drink from or step into.

'It's a death pool,' Jim said, smiling, as if it didn't frighten him. 'I'll die in water.'

I shivered, glad I had not taken the peyote myself. I didn't want to see even my imagined end. Jim's descriptions were disjointed and hard to follow.

In the morning when Jim wanted to swim in the ocean, I tugged at his hand, superstitious about his peyote dream. He laughed and pulled away. His swim took him close to a rock with sea-lions, but he thought better of being outnumbered by another species and swam back to me. He ran out of the water, cheerfully spent. Collapsing headlong into the sand, Jim laughed breathlessly.

'Don't take anybody's visions seriously,' Jim warned. 'Especially mine.'

We set up a camp near the boulders. Jim was determined to thread his own needle, despite the wear from visions. 'Are there any drunken tailors?' Jim asked. Finding the holes in the tiny beads he'd chosen wasn't much easier.

I left him to his own devices, since he had requested a necklace in tribute to his first album. He'd chosen the clear glass beads for 'Crystal Ship', bright orange for 'Light My Fire', and larger black beads for 'The End'. I'd been reading about numerology and how five was a balanced number. Since the old man who had talked to Jim about T'ai Chi insisted Jim was not balanced, I made the design's repetitions to come out to five.

I kept thinking of things I wanted to say to him, but every word seemed so final, I held each in, and happily settled for his holding me. No matter what we did that day, Jim's touch didn't leave me. When we hiked, he held my hand. When I made ink drawings of his bare body, brown ink on rose paper, he touched my foot with his. And when he held out his arms, I knew I would rather dance with Jim than share his visions. Leaning against his chest with his breath on my cheek mattered more than a hallucination.

Rather than record the days in Big Sur as I usually would, I made a list of images. At the end of the page, I wrote, '*Promise not to call until I've reached my destination,*' because Jim was reading over my shoulder and I couldn't speak the words.

Jim wanted me to sit so close to him on the drive back to Stockton, he drove one-handed. We passed the miles in silence, without even the radio. We didn't say goodbye or look at each other when I left the car to walk the last two blocks to my house. I forced myself not to turn around for a last look, because I believed it would be the last. I wanted to hold how it felt to sit beside him, not how he looked through a bug-splattered windshield.

Robert Kennedy was whistle-stopping his way down California. He was due for a stop in Stockton. My father and I had long ceased discussing politics. I imagined he was an Eisenhower Republican, though Eisenhower was long gone. But when I mentioned my best friend and I would like to see a Presidential candidate in person, my father volunteered to drive us downtown. Downtown Stockton, infamous for its roughness, was no place for young girls to wander alone.

Of course, when Kennedy was delayed, we wandered off to hear the death knell of downtown. Kress's still smelled of stale popcorn and had wooden floors. Between us, we could barely scare up enough to buy an apple to share. We returned to the platform where the candidate was to appear just in time to see him fending off fans like a rock-star. He made it to the stage with one shoe, but was good-humoured about it, and knew how to make a speech. My politics were left of his, but he seemed to be the strongest chance of ending the war.

My friend stayed over at my house. We stayed up late in my bedroom listening to music and talking, she stretched out in my bed and me on the floor in my sleeping bag that smelled faintly of Jim's sandalwood. We fell asleep with the lights on, music playing. When I woke up, I turned off the stereo and light, but could hear that my father had fallen asleep in the living-room in front of the television.

I wandered out to nudge him. Robert Kennedy's image was on the screen. I perched on the arm of the loveseat. This must be a nightmare, I thought. When I roused my father, he confirmed what I saw. We'd just seen the man alive and he lay near death on television.

12

We've Stepped into a River

'Darlin', I have to see you again,' Jim said. 'I really can't get away. Could you come down for a couple days? I'll fly you down. You can stay with Pamela and me.'

When we parted at Big Sur, we made a pact not to waste any more of our lives saying goodbye. I would call when we reached Florida as if I were just up the coast instead of on the wrong one. 'Just you and me . . . and Pamela,' I said.

'She'd like to meet you.' Especially since I was leaving California. 'Come on,' he sang the line that followed from 'The End' and chuckled.

I couldn't resist seeing Jim again. 'I'll take the bus.'

'*Blue bus* . . .' he sang. 'That will take forever.' I needed the time to buck up my courage. '*Blue bus tonight* . . .'

'I always meant to ask, is that one of those drug references of yours?'

'*Blue bus tonight*,' he sang again and then hung up. The song made for a nice exit, but I had to track him down at the third bar on his ever-changing list of phone numbers to give him the bus schedule.

The Greyhound pulled into the downtown Los Angeles station just before Friday noon. Weighted down by my rucksack and sleeping bag, I felt all the maturing done on the overnight trip down evaporate in the heat.

In the waiting-room, I spotted Jim leaning against the lockers. Relieved he was alone, I stared unabashedly at him. Hiding behind his aviator sunglasses, he looked like something hot the Santa Ana winds had blown in. That short haircut was grown out enough that wet tendrils framed his face. Even from the other side of the building, I could see great drops of sweat roll down his throat. Unbuttoned and dirty, his barely white shirt hung loose over low-riding brown pants held up by a belt whipped through silver rings. He sure looked more like Jim Morrison in Los Angeles, until he spotted me, then his grin turned his face from menacing to mischievous.

'You look like something the Santa Anas blew in,' I told him.

'They don't blow till the fall. You're a half-hour late,' he scolded in a dry rasp, grabbing my sleeping bag and pack just so he could drop them and hug me.

Tousling my hair in the way that reminded me of my older brother so greatly that it always left me feeling sad and pleased at the same time, he announced, 'I wrote a poem.' When I asked him to read it, he said, 'It's in my head. I was going to borrow a pen, but didn't see anybody I'd trust with a sharp instrument.'

I fished though my bag and handed him my ever-present blue mechanical pencil.

'Until now,' he said, whisking the pencil out of my hand and leaning down to kiss me. He took a crumpled envelope from his pocket and smoothed it out against a locker, shielding what he wrote with his arm, like I did when writing notes in school. He wrote a long time for a half-hour's musings. I sat on my up-ended sleeping bag, glad I had come, even if we spent the night like this, Jim writing against the locker and me watching one crowd spill out of the doors that led from the buses, and another drift in from the street, join for a few minutes and separate again. Like one of Escher's woodcuts where one object metamorphosed into another at their crossing. Like the paper I saved from the wrapping on the first gift for me in San Francisco. Like every day I spent with Jim that began as one thing and became something else.

Suddenly, I snapped to attention, fearing for a moment that Jim had gone. He was staring down at me. I felt a sudden wave of loss, having wasted time I should have spent memorizing him. I wanted to say, 'This is the last time we'll see each other,' but said an encouraging, 'Let's hear it.'

'Later,' Jim promised, lifting me to my feet and picking up my sleeping bag with a forward-moving sweep. 'Nice holding something that holds fond memories. This fits us just right. What say we meet in it around midnight?' When I asked about Pamela, he said, 'She hates sleeping bags. Are you starving? There's this great Mexican place. It's off Olivera, so it's kind of touristy while pretending it's a dive, but I asked, and they don't put lard in their refried beans.' He wasn't even making fun.

This time his car was a red GTO with a spotless white interior and fantastic speakers, which emitted commercials with great bass. Jim drummed on the steering wheel with his fingers. 'Which station am I on?' he asked.

'I'm not going to touch the radio.' I folded my hands in my lap like a schoolgirl.

Jim slid his shades down and eased into traffic. John's infamous drumbeat hit with static. Jim toyed with the tuning knob. 'No wonder.' He laughed. 'You're a witch.' He sang along with himself the way he had with other singers he liked while we drove. Particularly enjoying the instrumental section, he became something between a sax and a kazoo. 'Light My Fire' was long enough that the DJ went into a commercial right after the song. Jim turned the sound down, switched stations, stopped for Janis Joplin singing 'Down on Me' and sent the volume back up. Jim said, 'I hate to admit that's a good song.'

'It was real big last year up in the Bay Area. Maybe it wasn't on record. The FM stations sneak in a lot of tapes. I think the song's just getting air play other places.'

Jim looked a little puzzled. 'Oh, Janis is fine. I was talking about The Doors,' he said, as if he weren't one of them. 'I can't remember the last time I enjoyed that song.' He leaned over and gave me a sloppy wet kiss. 'Whew!'

We parked. Jim bounded out of the car and around to open the door for me. Met me with a quick kiss. 'Wanna tuck in my shirt for me?' he asked, like a sidewalk sleaze saying, 'Want some candy, little girl?' An echo of his stageside, 'Wanna show me a good time?' I unthreaded his belt just to shock him that I would take him up on his offer. His face registered faint surprise, which wasn't much of a pay-off for my embarrassment. I buttoned his shirt slowly, debating whether or not to unzip his pants at just past high noon on a Los Angeles sidewalk.

We locked our fingers as we strolled along the stretch of Olivera Street I had dim memories of from my childhood in Southern California. Olivera had seemed like Mexico then. I'd never crossed the border into real Mexico.

'What's that movie with Orson Welles, where there is this really long opening scene with no cuts?' A logical progression. The street. Mexico. Movies set in Mexico.

'*A Touch of Evil*,' Jim answered, making the connection easily. 'Decent experiment. I think that scene's minutes long. Hitchcock tried something similar in *Rope*, longer takes, but I don't think it was as successful. The camera was stiff. Because he kept repeating it, the experiment lost its impact. It's my least favourite Hitchcock film.'

A mariachi band overtook us. They wore tight black suits with intricate patterns drawn in white soutache braid and sang with stylized lament.

Asked, Jim explained the poignant song. 'Spanish is a romantic language, so it loses a little in the translation, but it's a lost love sort of song. This vaquero is telling his sweetheart that it's all over because he has fallen in love with her goat.'

'I take it that Spanish is a distant second language.'

'It's enough to get me a girl in Encinada.'

'Or a goat.'

'What's wrong with a nice goat?' Jim assured me it was only the billys who smelled, that they were, in reality, very finicky eaters, and while their legs were a little bony for his taste, their milk was naturally homogenized. How did he come to know goats so well? 'I read about them somewhere. In case you're wondering, I never dated one.'

'Then I guess that article I read was speculation,' I teased.

Suddenly solemn, Jim said, 'I asked you not to read shit about me.'

'I was kidding. Do people write weird stuff like that about you?'

'Pretty near,' he lightened his tone. 'But I suppose I encourage it. It's all a game, but I'd sure like to take my ball and go home.' He lowered his sunglasses, 'Or is it *balls*?'

Coming out of the sun, the shabby side-street restaurant was a cave. Even Jim pocketed his sunglasses. Almost as soon as the hostess seated us, we had freshly fried chips and fiery salsa. Jim ordered a Dos Exquis for himself and ice tea for me, without having to ask. He scooped salsa with a hot chip and downed it without much need for the beer. Then he sat for a few minutes, obsessed with removing the cilantro from the salsa.

Since Jim had vouched for the integrity of the beans, I ordered a burro and splurged on guacamole. The bus had passed avocado groves, and I'd developed a craving. After I ordered, Jim waved his hand at the waiter in dismissal without ordering.

'Aren't you going to eat?'

'This is fine. I'm not naturally thin. My weight is edging up.'

'Edging up to what? I saw you naked a few days ago.'

'That was nice, wasn't it?' He leaned over for a kiss meant to remind me how very nice it was.

'I could have played your ribs with a thimble.'

Jim straightened up. 'Why would you want to?'

'That was a washboard . . . um.'

'Analogy.' I'd miss Jim filling in my blanks. He complained, 'I gained almost five pounds since then.'

'Jim, I just tucked your shirt in five minutes ago,' I said, and remembered a quote from Rimbaud's *Illuminations*, a description of Pan, '*Your breast was like a lyre.*'

A bursting-with-pleasure grin broke across his face. 'You're reading Rimbaud!'

'You really can do that. Name a book from a line every time. Of course, with you, Rimbaud's no challenge.'

'Are you reading it in French or English?'

'Both. The copy I bought has the French on the left. English on the right.'

'How accurate is the translation?'

I laughed. 'I love your faith in me, Jim. But I think we can

199

safely assume that a Rimbaud scholar can translate better than a sophomore scraping through French class.'

'I'd trust your instincts over a scholar.'

'Well, the major difference is sentence structure. Where the translation shifts words around, I wouldn't. That's why I'm probably getting a C to be throttled over. Madame loses her patience. *Oh, mon Dieu!* My pronunciation is self-conscious. If I were editing your poetry . . .' I trailed off. What a bitchy thing to say. Pamela was *editing* Jim's college poems, which to her meant removing *fucks* and *shits*.

He asked, 'What would you do?'

'I wouldn't take the profanity out.'

'Why not?'

'Why not take the swearing out of *Howl*?' Well, stars.

Jim answered quickly, 'It's part of Ginsberg's angry rhythm.'

'Your own rhythm deserves its anger.' My voice was as loud as it ever became. My writing hadn't found its anger yet, but I was warming to it.

The waiter brought my plate, and a second beer for Jim. He poured it into his empty glass. 'I should give up beer.' But not food . . . 'Well, I like beer better. I guess it really doesn't matter. I can always get rid of either.' He declined to explain. 'I'll tell you after you eat.' When I insisted, Jim explained perfunctorily, 'Eat and drink what you want, then throw up. Romans used to do it.'

'Yeah, but look what happened to the Roman Empire.'

Jim laughed, 'A woman who used to be a model told me that's how she stayed thin. She's the editor of *Sixteen Magazine*. You see, it isn't detrimental.'

Delaying Pamela and me meeting, Jim drove me up to Griffith Observatory where part of *Rebel Without a Cause* was filmed. The city was hazy beneath us. He edged up to one of his shy teenage kisses I treasured. Then he drove me out to his old haunts at Venice Beach where we watched the sunset from a rooftop where he had written 'Moonlight Drive', saying goodbye to his California, not mine.

Inevitability followed us back into town. Jim shoved my sleeping bag under his arm rather than let go of my hand when he opened the door. Coming in behind Jim, I had to shift a little to his right to see Pamela. Only candlelight lit the room, so I had a brief hope that I did not look quite so much like her as my first flickering impression. Her hair was darker than mine. Her bones more fragile. I thought Jim perfectly capable of springing us on each other for the joke, and enjoying the awkward silence.

'Do you have the feeling,' I said a bit nervously, 'that you are looking in one of those distorted carnival mirrors?'

Pamela laughed. She had a warm and honest laugh. The tension broken, she came forward and hugged me lightly. Coming from staunch Yankee stock, I didn't hug easily. I never hugged friends in greeting. Only Jim ever hugged me. I felt stiff in her arms. Had Jim lightened his death grip on my hand, Pamela's embrace might have been easier.

'Jim said you were funny. Would you like to freshen up? The bathroom's this way. Why did you take the bus?' She took my hand, which made Jim drop the other, or the three of us would have been stumbling though the unlighted bedroom. I was beginning to think Jim had neglected to pay the electric bill until she switched on the bathroom light. In the mirror next to me, she looked like an ethereal mythical unicorn to my plough horse. 'I'm a tiny bit stoned,' she said, 'I was so nervous about meeting you.'

Her pupils were so big, I had to guess her eyes were blue. Green? She wore the artistically applied eye make-up I envied in *Mademoiselle* and could never quite duplicate.

'We can't seem to stop staring at each other,' she said with a giggle.

'I was admiring your eye make-up.' A half-truth, thinking I would have traded noses without a second thought. Her nose was perfect. Mine small and not worth notice.

'You don't wear much, do you? I can show you after dinner. It's like painting. Jim showed me some of your drawings. Would you like to see mine?'

My mouth actually dropped open. She drew? Jim apparently had a fondness for short, red-headed, Capricorn artists. 'Sure, just let me splash some water on my face and run a brush through my hair.' She closed the door gently. 'And jump out the window,' I said to myself. The square window was very small. I imagined myself caught at the hips like Marilyn in that porthole in *Gentlemen Prefer*

Blondes. I considered a treatise on the bathroom as haven. Often, that little room was hard to leave.

When I finally opened the door, the lamp was on in the bedroom. Pamela was sitting in the middle of the bed, a mattress and box spring on the floor with a flowered sheet and blue blanket thrown over it. Opened sketchbooks surrounding her, she patted the bed. I sat down and looked at the first sketchbook she handed me. 'Before I met Jim, I took some art classes at a junior college. I guess that doesn't count for much.'

'It's a good start,' I said. 'A lot of artists teach to support themselves.'

She brightened, 'I usually want to say I went to art school. Like it's more real or something.'

'These sketchbooks are real. They show a lot of work.'

I heard a swallow, and looked up at Jim leaning in the doorway, a bottle of beer in his hand. I wondered how long he had been standing there.

In the sketchbooks, there were a few studies. I recognized a chair I passed in the living-room, a collection of odds and ends that were in a different arrangement on the bureau, and the wayward philodendron I had spent time with in the bathroom. Most looked as if she had lost interest halfway through the drawings. More energy was put into the fashion illustrations. She hadn't quite found a style for her mannequins, but she was making an effort. 'You care more about these,' I said.

She turned around to Jim, 'She knows! Jim said you were . . . perceptive.'

Jim nodded. He hadn't said a word since our arrival. After I was sure he had swallowed his gulp of beer, I asked him, 'Is this your Gary Cooper impression?'

He stuck his tongue out at me. 'Smile when you say that,' he said in a slow, laid-back, Gary Cooper way that took us back to the night we met in San Francisco.

'It was a joke, Jim,' Pamela explained with exasperation. 'Like you were the strong, silent type Gary Cooper played in movies.' Jim pretended it was a small revelation. Finally, Pamela said, 'You've been such a moody son of a bitch all week. Why don't you roll a joint and mellow out.'

'The beer will do that. Don't need to feel any more paranoid than I do right now.'

'Roll me one then,' she dismissed him with her hand and he fell dramatically back into the living-room. She opened another sketchbook. 'These are better, don't you think?' The drawings, eight in all, were more consistent. 'Jim draws. Did you know Jim draws? He's not very good,' she whispered, 'but he showed me this little mistake I was making. I knew something was wrong, but couldn't put my finger on it. Then Jim suddenly saw it. That's why a teacher would be helpful. You see here,' she dragged back the previous sketchbook, 'the sleeve is supposed to be coming toward you, but it doesn't look that way because I have the . . .' she drew in the air.

'Arc? Curve?' I suggested, attempting to define her gesture. The damn sleeve.

'Yeah, going like a *u* instead of like an *n*. Did I say that backwards? Anyway, these are right. And these are wrong.'

Jim appeared with a lighted joint. He handed it to Pamela, and coughed out a puff of smoke himself. He squatted by the bed. 'Ginger's the one who showed me that.' He pointed to the head of the bed. Not many inches above the pillow, the line drawing of Jim's boots that we had done in San Francisco was tacked to the wall.

'You learned that in high-school?' Pamela sounded disheartened.

I hadn't had an art class when Jim and I had drawn the boots. 'No, I learned it in a book of drawings by Rembrandt I checked out of the library.'

'You don't draw like Rembrandt,' Jim told me. That was news.

'You don't write like Ginsberg.'

'Gotcha.' Jim winked and nodded in double agreement.

How easily Jim and I slipped into our shorthand way of talking. I didn't like the way it felt, with Pamela there, but Jim and I had little practice in sharing each other.

'Why don't you take a class in fashion design to help you put a portfolio together?' I asked Pamela, bringing her back into the conversation.

'Well,' she sighed, 'we travel a lot. It would be hard to finish a semester.'

Jim started to say something, then closed his mouth. I had the impression it was a contested subject between them.

'I better heat the oven. I'm ravenous. I made vegetarian lasagne. I just have to heat it through.'

'Thanks for going to all that trouble,' I said. Still stuffed from Olivera, I wondered how I'd get down lasagne. Jim neglected to mention we were expected for dinner.

'No trouble. I love to cook. Maybe I should go to that fancy cooking school in Paris.' She danced out of the room.

'With Sabrina,' I couldn't stop myself from saying to myself. Jim laughed as he fell on to the bed. 'I've gone through my whole life being able to say wicked things under my breath that no one ever heard and you go and take that pleasure away from me.'

'Adds *immeasurably*,' he said, making sure I caught he was using a word he considered my property, 'to mine. If it brings any solace, I seem to be deaf a little longer after every concert. In Santa Clara, I was reading your lips.'

Momentarily obnoxious, I nearly corrected him that it was the Santa Clara County Fairgrounds in San Jose. I stacked Pamela's sketchbooks in a neat pile and straightened the light blanket that was draped over the bed. Jim stood gracefully. He leaned to kiss me and I dipped out of his range.

'I'll be lucky to survive this visit without an *A* embroidered on some part of my body.'

'Can I do that? I know just where I'd like to put it.'

Pamela was buzzing around the little kitchen. 'Red or white?' she asked into the refrigerator. She turned, her arm gracefully draped over the fridge door. 'Red or white?'

'White,' Jim said tersely, 'if it's in there.'

'I only chill red in the summer. Who wants to drink hot things in this heat?'

Jim slipped between us for a bottle of wine, opened a drawer, then another searching for a corkscrew. Pamela closed the drawers after him. They seemed more comfortable in the small space of the kitchen than in the bedroom, even given that my presence added strain. Jim slipped the cork from the bottle with the same ease he showed in unzipping a dress.

Because it was too warm a night to light a fire, Pamela had placed an array of candles on a tray resting on the grate. A low table was set in front of the fireplace, a bowl of daisies at the centre. More candles. She had composed a striking stage.

When we sat down for dinner, she took my hand, and for a moment I thought she was going to say grace. 'I'm so glad you came. I've been asking Jim to invite you down.'

'Thank you. What a gracious thing to say,' I said.

'Oh, I mean it. Just ask Jim what I would say if I didn't.'

'Ginger blushes at swearing,' Jim said as if he never indulged in the profane himself. 'I think I heard her say *fishfeathers* once.'

I amused Jim by blushing anyway. 'Inherited that from my mother, though she insists God knows what she's thinking.'

I wasn't sure what I was supposed to call my hostess. Halfway through the dinner that Jim did not touch, it clicked that when he spoke to her, he called her Pam, and when he spoke of her, he called her Pamela. So I tried out calling her Pam.

Pamela disappeared occasionally, returning less coherent each time. During one of her absences, I asked Jim if I should leave. 'This performance isn't for you.'

On her return, she stumbled into the table and asked, 'Do you want to play jacks?'

'Shut up,' Jim snapped.

'Jim!' What if Pamela wanted to tease me about my age? 'I'm very adept at jacks even though my hands are small.' I rambled on about the technique of catching a ball on a hand filled with a rounded mass of jacks, hoping, given time, Jim's jaw would unclench.

'Jumping Jack Flash,' Jim said, as if it were an explanation and not the title of the new Rolling Stones song. I must have looked perplexed. 'It's a reference to heroin.'

That ended dinner. Still, Pamela insisted on showing me how to master the fine art of make-up. She took my hand and led me off to the bathroom. Until that night, I hadn't held another girl's hand since grammar-school field trips, but she was so comfortable about it, I relaxed a little. She unearthed all kinds of powders and liquids and little brushes, and tossed them into the sink for easy access. Jim wandered in and sat on the back of the toilet, slamming his boots down on the toilet-seat.

Pamela demanded I trade in my T-shirt and jeans for something more elegant. The closet was ninety-nine per cent Pamela's. A few of Jim's shirts hung in dry-cleaning wrappings. Pamela tossed an amazing array of the loveliest clothes I'd ever seen on to the mattress. Jim ploughed through the beautiful pile with suggestions. He held a flowing dress up to me and Pamela tugged at my T-shirt. I felt like the rope in a tug of war.

'We don't end the evening with the sacrifice of a virgin, do we?' I asked, at last winning the T-shirt war with Pamela.

Jim laughed. 'Slim pickings.'

'Slim Pickens?' I asked to get back at him. 'Wasn't he the actor who rode the bomb·in that Peter Sellers movie?'

Later, Pamela swept the clothes on to the floor and slipped gracefully out of her dress. 'You're welcome to sleep with us.' Jim didn't even look surprised. He said nothing, leaving the decision to me. No! 'If you change your mind,' Pamela assured me, 'I sleep like the dead.'

I backed out of the bedroom, closing the door. A suitably strange ending to an arduous evening. Gratefully alone, I surveyed the stacks of books lining the living-room. Jim told me that, more than once, Pamela had gotten into a frantic cleaning frenzy and thrown all his *messy* piles of books into the yard. The following day, they would haul all the books back inside. Something about their relationship was too complicated to let them buy a bookcase. After he had told me the story a second time, I sent a detailed schematic of a bookcase in sepia on parchment, as close as I could come to Leonardo da Vinci in style. I noticed Jim had taped the drawing to the wall, but ignored the hint.

Suddenly too exhausted to read the book I'd chosen, I pulled off my jeans, and inched into my sleeping bag. I started to cry. I cried off all the make-up Pamela had so painstakingly applied. I cried until my head ached and my nose was so stuffed up I had to breathe through my mouth, but felt no better. Crying was no release, I reminded myself, it just made you snore. That would be the final humiliation – to keep Jim and Pamela up all night with my snoring. Then it occurred to me, keeping them awake might be more like revenge. I buried my head in the sleeping bag and laughed. I couldn't quite believe her invitation for me to sleep with them. Maybe it was Los Angeles etiquette.

The bedroom door opened and closed quietly. 'You're having all the fun out here.' Jim kneeled beside me. He was barechested, but still in his half-zipped brown hip-hugging pants. A fine gold chain that held little trinkets I couldn't identify by moonlight dangled from his slender neck.

'Did I wake you?'

'Nope. I was on my way out to see if you were awake when I heard you laughing. You reading comics by flashlight under there?' He peeled the sleeping bag back a little. 'What's the joke?'

'This whole night!' I sniffled.

Jim smiled and clucked with concern. 'Are you catching a cold?'

'I'm hoping for pneumonia.'

Jim went in search of tissues and returned with a fresh roll of toilet paper. 'Sorry,' he said so humbly I was touched. He relit a few of the candles on the table, then worked at unzipping the sleeping bag.

'What are you doing?'

'Joining you.' Not with Pamela in the next room! 'She's the one who invited you to sleep with us.'

'Didn't you think that was odd?' I asked.

'Sure surprised me. Must have been her way of saying she approved of you.'

'You often bring girls over for her approval?'

'No. This is a very unique situation. Sometimes, girls show up. Usually they want to fuck me, so Pamela throws things at them.'

'Was she suggesting a ménage à trois?'

'No. At least I don't think so. Pamela's not a very physical person these days.'

'Why didn't she throw things at me? Did you tell her we are just friends?'

Jim bit his lower lip in that familiar boyish way. 'No, that would have been a lie. I told her that I loved you. We had a long talk about you before I asked you down. She said she could tell, after we met last summer, that a part of me had left her, and could always tell when I'd seen you because, for a little while afterwards, she liked me better. She thinks you are the only person I know who is a good influence on me.' He started to pull off my T-shirt and I stopped his hand. 'For a long time,' Jim said sadly, 'Pamela's been more in love with drugs than she is with me. She won't wake up until afternoon.'

'If she didn't mind my sleeping with you in your bed, she wouldn't mind you in my sleeping bag, but Jim, how do you think *I* felt when I saw Pamela? You really should have warned me.'

'I don't get it. Warned you about what?'

As he slid his pants down his beautiful thighs, I lost my train of thought. When I recovered I said, 'Pamela looks more like my sister than my sister does.'

He smiled and began evasively, 'I've never seen your sister . . .' She was the girl with dark hair in the family album. 'Your sister probably looks more like my sister than . . .'

Laughing, I said, 'Well, I thought I bore the evening pretty well feeling like Pamela's pale reflection.'

Jim sat back. 'Is that what you thought? You were thinking that all evening? I thought your remark about the mirror was just a great opening line. Darlin', I may have descended on you because of the way you looked, I have this weakness for redheads, but we became friends because you are a reflection of me, not Pamela. You and I are opposite sides of the same coin. I'm the dark side and you're the light. I feel as connected to you as that, like we were melted together. I keep hoping I will learn how to be light from you. My God, you shine!'

'Like a horse run too hard.'

'It's time we buried that old horse,' he said. 'My name's Jim, what's yours?'

I took the hand he offered and answered, 'Linda.'

He grinned. 'All this time and I didn't know my two favourite women have the same initials.' That night, Los Angeles and I were closer to Jim than the woman in his bed. I witnessed the reality of the poem Jim had cried over on the freeway that spring: Pamela's descent. The woman with the warm laugh had disappeared by the end of the evening. With his thumb, Jim brushed a tear from my

208

cheek. 'What's this?' he asked, holding his glistening thumb up to the candle-light.

A pang of loss struck like an arrow. Jim was one of few who still called me Ginger. I was saying goodbye to everything familiar. 'I'm just overflowing my banks.'

'Will you teach me how to be a river?' he asked.

'It's not something you learn,' I said, recovering enough to attempt a mock guru voice. 'It's something you remember. And you know what they say . . .' I watched Jim raise his questioning eyebrow on cue. 'You can't step . . .' I coached him.

'In the same philosophical moment twice,' Jim grinned.

The Los Angeles night was warm, and the two of us in the sleeping bag were hot. 'We are wet enough that we are going to start making those embarrassing squeaking noises if we move at all.' Then Jim started laughing so hard that our bodies made the loud smacking noises he had predicted. He wiped the sweat from his chest with his hand.

'Now I understand,' he said, in deep awe of his glistening fingertips, 'this is my first lesson in being a river. I am a river lapping against your smooth banks.'

Jim unzipped the sleeping bag and flung it open, the warm night air cool on our wet bodies. He kissed my neck and the damp space between my breasts. Each time he kissed me, the last time he would kiss me in that place. Soon, there would be a last kiss.

'No one else has touched you?' he asked, running his hand along the line of my shoulder. 'No one has kissed you?' Jim kissed me gently. He cleared his throat a few times, 'I feel like you've already left me, even though you're still in my arms.'

'Sounds like a country song,' I tried to lighten the moment, tears in my eyes, and sang, '*My baby has left me/Though she's still in my arms.*'

Jim grinned. 'That your own tune? Can I have it? I'm sorely tempted. Wouldn't that freak everybody out!' Jim sat up and slapped his bare thigh. 'Trouble is, I can hold my own in rock 'n' roll, but George Jones could drink me under the table.'

I giggled. 'The man has a B-side!'

'Where's that pencil?' Jim jumped up and flew into the kitchen. He opened drawers and rummaged through them, leaving them all open for Pamela to close the next day. He returned waving a piece of paper.

'Are you really gonna write a country song?' I asked after giving him a fat five minutes of silence while he stared at the paper in his hand.

He scooted up next to me. 'I talked to a lawyer last week. Don't get frazzled, I went *incognito*,' he said, drawing his hair back to demonstrate his clever disguise. 'He said there's a way you can go to court to get adult status, even at sixteen.'

Hope hit the ceiling.

'You've got to let me help you. I could front your court costs. Don't say a goddamn word! I know you'll have figured out how to pay me back with interest before the money's out of my pocket. I'm sure I can find you a job. That's part of it. You need to prove you can support yourself, that you can take better care of yourself than your parents do.'

I sat silent for a few minutes, trying to find my stomach on this swift ride. 'Jim, I don't think I can.'

'I know what I'm asking. There are still times I want to die. That part of my life, my past, is like this hitchhiker standing by the road. I keep picking him up even though I know that one day he's going to kill me.'

He drew that hitchhiker on the margins of his notebooks. At the bottom of his letters. His own ghost. I played with his hair. I wanted to go back to the playful country song and not know there was a way out if I were just brave enough to take it. 'In a year and a half I'll be eighteen. I can do it. If there comes a time I can't, you've done this for me.' I took the page of notes from his lawyer visit and folded it into quarters so it would fit in my purse. My eyes burned so badly, I didn't dare look at Jim. 'Don't hate me because I can't do this.'

'Of course not.' He kissed the top of my head.

'Do you think less of me, though?'

'No. I understand. There's another way for you to stay. I just wanted to give you this option first, because I thought, you know, that being legally emancipated might make you feel really free. There's something I've wanted to ask you for a long time . . .' his voice trailed off. He patted the pockets of his discarded cords.

His eyes met mine and held me in their intensity. 'I just feel crazy knowing you will be so far away.'

Crazy. We were going to say the things we swore we would not say in Big Sur. 'Before I lose my courage, can I talk about something first?' Jim nodded and I continued, 'I don't want to spoil the little time we have left, but there never seems to be a right time. Now, we are running out of time and I have to say it. That hitchhiker, Jim, I wish I could tell you how to leave him behind. You need someone who does.'

'I've talked to a shrink before. Scared him to death. He asked me not to come back.' Jim stared at his hands, avoiding my stare.

'Then he was the wrong shrink,' I said, lifting his face. 'You need to keep looking until you find one you can't scare.'

'I better start first thing Monday morning. That search could take a thousand years.'

On dangerous ground. 'If I might suggest a shortcut . . . Start with a woman.'

Jim lifted his eyebrow. 'Why a woman?'

'How many men do you trust?'

Jim smiled. 'One.' I was surprised the list was that long. Jim said, 'Yeah, well, Diogenes would have had an easier time of it if he was looking for honest women.'

'May I ask who it is you trust?'

'Bill Graham,' he answered immediately.

'I didn't know you were close.' Even though Mr Graham had apologized, I couldn't quite let go of his growl, '*And I'm not your pimp.*'

'You didn't ask who I was close to. That's a different question. A different answer. We had this really perfect day together up north. We talked about our boyhoods. I don't think either one had ever opened up to another man before. He told me about being herded across France. Children driven to exhaustion, living on oranges.'

We were quiet, remembering Jim's speech about living on oranges. You could always tell the SOB's where to go measured against Bill Graham's story of survival. 'Will you promise me something, swear to me on whatever is most precious to you?'

'That would be you,' he said, placing his hand solemnly on my head. 'What's the vow? I hope it doesn't have anything to do with

211

monogamy. I can promise you my heart, but my body . . . ooh, that would be tough.'

Duly sidetracked, I asked, 'How many women have you made love to?' The original line in 'Crystal Ship' was *A thousand girls* . . .

'Two,' he answered easily.

'Oh, we're playing semantics again.'

'We are playing truth. Pamela was the first woman I really made love with. You were the second. I never kept count, but I guess I've had some sort of sex with well over a hundred, maybe closer to two hundred women.

'Is that possible?'

His cheeks were a cherubic pink. 'Barely.'

I chucked his chin. 'This doesn't have anything to do with your sexual appetite.'

'That's a relief. Not that I wouldn't be willing to try, but I was going to ask if I could kinda taper off slowly. What's this promise?'

'I want you to promise me that if you ever stop teasing death, and really want to die, that you will get in touch with me, wherever I am. Wherever you are. Give me the chance to tell you why you belong in this world, and if you still want to leave it, to let me say goodbye, knowing it is goodbye.'

'It would be easier to promise to stop being promiscuous. Would you settle for that?'

'No deal.' I debated telling him something I had only told my best girlfriend. I took a few sort, sharp breaths. 'Do you remember my mentioning my older brother?' Jim nodded. I dug my nails into my knees to keep from ringing my hands. 'As a kid, I'd get to missing him so much that I would wish on a star for him. Like magic, he would call or show up out of the blue. I was very superstitious about it, and saved up my wishes until I thought I couldn't stand it any more if I didn't see him.

'A few years ago, I wished for him and he called that very night. I remember my sister had *Peyton Place* on TV and there was this continuity mix-up so that Allison, Mia Farrow's character, would be in one outfit, and pass through a door and be in another outfit. That's my clearest recollection of that night. I just talked to him for a few minutes about school and begged him to come visit. I missed him desperately.

'A couple days later, a call from the Florida police woke us in the middle of the night. My brother had blown his brains out in a bar. I was so stunned, I couldn't even cry. I felt I should have known from something in his voice. I was the sensitive one. Don't do that to me, Jim. Don't think I have failed you because I can't always tune you in like your music on the radio. If I know you're in trouble, I'll do anything to help you. But you have to tell me.'

Jim gently pried my nails from my knees. 'I won't make a promise that important if I'm not sure I can keep it. What guts it must have taken for you to call me when you read "Five to One". Your concern meant so much to me. at the time, and it means a hundred times more, now. If I had known, baby, I never would have written it . . . You told me once how old he was.'

'I'm hazy about the exact date of his death. It was around his birthday, so he was either twenty-seven or just turned twenty-eight.'

'So young. When was this?'

'Sixty-five.'

Jim shivered. 'That's when I had this incredible burst of creativity. Maybe I'm a soul collector. Do you think that's why I remind you of him? I usually only think like this on acid, but maybe that's what all of us who are ancient ones are. Why you know more than you possibly can from experience, while someone who is seventy still hasn't quite gotten it. And learning, like you teased about, really is remembering.'

We sat, facing each other, holding right hands, stalled out on a handshake. My brother was a mechanic, not a poet, but enough like Kerouac's Dean Moriarty to earn the epitaph.

'What was it you wanted to ask me?' I asked.

He considered for a moment. 'Do you want me to teach you to swim?' In the middle of painful confessions? 'Let's go skinny-dipping.'

'This was the question?' I asked.

'I'm keeping a promise. I promised that I'd teach you to swim.' Jim was on his feet, pulling on his pants. I found my T-shirt, skipped the bra and panties, and jumped into my jeans. Not wanting the place to burn down while Pamela slept, I stopped to blow out the candles and ran to catch up with Jim. The top of the GTO was down and Jim raced the engine, not impatiently, but excitedly, waking the sleeping street. I turned on the radio and caught a real look of disappointment on Jim's face that it was Credence and not The Doors, but Jim sang along anyway.

13

Witnessing the Wild Breeze

Jim pulled away from the curb into the silent street. I caught all my hair, gave it a couple of twists, and shoved it into my T-shirt to keep it from tangling in the wind from the speed of the car. Jim's turns were sharp and sure. We threaded our way into the hills. A two-lane road opened on the right to give a view of the city lights, then a couple turns later, the city vanished. The road was narrow, but smooth. Trees bent over the road, were briefly illuminated by the headlights, then gone. Up north, they might have been live oaks, but in Southern California, I didn't know. Jim slowed and made a left turn on to an ever narrower road. In a few winding minutes, a huge house appeared abruptly before us.

'This is a driveway?'

Jim kissed my naïve cheek. 'Belongs to an actor acquaintance.' He let his head drop back against the seat. 'Now, you have me alliterating.' And, I thought, lying.

I looked at the dark house. It must have been close to three in the morning. 'Won't we wake everybody up?'

'Stop being so damn considerate and have some fun.' Jim pulled me out of the car on his side and slammed the door so it resonated against the building. He sprinted around to the side of the house and ran up the side of a six-foot stone wall, grabbed the top stone and heaved himself over.

I hoped I wasn't supposed to do that. Jim answered by unlocking the gate and bowing like a butler long in service. He closed the gate behind us. There was enough moon to follow the path that led around the house and opened up on a large patio that climaxed with a pool where Esther Williams could have erupted in a water ballet. How bright the moon seemed, reflecting off the pool.

Jim hopped out of his pants and took a run at the pool. He dove in with a soft splash and swam its length with a steady grace, barely breaking the surface to breathe. When he stopped at my feet, he splashed my toes. 'Still dressed?' he asked.

I wiggled out of my clothes and sat on the edge of the pool, careful not to kick him when I lowered my legs in the water between his arms. He ran his wet hands up the outside of my thighs to my waist, and lifted me gently into the water. The fragile security I felt as he held me disappeared when he released me. My mother had called me the Little Fish when I was a child, but I'd nearly drowned in a shallow creek near our house when I was twelve. Thereafter, I accepted I was, in fact, a land animal. Jim walked me away from the safety of the pool's edge. My muscles stiffened.

'Trust me. I won't let go. I'm a dolphin, remember?'

Jim kissed me slowly. The water lapped around us, and for the first time in years didn't sound menacing. 'Let's make love like dolphins,' I suggested.

'You'd have to turn around for that.'

I made a fairly graceful turn in my new environment. Jim took my waist and continued my turn until I was facing him again.

'I want to make love with you before I go,' I whispered.

He kissed me gently. 'We aren't going to do that. You mean too much to me. It's not right to have one time and say goodbye.'

'If we rushed a little, couldn't we have two times?'

He laughed softly. 'We could have half a dozen times, but I don't want to rush. What we have is all we need for now.'

'When I was seven, seven being a mythological number,' I began, launching into one of my odd stories Jim found so amusing, 'I saw

216

Audrey Hepburn in *A Nun's Story*. All that self-sacrifice in the Congo really appealed to me. I told my mother I wanted to be a nun, but she said that, as far as she knew, the Methodist church didn't have nuns. Then I read that Albert Schweitzer and I shared the same birthday, some years apart.'

Jim blinked his silver moonlit lashes. 'Is that the end of the story?'

'Don't you get it? It was a call to the *Congo*, not to *God*.' Jim did his big laugh with the hees and snorts and added splashes. He wiped his eyes with his wet knuckles, then kissed me with that gradually increasing passion that made me want to breathe his breath. I let my legs float up around him. 'The point of the story *is*,' I said with an exasperated sigh, 'if I don't want to be a nun any more, why do you want me to be?'

'No,' he said softly and guided my arms around his waist. He pushed off from the bottom of the pool and swept a rush of water back with his cupped hands. My face rested in the small of his back, the way his so often did in mine when we slept together. The movement felt like dream flight, except for the sound of the water as Jim propelled us along. 'I make love with you every time I think of you. I'm not going to rush the rest.'

'You aren't rushing me. I've grown up quite a bit.' I was losing him. 'You wanted to make love to me the night we met, why not now?'

'I wasn't in love with you then. When you give yourself to me, I want . . . You are too good a woman to have it mean any less.'

'Jim Morrison! Your thinking about women is stuck in the fifties! You still think bad girls do and good girls don't.'

'Oversimplified, but close enough,' Jim said. 'I do want to marry a virgin.'

I laughed, 'Now, I'm speechless.'

'That doesn't happen often.'

'I'm sorry. I do babble.'

'It's one of my sweetest pleasures. Besides, you talk twice as fast as I do, so I figure we get the same airplay.' Jim lifted me on to the poolside cement and burst from the water to sit beside me. 'We are like Natasha and Pierre.'

I didn't want to fess up I didn't know who they were. Where

217

did Russia and France get together? Did it have something to do with that rogue Napoleon?

'*War and Peace*,' Jim said, when my long silence had given my questions away.

'It would be. Now, you are going to make me read *War and Peace* to understand the allusion,' I said, enjoying pretending to be unreasonable about his unreasonable hints. I learned my lesson with *Finnegans Wake*. 'I have other plans for the summer.'

'Don't cheat and watch the movie. It's lousy. Even if Audrey Hepburn is in it.'

I wondered if she were in the movie, or if he thought it a good joke. We did seem to be working our way through references to all her movies. Wordlessly, Jim stood and helped me to my feet. He led me around to the other side of the pool where there was a cabana. Inside, there was a little shower we squeezed into. We washed the chlorine from each other's hair, and let the cool water sheet our bodies. If I didn't shut off the water, Jim might have stayed under the stream until dawn. Finding no towels, we wrung each other's hair and flailed our arms a little, then settled for letting the warm air dry us.

Jim rocked me slowly. Not quite dancing. 'Natasha was too young for Pierre,' Jim picked up his explanation where he left off before the shower. 'While she was growing up, they were separated, but in the end they came together, because it was their destiny. We have that destiny. That's why I can wait. I hope you will wait for me.'

I shivered in the warm early morning air. Jim's wanting a marriage with me in a brutally distant future made me lonely. We dressed. Jim let me out the gate, locked it, and put the key in its secret place. I heard him take a running start to take the wall again.

Jim opened the car door on the driver's side. I crawled his hips' width under the steering wheel. Neither of us made a move to turn on the radio. When we reached the two-lane road, a hazy line of orange laid on the eastern horizon. Back at his place, Jim was naked before he reached the kitchen. He plucked a couple big strawberries from the basket on the sideboard, popped one into his mouth and tossed one to me.

'Your fielding isn't so bad,' he said when I caught it one-handed.

My giggle sounded hysterical in the quiet room. Jim poured himself the last half-glass of wine from the night before and a wine glass of orange juice. When I took the juice, he lightly touched our glasses with a high-pitched ping. 'To Destiny.'

The fine chain and charms glowed against his chest. At first, it seemed they were the source instead of the reflection from the light splintering in from the window. Jim broke the spell by moving. He crouched by a pile of albums, and not finding what he wanted, reached for another stack. He retrieved a couple albums in paperbag-brown sleeves and put the first on the turntable, one of those thick seventy-eights with a handsome dark blue label, changing both needle and speed before lowering the arm lightly. The record had the sizzle and eerie hollow sound of those old recordings. The first musical sound was a low wail, then a slide guitar that sent a chill down my spine in tempo.

'Robert Johnson,' Jim said, as if he hated to interrupt to say even that.

The name was new to me. I stretched out on the still open sleeping bag. Jim finished the wine in his glass and joined me. Unusually when Jim listened to music, his head bobbed and his hands were busy keeping time on anything in reach. That morning, he lay motionless but for his slow breathing, in exhaustion or reverence.

When the record ended, Jim drew himself up slowly, drifted out of sight into the bedroom, and returned with a book in his hands. He crossed his ankles, and sank beside me. The book's cover was missing and the spine broken, so all the yellowed pages were loose. 'This was the gift I bought for myself on my fifteenth birthday,' he said, entrusting the volume to my hands. Rimbaud's *Illuminations*. 'I want to hear it in French from you.'

Each letter had been individually set. Printed on thick paper. One side. Jim's treasure was a private edition. Reading aloud seemed a punishment, more cruel in French. Without Madame's disapproval, though, I fell into a reasonable facsimile of a French accent. Jim followed the print for a few pages, then lay on his back, gaze fixed first on me, then the ceiling. When he closed his eyes, I read, not sure if he had drifted to sleep.

'What colour do you think azure is?' he asked in a husky half-awake whisper.

'It's just French for blue.'

My answer disappointed him. 'I meant what colour do you see?'

'The colour the sky is a half-hour after sunset.'

He smiled. 'I love your specificity.'

I laughed. 'I didn't know anyone could say that word.' I lisped through several attempts to prove his remarkable feat.

He tapped the book, and I continued to read. When I read the *Parade Sauvage*, Jim brushed my knee with the back of his hand. 'What does that translate as?'

'Sideshow.' If I remembered from my less precious copy.

'Yeah, I believed that when I was fifteen. I see humanity differently since I've known you . . . *Soft*. You know. *Soft*,' he repeated with a gentle wave of his hand, enjoying the sound of the word. 'It comforts and scares me at the same time.'

When I finished the book. Jim cradled me with the book between us. The sun forced the room into an uncomfortable hot summer morning, but neither of us shifted until we heard movement in the next room. There was talk of a party which Jim and Pamela had promised to attend.

Pamela slid behind the wheel. I took the cramped back seat, and Jim stretched out in the passenger side, looking like he would rather take a nap than go to a party. Again a little stoned, Pamela's right turns were dangerously wide, but Jim didn't make any comment. If lucky, his eyes were closed behind his shades. I squinted against the bright white sunlight, never quite cool enough to remember sunglasses.

The traffic had been so dense, when we pulled to a stop behind a line of cars, it took a moment to connect that we were parking. Jim eased himself out of his comfortable lounging position, and offered a hand to help me out of the back seat.

A hush followed a rumble when Jim and Pamela made their entrance. Men wanted to slap Jim's back and shake his hand.

220

Girls wanted to brush some part of their anatomy against his. Pamela pushed at them a little. Jim shrugged and smiled. A young man, dark-haired, and a few inches shorter than Jim, said, 'Good seeing you again, Jim.' Jim looked like he was trying unsuccessfully to place him. The man handed him a bottle of cognac.

Pamela was still holding my hand, which made me feel a little odd. A woman asked if I were Pamela's sister. Before I could answer, the woman pushed between us to get closer to Jim and our light hold broke. For a moment, I felt I had lost my life preserver and was swept away in this sea of strangers. I'd never been to a big party. I'd never been to a party that wasn't a birthday party.

Calmer on the edge of things, I sought escape from the smoke, equal parts grass and cigarettes. Just outside the sliding glass door, I saw someone I thought I knew. I smiled and started to say hello when I realized he looked familiar because he was Stephen Stills of Buffalo Springfield. I started to ease around him when a hard blow against my back pushed me straight at him. Stephen caught me and growled at the drunk over my shoulder, 'Watch the fuck out!' Returning his attention to me, he said, 'Good thing the door was open.'

I was too shaken to more than nod. He picked up the purse I didn't realize I had lost and handed it to me in the sweet, awkward way men have of handling purses. I thanked him and he said, 'Glad I was here,' and tugged my hair the way Jim did. Men had been playing with my hair ever since I could remember. Boys at school would compare my hair to a Botticelli painting if they wanted to impress me. Or Cousin It from *The Addams Family* if they were honest.

I wandered around the yard, listening to snatches of conversation, and trying to stay just visible enough that someone wouldn't run into me again. Back inside, I skirted the edge of the room to make it to the kitchen for something to drink. Jim and Pamela were holding court. An awed group circled them. All that was missing was the kneeling and bowed heads. Jim caught my eye and winked. I wished I had had them drop me at the bus station early.

A woman said, 'Excuse me.' I automatically tried to flatten against the wall to get out of her way. She was quite tall with

221

dark hair. 'You look a little lost here. Could I introduce you around? Would you like to meet Jim Morrison?'

'No, thank you.'

'A young woman not interested in Jim? I'm intrigued.' She leaned in close to me. 'Would you like to take a little trip with me? Upstairs I mean. There's a better party upstairs.'

'No, thank you.' It seemed the best answer to any question at that party.

She leaned so close, I could only smell her Shalimar. 'Come upstairs, let me show you something new.'

'I'm really not interested,' I said, never having tried to be rude to anyone before. She pressed closer and whispered something I couldn't catch. I made the mistake of asking her to repeat it.

The young man who had given Jim the cognac stood in the kitchen doorway. As I passed through, I heard him say, 'Morrison is such a falling-down-drunk asshole.'

Defensive about the slur against Jim, for the first time in my life I wanted to punch someone. I stood in the kitchen sucking up deep breaths in an effort not to cry.

A melodic voice whispered, 'Are you gonna be okay?'

A delicate hand lit on my shoulder. I turned. The face from movies surprised me. Recognition came in waves. Brandon de Wilde had been in *Hud*, the film that made me want to make movies. 'You look different in colour.' Jim's approval of my saying the first thing that came into my mind had its embarrassing consequences.

Brandon grinned. 'I'm better looking in black and white.' He played self-consciously with his gold-rimmed glasses.

I thought not. 'Just different,' I said. Brandon was not tall. His golden hair fell past his collar and he had a good start on a moustache. 'You were wonderful in *Hud*.'

'Thanks, that's nice to hear.'

I tried to think of something polite to say, but had one real interest. 'I guess everyone asks what James Wong Howe is really like.'

Brandon laughed, a light, rhythmic laugh, and shook his head. 'You're the first. Most people ask what Paul Newman is like.'

'Oh, he made *Cool Hand Luke* up near where I live in Stockton.

The word was, he was reserved, but nice. An average tipper. And wouldn't give autographs. Of course, that's by way of waitresses.'

He laughed again, 'Sounds about right. What were the tears for? I'm a pretty fair listener.'

'Thanks,' I said, not knowing how to explain I was on the emotional edge trying to survive the party where drunks pushed me and attractive women made sexual innuendoes I didn't understand, when I would rather have been saying a private goodbye to Jim. Or better yet, have the goodbye said and be staring out a bus window.

Brandon ran a beautiful finger along my jawline in a way that seemed intensely personal. I stepped back. No man but Jim had ever touched me. 'Let's find a private place to talk,' he whispered. His lips brushed against mine and his tongue made a flickering pass along my teeth. I pushed his chest gently. He took a theatrical giant step back and leaned comfortably against the tiled counter, shoving his hands in the deep pockets of his jeans to look harmless. 'I really want to make love with you,' he said with a winning smile. Not so harmless.

My first thought was to run, but there were half a dozen other people milling in the kitchen and his relaxed pose was less threatening than the woman in the other room. 'Thank you, but no.'

He grinned. 'What idiot left someone as sweet as you stranded with these piranhas? *Us* piranhas.'

I didn't answer, but leaned against the facing counter and listened to him talk about having given most of his life to acting, which sounded so strange from such a young man. He was about Jim's age, though he looked younger. He spoke of giving up movies until he could come back as a forty-year-old character actor. All that had been in his favour as a child, his being small for his age and a bit too pretty, had worked against him as an adult.

Unfortunately, he had exchanged very few words with the cinematographer. Most of the communication was between Howe and the director. Actors weren't, as a whole, very important, especially former child stars. He wanted to try music. His marriage had hit a plateau. He was lonely. He was considering a career in country music. I didn't remember his singing being so great in *Hud*, but that was acting. He offered me a bottle of Coke out of the fridge and opened it, apologizing for no glass.

Jim entered the kitchen. Brandon and he nodded at each other, without speaking. 'Seems like you have a weakness for blondes the way I do for redheads.' There was a nasty edge to Jim's voice. 'Making your way through every one of them here?'

'Is this the idiot who let you out of his sight?' Brandon asked, looking at Jim, not me.

Jim laughed, 'Yeah. Don't suppose he told you that he has a worse reputation than I do? Did you introduce yourselves and all that?'

Jim did the honours. Brandon shook my hand. I was taken by his firm, but not finger-crushing, handshake. 'Real nice to meet you,' he said in an affected western drawl.

'Same here.' I was such a fan. 'I still cry at *Shane*.'

'Me, too,' Brandon whispered. 'I'll tell you why sometime.' He grabbed a fresh beer, saluted Jim with it, and strolled out of the kitchen.

I set my gaze on Jim. 'Exactly what is S and M?' I knew I had heard the expression with snickers before. I knew it had something to do with dirty sex.

'Sure, ask me when you are leaving town,' Jim laughed. 'Now wait. Brandon didn't bring that up. Never heard that about him. Actually, I heard he was "Some kind of wonderful".' Jim sang half a line. He scratched his nose with the lip of the bottle and broke into laughter. He spun towards the living-room. 'Is Gloria here?'

'Tall? Dark hair?' I asked. 'Why is it that the women you know want to go to bed with me?'

'The men do, too.' He nodded at the doorway where Brandon had exited. Brandon glanced back at us. 'Sado-masochism. Marquis de Sade. Heard of him? Hurt and be hurt. Only being up front about it instead of killing each other in the name of love.' That seemed to be what he and Pamela were doing. Jim was good and drunk.

'Why would she think I'd be interested?'

'Oh, she just wanted to shock you. You look every bit as naïve as you are.'

When it was time for me to leave for my bus, Jim was leaning against the living-room wall, Pamela staring up at him. I hated everyone in the room who seemed to say one thing to Jim's face and another behind his back.

'It was good to see you again.' I extended my hand for a public farewell, feeling awkward in front of the audience surrounding Jim. He ignored my hand. I pulled it back.

Pamela gave me a swift little hug. 'Oh, can't you stay a while? Why don't you spend the weekend with us?' She'd found some energy and seemed once again the Pamela who had greeted me in their apartment.

'Thank you, but I have to go. Could I have the car keys?' I asked.

Jim patted his pockets, then fished through Pamela's purse. He dropped the plaited leather key-ring with its roach clip and feathers into my hand.

Jim pushed away from the wall unsteadily. 'Let me drive you.'

'No, thanks.'

'It's a long walk. I'll call you a cab if you don't trust me to drive.'

'I like to walk. I just need to get my things.'

'I'll see you out at least.' Jim swept up the nearly empty bottle of cognac from the coffee-table. He staggered halfway across the lawn, his drunken walk an exaggeration of his normal one-foot-in-front-of-the-other tightrope walk. We stood a few feet from each other unable to speak.

At last he said, 'I thought it would be easier this way, but I just feel cheated.' He set the bottle in the grass and nearly followed it. I caught him and staggered myself. He rested his head on my shoulder. 'I wish you hadn't touched me. It only makes it harder to say goodbye.'

The word stung. I released him slowly to make sure he could stand on his own. I fetched my pack and sleeping bag from the car and slammed the door. Jim held out his hand for the key. 'Neither of you should be behind the wheel. I'll leave them under the mat.' Jim frowned and shrugged. 'Jim, I need to tell you something,' I said, knowing I needed to do more than confiscate his keys once and walk away. He raised an eyebrow, waiting. I searched for the image I wanted him to see.

'It's like *The African Queen* . . .' I began.

Jim gave me one of his slow smiles. 'I hope this doesn't mean I have to drink gin. Don't care much for gin. But at least this time I'm sure I *do* get to be Humphrey Bogart. I'm a drunk, and you're Kate – and so much better than me.' He heaved a dramatic sigh.

'Rose wasn't better than Henry. They were different. That's not my point. I'm not in the boat.'

'Not in the boat? I must be a little too wasted to follow you, honey,' he half-apologized, then he laughed. 'My God, Albert Schweitzer in the Congo again? You just can't be Robert Morley! I won't allow it!' Robert Morley played Rose's bonkers brother, an evangelist, as I remembered.

I smiled. His drunken laugh was charming. 'No. I'm the camera. You are up to your waist in water and covered with leeches. Hovering over you I can see,' I said, my eyes following the gesture I made to the imagined lake to my left, 'that you have taken the wrong tributary, and just through those rushes is where you want to be.'

My hand was still suspended in the air when my eyes returned to his face. His eyes were unrecognizably dark and his clenched jaw rippled white and pink. Jim scooped up the bottle from the grass and flung it at a tree across the yard, where it shattered with a dull clank. He reeled back to me. Three inches from my face he screamed, 'I could pick up any sixteen-year-old on Sunset and she would know more about life than you do! What right do you have to tell me how to live my life?'

'Yeah, I know,' my voice trembled, 'but she wouldn't know more about you, Jim. I may have said it all wrong, but I have the right because I love you.' I touched his cheek and he rested the weight of his head in my hand. His jaw relaxed, and its colour returned. Tears spread in a wash down his face. 'I hated what I saw in there,' I said. 'The guy who gave you that bottle was calling you a drunk on the other side of the room. He wasn't the only one who said one thing to your face and another behind your back. I couldn't

226

go without telling you that I'll never pour you a drink, but I will pick you up off the floor as many times as it takes.'

Jim had to take a step back to keep from bumping into me when he marched back towards the house. At the steps, he stopped. I thought my heart would break if he didn't turn around. 'For almost a year, I've been the one to say you loved me. This is the first time,' he said softly, still facing the door, 'that *you* said you loved me.' He turned, eyes diverted, his curls shading them from me. He raised his head slowly. 'My God!' he screamed. Startled, I looked behind me.

Jim rushed at me and sunk to his knees. He caressed my right knee. Blood seeped through my yellow tights. In a bank shot that would have had Minnesota Fats shaking his head, Jim's tossed bottle had sent a fragment of glass across the yard.

'Get up,' I said. 'I feel silly with you down there. You know how knees bleed. I didn't even feel it.' My knee stung a little since he drew my attention to it. I tugged at the yoke of his shirt, but he wouldn't budge. 'Jeez, I thought a spaceship had landed. Imagine my disappointment.'

'Is it really okay? I couldn't bear it if I hurt you.'

'It was an accident. Bet you couldn't do it again if you tried.'

He smiled up at me. 'As long as I'm down here I feel I should ask you to marry me.' We laughed together. With me to steady him, Jim struggled to his feet. He pulled the gold chain over his head, and fidgeted with the fastener. 'Could you undo this?'

I obliged and returned it to him. He let the charms drop into the grass. When I stooped to pick them up, he said, 'They don't matter.' He searched his shirt and pants' pockets until he discovered a crunched piece of tissue paper, unfolding it to reveal a ring with a large emerald-coloured stone in a sleek gold setting. He slipped it up the first joint on his ring finger so we could both look at it, beautiful in the fading sunlight.

'I bought this after Big Sur. Stuck to the rules. It's just a pretty piece of glass. I meant to give it to you last night . . .' Jim trailed off, threading the ring on to the chain with as much concentration as he used threading a needle in Big Sur. He gathered my hair and lifted it so I could slide the chain under and fasten it. Jim sang a couple of lines of 'Wear My Ring Around Your Neck', not paying much attention to the way Elvis sang the song. His hands held my waist. He kissed me gently, then deeply. 'How do I let you go?'

'You just let go.'

Jim dropped his hands to his sides. I felt like one of those papery husks beetles leave behind. I took a few steps back, jumped the gutter to show him my knee still worked. Determined not to look back, I watched the toes of my Mary Janes as I coaxed one foot in front of the other up the street.

'Ginger!' Jim called. I smiled at my shoes. He was having as much trouble as I was burying that old horse. Though he asked my name, he hadn't yet called me Linda. I pretended I hadn't heard. He called louder. I twirled on a toe.

To stop myself from running back to him, I walked backwards, and called to him, 'I'll come back when I'm eighteen. We'll knock them dead with a musical version of *The Razor's Edge*.'

Jim's laugh sounded good. 'You'd be perfect, except for this one flaw. You have absolutely no sense of direction. You're going into the hills.'

Feeling silly was so much better than feeling empty. As I walked by him, he stepped off the curb, close, but not touching me. His breath moistened my cheek as he whispered, 'I promise.' His eyelashes brushed mine. 'What you asked last night, I promise.' He stepped back up on to the curb, drawing a cross over his heart and raising his right hand.

The house was sold, contents boxed, red lines drawn on maps. There was a last impromptu camping trip in the Sierra Nevadas with a friend's family. I borrowed a blue and white gingham two-piece swim suit with ruffles on the bottom like little girls' panties, but it didn't get wet. My new confidence about water stayed in Los Angeles with Jim.

The phone rang late the day I returned. I rushed to hear Jim's voice. 'Hello,' a silky voice that was not Jim's said, 'this is Brandon. We met at a party a few days ago.'

I had a crush on Brandon de Wilde since I was five years old. Amused he felt he had to explain, I said, 'You were going to tell me why *Shane* makes you cry.'

'Was I? I never told anyone that story. Can't believe I'm going to do this. I was nominated for Best Supporting Actor for that role. A few years before, I'd won an award on Broadway for *Member of the Wedding*. No kid had ever won that particular award. I thought that's how it worked. You just got handed these trophies and everybody shakes your hand and takes your picture and you get to stay up late.

'When they didn't call my name for the Oscar, I started to cry, and this adult who really meant a lot to me pinched my arm and said, 'Don't you dare cry. Maybe next time you'll work harder.' Whenever I catch that film on television, I watch every frame, wondering if I could have done a better job.'

Brandon had to swing through Stockton on the way to the Sierras for a camping trip and thought he might pick me up. A run on nature. I knew from Jim that there was no such thing as first dibs on a heart, but the man was married. I declined. 'I wish you all the best with your music.'

Asked if I were behind Morrison's success, I answered, 'No. Morrison is behind Morrison's success. Also, in the way of it.'

Brandon laughed. 'I run into that myself. Can I ask just what you two are?'

Blood brothers. 'A couple of Navy brats in search of a dock.'

14

Waiting for the Sun

We had moved West in the early sixties. I remembered Route 66 and the deserted mining town of Jerome, Arizona, waking at dawn in the Joshua trees of the California desert. My sister had decided it was time to strike out on her own, but my parents, two dogs, and I were crammed into the station-wagon with suitcases and lunches.

The car flew down 5, the artery that connected Jim and me for nearly a year. As the car turned east, my first roots, which were sunk into California and my friendship with Jim, strained and broke. I looked out the back window as if I might see Los Angeles and a last glimpse of Jim. All I could see was the U-Haul that held our pared-down belongings. My father's idea of travel was to deadhead on coffee and cigarettes, so we made it to Florida in four days.

We stayed with friends of my parents a few blocks from the beach near Daytona. I walked there every day, mumbling to myself about the clean white sand, the lack of cliffs, and the ocean being on the wrong side. There were perfect pastel shells that looked like tiny slippers and scurrying sand crabs. The air was so humid, I felt I might sprout gills.

One night, a band played on the beach. They did rowdy versions

231

of top forty hits. Of course, they had to take a mad stab at 'Light My Fire'. I left the beach early and went back to the house to read. Working my way through our hosts' bookcase, I was a quarter of the way through James Joyce's *Ulysses*, obviously not reading alphabetically. The phone rang. I answered formally, the way I was taught to do in other people's houses.

'It was a real bus,' Jim said.

I'd heard no word from him since our spoiled goodbye in Los Angeles. When my heart settled down, I asked about the cryptic greeting.

'You asked if it was a drug allusion,' he explained. 'The bus that went to the beach was blue, though if I was a chemist, I might have a go at a blue bus tonight.' Jim laughed his silliest laugh. 'Whatcha readin'?'

'*Ulysses*,' I answered, my voice shaking from the excitement of hearing his voice.

He chastised me, 'You call that beach reading?'

'It's the only book too heavy for the crabs to carry off.'

Jim chuckled. 'I see I went all wrong with Steinbeck. Never did find out the end to *Tortilla Flat*,' he said as if he lost the slender volume to Florida's crab population. 'Oh, God, it's good to hear you! I loved your letter. Came today. I felt like I was on the road with you, being snubbed by snobbish waitresses and dodging Texas cockroaches. We have to *really* travel together sometime. We'll make a book of it. I'll do the words and you do the pictures.'

'Yeah. We pretty well covered Big Sur,' I said, though not on the page. He'd written a song about Big Sur called 'Waiting for the Sun' with a UCLA friend, but I hadn't contributed beyond holding a flashlight. The Doors' new album was named for the song, but the song wasn't going to be on it through some argument with Robby about which Jim mumbled, but would not elaborate. Elektra couldn't waste all those album covers even if they were emblazoned with the wrong title!

'I was afraid I said too much when you didn't call before I left,' I said softly.

'I tried. Baby, I tried. First you weren't home, then your line was always busy, then it was disconnected,' he drew in his breath.

'God, I hated that. It made your being gone so real. I was only angry that what you said was true. A lot of them at the party were there to worship the *hollow idol* or ask for alms. I think you are the only person I know who hasn't asked me for money. I don't have any real friends. Except you.'

'You're just feeling lonely. You have people who care about you,' I said, then added the list, 'Pamela, the band, your friends from college.'

'Yeah, well, I'm not so sure. You were very wrong about something, though. You're no camera.' I had been certain I was the observer. Jim said in a childlike voice, 'You're the rain that lifts me from the mud.'

Jim remembered that when Bogart's character in *The African Queen* had given up, a night of rain had rescued his mired boat. Until he put it into words, I didn't realize that was what I wanted to be for him.

'I've been trying to write a song, but I feel too much to put into words. Besides,' he added, 'I used up that *mire* line on Robby's song.'

After a silence, I asked, 'How are you doing?'

'Let's see,' he started, then made stretching and yawning noises. 'I sauntered into the old office and resigned.' His was a response that answered both *how* and *what*. 'You know I've wanted to since the first of the year. I expected this collected sigh of relief to blow me out of the door, but the guys were shocked. Later, Ray and I had a long talk,' Jim sighed. 'It's been so long since we really talked, I was mostly trying not to cry. He asked me to stay with the band for six months.'

'Are you going to?' I asked.

'Yeah. I'll do it for Ray. He's very nearly as much my brother as Andy,' he said quickly, then hesitated. 'We don't always have to like each other. We aren't the buddies we might have been, but I love Ray. I'd lay down my life for him.'

Obligated to ask the hard questions, I asked, 'Staying won't be doing that?'

'You carve close to the bone. No. I'm gonna look for a shrink. Try to drink less. Anybody would think it was New Year's, the resolutions I've been making. Thank you, baby. I may not be able

233

to pull this off, but at least . . .' Jim chuckled, 'I'll never be able to watch *The African Queen* again.'

'I'm sorry. What a terrible thing to do to a Humphrey Bogart fan. I just wanted you to see . . .'

'What you were seeing. Hey, it was exactly right! That leech scene always made me shiver. I think that's why I reacted so violently. You know, don't you, how sorry I am?'

'Yes, I know. You were right, too. I don't know much about life. I definitely know more about movies. Was that your Australian/ Robert Mitchum lizard?'

Jim laughed, 'And you didn't even blink! *Intrepid friend.*'

I asked if things had improved with the band. 'A little. Like couples after a big fight. They make up and try. We haven't tried very much for a long time. Especially me. We have a lot of touring ahead, which I hate. The single's out. It's doing great. Getting flak from the press saying it's a sell-out.'

'I think it's fun. I bet you cleaned up the beach with that line.' 'Hello, I Love You'.

'I'm too bashful to admit the truth.'

'How can they say it's selling out?' I couldn't see anything wrong with a catchy tune. 'Didn't you write that a long time ago? It's in the same spirit as "Foxey Lady".'

There was a pause on Jim's end, then a little chuckle. 'You mean "Twentieth Century Fox".'

'What did I say?'

'Hendrix's song.' So much for cheering the guy up. 'Yeah, well. Reviewers only remember "Light My Fire" and "The End". Tunnel vision. "Hello" isn't my favourite song of all time, but at least it has some energy. I don't know where it came from, because I sure didn't feel any. "Five to One" is a superior song. It's just "Unknown Soldier" didn't do much as a single.'

'Will you send me a copy?' I was a little hurt about not getting an advance copy. 'Send me an album, okay? That way I can save my allowance for stamps to write to you.'

'I'll think about it. Your money is better spent on stamps. I'd send self-addressed stamped envelopes if it would get me more of them.' There was a long mutual silence.

Finally, I said, 'You're so critical of your work.'

'That's not always true. The Hollywood Bowl went well. It was filmed by my friend Paul from college. So you will be able to see it. Before the show, I met Mick Jagger. Jesus, we were a couple of cobras eyeing each other. Great fun! He sat a few rows back. The band was grim because I dropped acid. If they were going to film the thing, I wanted to capture July 1968.'

He said he screamed and crooned as best he could. 'What was really fascinating was I had the feeling that the music was coming at me slower than it sounded, so I had to compensate. I did some of *Celebration of the Lizard*. I had a really hard time getting through the last verse of "The End" because I felt like I was saying goodbye to you. I nearly broke. Anyway, I was really happy with that show, so don't say I'm critical. I take a bow now and then. It's just the album *is* crap.'

When I asked him about the poem he'd written on the envelope at the bus station, he said it wasn't full of the brilliance he hoped. I felt liked telling him I'd kick him if he put himself down one more time . . . a long-distance verbal kick if that were the best I could do. But I said, 'Read it to me sometime.'

'Well, if it wouldn't spoil your day, I could read it to you now.' There was a brief silence, a crackle of paper. After he'd speed-read his way through a poem I wanted to take in slowly, Jim said, 'Would you do me a favour? Watch the sunrise at the beach tomorrow. I used to do that when I lived in Florida. There's this stretch of beach near you I remember . . .' He described the section of beach with such detail, I felt we were on our little imaginary trips together.

Because I was sleeping on the sofa, attempts at sleeping late weren't very successful anyway, so I beat the sun to the ocean. Ridiculous for the sun to rise up from the sea instead of dropping into it! No cliffs! I walked from the road into the soft sand. At the water's edge, tiny lemon- and lavender-coloured shells littered the beach. I heard the crunch of sand behind me, and turned to view Jim's unmistakable Frye boots.

Wanting to tell him I loved him, I simply held his hand in both of mine, studied his veins, a nail he'd blackened slamming it in a car door, the surprising softness of his palm when I kissed it. We walked south along the unbroken coast.

When weary, we checked into one of the endless pastel-coloured motels. I peeled without thinking what should come off first. Then Jim let me undress him. I sat between his thighs, my legs over his as if we were bordered by the confines of a bathtub, instead of having the expanse of a bed. We held each other for a long time. I felt fiery whenever our skin touched whether it was intimate parts of our bodies or our hands.

At last, Jim lay back and I caressed him with my small hands. When he quickened, he pushed me back to tease me. Then Jim was up and dancing around the small square room. He beckoned me, pulling me to him. Dizzily spinning, he lifted me off my feet as if I were a feather, then accidentally slammed my back against the wall with a thud that proved I was not.

We kissed until breathless, then he moved delicately, slowly between my legs, careful not to enter me. 'Yes,' I whispered. I wanted him so much I would fly off the planet if he didn't make love to me. The thought jogged for a harsh second with his pinning me on the sofa of that terrible Stockton night he had lost touch with the world. So often, I defined Jim as out of control, but his rhythm with me didn't wander as he complained it did musically, it built.

The wall felt cool against my back, Jim's chest moist and warm against mine. When he heard my shy sighs, he came, screaming instead of low moans. He whooped and swung me around falling crosswise across the bed backwards with me, all elbows and knees, sprawled on top of him. Jim locked his hand over his wrist to hold me against him.

Pleasantly spent, we engaged in slow kisses. Jim raised his head, becoming aware of the beach noises outside. I lazed against the two pancake pillows. Jim crept between my thighs to begin the dance again. 'Shouldn't we talk?' I asked, not really wanting to.

Afterwards, Jim fell asleep on my stomach. I held him and watched what light there was glisten against the wet art of his semen arc on the wall. On waking, Jim followed my gaze and shouted, 'A poem!'

'Now, that's the difference between us, Jim. I see your ejaculation as art and you see it as poetry.'

We showered a sexy shower, dressed, and hailed a cab. Shy in the sun, I took a step back when he ran his lovely fingers through my hair. He kissed the top of my head as if to turn me into a child again, but whispered, 'Perfect passion,' in my ear, humming a new tune as he ducked into the cab.

Jim sneaked in another visit before he had to be off on tour – creeping up behind me on the beach singing 'Strange Days'. He kidnapped my straw beach-bag and put his finger to his lips for my silence while he impersonated my transistor radio. Wearing swimming trunks under his cords ruined the impact of his oceanside strip. He strode into the surf until he could propel himself into a dive in the turquoise water.

Another motel room. We had the day, but rummaging through notebooks, running out for what he called *supplies*, Jim was troubled and not wholly with me. He returned with a bottle of Pepsi for me and whiskey for himself, silent from confusion, not passion.

When he left, he was drunker than I'd ever seen him. He cried over our goodbye even though he had proven we could see each other as often as before. A few days later, in an otherwise empty mailbox there was a poem from Jim about the sound of sparrows he had fed on the window-sill of the motel room and the pull of childhood.

Just when I felt the all-night flights for a few hours with me might wear Jim out but make Florida bearable, my father, restless with retirement, decided to return to his native New England to work. Both of my parents were born in Maine. They had family there. My brother was buried there. They bought wooded land from my uncle, a trailer to live in while they built a house, and a horse for me as my summer friend. Across the road, down a gently rolling hill, lay woods, and glimmering through the trees, the Kennebec River.

As soon as Jim had my address, he sent six lines on the back of a postcard, Jim's poem-way of saying he missed me. That gold glimpse was never me. I, too, turned when I saw dark hair, the way he did for light a continent away.

Jim phoned a couple times a week, always before five-thirty when my father got home from work. With the time difference, it often meant that Jim had just woken up after another all-nighter and crawled sleepily to a phone.

'Something I want to do while we're separated,' Jim began, warning, 'Now, don't say *no* before I get it out. I want to use this time to teach you a few things I've discovered about writing.'

The rest of my summer was divided between the woods and Jim's correspondence course in writing. Knowing he wanted to give me the encouragement he'd never had, I'd spread out a blanket in a opening among the trees for my lessons. My horse preferred one near an apple tree so she could reach up for a snack, and my dog liked it deeper in the woods where she could sniff for hours.

I collected all Jim's writing insights I'd scribbled among the Jim saids and I saids in my diary into a small spiralled notebook like the ones Jim carried. Sometimes, it was a tough call on whether something he said was about writing or about life. When I wrote this to him, he wrote back that writing and life were the same.

There was a rediscovered quote from Schiller: 'Truth exists for the wise; beauty for the feeling heart.' Jim had written me I had both. I laboured at making my writing have both. Dissatisfied with my poems which seemed so young and shallow, I diligently tried to copy the mode of an admired poet: Jim.

Jim flung – there was vehemence in the mail that day – the poems back at me with the concise note: 'These suck.' Jim was back to telling me at that rate my poems would never be as good poetry as my letters. After a good cry, I tried again.

He sent books by other writers and a long poem he'd written in Hawaii in between concerts and breaking drinking records in local bars. He sent a note, block-printing a quote from Mark Twain about the difference between the right word and the nearly right word being the difference between *lightning* and a *lightning bug*. I wrote back, 'Is a lightning bug the same as a firefly?' As if we were passing notes in school, we began to ask and answer on each other's stationery.

I cried watching the Chicago Democratic Convention. Jim wrote a song about it. I couldn't put the big things on paper. 'No wonder my teachers say I write about unimportant things.'

He answered my letter with a ten-second call, 'Yeah, you write about unimportant things like people.'

Although the summer tour had loomed over Jim, he looked forward to the European tour with the Jefferson Airplane. The

238

clock had swung the other way, and his less frequent calls were usually before a show. His speech was often slow and slurred, I felt helplessly far away. During one of the first calls from England, Pamela walked in on his proclamation of love.

I heard the explosion over the phone. I wanted to hang up, since Jim hadn't, but was afraid he'd think me angry. Jim had only just said they had been getting along better than they had in a long time. They fared better when they travelled than when they were in Los Angeles. 'Look,' he shouted at Pamela, 'I need to talk to Ginger or I'm not going to make it on stage tonight.'

Pamela said, 'Why didn't you say it was Ginger? I thought you were talking to some piece of ass you picked up here.' Then Pamela was on the phone apologizing to me. 'I'm sorry,' she said, 'we do this.'

Jim came back on the phone with a deep sigh. I didn't know how talking with me was going to get him on stage when he sounded too drunk to stand up.

A couple weeks later, on top of the pile of mail in the roadside mailbox, was a postcard of one of Van Gogh's iris paintings, postmarked Amsterdam. Jim had written:

Having an *EXCESSFUL* tour.
Best you're not here.

JM

After the tour, Jim stayed on in London with Pamela. He met Michael McClure, one of the beat poets who had been at the first love-in, a Human Be In, in San Francisco, held on my fifteenth birthday in 1967. Michael had been surprised at the quality of Jim's poetry. The positive reaction from a poet he admired lifted Jim's spirits.

In addition to his loftier poetic pursuits, Jim began reading P. G. Wodehouse. A patron had left a book behind in a pub and Jim delighted in the splendid world of flighty Bertie Wooster and his practical Jeeves forever extricating him from difficulty. Wodehouse made, Jim said, the room-temperature beer go down more easily.

Jim would call in his newly acquired Bertie Wooster persona, *quite whiffled*, Bertie himself would have cautioned. 'Better to drink and telephone, than drink and drive,' I suggested in my best

Jeeves. Surely Jeeves, like me, was a Capricorn. Jim promised a set of Wodehouse so I might investigate the point.

After a pleasant week of alter-ego conversations, the phone woke me. Foggy enough to sense it was the middle of the night and not sure how many times it had rung, I sprinted to the kitchen. My father was swearing about drunks calling wrong numbers at all hours. My guess it was a drunk calling the right number. 'I'll get it.'

'They betrayed me,' Jim hissed. 'They sold out. They sold "Light My Fire" for a fucking car commercial!'

'Jim . . . Jim, it sounds like a really lousy business decision, not a betrayal. They aren't the same thing at all. How could they out-vote you?' Jim had said band decisions were always a unanimous 'yea' or 'nay' by default.

'No vote. They waited until my back was turned . . .'

'The way things are going with the four of you, that's pretty nearly all the time these days.'

Jim managed a little laugh, 'Don't make me laugh. I'm really mad. Don't they know that half a dozen times I've been offered three or four times what they are getting to sell the song we will always, right or wrong, be identified with?

'One record company offered me a house in Beverly Hills, a goddamn Rolls-Royce, and a $250,000 bonus if I let their lawyers break my contract with Elektra, and sign with them as a solo,' his voice rose with every line. 'I laughed at the son of a bitch. And they sold me out for fucking peanuts, like the band was about money. They were hemming and hawing about it being Robby's song anyway, and I thought, "Don't they remember? It's a Doors song. *We* are The Doors."

'From the beginning, I said we'd divide the royalties on all the songs even though I was doing most of the fucking writing, because we were an entity. Now they pull this. I should never have promised Ray this six months.' Jim's voice expressed more pain than anger, and dissolved. 'They broke my heart. I'll never forgive them. Never.'

'Ah, Jim,' I sat in a kitchen chair, pulled my cold feet up under my nightgown and hugged my knees. 'I think you are so upset, not just because of the song, not just because of your integrity, but you

240

feel you've lost your second family. Because this bond you had with the band happened magically, you expected it to mend magically. Maybe you have to talk to each other and work things out. Things could have ended for us when I screwed up our goodbye so badly. You forgave me.'

'You always act out of love. And you were right.' We were both quiet for some time, then Jim asked, 'What would you think if I just quit the business and taught college?'

Jim was an amazing teacher, but I couldn't imagine him showing up for class regularly. Maybe that wasn't as important as what he could do when he did show. 'Well, I'd hope you'd be drawn to one of these quaint vine-covered New England colleges.'

'When I asked Pamela, "What if I got my Master's and got a job teaching English for a living and wrote the poems I want to write?" she said that sorry old, "Those who can, do, those who can't, teach." Ginsberg teaches. Pamela thinks the way out is for me to quit the band and write poetry. Ever since Michael McClure gave my poetry a little recognition, she's off on this kick of "Let's quit rock 'n' roll and become bohemian poets." She thinks it sounds romantic.' He grew more cynical. '*We* are going to quit rock 'n' roll? *We* are going to be poets? She likes the idea, not the reality. She's not willing to live on what a teacher earns, much less a poet. I could go back to living on the street since I know that, like you said last summer, I'm mired in the wrong tributary. Rock isn't the way to get my poetry read. But Pamela wants comfort, and all the money and fame.'

'Ooh, you have the blues something awful. When you hang up, put some Billie Holiday on the stereo and sing the blues with her a while.'

'Don't think I won't!' he relaxed with a soft laugh. 'I wish I could snuggle up to you. That would do me more good than anything. I dream about you.'

'This is cruel, Jim. Do you know how cold it is at,' I looked at the little clock on the stove, 'one o'clock in the morning . . . in Maine . . . in the winter . . . without you?'

'Ah, shit. Jesus, I counted the time backwards, like I was calling from England, not LA. I'm sorry. I thought I was just calling a little late. Not a lot late. Is your dad going to be furious?'

241

'He grumbled some. With luck, he won't remember in the morning. By the way, I keep telling you I wasn't encouraging you to quit the band last summer. I think you can have it all. You just have to be willing to have a smaller audience for your poetry. You can't expect to drag your young audience, who buy your music, to poetry written for people your age. You had a clearer view of this that time we talked in Carmel, when you understood that a lot of your fans bought your music because it matched their sofa. I'm not sure I agreed with you that a good beat is the same as a blue painting over a blue couch. I guess I was too shy to contradict you then. Rhythm is a soul-touching thing.'

Jim sighed, ' "Dance on Fire", thanks for reminding me. You're the ballast in my life.'

'Is that a weight joke?'

'Nah, it's a "Horse Latitudes" joke. You would have saved the ship without losing a single horse.'

I flushed with the warmth of his compliment. 'Is this sale of "Light My Fire" settled? Is it something that can't be undone?'

'I'll find a way,' he said bitterly.

'Would it help if I talked to Ray or Robby for you? They probably think I'm one of those Maine loons they've heard about, but I'd do anything, Jim, to make you feel better.'

'Thanks, honey. I'll fight my own battles.'

'I was thinking more of an armistice.'

Jim laughed, 'You would.' With that, he hung up. I imagined he'd finish whatever bottle he'd started and sleep more peacefully than he would have without the call. I had no idea of how to get him to put the unfinished bottle in the cupboard.

A few days later, an album-shaped packaged arrived from California. I thought, 'At last!' He'd sent me *Waiting for the Sun*! I knew how to talk sense to Jim. I felt so proud of myself – until I opened the package and it was the other Morrison's album: *Astral Weeks* by Van Morrison. The note was one line. 'This Morrison can be proud of his work.' Jim was still sulking. I made no miracle. He was right about Van, though.

The Doors were set to appear on the *Smothers Brothers Show* on Sunday, the 15th December. The show requested them to do 'Touch Me', which was on the radio, even in Maine. Jim had found

242

more music than the lament by the highway in California, which changed 'Wild Child' from a poem into a song. Jim wanted me to *see* him when I heard it for the first time, so he had arranged for that to be the band's other song.

Sitting cross-legged on the floor, as if I were a few feet from Jim, instead of the television, I hung on the Smothers Brothers' introduction of the band. In the five months since I had seen him, his hair had grown long again. He wore a black shirt and pants and a suede coat that appeared grey on our black and white set. 'Wild Child,' Jim wailed. I blushed. He had added a delightfully evil little laugh after the spoken *ancient lunatic* line. The middle verse was eliminated. No *beautiful child, mystical child* verse. Thank goodness and Jim's brush with good judgment. I wished he had been looking into the camera for his spoken last line.

Between The Doors' songs, George Carlin did his Indian sergeant. There were a few other comedy bits that didn't quite make it, unless it was just my impatience to see Jim. Then the Doors, backed up by a horn section, did 'Touch Me'. Jim smiled early in the song, then missed a cue, so there was this little space that hung where the second deluge of *C'mon's* belonged. To make up for it, Jim visibly pounced on the rest of the verse.

Jim called me after school the next day. 'At least I didn't fall,' he said sheepishly. 'I was concentrating so hard on making you like "Wild Child" that I was still on a high when it came time to sing "Touch Me". I just wanted to smile. I was telling myself, "Jim, keep that silly grin off your face, you're gonna ruin your reputation," and forgot where I was in the song. That's what I get for thinking about you. I had to listen to the band for a couple seconds to figure out where we were. Robby probably thinks I did it intentionally because I don't like the song. Was it terrible?'

'It was wonderful. Especially the smile.'

'You're supposed to say, "Especially my song."'

'Especially "Wild Child",' I said obediently. 'I do like the song. It just embarrasses me. I still can't scream.'

Jim let out a loud yelp into the phone. 'You'd be perfect if you could scream.'

'My faults are doubling. Before you said I'd be perfect if I only

243

had a sense of direction. My sister gave me a Girl Scout compass.'
One thing at a time.

'I never did teach you to scream. We'll take care of that
next time I see you. He sang about screaming in a teasing little voice. Jim laughed, 'It's unfair. You got to see me, but I
didn't get to see you. Sure wish I could say, "Cut school tomorrow. Meet you in Eden. Or Monterey." We could watch the
sea-lions.'

For Christmas, Jim gave me the Beatles' double *White Album*.
The first album I ever bought was the Beatles' *Rubber Soul*.
Before then, I just listened to the radio. *Sergeant Pepper's* had
been heavy competition for Jim's first album. Nice to know he
didn't hold grudges about everything. Jim had slit the cellophane
wrapping just enough to slip in a note that he gave me the album
for one song, 'Blackbird'.

He gave me a heavily underlined paperback of Lenny Bruce's
book, *How to Talk Dirty and Influence People*, a collection of
e. e. cummings' poems in hardcover, complete with a hand-painted
bookmark, and a pale pink sweater with intricate cables that,
according to its label, came from London. Best of all, he called
in the early afternoon. 'Merry Christmas. Ginger? Are you there?'
Jim asked with a discernible slur.

'Merry Christmas,' I whispered.

'Can you talk?'

'I can listen.'

'Thank you for the vest. It's beautiful.' The basic vest was black
velvet. Two beaded panels in the red, white and black of a king
snake met in front to form a single pattern. I traced a drawing of a
snake from one of Jim's notebooks, made a graph of it, and wove
the pattern in beads. 'Pamela wants one.'

'Well, you're welcome, but Pamela can make her own. I'll send
her the pattern.'

'You made this?'

'You asked me to weave some beads for you.'

'You made this!' I warmed to his surprise. He just wasn't
accustomed to people who did things other than music.

'Thank you.' I slinked down the narrow hallway as far as the phone cord would stretch. 'My wings aren't broken,' I whispered. 'They've just been clipped.'

Jim laughed. 'Why can I picture you whistling the theme from *The Bridge on the River Kwai*. How are you doing?'

'Cold. Lonely. Maybe I'll hum something from *Dr Zhivago*. They are having the worst winter in anything from ten to forty years, depending on the teller of the tale.'

Winter became familiar. I was back in school and staring out the windows at snowfall. The hallways filled like cattle cars at every bell. A bad time to be short, I could never see much more than the back of the person in front of me. One morning, a little hole opened. I edged through sideways, and caught a glimpse of a new face. The event wouldn't merit much notice in California, but in this small town, where, for the most part, everyone had known everyone else since kindergarten, I was an oddity. Suddenly, there was another. He was a few inches taller than me, hazel eyes, and long dark blond hair, with bits of sunlight in it. I missed the sun.

The week before my birthday, Jim called again. Just in from the long bus ride home, I was still juggling books and muffler and coat while trying to hold on to the phone.

'You sound sexy breathless,' Jim mocked the Marilyn Monroe wispiness of my voice.

'Sounds sexier from you.'

My mother, with her marvellous discretion, ran off to fold laundry, giving me the few feet of privacy the trailer could afford. Jim and I flirted a while, our small-talk.

'Got two letters from you today,' Jim said with a yawn. 'One's postmarked two weeks ago. The other a couple days ago.'

'They were probably waiting for the mailbag to fill up before they sent the sled team out.'

He laughed. 'I wish you could deliver them under my pillow yourself. I just wanna talk to you all night.'

I checked at the clock on the stove. 'How about a nice hour?' I needed to be off the phone when my father returned home from work.

Jim sighed. 'I miss you so damn much.'

'Yeah. Miss you. What have you been up to?'

'Oh, the band is rehearsing for the new album,' he said flatly.

'You haven't even mentioned that. Jim . . . what are the new songs like?' I missed being a part of them.

'I'm too lonely to sing them to you. What have you been up to?'

'I wrote a poem,' I said tentatively.

'Recite!' Jim commanded.

'I'll read it. I'll probably drop dead where I stand from the embarrassment. You have to promise not to laugh.' Or say it sucks.

'Would I laugh?' he asked, trying not to laugh.

'Yes. You would snort and haw and all of that.'

'I liked your haiku very much. I have them memorized.' He promptly recited one. I had sent him haiku, written on squares of origami paper, and folded into cranes. I considered them art pieces.

He had written, when he received the fourth, that at least they had the sense to fly south for the winter. By refolding my poems, he had learned to make cranes, and had made a mobile out of them to hang over his bed. I had asked, 'Which bed?'

'A whole poem?' he asked in his most encouraging voice. 'Give it a whirl.'

I thought it the best thing I had written and wanted Jim's approval. When adrenalin hit my system, my body idled roughly. My voice shook a little. My hands shook a lot. When I read the last line, the ensuing silence over the phone hung more heavily than in person. After a long pause, Jim cleared his throat.

'So,' he sighed the word into several syllables, 'you've fallen in love. Got this big taste of what you must feel about things I write for Pamela, and I don't like it very much. Give me a minute. Hold on.' I heard him set the receiver down. How did he know it wasn't written for him? I could hear the radio in the background. Cream's 'White Room' was just ending, and Creedence sang 'I Put a Spell on You' before Jim returned to the phone. 'Was it wonderful, making love with this boy?'

I giggled. 'Where did you get *that* idea?'

'Read that part about *night island* again. Sure sounds like making love to me.'

I enjoyed his misinterpretation. 'Jim, it's all your fault. You told

me to be less linear. Brian,' I explained giving the boy his name,
'lives in his grandmother's house on what's called the Island. On
the Kennebec. Gosh, we've only just met. We pass notes in the hall
at school. We held hands for about a minute once, then stuck our
hands back in our pockets, because we were both so shy.'

'You're in love with him, though,' he stated, not asked.

'I have feelings for him. You're the one who's taught me about
love. Wouldn't mean much if I couldn't carry it with me. Until
now, I couldn't understand how you could love both Pamela and
me. I thought one or the other had to be a lie. I thought maybe
that was the lie you keep looking to define. I've never felt divided
before.'

'Then you still love me?' he asked.

'Always.'

'Happy birthday,' he said sadly. 'I wanted to wish you a happy
birthday.'

My birthday was more than a week away. My thanks was met
with a click, then that lonesome dial tone. There wasn't time to
call Jim back even if I could locate him. He was so rarely home,
it would have been useless to try.

The station-wagon pulled into the drive. I was in my room
before I heard my dad stomping the snow off his shoes on the
front steps. *Strange Days* was on the record-player from before
school. I hadn't been able to put the needle down. Since leaving
California, I couldn't listen to Jim sing very easily. Some days, I
felt lucky that I had a way to hear him when he was so far away,
but the records were never quite Jim. They were always the same,
Jim always in flux.

PART III: *1969*

———————

15

Can You Give Me Sanctuary?

That Friday, when the bus rolled out of the school parking-lot, the air was so cold, ice crystals danced in the air, glittering like fairy-dust, but by the time the bus groaned to a halt at the end of my driveway, the clouds had closed in and it had warmed enough to snow. I waded through the hard snow wake the road plough had left.

My mother was on the phone. My favourite aunt, her sister, lived in the next house down the road. They talked daily about the weather, the town, what they were cooking for dinner. Sometimes, I would hang out in the living-room, staring at an open book so I could listen to my mother's side of these feminine exchanges. My mother hadn't lost much of her Maine accent during all her travels. She put r's in the middle of words that had none, and left r's off the end of words that had them. In the months we'd been back in her neck of the woods, her accent had deepened. She finished commiserating about the weather, then held the phone out to me, 'It's your friend, Jim.'

I felt a great rush of surprise and pleasure. 'Hi,' I said in a high-pitched voice I didn't recognize. The *happy birthday* at the end of our last call, three days before, had sounded like *goodbye*.

'What do you want for your birthday?' Jim tried to sound cheerful, but his voice was lifeless.

'Besides you?' I asked, my attempt at cheerful more successful than his.

He laughed wearily. 'No, including me.'

'Well, then, *you*.'

'I'm so glad you said that. Otherwise, this could be very awkward. I'm soaking up all this knotty pine atmosphere in the little motel you have here.' My excitement took no acting at all. 'I was beginning to think a desperate man couldn't get here from there. Wanna pack a bag and spend the night with me?'

'You're really here! I'm going to cry.'

'This is supposed to make you happy. Make your excuses. I'll pay for a cab – and don't show up with red blotches all over that beautiful face.'

He gave his room number and hung up. I danced around the kitchen table, trying to hold in my excitement. 'Can I spend the night with Trina?' Trina was my ally in enemy territory. When she accepted me as a friend, other kids were less leery of me. I hadn't told a lie in a long time. I started to tell myself that it was a question, not a lie – Trina had asked me to her house, if not that particular day. Lying didn't seem to matter as much as it once had. I was going to see Jim!

One car, a dated Rambler, white except for its rust skirt from too many salted winter roads, collected snow in the motel parking-lot. My fist was raised for a solid knock, when the door opened. Jim, dark circles under his eyes, unshaven, beautiful, was really there. His eyes, like mine, brimmed with tears. He fluffed some of the snow out of my hair, then raked both hands through it, pulling me into the room. The door slammed and Jim slammed me against it. His knuckles rapped hard against the wood. He pinned me against the door with his hips. After months of distance, he couldn't get close enough.

His clothes looked like those he had worn when he had sung 'Wild Child' on the *Smothers Brothers Show*. Beneath the heavy odour of the suede jacket, Jim's body smelled rank, like he had been on the road for days. 'Did you drive across country?' I asked before I worked out he couldn't possibly have made the drive since the last time we spoke.

'No, I flew to Boston, then drove up.' His voice was soft and faraway.

When my watch snagged in my coat lining, Jim tugged helpfully here and there. By contrast, he let his jacket slide down his arms in a graceful movement which climaxed with his flinging the jacket over the back of a chair like a toreador's cape.

His hands glided down my arms. He took my hands in his. A wet kiss on my ear made me shiver with pleasure. 'I need a bath,' he whispered.

Badly, I thought, and some fresh clothes. 'Have you changed since the *Smothers Show*?' I joked. Nearly a month had passed since then.

There was no sign of the expected smile. He scratched his shoulder. 'Just the beads,' he said, holding out from his collar the fine strand we had strung in Big Sur. The crystal beads for 'Crystal Ship', the orange for 'Light My Fire', the black for . . . He kissed my cheek and said, 'Undress me.'

Jim's only assistance was to sit on the edge of the bed while I pulled off his boots. He didn't bother with the game of clinging on to the inside of his boots with his toes which always ended with my falling on the floor. The dried salty snow embroidered vines on the suede. He made no effort to lift his body when I struggled with his leathers. When he didn't grab at my clothes, shyness swept me, and I decided to undress in the bathroom.

After the long six months, did he feel a little shy, too? Jim wandered out of sight. I kicked off my boots and stepped out of my jeans, then sat on the edge of the tub watching it fill. When the water stopped running, Jim returned. He closed my hand around the cake of sandalwood soap from San Francisco. Jim cared so little for possessions, I was caught in my own feelings of pleasure over his saving the memento of our meeting, until I met his eyes. He needed a ceremonial cleansing like that first one. He held his body so rigidly, my own shoulders ached in empathy. 'What's happened? How long has this been going on?'

'Could we talk later?' he asked, brushing my lips lightly with his.

As he stepped into the tub, he grabbed my arm for the balance he had never before needed. He lowered himself so slowly into the water, I dipped my free hand in to test the temperature. The water felt comfortably warmer than my skin. Whatever pained Jim was in him. I flicked off the bathroom fixture. Light spilled in from the other room to soften the harsh tile. I kneeled by the tub, rolled a towel for a pillow. When I slipped the makeshift pillow under his head, I noticed his long hair was a nest of tangles. He closed his eyes. I pushed my sleeves up with a sigh that reverberated off the tiles. The hint of a smile briefly lit Jim's sombre face.

His body was less boyish. His shoulders were broader. I could no longer count his ribs without touching him. I didn't know how to recreate what had been a spontaneous gesture of kindness to a stranger a year and a half before. Since then, our baths had become a mutually sensual pleasure. I dipped my cupped hands into the water, let it spill over his face, and followed the water's course with my fingers. I loved the body I was touching and feared he came to tell me he wanted to die. When I asked for his promise in June, I thought it would act as a charm to keep the need from approaching. I had believed that my love alone was strong enough to hold him in the world.

My hand on his foot signalled Jim to open his eyes. The water must have been uncomfortably cool, but Jim remained motionless, watching me intently. At last, he sighed dramatically, as I had at the beginning of the task, then touched my hand without taking it. '*Nobody, not even the rain, has such small hands,*' he said softly.

I looked at my short, broad, practical hand next to his elegant one. We remained silent. I pulled the plug, embarrassed by the rude sucking sound. Jim watched the water go down the drain until he was sitting in silt.

He grabbed my hand and led me to the bed. He ripped my turtleneck over my head and smiled when I shook my hair loose. As he combed my hair with his hands, he examined the strands between his fingers. I tried to catch his gaze. 'Are you high?'

'No. I'm straight as an arrow. I'm just enjoying you. Your hair is redder without the sun. It was nearly blonde the last time I saw you.'

I laid back along the foot of the bed. After months of mailboxes and telephones, we stared at each other in disbelief as Jim stretched out on top of me. He lightly traced the lines of my face with his thumbs, then rolled off me on to his side. Jim reached behind his back with a groan, and bopped my nose with the barely opened bud of a long-stemmed white rose. Its delicate scent lingered as he let it drop in my hair.

'Happy birthday,' he kissed me gently. I fumbled for the rose in my hair. He'd brought me a white rose when he climbed through my window in Stockton for my sixteenth birthday. I wouldn't have thought Jim cared for sentimental tradition. He produced another rose with a magician's dexterity and brushed its petals over my lips, 'Happy birthday.' I raised up on my elbows to look over the wall of his body. With all my attention on Jim, I hadn't seen the bundle of white roses, their heads lost on the white pillow, their stems tucked neatly under the covers.

'Jim!' I crawled over him to gather the flowers in my hands. I could barely hold them all. 'How many are there?'

'A dozen and a half. One for every year. One to grow on.'

'Thank you. I've never gotten a bouquet of flowers before.'

'I want to be the first to give all the good things.' Jim ran his hand along the curve of my back. 'You look like one of those Impressionist paintings. Renoir.' He reached around me and produced four wrapped packages. 'How nice you never took your eyes off me! Open this one first.' I let the roses fall back against the pillow with a sweet-scented flutter.

'You *and* presents! And it's not quite my birthday.'

'I believe in long celebrations.' He set the box, just the right size and weight for a pair of hiking shoes, in my lap, then lay back on the unoccupied pillow. The paper was hand-marbled, not printed; its blue and gold swirls silky against the tooth of the paper. The plain white bow was a satiny hair ribbon.

'The roses will die before you get the box open,' he prodded.

'I don't want to tear the beautiful paper.'

'I appreciate that. I made it myself. The kitchen sink will never be the same.' No doubt. To make the marbled paper, he had to float and swirl oil paints over water. Jim prompted, 'The suspense has reached its peak and the audience is getting restless.'

'Who would know better?' I laughed, relieved his mood had

lifted and he had begun his brotherly banter. Inside the box lay a rectangular clear-crystal vase. 'Jim. Can a vase be sophisticated? I think it's the most sophisticated vase I've ever seen.' Sharp edges caught the light like a prism.

'Maybe classic. I knew you would be worried all night about those roses going thirsty.' I bounded off to the bathroom to fill the vase with water. When I lowered the stems into the vase, the roses arranged themselves. I sat them on the dresser. Jim wouldn't allow me much time to admire them, but tapped on a flat box, 'This one.'

The box held a white lawn poet's shirt. The neck and sleeves ended in fluid bias-cut ruffles five inches wide, the edges rolled and delicately hand-stitched. Jim kneeled to slip it over my head. I studied myself in the mirror on the wall opposite the bed. It looked a looser version of something Jim might wear. 'It's beautiful. Thank you.' When I caught the reflection of my arm gesturing, its grace surprised me. I crawled back on the bed to be close to Jim and moved my arm again to watch the fabric move. Charmed by the unaccustomed feeling of beauty, I repeated the movement.

'I found it in Amsterdam. I wanted to bring you Van Gogh's irises.' Jim had sent me that postcard from his European débâcle. Apparently, he was not unconscious the entire trip. 'One day, I'll take you there and at least let you visit them.'

Jim tapped on the next-to-the-smallest box. On a bed of tissue lay a hand-made book, four inches square, held together with two rings that opened and closed. With no cover or title page, in neat printing, the book began with 'She Looked So Sad in Sleep', the next page was 'The Spy'. Jim included poems or songs he had written with some thought of me, and pieces that he had written before we met, but had meaning for us, like changing the line in 'Crystal Ship' to *gentle reign*. A tear rolled off my nose and blurred the ink on *reign*.

'Should I change that back to *rain*?' Jim reached over and wiped my face with the heel of his hand.

'You can read it in a real circle. Better than Joyce,' I said. 'Because any page can be the first page. It's wonderful. Thank you. "The Spy" means more now than when you wrote it.'

Jim nodded. I hoped he would burst into song, but he said, 'Some day, there will be enough pages to make the book a wheel.' He flipped through the book and handed it back to me. 'I started to copy new poems into it, but ran out of time. I brought some paper. I'll do it tomorrow.' Looking through the pages a second time, I saw one new four-line morning song his seeking for sanctuary.

'Is this why you're here?' I asked.

Jim took the book, tore that page out, crumpled it, tossed the crumpled page over his shoulder, and put the last small box in my hand.

'This is why I'm here.'

The box was empty. I looked at the box, then at Jim's face for a clue. I was disappointed I'd lost my ability to guess his riddles. 'Too small for Van Gogh's irises.'

Jim nodded amiably. He kneeled and toyed with the fastener on the gold chain I had worn since he had given it to me when we said goodbye in LA. 'I'm sorry, even sober, I can't get it,' he said. I brought it around so I could see the clasp and opened it for him. He held out his hand and I dropped the chain with the ring into his palm. He slipped the ring off the chain and on to the little finger of his left hand, fastened the chain, and put it over his head. 'The chain was a loan,' he explained. He took the ring off his finger, placed it in the box, and closed the lid. 'I didn't do this right the first time.' He opened the box and held the ring between his thumb and index finger. His hand trembled, but his eyes looked steadily into mine, 'Will you marry me?'

I wrapped my hand around the ball of his thumb. We became one quivering animal. My tongue was too dry to wet my parched lips. I studied our hands, unable to look at Jim's face. He lifted my chin so I met his half-closed eyes and kissed me as if my mouth were a welcome new discovery.

He removed the loose silver friendship ring from my finger, and replaced it with the gold ring. The metal was warm from his hand as the friendship ring had been in San Francisco when he told me it was to keep his place. Jim wrapped his fingers tightly around mine, afraid I would rip it off and fling it in his face. 'The stone is a real emerald. I didn't want you to refuse it on principle out there on the lawn. I designed the setting.' A gracefully arched bridge, like those in Big Sur, held the stone on a wide band.

'I'm always burning bridges. About time I built one,' he said softly, then stuck his tongue out. 'That was awful! I want you to know, when you're eighteen, I'll let you go without argument.' I tilted my head like an attentive parrot. He grinned and elaborated, 'This will get you out from under your father's control, and put you under mine . . . which is enough to strike terror in mothers across the continent.'

I asked, 'Have you had a fight with Pamela?'

'Which fight?' he smiled. 'This isn't about her. I'll take care of her.'

'Sounds like a mob hit.'

Jim's smile broadened. 'I meant financially. She'll never make it on her own. I'll always care about her. We talked it out last summer. This was always an engagement ring. She knew I asked you down to LA to marry me.'

'So, you *were* planning a virginal sacrifice!' I sought to be clever while my mind ran in crazy circles.

Jim laughed for the first time. 'Well, yeah. Something in a Mayan temple.'

'This was the other way I could have stayed in Los Angeles? I love you for this offer, Jim, but when the time comes, I want a once-and-forever marriage.'

'I'm not saying ours won't be. I should have rehearsed this. During that beautiful time we had in Big Sur, I convinced myself that you were in love with me, but were too shy to tell me. I had this ring made, and invited you down to LA. I wanted to offer you the emancipation because I thought it was important to make you feel free. You don't know how many times I've rewritten that night, so that I ask you to marry me, before you ask for the promise that told me you loved me more than I have ever been loved, but as your brother. I was in shock. It's taken me all these months to know that it's okay if we love each other differently.'

Jim tightened his grip around my fingers, the stone cutting into both of us.

'When was the last time you slept?' I asked.

'Have you forgotten? I don't sleep. I pass out.'

'Jim . . .' I ran my hand through his long hair and caught the ring in its tangles. 'When was the last time you brushed your hair?' He fell back laughing, leaving a few strands of his dark hair in the ring.

'Ouch,' he said a few beats late. I fetched a comb from my bag and stood beside the bed. His hair was badly snarled underneath. 'You can cut it all off if it's easier,' he said. 'That's what I do.'

'Good thing I didn't pack scissors, then. Your hair *is* beautiful. I love it long. It's just in a bad mood.' I worked gently at the mats with my comb. He leaned back against me. 'Want me to do this later?' I was afraid the fussing and tugging, no matter how careful I was, taxed him. He shook his head slightly, and sat up, eyes closed. When I finished, Jim ran both hands through his hair and shook his head. It needed washing.

Jim objected. 'We'll do that later. Come to bed. I want to hold you.' The sweet feeling of beauty that had come with the shirt stayed with me as I slipped under the covers Jim raised for me. Sharing a pillow and half the bed, we lay facing each with a hand on the other's hip. Jim's eyes fluttered, then closed. His head dropped a little closer to mine. I listened to our breathing, concentrating on stillness, afraid if I moved, I would wake the lions that stole his sleep. He stirred once, nuzzling against my chest like a kitten drawn to my warmth. In the hour Jim slept, I changed my answer to his question a dozen times. Jim woke slowly, cosy and content. He found my mouth without opening his eyes, and ended the kiss with a small yawn. 'Will you marry me?'

'We need to talk when you're rested.' I was the one who needed the time.

He sighed back against the pillow. 'Don't suppose they have room service?'

'Not unless the guy in the office has a hotplate.'

Jim grumbled as he shaved, grumbled as he dressed. His grumbling fell into a pleasant rhythm and by the time he was looking for his car keys, he was singing Willie Dixon's 'Backdoor Man'. In the car, Jim turned the ignition and it grumbled. 'Oh, shit.'

'Dead battery?'

'That wouldn't make any noise. If the engine's like me it's too damn cold to start. How do you stand this fucking weather?' He turned the key again.

'Was this the only rental car left?'

'I left my driver's licence in LA. Nobody would rent me a car without one. There was this one girl behind the counter who had every record, wanted my autograph more than anything, probably practised kissing with my picture.' Jim grinned. 'But she wouldn't rent me a car without my licence. All was not lost. She loaned me her car.'

'Loaned?' I couldn't help raising my eyebrows with my voice.

Jim only raised one eyebrow. 'Are you implying I fucked her for it?'

'That never entered my mind. I thought you might have stolen it.' I'd wondered about his mysterious series of cars.

'Joyridin', yeah. What a rush!' He hammered the wheel with his hands. 'I did that once when I was sixteen. An old burgundy Mercury. The guy who owned it smoked fancy Cuban cigars. I found one in the glove compartment and had to try it. Got so damn dizzy on that heady cigar, I nearly crashed. That's why I love a good cigar. The smell of that old Merc. Holds a little of that rush.'

I looked at him wondering if the story were true. I'd never witnessed his smoking a cigar. 'Did you get caught?'

'Nope.' He sang to the tune of 'Backdoor Man', *Drove into DC and got myself a whore . . .*' He made up verses, until on the fourth try, the engine rattled. Jim let it warm. Downtown was a one-way street that looped around a narrow block and gave you a chance to leave town again. Not much was open. Jim had just killed the poor Rambler's engine when a small band of teenagers straggled by.

Jim asked, 'That's him, isn't it, the kid in the fringed jacket?'

I look up, startled to see Brian Le Blanc hunched against the cold in the midst of the group of kids. I'd give him being able to pick out Nick Isaak. I had told Jim he reminded me of Kurt Russell, but I'd never described Brian in any way. Incredulous, I asked, 'How did you know?'

'I know you.' I asked if he wanted to meet my new friend. 'No.' He inhaled slowly. 'Is he what we have to talk about tonight?'

Brian and his friends turned right at the corner, probably heading to the one small music store in town. If it were closed, they would just cover ground. You could clock a lot of miles in a small town with no place to go. Jim opened his door which let out a plaintive creak. He slid about three feet, making good use of the balance he didn't seem to have a couple hours before. I pulled his door closed for him to save him the slide back. I climbed out cautiously, avoiding the ice patches. We met on the dry bit of sidewalk close to the buildings.

'Chances are, we'll meet somebody I know. Are you Jim Morrison?'

'Doesn't he have brown eyes?' Jim blinked his blue-grey eyes. 'Don't suppose you have a college handy.'

'Colby. Look rich.'

'Do you have any idea how much this coat costs that I'm freezing my ass in?' He petted the suede fondly.

'Are you rich?'

'Was before I bought this coat.' He put his arm around my waist, then retrieved it self-consciously.

Booths lined the left side and a counter ran down the right of the little café. It belonged to the father of a friend in my class, who I hoped hadn't been cornered into waitressing Friday night. I didn't recognize any of the farmers or shoe factory workers, with their caps still on and their wives with caps of tightly curled hair. 'Must have been a special on perms this week,' I whispered to Jim.

Jim turned back to the door to laugh, and was wiping his eyes when the waitress, a senior at school, beckoned us with laminated menus. She seated us at the next-to-the-last booth. 'Good-evening. Cold enough for you?'

I knew Jim was thinking, 'She didn't seriously ask that?' I imagined the locals answered with a succinct, 'Pretty near,' or 'Not hardly.'

'Sure is,' I said before Jim decided to say something that would send her screaming into the kitchen.

'Warm you up with some coffee?' With her hair pulled back into a ponytail and bangs halfway up her forehead, she looked as if she had time-travelled from the fifties. I wondered how she had developed the style of a hard-boiled waitress at eighteen.

Jim was red, his cheeks about to pop. 'He'll have a cup,' I ordered for him since there was no beer on the menu. 'And I'll have tea, please.' When she whisked efficiently around the counter, I begged,

261

'Play the game.' The small-town reality was that if Jim berated the waitress, it would be telegraphed back to my mother by Monday. I didn't have to recognize a face for one of them to know whose daughter I was.

'Happy to.' He lifted his hand, to make room for the coffee-cup. 'Thanks,' he said in his sweetest voice, flashing his delectable smile. The waitress was temporarily mesmerized, transfixed by his beauty. 'I'll have a hamburger.'

A safe choice for an omnivore in a little diner. Flustered, it took the poor girl a few minutes to find the pencil in her pocket. I ordered a grilled cheese. Gooey processed cheese on white bread. That or mashed potatoes and limp green beans were the winter vegetarian choices in town. Vegetarianism was frowned on as a bizarre cultist practice. Best not to let on that you were one by special requests.

'Do you think she recognized you?' I asked Jim when she released him from a long stare.

'No, I think she wants to fuck me.'

'Mutual?'

'No. I'm saving myself for my honeymoon.'

I asked him, 'Did you really find a whore in DC when you were sixteen?'

'A whore would have scared me to death at sixteen. Met my first whore in Ensenada when I was maybe twenty, but I couldn't afford her. She gave me a considerable discount 'cause I was so young and handsome.' Sounded like a good short story. 'What's the matter? Didn't like the song?' He whisper-sang a few lines from 'Love Street'.

I felt embarrassed that I'd assumed the song was about Pamela. 'If I tell you it was kind of nasal you might get the idea I have the album.' He never did break down and send my a copy of the album, so I traded a friend two albums for it.

He winked. 'Be a better short story. Yeah. Maybe I should write one about going joyriding. I haven't written a short story in a long time.'

'Maybe you could weave the two together.'

'I love your mind. I just wrote a song about that. He sang a line softly. 'Remind me to sing it sometime. Tell me about him.'

'Brian. I call Pamela, Pamela, not her. You call Brian, Brian, not him.'

'If I can figure that out. I've missed talking with you. Nobody talks like you. It's good on the phone, but better in person. Tell me about Brian.'

'He and his mom moved up from Worcester. That's Massachusetts. As outsiders, I think we were drawn to each other. And he's . . .'

'Yeah, *spiders across the stars*,' he interrupted to quote Kerouac on those who burn to live from *On the Road*. 'That's how I spotted him. There were a couple in that little parade, but you have a weakness for blonds the way I do for redheads.'

'It's not how he looks,' I insisted, then flashed on the first rush I felt when I saw the sunlight in Brian's hair. 'We just hit it off.'

'Love at first sight?'

I squirmed against the green vinyl. 'What do I know about love?'

'Quite a lot. You're just terrified of the word. You love mankind, the earth, probably the universe in some exponential way only Einstein could unfold.' Jim took a minute to smile about that. I'd picked up the word *exponential* from him. It made me sound so bright, because I could use it in sentences nearly as well as he. The irony rested in my lack of any mathematical ability. He began again, more earnestly, 'And you love me more completely than I've ever been loved. I can say *love* so easily when it doesn't mean anything. *Hello, I love you*,' he sang in a low growl. 'Sure, baby, I love you,' he whispered breathlessly as he probably had to many young fans. 'See? But really, I only love writing and,' he counted, touching his thumb to each finger, then adding the thumb of the other hand, 'six people.'

'Who's on the list?'

He repeated the process with names. 'You, Anne, Andy, Ray, Pamela. A friend from the old days. I like a few other things. A few other people quite a lot. How did you meet?'

'In the hall at school. We looked at each other. He's shy. I'm shy. It took us a while to say anything. We pass notes. The first note he handed me began with 'People Are Strange'.'

'Did you tell him you gave me the idea for the song?'

'Your life gave you the idea for the song.'

'It was about that conversation we had. About being the constant stranger. I told you when I first sang it over the phone to you. Don't you remember? I want you to remember everything I ever said to you. Did you tell him you know me?'

'No. I've never told anyone about you. We are private.'

'Yeah. I feel that way, too. Well, Pamela and Bill Graham know.'

'My mother and Mr Graham.'

Jim returned to Brian. 'Do you sit next to each other in class? I would have killed to sit next to you in class.'

'We don't have any classes together. We have lunch together sometimes. We pass each other a lot coming and going from the vice-principal's office.'

'What are you doing in the vice-principal's office? You sweet thing! Are you organizing protests and sit-down strikes?' Jim teased.

'And "Wild Child" wasn't a good ribbing? There was that time when the vice-principal told me to leave Lenny Bruce at home. I think he looks in my locker to see what books to ban.'

'I'm so proud of my little girl.' Jim swelled in cartoon proportions.

I decided to ignore him. 'Mostly though, he calls me out of my favourite class to torment me. I look like everything he thinks is undermining the country. He's determined to convince me that Gandhi was a fool, King was a communist, and Bob Dylan can't sing.'

'How's the conversion coming?'

'His or mine?'

'That's my girl,' he patted my hand as our food arrived. Jim edged the pink and green tomato out from under the bun, surveyed the remains suspiciously, then took a bite. 'Back to Brian,' he began with a full mouth. 'What's he in there for? Is he a hippie pinko radical subversive like you?'

'*And* has the longest hair of any boy in school. Boys' hair is not supposed to be past their collars, so he wears T-shirts and wins a couple inches.'

'Yahoo! I missed all that. When I was in school, I had short hair.

The Beatles hadn't landed. Did I ever show you a picture?' I nodded. He continued, 'In college, it was my father who thought my
hair was girlish. He wouldn't let me in the house unless it was what
he considered a suitable length for a man. If he saw a picture of me
now, he'd probably think I was a transvestite.' Jim blinked hard as
if the lights suddenly bothered him. 'Does Brian do drugs?'

'Not around me.'

Jim laughed, 'You have that effect on people.'

'Are you on something? You've done a one-eighty since I first
saw you.'

'Just you. Remember? You are my favourite drug. I get high on
you. When I got back from San Francisco after we met, I was high
for days. Pamela kept asking, *What are you on? I want some.* I
told her I wasn't sharing. *Stoned Immaculate!*'

When he told me the same story a year before, he only said,
people asked. More honestly, it was Pamela. 'I don't know where
you'd get drugs here. There's a little pot around, but I haven't seen
much else. A little evidence of harder drugs. No word about acid.
If I were interested, I would've found out. Not easy. We're sort of
isolated.'

'That's for sure. Forget airplanes, you can't get a bus or a
train here.'

'Makes a thumb the only way to run away, and after that
incident . . .'

'What incident?' he asked.

'I told you.'

'Well, tell me again.'

'I was hitchhiking to Portland, which is,' I hesitated, 'south-east
from here.' Jim gave me a look that let me know he wouldn't
trust me to find our way back to the motel, let alone Portland.
I pretended I hadn't noticed. '*Because* I heard that Janis Joplin
was going to be there. I felt so homesick, I thought I'd die if I
didn't see her. Not only did I see her sing a lot, but it seemed like
I'd see her almost every time I went to San Francisco. Once, in a
bookstore . . .'

'What was she buying?'

'She had James Agee's . . .' I drew a blank. 'The one published
after he died . . .'

265

Jim nodded. 'Good for her. Go on.'

'Yeah, I love his writing, but no one can see inside someone's creative mind. I felt uneasy about the editor putting the book together.'

'Nobody better fuck with my writing after I check out. I'll haunt them.' He laughed. 'But I meant go on with your story.'

'Oh. Janis asked if she could have the beads I was wearing. She gave me her twisted silver bangle bracelet in trade. I loved it. Somebody stole it from my locker at school. In Stockton. Not here. Here, I share a locker with a girl from this place for troubled teens. She was in that group of kids. She loans me shoes when I forget you're supposed to wear these clunky boots and change into shoes at school.' I'd babbled off again. 'People keep saying Janis is fat. I think she just wasn't blessed with cheekbones.'

Jim grinned. 'I think she's very attractive.'

'And a Capricorn.' I suddenly remembered Jim's telling me that.

'You were hitchhiking . . .' he prompted me back to the story he intended I return to earlier.

'Oh.' I blushed and he tugged my hair in his big brother fashion, making it feel all right to be distracted. 'I got a ride with a couple. Couples always seem safer, but this time, the woman pulled a knife on me.'

He dropped his limp hamburger. 'Shit! You never told me this. What happened?'

'She told me to hand over my purse and shoes.'

'Shoes? Who would want *your* shoes?' Jim laughed. 'I mean . . .'

'Goes to show she wasn't in her right mind.'

'I'm sorry,' he smiled. 'I know you have very,' he paused, searching for a description, '*ethical* shoes. She didn't hurt you?'

'They just dropped me at the turnpike.'

'Did you get to see Janis?'

'No. I was in fear of frostbite. A nice guy gave me a ride back. He even loaned me a pair of socks. I washed them and mailed them to him.'

Jim shook his head. 'Probably didn't miss much. Janis's performances have become unpredictable. Mine are worse, so I can say that. I have a show in New York in a couple weeks. I decided I'm

266

going to *be there*, not just show up. The six months I promised Ray will be up, and I want to give him that as a going-away present. Want to honeymoon in New York? We could go early. Maybe they have a canvas of Vincent's irises at the Metropolitan to hold you until Amsterdam.'

'Jim . . .'

'So, you love Brian.' The cold grilled cheese crawled down my throat. I helped it down with some water. Jim guided a French fry into my mouth. 'At least they're edible. Help yourself. I'm not going to eat them.'

The waitress returned to offer us dessert and slapped the check on top of Jim's hand. She let her hand rest there, while she hoped everything was satisfactory, ignoring our barely disturbed plates. The café was one of those places where people took their checks up to the register, but she offered to make the trip herself. With the change, she included a scrap of paper with her phone number. As Jim stood up, he touched her back lightly to edge her out of his way. Goose bumps ran down her arms. When Jim reached around her to take my hand, she flashed me a look that was meant to melt me into a puddle on the floor.

On the sidewalk, I asked, 'Does that bother you?'

'Not like that. She just thought I was the best piece of meat in town. She probably hasn't met Brian,' he interjected, bumping my hip. 'What bothers me is when thousands of women in an audience want to fuck me.'

I giggled and leaned against the wall. 'Do you remember when I ran after you that first night in San Francisco and you asked, *Wanna* . . . Well, you know. I wasn't quite sure what it meant. I knew it was something sexual, but not what base.' Jim toyed with a button on my coat. 'Why does that part of fame still bother you. It's just some fantasy.'

He grunted and stepped back. 'They're like vampires. Bleed me dry. Don't know what's so special about my cock that they all want to swallow it.'

How gross! 'Well, Jim, I don't have any means of comparison. Yours is the only one I've seen. But you make your fans sound more like cannibals than vampires.'

'We *do* have some things to talk about,' he grinned and leaned

267

closer to whisper, 'I'm kinda relieved you and Brian haven't gotten around to show and tell.' He jumped a patch of ice and opened the door for me. The car didn't complain quite so bitterly when Jim turned the key. While we waited for the engine to warm up, Jim asked, 'What do kids do for fun around here? The freaks I mean.'

'Oh, look for their own kind. If we can find a house where parents are out, we play Jimi Hendrix to see if he can melt the snow. Walk. A friend of a friend has use of a car sometimes, so we can drive. We spent an evening skidding on ice in a parking-lot.'

'Sounds good to me. For kicks, I used to like to drive winding roads with my eyes closed. Stoned. High. I don't think it occurred to me until just now that there could have been oncoming traffic. There's nothing like an immortal acid high. Where's good ice?'

Using no judgment at all, I directed him to one of the bigger parking-lots above the motel. Jim drove much faster than we had and he just gave up control, letting the car careen. 'Well, that was fun,' he said after a few runs, crestfallen he hadn't made the car roll.

'Imagine if they let you design your own Disneyland.'

'Whew! Have to have a Dante's *Inferno* ride.' Jim shook his head. 'Wouldn't be any fun, though, if the risk weren't real. Fuck!' he said suddenly, and threw the car door open, stumbled out, and vomited what little dinner he had eaten. He washed out his mouth with snow a few times and took a deep breath before climbing back into the car. 'You were right about the fall of the Roman Empire. Got into doing that to keep my weight down on the tour, now I can't keep food down very reliably when I want to.'

I rubbed his shoulder. 'Do I have to ask you to try not to do that any more?'

'No. I think I figured that one out on my own.'

Instead of heading back to the motel, Jim went back into town and veered right. 'The white church in your poem,' Jim said. He pulled around the simple white church and parked. 'I need to walk on that footbridge you wrote about.' The wooden bridge was painted white and frosted fresh snow white. Halfway across, he brushed the snow from the railing and leaned his arms on it, eyes on the frozen river below.

'I have an incredible urge to walk the railing. I like the way it sways.'

'Would you mind waiting until the river thaws?'

Jim turned to face me. 'How do you make a church with fingers?' He referred to the imagery in the poem I'd have wished I'd never read him, except it brought him there.

'It was just a way of saying we held hands, you know how you lace your fingers. There's this children's game.' I demonstrated by lacing our fingers together, making a steeple of our pointing fingers, and doors of our thumbs, *Here's the church and here's the steeple. Open the door and see all the people.* I wiggled my fingers.

'Oh, yeah. I remember my sister doing that. In the car. Going someplace,' he said thoughtfully, nodding and keeping my hand locked in his. He studied the lacy-white trees, the clapboard houses, the brick shoe factories. Making his own notes on winter in a New England town. 'Brian's hand would fit yours better than mine,' he said, tightening his grip until it hurt.

'Actually, his hands are bigger than yours.'

'I'm so jealous I want to scream. I want to be the only one. I know it's unfair to ask when we're apart. But if we were together . . . Say *yes*,' he begged. 'Come with me. Please.'

'Let's go get naked and warm,' I said, without a complete thought in my head.

16

---·◆·---

Trainyard Nursing Penitentiary

Naked and warm was wonderful. Jim fell asleep, his face against my stomach, and woke me later with wet kisses on my thigh. 'I'm ready to listen, if you're ready to talk,' he said, bringing the covers up with him. He rested his head against mine on the pillow.

'What happened, Jim?' I asked. 'How long has it been since you've taken a bath?'

After a long pause, he said with a smile, 'Didn't we decide it was just before the Smothers show?' He frowned. 'Nothing's wrong, baby, except I miss you.' He rubbed his forehead with the palms of his hands. 'Gotta take a crap,' he said, stumbling to the bathroom.

I heard his retching, and followed him. I put my arm around his waist and held his hair back. He was racked in dry heaves until he was so dizzy I could barely keep him on his feet. Just as I was about to suggest he sit on the floor before he fell, Jim straightened painfully, and rested his face against the cool tile wall.

'Sorry,' he rasped.

'You don't have to apologize for being sick.'

He shivered. 'This is one hell of a fucking cold place.'

I walked him back to bed, his arm leaden across my shoulders. He crawled into bed and lay on his side. I settled in against

271

his back and stroked his head. My body seemed too small to warm him.

'I thought you were in pain earlier. What's wrong, Jim? Do you need a doctor?'

'No, I guess I have the flu.' With his thumbnail, he scratched the vertical furrow that ran up his forehead. 'I feel like I've been hit dead centre with a wrecking ball.'

'Thank heavens.'

Jim chuckled and winced, 'Some comfort.'

'I'm just relieved it's the flu. I was afraid it was a death rattle.' He reached back and squeezed my hip. I stroked his head. 'What can I do, Jim?'

'What you're doing feels great.' He patted me gently.

'Wanna see if my giving you back the ring helps?'

Jim began a long laugh ending in a low moan. 'I want you to be Mrs Morrison. Unless you want to keep your own initials. I'm real fond of your LA at the bottom of your letters. Just promise not to say anything funny until the room stops spinning. Come around so I can see you. Talk to me.'

I asked the question that plagued me. 'Can we be what we are?'

Jim smiled. 'Can we be anything else? Are we waiting for Godot? Our marriage can be anything we want it to be. At the end of the year, we can renew our vows, or dissolve them. Either way, we'll have been blessed with an amazing year.' He lifted my bangs from my eyes. 'I love you. Will you marry me?'

I played with his hair a while, too. 'I'm having trouble picturing the Pamela that inspired "Five to One" accepting your choosing me over her.'

'The fight we had was about you. She was used to my fucking around, even though we fought about that, but it was the first time I told her I was in love with someone else. When she cooled down, I showed her your letters, told her about you, and she said you were better for me than she was. After all, I'd never asked her to marry me. She asked if she and I could be friends, and I thought so. We would just change. You and I would be lovers. She and I would be friends.'

He once told me they had taken out a marriage licence, though he had filled in his half as Elvis. Maybe she had asked him. 'Dosey Doe,' I said, drawing the symbol for infinity with my finger on his chest.

'That upsets you? I would like to stay friends with her. I don't have to if you'd rather I didn't. It would save me a lot of wear and tear.'

'Jim, you were in shock when you found out I loved you, however it is I love you. It's not just as a brother, because I'm drawn to you physically. But I'm still trying to grasp that you don't love me the way I thought you did. In "Wild Child" you say you love me like my father . . .'

'I've never loved anyone in such a complex way. I do want to take care of you, protect you, teach you about life. In that way, I love you like a father. My old soul loves yours, the way you understand me. And I love you carnally.'

'If you wanted me,' I asked shyly, 'why did you turn me down when I threw myself at you in that swimming pool?' I sat up. 'It's hard for me, Jim, that my father treats me like I'm Mary Magdalene and you treat me like the Virgin Mary. What's so good with Brian,' getting to the point at last, 'is that he thinks it's fine if I'm just trying to figure out how to be seventeen.'

'You still have a couple days to figure that out.' Jim held my hand. 'Brian sounds sweet. I don't think of you like that. The reason I told you I didn't think that was right for us then, was because I was treating you the way I wished someone had treated me. I think it's a lovely thing for a woman to share her first time with her husband.'

'I thought you were kidding. Is that why we haven't made love?'

'We've made love. I told you, we make love every time I touch you. That swim with you was the most erotic experience I've ever had. Like an orgasm that lasted for minutes. When I am an old man, it will be the physical experience I'll cherish. I dream about it a lot. What's painful is I wake up and you aren't there. That's why I'm here. I can't take it any more.' Like the line in the new poem.

'You really want to marry a virgin?' Men and their double standards. 'Why, if you find it so beautiful, didn't you share your virginity with a virgin bride?'

273

'There's a condition,' I said, realizing I was accepting his proposal.

'Ouch!' He laughed and pulled me down to him. 'I'll give monogamy a try. Or at least discretion. Do you want me to give up drugs and drink and . . .'

I interrupted, 'I don't want to lose my family. I can't run away with you. I need my mother's approval.'

He waited. 'That's it?'

'That's a big thing,' I said.

'Your mother likes me. We'll just leave out the part about my being a drunken womanizing rock cock until after the ceremony. Then I'll fly her down to New York, give her earplugs, a front row seat, and break it to her as gently as possible just how this sensitive poet prostitutes himself. Does she have a strong heart?'

I giggled. 'When are you going to make peace with the music in your head? Why do you think it's there if you aren't supposed to do something with it?'

Jim looked beyond me to the ceiling. 'My current theory of the universe runs along the lines that you're my peek at heaven, Pamela my descent into hell, and music, music is purgatory.'

Sharply at 7 a.m., I startled awake, escaping from an immediately forgotten dream. I called home to ask Mama if she would beg off the planned shopping trip with my father to the naval base in New Brunswick so we could talk. Though she didn't ask why, I added, 'Jim's here. He's asked me to marry him.'

'Then we do need to talk,' she said stiffly.

I watched women fussing with their men in public with decided disdain. Yet I stood by the car in the parking-lot outside our room, bundling Jim with my muffler and arranging his hair over his collar.

'I can cut it if it will make a better impression,' he offered.

'Oh, that won't matter to Mama. She'll just wonder why such a handsome man wants to hide his face. It's me. I'm sorry. I just can't stop touching you. I hate it when I see women do that. Like men were children.'

'I wasn't complaining. I'm finding it is possible to get a hard-on when my ass is freezing.'

'Let's leave that out of the casual conversation.'

274

'Don't worry. I'm great with mothers. I won't mention my ass or cock once. I'll keep my hands in plain sight at all times. She'll be thinking what beautiful grandchildren we could make for her. It's this odd thing mothers can do. They can think of grandchildren without thinking of sex.'

I looked up at him. 'Have you done this before?'

'No. Never been in this situation.' He shivered. 'You're the only one I ever asked to marry. I'll improvise.'

We drove down to the stone church, turned on to the back road to Norridgewock, up past the town library on the right and Margaret Chase Smith's home on the left, down where you could catch glimpses of the frozen Kennebec River through the bare trees. There were a few houses on alternating sides of the unmarked two-lane road, mostly painted white, differentiated by the colour of the shutters.

'I have this incredible sense of *déjà vu*. I've been here before in your letters. That's your aunt and uncle's house,' he pointed to the narrow two-storey clapboard house and its train of asphalt and shingle outbuildings.

Jim pulled into the next driveway as if he had visited me there a dozen times. 'That's my horse.' Gypsy was a furry buckskin with icicles in her dark mane, straining at the fence to greet me. 'She has a nice stable, but prefers the outdoor life. If you get close to her, she'll grab a finger and hold it for a carrot ransom.'

'She bites?' A car width away, he hid his hands in his pants' pockets.

'No. Just holds on. I'll introduce you later.'

We announced ourselves with the traditional stomping of the snow off our boots. My mother opened the door for us, shivering a little. We were three cold and nervous people. 'Nice to see you again, Jim,' my mother said, closing the door behind us.

Jim smiled his smile to ingratiate himself to mothers. 'Thank you,' he said, taking her arthritic hand gently, not to shake, but to hold as long as she would let him.

My little mutt Joey made a dash for Jim. 'Remember me?' He picked her up and scratched her ears just the way she liked. He set her down and gave my parents' German Shepherd a solid pat. 'How you doing, girl?'

My mother offered Jim coffee. We all sat around the little dinette with the plastic wood-grain table-top and uncomfortable chairs. Jim looked cool, but dumped cream and sugar into his coffee. He reached across the table to light my mother's cigarette.

My mother must have had a hundred questions running through her mind, but, I thought, was too well-bred a Yankee to ask any of them. She adjusted her glasses, wiped the lipstick from the corners of her mouth, and straightened her already erect posture.

Jim spoke in his cultured Southern gentleman's voice. 'I guess it's not much of a surprise to you that I'm in love with Linda.' He never got around to calling me Linda before. 'This separation has been hard on . . .' *Hard on*, even in a different context, made me giggle like a twelve-year-old. Jim stepped lightly on my toe under the table. '. . . both of us.' Fortunately, my mother had never heard the words in their sexier context, and was focused on Jim. 'We'd like very much to have your approval of our marriage.'

My mother's lips tightened. She adjusted her glasses again. 'Did you spend the night together last night?'

The directness of her question startled me. Jim answered, 'Yes.'

'My daughter led me to believe, when we talked about her relationship with you this time last year, that you were just friends.'

'We were friends. I have always treated your daughter with respect. I care deeply for her. This separation made our feelings clearer.'

My mother asked, 'How old are you, Jim?

'Twenty-two last month,' Jim said immediately. Math would never be a waterfall for me, but even I could calculate that if he were born in 1943, he was twenty-five, but he was right in his assessment that the difference in our ages would be a problem.

'That makes you more than five years older than Linda.' Better than eight years and, I counted on my fingers, five weeks. 'Why are you interested in such a young girl?'

'I understand your concern about the difference in our ages. I didn't set out to fall in love with a teenager. You know your daughter, though. I've never met a woman who was my intellectual equal. Ginger . . . *Linda's* bright and talented and funny. And none of that speaks to those intangible things that make a man love a woman.'

Jim's ease with improvisation was breathtaking. Relaxed and believable, he showed no sign of the man who had lain in a foetal position the night before.

'She's not a woman, yet,' my mother corrected him. 'I like you very much, Jim. I know that my daughter's IQ is in the genius range. I've had it literally thrown in my face on more than one occasion when I had conferences to discuss why she isn't living up to her potential. I usually say that they are just using the wrong yardstick.'

Jim laughed, 'Yeah, schools don't know what to do with creative minds.'

'*But,*' she continued, 'I don't think that means she should drop out of school at not quite seventeen and marry. I would rather we had this conversation a couple years from now. Why the hurry?'

'Well, it's not feasible for me to live here, so the natural solution is to have Linda return to California with me.'

'If you love each other,' my mother said through tight lips, 'marriage can wait.'

'Are you aware of what is going on between Linda and her father?'

I couldn't believe Jim asked that. I nudged his boot with mine.

'I know they lock horns,' she said. 'They look at the world so differently.'

'It's taking its toll on Linda.'

'It's taking its toll on her father, too. You don't throw families away. You have this romantic notion of carrying her away like a knight in shining armour. What happens if you're disillusioned with this romantic notion six months or a year down the line?'

Jim didn't hesitate. 'I love Linda. I'm never *not* going to love her. I'll always take good care of her. She can finish school in Los Angeles if she wants to, but she could pass a high-school equivalency test with her eyes closed – as long as they don't count too much on spelling.' He smiled his most charming smile. 'To make her plod through high-school is unnecessary. She should be in art school.'

Were Jim's debating trophies collecting dust in his parents' attic? I'd watched his temper flare under pressure, but when it was so important for us, he spoke softly and confidently. We hadn't discussed any of that. I liked his idea of my abandoning high-school for art, and hoped it wasn't merely a part of his sales pitch.

'I'll have to talk this over with her father. It's not my decision to make. Jim can talk with your father tonight.'

'Fine by me,' Jim said easily. 'Do we have your blessing if your husband agrees? That's what's important to Linda.'

Her feelings wouldn't matter up against my father's. I was anxious to talk privately with Jim. I knew he felt he could manoeuvre my father the way he had my mother. I wanted to tell him he had won the battle, but lost the war.

'Let's take Gypsy for a walk.'

'I thought her name was Joey.' At the sound of her name, Joey threw herself at Jim again.

'Gypsy's the horse.'

'You *walk* your horse?' Jim asked.

'She injured her knee on some farm equipment last fall. I like to keep her moving, but she doesn't need to carry my weight around.'

I found some weatherproof boots for Jim that cramped his toes, a warmer jacket that stopped short of his wrists, and gloves that were plain ugly. I broke a few carrots into my pocket. The dogs gambolled through the snow out to the stable. Gypsy stuck her head in, but, as always, wouldn't cross the threshold. I slipped a plain bridle over her ears.

Jim stroked her velvety muzzle, and barely flinched when she grabbed his knuckle. I handed him a carrot. She traded him his index finger for it. 'I think she's the only horse I've seen with a sense of humour,' I said. 'She really thinks that's funny.' I struck out through the newly fallen snow towards the woods behind the stable.

'This is what you do?' Jim asked, stopping a few yards behind me. 'You, with no sense of direction, walk in the woods with no sun. What if snow covers your tracks?'

'There's a fairly clear path ahead. And Tanya, the German Shepherd, has a great sense of direction. I got lost a few times in the summer when all this was dense green. All I have to say is, "Let's go home," and Tanya wags away.'

Jim Morrison at the Hollywood Bowl/Photofest (Henry Diltz)

Jim Morrison stands among a group at the original Hard Rock Café in the skid row area of downtown Los Angeles, 1969/Corbis-Bettmann (Henry Diltz)

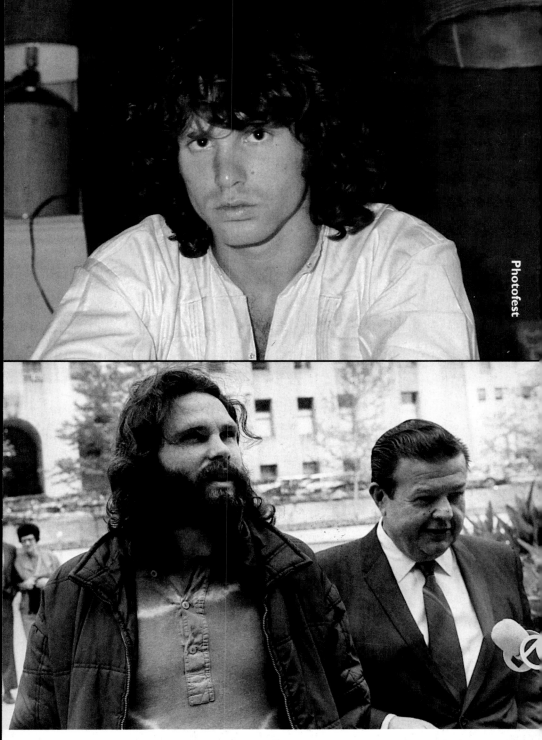

Jim Morrison and attorney Max Fink as they arrive at the Los Angeles Federal Building to appear before the U.S. Commissioner for extradition proceedings to Florida, 1969, Los Angeles/UPI-Corbis-Bettmann

1968, Los Angeles/Corbis-Bettmann (Henry Diltz)

The band poses for their album cover inside the Morrison Hotel, 1969, Los Angeles/Corbis-Bettmann (Henry Diltz)

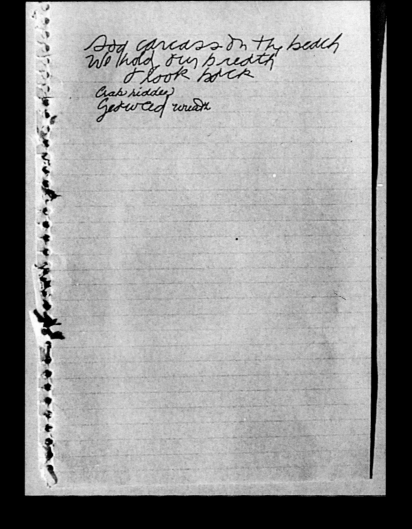

Dog carcass on the beach
We hold our breath
& look back
Crab ridden
Seaweed wreath

**A page Jim Morrison gave Linda Ashcroft from his notebook—their
shared writing in Santa Cruz, November, 1967/Collection: Linda Ashcroft**

Watching The Skies
J.M. / L.A. / D.H.

J I am a brother of the skies
L it wanders over earth
J O thou joy the realms of God
D shed leisured what they new worlds

J Since you fled to that distant shore
L its dreamcoat of our last embrace
J The whisper of foaming sands
D Recalled your morning grace

J Come back to my Baby
L (come on back around)
Come back to me, baby
(come on back around)

J Together we confess the stars
D it only make it alone
L How can you say you won't return?
J My heart is if turn to stone

Repeat 1st

Siddhartha

The song Jim Morrison, Dennis Hopper, and Linda Ashcroft wrote in an hour in a Los Angeles parking lot on a hot August night, 1969/Collection: Linda Ashcroft

Globe Photos (Jay Thompson)

We walked, the dogs bounding ahead of us, Gypsy crowding us in the narrow path that was the remnants of a logging road. Years before, my uncle had sold off the hardwood. The loggers had abandoned huge stumps. Bracken sprawled over them. Their shapes were softened by the snow in winter and covered with luscious raspberries in the summer. I showed Jim deer tracks and rabbit tracks where the dogs hadn't obliterated them with their sniffing and wagging.

Jim asked, 'No bears?'

'Not any more. All but my bears would be napping for the winter.'

'*You* have bears?'

I nodded to the clump of trees in front of us where I kept my snow sculptures. I picked the pine whose lower branches were cut away, giving headroom for the mother polar bear, and protection from new snowfall. The mother arched her neck and the two snow cubs were pushed against each other. Jim crept up on them as if he were afraid to startle them. I never liked Jim so well as that moment. My love for him doubled. He squatted down in front of them. Caressed the ear of the closest twin. 'Do they have names?' I stood behind Jim. He rocked back against my boots, and reached behind to stroke my thighs. 'Where did you get the idea?'

'Who could resist all this free sculpting material? But to try sculpting at all, from a book by Shelby Hearon called *Armadillo in the Grass*. I bought it because of the line drawing on the cover. It's a beautiful little book about the differences in the way men and women experience the world. The woman in the book wants to learn to sculpt a particular possum. Not *essence* of possum. Her husband is a professor writing a history book. Anaïs Nin wrote that the very personal becomes universal. Men tend to look at things from the other way.' I remembered when we met, I was attracted to drawing the essence of things, but the need to be very specific struck like lightning that summer. 'I'm off on some tangent, aren't I?'

'Nope. I keep trying to write things that go beyond the personal to somehow explain the world, but my most successful writing is the very personal. My love poems. Yeah. So . . . I must have a feminine sensibility.'

He stood slowly, fixed on the bear cub he liked best. 'Doesn't it kill you that they won't last?'

'My ego wants a professional out here snapping shots to blow up into eight-by-ten glossies to leave out on the coffee-table for people to drool over, but most of me likes they will water this pine in the spring.'

I scratched Gypsy under her forelock. She nudged my carrot-filled pocket. I edged one out from its depths, so she could pretend she'd stolen it. The five us walked back down the road. Jim was humming, occasionally interjecting a sung line. The horse, back in her pasture, kicked up her heels. I returned her bridle to its hook. You could see our breath in the cold, still air.

'We could board her,' Jim said softly of my horse. 'I thought I caught a tear in your eye when you watched her run. You don't have to give her up to be with me. Joey's welcome, too.'

I did my best not to cry. 'Jim, my father isn't going to let me go with you. You were wonderful with my mother. She was against you when we sat down. I know how hard it was for you not to just say . . .'

'Fuck it!' Jim filled in the blank. 'Well, if it comes down to it, I can say it to your father. There are states where it's legal to marry at seventeen. Is it here? Hell, it's legal in some states to marry your cousin at fourteen. I'm just your blood brother.'

I smiled despite the knot in my heart. 'Did you understand what my mother was saying? It's not just that this is traditionally something a girl's parents should decide together. She's afraid of crossing him.' I couldn't bring myself to tell him I was, too. I wanted to stretch out this time Jim had given me. We followed the dogs back inside.

When he saw my cold little room, Jim didn't say, 'I've had closets bigger than this.' He nodded at the Camus poster transplanted from my bedroom in California and admired the collage done, at Jim's suggestion, in lieu of a book report on *Portrait of the Artist as a Young Man*. 'It would make a great book jacket. Ever think of designing album covers?'

'No.'

'Then I won't beg. Eleanor Roosevelt,' Jim read her name at the bottom of a little banner I had made. '*You must do the thing you think you cannot do,*' Jim read aloud. 'Sounds like old Eleanor, all right. She should have been president.'

'I thought she was,' I said.

Jim grinned. 'Why this quote?'

'My next-door neighbour in Stockton, who emigrated from the Philippines, gave it to me when I was a kid in thanks for my helping her pass her American Citizenship Test. I ran over to her house in tears after my first boy/girl party because I couldn't dance. She told me a story about young Eleanor not being able to dance, and her resolve to learn for this cotillion, even though she felt like a horse.'

'I love dancing with you.' Jim moved his hips ever so slightly.

I declined the invitation with a smile. 'I came across the quote unpacking, and made the banner. When I'm being kind to myself, it reminds me to write when I think I can't write, and to practise guitar knowing I'll never be Eric Clapton.'

Jim grinned. 'And when you're not being kind to yourself?'

'I've rewritten that last night in Los Angeles, too, Jim. The banner is my version of a hair shirt for not being able to trade my family for freedom in California last summer.'

Jim asked, 'What about now? If I can't pull this off and it really comes down to a choice between your family and me.'

'If I have to choose, I'll choose you.'

'Thank you, that means everything to me. And thank you, Eleanor Roosevelt,' Jim gave the banner a Boy Scout salute.

He picked up the Shelby Hearon book, and read for fifteen minutes without looking up.

'You and my father are going to come to blows in about an hour, and you're reading.'

'I'd rather be drinking, but I thought we agreed to leave out the part about my being a drunkard. Whatever your father says, we leave together.' Jim stuck his nose back in the book. A half-hour later, he pushed it back into the bookshelf, and said, 'I like the part where the guy says he could tell whether he slept alone or not by the grass stains on his jeans. Had a lot of those nights myself. You're my favourite mattress.' He pulled out Richard Farina's *Been Down So Long It Looks Like Up to Me.*

'He's married to Mimi, Joan Baez's sister,' I explained, knowing that folk music was not his forte. 'There's a line in one of his songs, "Hard Lovin' Loser" about the guy having no sense of direction, that gets sent to the jungle alone.'

Jim poked me. 'Good thing you're not 1A.'

I'd never wondered before why Jim hadn't been drafted. 'Why aren't you?'

'Rapid heartbeat,' he explained coolly. I expressed my real concern. 'Oh, I faked it. And to make sure, I told them I was a homosexual, hoped they didn't mind.'

I handed him my guitar. I manipulated his fingers through the chord changes of 'Love Is Just a Four-Letter Word', and showed him a simple fingering pattern I hadn't quite mastered. 'Amazing,' he said. 'How many things are bebopping around your head you don't know are up there.' He sang, accentuating the words at the chord changes, like everyone does at first, because it seems so important to get *there*. It didn't seem to be in his key, but I had no idea how to change it so he didn't have to strain for notes. After half a dozen times through, Jim stopped to suck the bright pink fingertips of his left hand.

Tapping on the open door with her nails, my mother said. 'I'm sorry to interrupt. You have a very pleasant voice, Jim.' Jim thanked her. She said, 'Your father's going to be home soon. I thought you might like to think about dealing with all of this tomorrow.'

'What's that great quote about cowards?' I asked.

'A coward dies a thousand . . .' Jim began helpfully. I don't think we want that one. Jim laughed, and suggested, 'He who runs away, lives to fight another day.'

'That has a certain ring.'

'I appreciate your concern,' Jim said in a formal tone. 'But I don't want to leave Linda here.'

'In that case, you should both go. Quickly.'

Back in the sanctity of the motel room, Jim jumped up and down, stretching his back. When he stopped, he took a deep breath. He was feeling better than the day before. A smile flashed through his eyes, then across his face. 'We'll buy some marble and you could make polar bears that won't melt. Oh, yeah. Music. Like it's easier for me to put words to music, you prefer to start from scratch, rather than a block. How's clay?' Jim started singing, 'A Hundred Pounds of Clay.'

'Jim, I love you so much. Don't. Please. I don't want to pretend.'

'Who's pretending? I'm not leaving Maine without you.' He slipped his arm around me and kissed my forehead. 'We'll tell your mom you're pregnant.'

I laughed. 'Immaculate conception is right in line with this insane Madonna vision you have about me.'

'We'd have to have a story about our getting carried away a month or two ago. It was, of course, all my fault. Your mother would think I was doing the right thing to marry you. Wouldn't your father? After they are hurt and disillusioned, they would be grateful we were rushing into marriage.'

'I think my father would spend about thirty seconds deciding which of us to kill first.'

'I wouldn't let him hurt you.' Jim sounded so confident. 'If you're worried about my hurting him, we could do it by phone from California.'

'Jim, I hate to add that lie to all the other lies I tell so I can have you in my life.'

'After we are married, the lying can stop,' he said, rubbing my back reassuringly.

'What about no baby?' I asked.

'Well, we can have had a false alarm. We could try to make one real fast. Well, okay. That's not likely. To be more honest than I've ever been with anyone,' Jim stopped to clear his throat, averted his eyes, 'my sperm count is on the low side. I thought I remembered having mumps when I was a kid, but had a real bout when I was twenty. Might take some doing to get you with child. It would take a hell of a lot of sex and the UCLA Medical Center for me to father a child . . . Do you want kids?'

'Yeah, but not real fast. Not before we decide to renew our contract,' I rubbed his back to reassure him. 'Until then, a hell of a lot of sex intrigues me.'

Jim smiled and kissed my cheek 'You'd be a great mother. Imagine a mother who makes snow bears!'

'Better yet, a father who believes in them.'

283

Jim kissed my mouth. 'The best memories of my family have to do with nature.' Without announcing a change of subject, he said, 'Maybe we could find a studio in Venice. California. Not Italy. There's a good art school in LA – Otis. Maybe it would help circumvent the rules if I asked Andy to write you a recommendation.'

I was puzzled. 'I didn't think Andy was old enough to be a teacher.'

'Not my kid brother. Andy Warhol. I was name-dropping. I *do* know Andy Warhol. He wants my bare ass in a movie.' Jim paused to smile. 'He wants my bare ass. He liked the boots we drew. Well, you drew. He loved the little book you drew for me. He said you have a beautiful sense of line and space. Something like that. He thought our drawing together was very cosmic.'

I was trying to imagine Jim pulling out my bits of amateur art at one of the wild Andy Warhol parties I had heard about. 'You really know Andy Warhol? What's he like?'

'Andy is odd.' I laughed, wondering what Jim called odd. Jim smiled, and rolled his eyes, thinking. 'He never finishes his sentences.'

'We do that all the time.'

'Yeah, but who knows where the hell his are going?'

I liked the possibilities. 'That would make it more fun to finish them.'

'I *know* he'd write you a recommendation. If I'm not with the band, we can be together all the time. I keep doing one more thing for them. Now, it's this album. Then they will want to tour to promote it. I fucking can't do the road any more.'

'Can't you just make albums and not tour? It would give you time to write. And it's touring that grinds you down. Do better albums and sell less of them.'

'The music business pretends it's a creative entity, but it's all bottom line.' Jim sat on the bed. 'Do you have that poem with you? I'll show you how you could make it better, other than have it be about me.'

'Luckily it's in my room.'

'I just thought it could use some colour. Let me show you what I do.' He picked up a novel from the nightstand, and grabbed his

284

notebook. 'Do you remember the first time you read my notebook in San Francisco? You told me I put words not normally used together to create my own meaning? Some of that is right from the unconscious. Acid. But even your unconscious is limited by your experience.

'A writer tends to repeat certain words. They are comfortable or important, whatever. Or I can be sitting with a pen in my hand and no muse on my shoulder. This is what I do.' He opened the book at random, reading the word his thumb happened to hit. He wrote down *dog*. He repeated the process two more times. What he had written on his notebook was, *Dog Speaks Rage*. In San Francisco I had told him my voices were neither God nor dogs. Funny coincidence.

He laughed. 'Maybe this isn't the best example. Sounds like something I would have written anyway. Usually my first look at them, they seem to be some accurately translated Japanese poem. But what I have is a dog speaking, not barking, howling, whining, yapping or growling.' Jim stretched out across the bed. 'This dog isn't a pooch. He's a seer. Maybe this dog is me on peyote. Maybe he's someone I'm afraid to face in his true shape. A minute ago I didn't have a single thought in my head about that. I have something to play with.

'Often, they don't wind up anywhere, but kick me into gear. I'm not looking at a blank page. Never look at a blank page longer than it takes your pen – or pencil – to hit it. This way, I have a new arrangement of words in my head. I can do this over and over and it will always be new. I can do it with a newspaper or Yellow Pages, but the vocabulary sucks. I don't like to use a dictionary, because you can tell where in the alphabet you are, and slant your choice towards a letter you know you like. Random. Random is best. I use this once per poem. I've tapped the great unconscious. What I would write from *Dog Speaks Rage* and what you would write would be entirely different.'

We played. Laughing over the odd combinations. Bewildered when they seemed poetic and truthful, as if they provided proof of the inexplicable nature of creative beauty, and the possibility of monkeys typing Shakespeare.

'I have a little condition about our wedding,' Jim announced after some time. We'd had no discussion about the details of getting married. My first consideration of the word. A ceremony. Jim said solemnly, 'I want to get married in a church.'

Believing the request a joke, I asked, 'Weren't there rumours of a Mayan temple?'

'That's where I want to ravage you, if possible by moonlight, but I'm talking about exchanging vows in a real church, becoming husband and wife in God's eyes.'

'On a year's lease? I thought God was pretty much an expletive in your vocabulary.'

'When I was younger, I went through a very contemplative, religious period. I felt angry that my prayers were never answered. I feel this tug back to that childhood hope for a God, because it seems like you're the answer to all those prayers I so carefully worded. Would you do it for me? I want it very much.'

His eyes were seriously blue. 'Could I think about it?'

Jim edged off the bed and pawed to the bottom of his suitcase.

'Another birthday present?' I rested the near-weightless box on my lap.

'I thought it might be the answer to your next question.' Jim looked as patiently as he might at a slow child. 'Aren't you going to ask what you're going to wear?'

Within the slim box lay a white dress from the twenties. The outer fabric was silk georgette, the matching slip less diaphanous, but incredibly light. Wisteria blossoms made from tiny seed pearls fell from the shoulders.

'I thought you'd forgive the silk since the dress is second-hand. There are shoes to match. Let me see you in it.'

'Isn't that bad luck?'

The phone woke us at 8 a.m. I picked it up on the second ring. 'Hello.'

'Honey, you have to come home,' my mother said. 'Someone told your father that they saw you holding hands with a hippie in town.' I giggled. Of all people. Jim a hippie! 'Anyone with long hair is a hippie here. Your father is livid. I think that your friend should go back to California. We'll take some time with this.'

'What's happening?' Jim asked sleepily.

'My father is upset. My mother thinks you should go home, and let us take some time to work this out.'

'Let me talk to her.' Jim took the phone. 'This is Jim. I'm sorry Lin's father is upset, but I'm sure we can talk this out.' Just hearing Jim's side of the conversation was nerve-racking. 'What for? . . . Well, that isn't true . . . Shit . . . Excuse me, mam . . . I don't feel right about that . . . We'll talk it over and call you back.' Jim tossed the receiver into its cradle, bolted for the bathroom for another round of dry heaves.

I held his forehead, and when he stopped heaving, helped him back to bed. He settled on his back with a little groan. I asked, 'What should I do?'

'I think we should drive to Boston, fly to Mexico, and get married.'

'I meant to make you feel better.'

'That would make me feel better,' Jim said hoarsely.

'What did my mother say?'

'Your father is upset.' He stroked my arm. 'Do you have a learner's permit?'

'No. And I've never driven in the snow. I've watched a lot, though.'

'Hell, I'd settle for you having read a book about it.' Jim lay quietly, then said dreamily, 'I was thinking about learning to play the guitar. I enjoyed that yesterday.'

My father was on the rampage, Jim really needed to be a short run from a toilet, yet he was daydreaming about guitar lessons. 'Better get Robby to teach you. We've exhausted my repertoire.'

'I can't remember if we're speaking. Neither one of us talks much, so it's hard to tell. I'd like to have someone teach me about music theory, composition. I still have this music in my head I can't get out. What do you say we hit the road?'

The phone rang and I jumped a foot. Jim took my wrist. 'Trust you instincts and let it ring.'

My mother's voice was panicky. 'Your father called the police.' I couldn't imagine why. 'Didn't Jim tell you? He wants to have him arrested for rape.'

I stared at Jim's passive face. He didn't even blink. 'That isn't true,' I said, and flashed on Jim saying the same words. Such rage because I held hands with Jim in public?

'Statutory rape is based on your age, not consent. What I told Jim is that if he goes back to California, I think I can calm your father down.'

I felt like I'd been running. I asked breathlessly, 'Does he know we're together?'

'No, he thinks you're at Trina's.' She defended my father, 'He's just being protective. He loves you. When he calms down, we can talk about this rationally. Get to Trina's by ten.'

I hung up the phone. 'Why didn't you tell me?'

'You're coming with me.' He took my hand. 'Don't panic.'

'What will it do to you if you're arrested for rape?'

'Enhance my image. The press loved my being unfairly busted in New Haven. Look, it's obvious we can't handle this by your being in the family way, if your father is this crazy. But I'm sure as hell not going to leave you to handle this alone.'

'You're not leaving me. I'm asking you to go.'

'You said yesterday that if it came down to a choice, you'd choose me.'

'I am, Jim. Look how the police roughed you up in New Haven, for what, a joke? What are they going to do to you in this conservative little town if you're charged with rape? I'm worried for your safety. I couldn't stand it if you were hurt because of me.'

Jim paced to the door and back. 'Shit! How am I supposed to feel if something happens to you?' He studied the floor. After a few minutes, he looked at me. 'This is just temporary. When things cool down, you'll come to me. Just a couple of days.'

'Are you going to be able to make the drive?' I asked. He was pale and shaky. 'If you have any doubt at all . . . that friend of Trina's has a licence.'

'I can drive. I just wanted to curl up and enjoy the ride.' Jim pulled on his pants and boots. 'Jesus. I don't want to do this. It's not right.' Dressed, he stopped to give me a hug. 'Much as I hate to say so, you better get dressed.'

I felt numb pulling on the Christmas sweater. Jim's hand followed the trail of a cable down my chest before he repacked my presents in their boxes and put the boxes into a Gumps bag. 'Gumps in San Francisco?' I asked. Gumps was one of those ritzy stores that didn't put price tags on things, because if you had to ask, you couldn't afford to shop there.

'Yeah. Got the vase there. I spent a day in San Francisco before I flew out. I was hoping to see McClure, but missed him.'

By car, it only took two minutes to reach my friend's street. Jim stopped. I kissed his cheek. I eased the emerald, beautiful in the winter light, off my hand and rested the little piece of Big Sur in his hand. Every minute I stayed in the car seemed dangerous. I forced myself to open the door and climb out into the snow. Trying to sound as brave and plucky as he expected me to be, I leaned down to look at him and said, 'And I didn't think you could top climbing in my window for my sixteenth birthday.'

Jim scooted across the seat to kiss me a last time. 'We'll be together soon.'

17

Coda Queen Be My Bride

Six hours later, when Jim should have reached Boston, he called, but my mother wouldn't let me speak to him. He called the next morning to catch me before school. My mother grabbed the phone. I was so close, I could hear Jim's plea, 'Please let me speak with Ginger.' That poor horse. My mother said to him, 'It's best we let things cool off.'

On the bus, I dashed off a letter telling Jim that my father believed that I had been with a local boy, and my mother, bless her, kept her silence. I thanked him for all the gifts, including himself, assured him there had been no fallout from the visit, but felt I could safely assume I was grounded for the duration. *After all, who could tell the difference?* Seeing the letter personally to the post office, I made myself late for my first class.

My birthday passed without much notice. At school, a friend going down the stairway as I was going up, sang, 'She was Just Seventeen'. Trina gave me a handmade birthday card illustrated with her relentless flair pen. A mushroom with birthday candles lit up the front. Inside, she misquoted 'The End', but her point was, The WEST was the BEST. There was no poem in the mail from Jim.

There was no discussion of Jim's visit or our plans within my family. I gave Jim a few days for him to shake the flu. He normally received my letters four days after they were mailed, unless they were held up by slow sled dogs, but he didn't call on that day. Days went by with no word from Jim by phone or letter. No belated birthday poem. As was my custom, I was writing a page or two every day to collect and mail in a single envelope at the end of the week. Since I left California, Jim had become my journal.

Late in the week, I came home to find my mother in tears. She had spoken with Jim. Having thought things over, he had realized our relationship was a mistake. He thought we were a mistake? The friendship, too? She said he asked I not contact him. Although I couldn't hear Jim's voice in my mind saying that, I believed her tears.

Brian and I still passed notes and smiles in the hallways at school and ate lunch together. I tagged along with other friends to his house when no one was home. He had a tiny attic room with an American flag curtain and a mattress that took up most of the floor. We talked music and California as if they were forbidden words. Everything seemed forbidden. I talked less and less for fear a secret would spill out.

By March, some snow had melted, but the wind was cruel. My lips and knuckles cracked and bled, no matter how much balm I applied to soothe them. I hadn't felt warm since Jim held me. After a year and a half of Jim's at least twice-weekly phone calls, envelopes stuffed with poems, and spontaneous appearances, the stillness was savage.

Late one night, the phone woke me. I flew out of bed. Silence. Either the phone had rung once or it was a dream.

The next night I fell into bed without undressing, turned on the radio, and Jim was singing 'Light My Fire'. I hadn't heard his music since he left Maine. How many kids got by waiting to hear Jim's music one more time, like he had lived for Bo Diddley, when being fifteen was so very hard for him? I'd tell Jim that the next time he called. Maybe it would make him feel better about the band. Just before sleep, I remembered there would be no call.

Shaken awake in the dark by my mother, my first thought was some catastrophe had struck. That the trailer was on fire. 'What's wrong?'

'Daddy and I were talking tonight, he wants to move back to California. Who wrote that book, *You Can't Go Home Again?*'

'Thomas Hardy. Virginia Woolf. I mean Thomas Wolfe.' I knew it was somewhere in there. *California.*

'Well, he was right. Daddy isn't happy here.' He wasn't happy anywhere. 'You've been so quiet since things didn't work out with your friend. I'm trying to do what's best for you. I know it doesn't seem that way. I understand how Jim could sweep you off your feet. He's probably the handsomest man I've even seen . . . even with all that hair! And he's as bright as you are. Did I tell you that when I was about your age, I was at a local resort and Douglas Fairbanks asked me to play tennis with him? He was so smart and witty. Jim has that charisma. I'd like you to promise me that if I let you go ahead to California, you won't do anything headstrong. Promise you won't marry your Jim until you're eighteen.'

He wasn't my Jim any more. 'I promise,' I said easily. 'What happened with Douglas Fairbanks?' I wondered if she meant Junior or Senior. Jim was more like Senior.

She smiled. 'I'll tell you when you're older.'

My mother didn't often talk about her life. I enjoyed her thinking Jim handsome, and delighted in her comparing his intelligence to mine, instead of mine to his. Mothers!

English. The teacher looked like pictures I'd seen of John Updike, except that a little cloud of chalk dust followed him everywhere. I had seen him in the A & P once, and he had chalk dust on a sweater I had never seen him wear to school. Trina thought she spotted chalk dust on his Sunday dress-suit. The class was in the midst of reading a collection of any chosen author's works for the purpose of writing a comparative analysis. I chose J. D. Salinger because *Catcher in the Rye* was barely allowed into the hallowed halls. And I'd read all his books that summer when Jim gave me a set of paperbacks to go with *Franny and Zooey.*

After class, I navigated the sharp front walk and took refuge in the first phone booth I saw. The door broke the blast of wind, but let it whistle though the cracks like banshees. I emptied my heavy change purse and stared at the pyramid of coins.

Swallowing my pride, I dialled Jim's number. He might yell at me like he did on the lawn when we said goodbye in LA, but that would be all right. I just wanted to hear his voice. When no one answered, I let it ring a long time, so I wouldn't have to hang up and start over. I called The Doors' office, and left the number of the phone booth. I left the same message at several of Jim's haunts. Each time, I felt more humiliated and more desperate.

After six calls, I was too exhausted to try again. The phone rang in my hand. 'Jim?'

'Thank God!' Jim screamed.

'That Merry Prankster,' I whispered back. I held my composure for a few seconds, then fell into sobs. Jim let me cry, saying, 'Shh, hush.'

'I won't bother you again,' I assured him, 'I just needed to hear your voice one last time.'

'Bother me? I've been going crazy!'

'My mother said you changed your mind and wanted me to leave you alone.'

'Jesus Christ! I love you. I never changed my mind, baby. She lied to you,' his voice rose passionately.

'She lied?' I couldn't believe it. My mother loved me and sincerely liked Jim.

'Did she tell you I called last night?' Jim asked.

'No.' She *lied*. 'You love me?'

'Oh, yes! Did you know I called the day I left, as soon as I reached the airport? I called the next morning, too. Your mother asked me to give you some breathing room and let things cool off. When I got your letter, I called, and she said you were sorry, but you'd been impulsive, that you really didn't love me. I begged her to let me talk to you so I could hear for myself. She said you were standing right there and didn't want to talk to me. I wouldn't have believed her, but I knew I had pressured you. I thought that was why you gave me back the ring. That's why I believed her. You gave me back the ring.' He repeated with building anguish. 'You gave me back the ring. You gave me back the ring.'

'I was afraid of being caught with it once I knew what it meant. I only gave it to you for safe keeping.'

'I called almost every day, but stopped when your mother said she'd have me busted for harassment. I carried that last letter around until it fell apart, then I fell apart.'

Jim had fallen apart. 'Are you okay?'

'Yeah, *now*,' Jim whispered. 'I feel like I just woke up from the worst nightmare I ever had.'

'Me, too,' I agreed, unsure if I had only awakened within a dream.

'Night before last, I started calling again. What's one more charge, right?' Jim asked with a forced brightness.

'What? Oh, God, Jim, I thought my father never went through with pressing charges. Is that a lie, too?'

'No, baby. As far as I know, he didn't. Don't you get papers up there? I got myself into this one. I'm so excited I can't think. Can I come get you?'

'You don't have to, Jim. My parents are moving back to California. They're sending me ahead while they clear up things here. I'll be in California in a few days. I'm going to be staying in Stockton with a friend and her family to finish out the school year. It might be difficult to see each other for a while.'

'I've got to see you,' he said excitedly. 'There must be a window I can climb into or you can climb out of. I've been lost without you.'

The high windows in my friend's house were unwelcoming for midnight visitations, but not as insurmountable as a continent. 'Why are you wanted? Is that a joke?'

'Pretty much. I like to say I was too drunk to remember, but the only blackouts I have of that nature are matters of convenience.'

'What happened?' I asked, wondering how true that was, since he had once said he wondered between his and Pamela's memory lapses if they had the same relationship.

'Let's see. A couple weeks ago, we played Miami. I misbehaved,' he sounded a mischievous boy. 'I showed up late, too drunk to remember any of our songs. I coulda done a real juicy set of the best of the Rolling Stones, but couldn't remember a damn thing *I* wrote. I started this little rap, figuring somewhere along the line I'd kick into autopilot.

'The place was so hot and packed, it was a miserable place to be. God, I hate Florida! We all should've gone home. I had no business being on stage. I'd been in this who-the-fuck-cares mood. This guy, can't remember his name. He's an animal rights freak. Well, he handed me this lamb. You'd think it would have been scared to death with all the noise and lights, but it just lay real calm in my arms. I could feel its heartbeat. Reminded me of you that first night in San Francisco. *It's like the wolf* . . . Remember? I was going though the words of "The Spy" to myself when I realized the *band* didn't know that one. Then I said something like, *If she wasn't so young, I'd fuck her.*'

I giggled. 'Now, I'm even too tough for mutton stew. Finish your story. Why are you a wanted man? Did you steal the lamb or have sex with it?'

Jim's laugh was wonderful to hear. 'What I did and what I'm accused of are kinda different things. I planned, at some point in the show, to take everyone into a Fellini dream, and drop my pants. I bought some boxers for the occasion.'

'You did a striptease like the one in San Francisco so you wouldn't offend me?'

'Well, not exactly. I wanted to offend them. I took off my shirt, and was playing loin peek-a-boo with it. I was acting about six ounces drunker than I was, but was drunk enough that I thought I was funnier than I was.

'Looking back, I was just so damn pissed. All they wanted was to fuck me to "Light My Fire". I did this sleight-of-hand thing.' He giggled, enjoying his own tale. 'Literally. I showed them my thumb. I figured they'd see what they wanted to. I said I was lonely – God, I've missed you – and invited them on stage to fuck me. All hell broke loose. They really wanted to fuck me! And you told me is was just a fantasy. I was dragged off stage. The cops stopped the show. I think if they'd rode along with me they might have gone away with something, not what they wanted, but something.'

'Did the cops hurt you? Arrest you?'

'Not then. As far as I knew everything was cool. We, the band, went to Jamaica. I picked a fight with Pamela so I could be alone. I wrote. I had this amazing dream about you: a visitation. Done any out-of-the-body travel? It made me so fucking lonely, I flew back to LA so I could fight with Pamela some more. That's when I found out that the Miami police had a warrant for my arrest. Or

maybe Siddons told me when I said I was coming back. I forget.
Jesus. It's all a joke.'

Three friends came out to visit for the first time and say goodbye.
My father glowered at the long-haired boys and my mother loved
our happy noise under her roof. They sang every song about
California they could even half recall. Before they piled back into
the red Porsche to head back to town, Brian gave me the fist he'd
cast in lead to the detriment of his grandmother's stove. I didn't
have much memory of the long drive to the Boston airport or the
long flight back to California but, nearly a year after leaving, I sat
at a friend's kitchen table while her mother read the tea leaves in
the bottom of my cup.

A few nights later, I waited for the house to sleep. After midnight,
I walked out the front door, closing it silently behind me. As I
walked the half-block to where Jim and I arranged to meet, I saw
him, lit blue by moonlight, leaning against the trunk of a car.

He didn't run to me, but waited, almost shy, until I reached
him. 'Welcome home,' Jim said, spreading his arms just enough
for me to walk into them, his chest the best welcome mat I could
imagine.

His usually silky hair was dry and wild. I'd seen him in various
stages of war with shaving, but this was the first beard so full that
I couldn't trace the beauty of his jawline. Grey or blond hairs, I
couldn't tell which by streetlight, surrounded his mouth. His beard
felt soft against my face. We held each other, crying. After I had
been leaning against him and he against the trunk for what must
have been ten minutes, Jim said, 'I rented a room.'

I asked, 'Can't we just drive like we used to?'

'Honey, I've been driving all day. I'm beat. All I want to do is
hold you.'

Never having the need for one, I couldn't recall ever seeing a
motel in Stockton. There were sleazy hotels in the older part of
downtown. I hoped Jim hadn't gravitated towards them with that
need of his to live out a Raymond Chandler novel.

As we drove, he stroked my thigh. We hopscotched from one
red light to the next. At the latest, he tilted his face to me and we
kissed for the first time. The car behind us honked. Jim stepped

on the gas and the car lurched forward. Jim emitted an odd little sound, followed by a yelp and laugh.

'What's so funny?' I asked.

'I came in my pants. I *am* excited to see you.'

I blushed in the dash light. 'You need to have your brakes relined.'

He whooped and snorted. 'I love the way your mind works.'

I could only claim the timing, not the line. 'Not mine. It's more or less from *Foreign Affair*. Jean Arthur said it. Can't remember who wrote it.'

'Good to hear you're still doing your homework in front of the TV.'

We exhibited the restraint not to kiss at the other red lights. Jim drove Stockton better than I could have directed him. He slowed in an older neighbourhood and turned into the driveway of a large house with a porch running in an L across the front and down the side. Jim ran up the three steps at the back of the porch and unlocked the door.

'Want me to carry you over the threshold?'

I said, 'I think we'd both be in better shape if you didn't.' He hadn't felt awkward about alluding to our squelched plans. The room must once have been just a good-sized bedroom in the old house. To make an efficiency unit, the basics of a kitchen and a bathroom were added along the right wall. Under the window by the door was a small table with two unmatched wooden chairs in need of paint. Straight ahead, lined up against the blue wainscoting, were a long low dresser, a double bed, and a little nightstand.

A tiny fireplace was centred on the left wall. On the narrow mantle, a curious collection of books lay on their sides: Jean-Paul Sartre's *No Exit*, Gertrude Stein's *Autobiography of Alice B. Toklas*, William Burroughs' *Naked Lunch*, a translation of Sappho's poetry, a Norman Mailer book, and *The I Never Cooked Before Cookbook*, like one of those tests, 'Which does not belong?' Next to the books lay a black bound sketchbook, Jim's latest notebook, with a pen clipped to the cover, a pair of very dark sunglasses, a bottle of whiskey, and a large manila envelope propped up against the wall.

'Looks like you've moved in,' I teased.

'I have,' he tossed me a key. 'And so have you. While you finish the school year, I thought my fiancée deserved better than a choice between a motel or the back seat.'

I turned the key over in my hand like a worry stone, while I surveyed the room trying to feel some part of it was mine. Beyond Jim's weary face, I saw my reflection in the mirror above the dresser. We looked like we both needed to sleep for a week.

Interpreting my confusion as judgmental, he said, 'I took the first place that was available. We can get something better, but I wanted to really welcome you home.'

Jim stepped on the heel of his right boot to give himself an edge in pulling it off. New boots! Thought he'd die with his homely Frye's on. He struggled with the second, unzipped his cords and pushed them around his ankles. 'This is why boys in high-school only go out once with a girl. They want so desperately to go all the way they don't even get out of their pants. Who can ask the girl out again? Being old enough to know that embarrassment is rarely fatal, it was kind of fun. I haven't gone off like a Roman candle since I was a teenager.'

'You are a Roman candle in so many respects,' I said, admiration in my voice, Jim's favourite quote from Kerouac in my head. Jim fell on his butt laughing. He jumped up and skipped into the bathroom.

On his return, he fell back into the marshmallow mattress. 'Still find me attractive?' I tilted my head like the RCA dog. Jim laughed. 'Thank you for that look. Everybody revels in telling me I'm fat. I haven't felt so sexy since the last time I saw you.' He drummed his thighs. 'Sit here.'

I straddled Jim's lap on the too-soft bed. He sat up to meet my mouth for a sweet kiss. He tousled my hair. 'You have the most beautiful hair. It's always changing. Your hair has seasons. My little Wood Nymph.'

'I feel more like a frog on a lily pad,' I said. His grin, not so easy to see behind the beard, lit his red-rimmed eyes. 'You look so tired. I'm sorry about the long drive.'

'I could have flown up, but I needed to feel the distance between me and LA.' He looked at the wall, then let his eyes settle on me.

'*The Doors are dead. Long live The Doors.* I am sorry that the Miami massacre was my resignation.

'I did the show I promised I would do at the Garden, New York,' he explained. 'Even though the band had been trying to manipulate me. I'm supposed to be a fucking genius, but I'm not supposed to see that? I was so depressed about us, I didn't want to get out of bed, let alone get on a stage.'

Jim faded back into the soft mattress, studying the ceiling. He was probably making animals out of the cracks and patches, like he did with clouds. I expected him to notice the elephant, but instead, he sat back up and continued with his story.

'I realized, a little late, that Bill Graham was right. The magic would have been keener at the Fillmore. East. Do you know there's a Fillmore East?' I shook my head. 'But it was still a good show. It was important to me that Ray have good feelings about the end. The band acted like it was a turn-around. I couldn't tell them it was just one show I pulled out for them. I gave them all I had left. Jim hugged me to his chest and I gasped. 'Oops. Sorry. Did I pull your hair? Have I forgotten how to do this?' He grinned and rearranged my hair so it was, he thought, out of his way.

When he lowered the zipper of my dress a few inches, I sat up. 'Jim. I'm not feeling very . . . attractive,' I said. I retreated from his lap. The hardwood floor was cool under my feet.

Jim sat up and took my hands. 'We're talking about the wrong things. I'm sorry. It's just that I haven't had anyone to talk to about this. About anything.'

'I want you to talk to me. I've missed your voice. Our friendship.'

Jim swung our hands away from my sides. 'How about we drive down to Mexico and get married?'

I hedged. 'The magistrate's wouldn't be open.' I guessed that's what they had in Mexico.

Jim played along. 'Even worse, the bars might not be,' he said, though I imagined he knew every all-night joint in Ensenada. He squeezed my hands. 'We belong together. I want to marry you.'

'We belong together,' I agreed. 'Jim . . . the condition of my coming here was a promise to my mother that I wouldn't marry you until I turn eighteen.'

'You'd honour a promise after what she did?' Jim stood so close our breathing fell into rhythm. 'Didn't you make the promise believing I had deserted you?'

Deserted seemed the wrong word. 'This is about *my* honour.' Jim wrenched away and grabbed the mantle. He did a couple push-ups against it, then stood motionless with his back to me. The promise was much easier to make than it would be to keep. I asked, 'If I keep my promise to her, do I lose you?'

For an answer, he grabbed the big manila envelope from the mantle and dumped its contents on the bed. There were more than a dozen envelopes. Through heavy black pen scratches, I could see enough to tell it had been addressed to me in Jim's boyish handwriting. An arrow directed the post office to *Return to Sender*. Every envelope was mutilated in the same way. I picked up each one, arranging them in order in my lap according to the dates on the postmarks. They were from Boston, Los Angeles, New York, New Orleans, Jamaica, and Los Angeles again.

Jim kneeled at my feet. 'I did not *consent*,' he whispered. He had not given up as he had in 'Horse Latitudes'. He hadn't given up! I counted the envelopes, eighteen, and felt overwhelmed by them, even unopened.

'My heart broke when there was no birthday poem,' I whispered, unable to look up from the envelopes filling my lap.

Jim plucked the first envelope, the one postmarked Boston, and ripped it open. I wanted him to show more care. 'It's not a poem. It's a song,' he said. 'I wanted to save one special gift for your real birthday. When I couldn't speak to you, I mailed it from the airport. I thought you'd get it on your birthday.' He snatched one of the wooden chairs from across the room and twirled it in front of me. He swung his leg over it, like he was mounting a horse, and leaned forwards against its back.

'Bareback riding?' I asked.

He rubbed his thighs as if to warm them, dismounted, and opened a drawer stuffed with jeans. He had moved in. He looked so handsome in unzipped jeans, laughing and running his hand through his mane. 'This sounds full of irony now, but when I wrote it I felt this joy, this anticipation, of being with you. And it's as close as I'll get to a country song. Remember that little tune of yours?'

'You can hold your own in rock 'n' roll . . . no, that was the B-side.'

He smiled. 'My voice is a little rough.' Jim sat down, closed his eyes, and tapped his thumb against the arm he rested on the chair back. He sang a zippy 'Easy Ride'.

I couldn't hold in a peal of laughter. I held my ribs like I expected them to crumble. 'Don't you know when you ride *insanity's horse* you're bound to be thrown?' Jim opened his eyes and stuck out his tongue, not losing a beat with his thumb metronome, waiting for his rowdy audience to settle down. When he finished the song, he spread his hands open. He repeated a Coda Queen line as a challenge, as if it were the last line of 'Wild Child'.

'From child to queen in just a year,' I said. When his face flattened with disappointment, because I had not been able to say a simple *Yes*, I said, 'I love you, Jim.'

'I know that isn't easy for you to say. I think that's a grand total of three times you've said it.'

'What does *coda* mean?' I asked. It sounded negative to me. 'Is it a slight?'

'Oh, no! Musically,' Jim began, brushing my hair back over my shoulder, and leaving his hand there to caress my neck, 'a coda is the little piece at the end . . .'

'Like little piece of ass?' I pretended offence. 'Tail end?'

Jim grinned. 'I do think it comes from the Latin for *tail*.' Ahah. 'And you have a real sweet ass, but in this instance, I am talking about this *separate* piece of music that completes the whole composition. *You* complete *me*.'

Amazed to be close to him again, my eyes burned with tears. I tried to make out the words floating on the paper. 'Rage. Like a river? Thank you, Jim.' I couldn't feel what I felt that night in Los Angeles. My body still felt three thousand miles away from him.

'I wrote another song . . .' Jim shrugged and wandered in a circle, humming, looking as if he were trying to locate a tune he'd lost. He stopped and sat on his heels in front of me. He sang the song he had mentioned in Maine, growing more flirtatious with every line.

When he finished, he had tears in his eyes and a big grin shining through his beard. He flipped through the envelopes in my lap, presenting one to me. 'I hoped, each time I mailed one of these, *that* would be the one you'd open. Obviously, you never saw them. I think there is a federal charge in that. When I sent the song to you, I wanted you to be so absolutely charmed, you would take me back.'

He titled it 'Shaman's Blues'. Reading it, I smiled, catching something I missed in his performance. 'Gleanings of the great unconscious?' There was a line of disjointed words. Doing time.

Jim rubbed my knee. 'I was worried about the time *you* were doing. How did you swing the early parole? It makes no sense to pull you out of school this time of year.'

'I wasn't in on the board meeting,' I said, feeling that was honest enough. I may have been his lie detector, but he was never mine. 'Grizzlies are western bears. My father would be a black one.' I wanted to ask him to leave that part out. I resented my father being in our song.

'Grant me some artistic licence.'

'Anytime,' I smiled. 'Was it a Saturday when we said our June goodbye?'

Jim looked misty-eyed. 'Yeah, baby, by the time we got around to regrets.' We had both rewritten that night in LA countless times. 'I still dream about our swim, sleeping dreams, waking dreams.' Jim collected the mass of envelopes from my lap and fanned them on the dresser. He climbed into bed behind me, searching for my zipper under my hair.

'Could we turn out the light?' I asked, then added, 'I'm feeling shy.'

'Sure,' Jim smiled, giving me a little kiss on my cheek to let me know it really was okay. He reached over and clicked off the bedside lamp. In the dark, he slipped the dress from my shoulders. Every few inches he lowered my dress, he paused to kiss the exposed skin.

18

Your Hands Upon the Wheel

For the first time, I had returned to a place. I'd never back-tracked. I felt comforted by the familiarity of the streets and confused by the changed alliances of the people I had known. The young trees around campus were less lissome, and so were my old friends.

On little sleep, I struggled through the first few classes, watching the clock. I told my friends I was going to have lunch off campus, which wasn't allowed. No telling what the lot of us could do to the town over the lunch hour. The announcement was met with a mixture of disapproval and envy. I'd asked Jim not to pull up to the flagpole, but park down the street. Jim leaned, as he had the night before, against the trunk of the blue car. In daylight, though, he had his face in an open paperback.

'Whatcha readin'?' I asked, though I could see it was the Sartre play.

Jim looked up and smiled. 'You do sleepless nights well.' He bowed to kiss my cheek. Jim appeared fuzzy around the edges, happily languid, as if he had awakened from a satisfying nap. He escorted me to the car door, then leaned over for a second kiss.

'What do you say we drive down to Mexico and get married?' he asked two inches from my face.

'By the time we get there, the magistrate's would be closed.'

He rolled his eyes to the bright blue heavens. 'Ah, but the bars would still be open.' When he sank in behind the wheel, he said, 'Lunch then?'

That night, I fell asleep waiting for the household to fall asleep. I woke with a start. After puzzling over which was the big hand and whether it was twelve twenty-five or five in the morning, I pulled on my sandals and slipped out of the house.

Jim leaned against the trunk of the car, his arms folded across his chest. I asked, 'Do you remember that *Twilight Zone* with a woman going through this same waking dream over and over, and it turns out that she is a character living an author's rewrites?'

Jim laughed. 'Oh, yeah. Did the writer type you in late?'

I fell asleep on the short drive. Jim woke me with the back of his fingers stroking my cheek. 'You can sleep inside. I don't care if you sleep, just so it's beside me.'

Jim tucked us into bed together, humming me to sleep. When I opened my eyes, Jim was out of bed and searching for matches in the dark. He struck a match and lit a cluster of candles on the dresser. Jim's body reflected the warm light. He stood golden, watching the candles burn before rejoining me.

He kissed my hair, and split half to make a braid. 'When you're eighteen, and have kept your promise to your mother, will you marry me?'

'That's really sweet of you, Jim. Your coming to Maine to rescue me, well, it means more than I can say. But you don't have to feel an obligation.'

'I don't feel an obligation.' He reached the end of the braid. 'I'm in love with you.'

'But you came to rescue me.'

'Yes,' he said. Then, 'No. I'm not sure when I knew it, maybe not until everything fell apart, but I came to Maine to rescue myself. With you gone, things just chipped away at me. Everything that you thought was right. That *was* my death rattle. I hadn't taken a sober breath in six months. I didn't have the flu, baby, I was going through withdrawal from alcohol. If you asked, I wanted to be able to tell you that I hadn't been drinking. If I'd known how rough it was going to be, I would have waited until after the honeymoon.

306

'Remember when I was so upset about the band selling the song, and you said it wasn't just about the song, or integrity, but that I felt I'd lost my family again? Instead of trying to get Ray and Robby and John back, I got it in my head to try to get my first one back. Not really be in their lives, but just to say, "It was a mess and everybody's probably sorry." More so I could have Anne and Andy back. I miss them. I seem to need them more the older I get.

'I tried to call a lot of times.'

'You saved my life, honey. Twice now. You kept me off that plane. And you taught me not to give my consent. I don't know it every day. I still think death is easier. But with you, life is better, no matter what the struggle.

'I thought if we had a year together, where you felt free to stay or go, that you would come to love me the way I love you. I want to know you at twenty and thirty and fifty. When I'm an old man, I want to wake up next to you, and if I can still get it up, make love with you, and if I can't, to hear what the hell you'd have to say about it. I know I can be more with you, both as an artist and a man, than I can ever be alone, or with anyone else.' When he finished his speech, he lay back against the pillows.

'I'm more with you, too,' I said gently. 'But you pretend Pamela doesn't exist.'

'She doesn't most of the time. Pamela is just something she passes through between one drug and the next. Things have only gotten worse.'

How could they be worse than overdoses and fights?

'She won't admit there's a problem. She just thinks if I was there all the time, she'd be happy. But when I'm there, I'm the problem. It's exhausting to be with her.'

'You love her.'

'I love her. Or who she used to be. I guess I haven't stopped loving her.'

'Do you think, Jim, you should be asking Pamela to marry you instead of me?'

'No. I don't ever think that. You're the only one I want to marry. It's not as if it's a choice between the two of you. During these last three awful months, when most of me believed I would never see you again, I didn't ask Pamela. If I told you the truth about Pamela and me, you'd never let me near you again.'

He never did tell me the end to the story he started in San Francisco the year before. 'I know you are tied to each other in some way that you both need. And that it causes you both pain.'

'You are afraid to tell me something you are caught up in and have no control over.' Jim took a deep breath. 'I have control over this.'

I sang a line from 'Unhappy Girl' and disliked myself for doing it.

Jim laughed. 'Ouch. I may have written that about Pamela's drug use, but I helped build this prison with her.'

Jim stammered through a few false starts. 'Here goes . . . I thought I'd passed out with somebody, but woke up alone. So, I hauled myself to answer this banging at the door. There was Pamela all dolled up with a biker as big as a Harley on her arm.

'Pamela locked the door. She said, "I thought we'd play ham sandwich." I laughed. She thought I was a ham on stage. We'd played around with a threesome in New York, but it was with another women, and I thought it was pretty boring when they were occupied with each other, so I figured I'd like it even less with another guy. I told her, you know, I wasn't interested. Too beat. There must be a vacancy somewhere, but since they were there, I told 'em I'd be a gentleman and give them my room.

'Then Pamela says, "He's not for me. He's for you. I just raised the stakes." I hadn't taken her ham sandwich literally enough.'

Chills ran up my arms. Jim rubbed them to warm me. 'I spent the longest two hours of my life getting that huge son of a bitch drunk enough so I could get by him. Pamela came running after me laughing. I told her that was the end. Not funny. Not a game. Just mean. I got a cab and left her hollering at me in the street.

'That Sunday, a friend of hers called and said she couldn't get Pamela to come around. I called her doctor. Saying all this, you gotta wonder how we can say we love each other, but we do. It's just that we are so bad for each other. Because she was the first woman I loved, I thought that it had to be forever. I do love her. Maybe neither one of us would have gotten so bizarre if we hadn't gotten together.'

He told me when the first album was successful, she wanted to be on his arm. She wanted people to know she was his steady girl. He didn't mind. Since she made a point of telling all of LA that they were married, he had a built-in excuse to put off girls who were making demands. He said, 'In private, she was so distant that when she'd hang on me and kiss me and be so sexy in public, I took what I could get. I loved her.

'Then I saw you. And I felt that same wash of warmth as I did when I first saw Pamela. And I thought, "This can happen more than once?" Drunk as I was, I had that one coherent thought. You glowed. I'd never had such a perfect time as that evening we spent talking. I left because I didn't want to hurt you. When you came running after me, my heart just went wild. I never felt that. God, I knew I met the wrong one first.

'I'm sorry,' he said, eyeing me. 'Did that hurt your feelings? I mean, this is what I thought in the beginning. We were still in the street, and I wanted you so badly I was busting out of my pants, and you were so damn sweet. What happened was that I found myself in you. I got stripped right down to fifteen with a chance to do it right.

'My heart says yes,' I said, as if he had just asked me to marry him.

'Then listen to your heart. You trust your heart in everything else.'

'I'm afraid.'

Jim looked pained. 'Afraid of me? Because of what I said?'

'No, afraid of marriage. My parents. Your parents.' I hesitated. 'You said you were afraid of that yourself.'

'But not with you. We can make up our own marriage. I don't know any man who has the kind of friendship with a woman I have with you. I don't see why the same won't be true if we marry.'

Finally, Jim backed off and put Neil Young's new album on the record-player, *Everybody Knows This Is Nowhere*. Seems like it had just come out, but Jim knew every song by heart and sang along at full throttle.

'You need some sleep and I need to go back to LA for a couple days. I have to check in with the band. We're trying to put an album together.'

'You're doing an album? I thought, *"The Doors are dead. Long live The Doors."* '

'We are. This is a contractual obligation, the one we were rehearsing for in January. Your songs will be on it. That's something. I'll be back Thursday. Rest.'

I caught up on homework, not sleep. I was behind in everything and finding I couldn't breeze through as I used to.

'How can you look worse?' Jim asked the next time he saw me.

'Thank you,' I laughed, but felt hurt. 'One of the difficulties in changing schools mid-term is that I have pages and pages of a comparative analysis on the writing of J. D. Salinger that no one here is interested in, and nothing for a history paper due practically overnight. I may cut my loses and cut the rest of the year.'

'Aw. I've never watched you do your homework.' Jim was incorrigible. 'Do you ever do your homework naked?'

'Never.' I shook my head defiantly.

When we reached the room, Jim's notebook lay on the table, closed, bits of paper sticking out everywhere. Once in a while, he would collect all the notes he had made on napkins, envelopes, and assorted scraps of paper, and copy them into a notebook.

He picked up a rolled poster and brandished it like a sword. 'You can't impress me with your pirate, Jim. My mother knew Douglas Fairbanks.' We both stopped, awkward grins frozen on our faces from the mention of my mother. His melted first.

'Is that so?' He took me in one arm for a pirate pose.

'Yeah. She told me that you have the same charisma. What's the poster?' I asked.

Jim unrolled it. Kandinsky's horse painting! 'I got it in Europe. Goes on the ceiling over the bed, don't you think?'

Standing on the bed in his boots, Jim still couldn't reach the high ceiling. Undaunted, he pulled the bed away and dragged the table over, and bounded on top of that. Once he'd proved his balance infallible, my New England blood got the better of me.

I said, 'Jim, your boots!'

A thumbtack in his mouth, he mumbled, 'If Fred Astaire . . . can dance . . . on a piano,' he spat the tack out and continued, 'the Lizard King can dance on a table.' He did a little jig, one hand holding the poster to the ceiling.

'And I thought the Lizard King had lost his tail.'

He put a final tack into the poster. 'Is that a Coda Queen joke?' he asked with a hand on his hip in a remarkable impression of my exasperated self. He leaped off the table to give the light fixture a good shake and intimidate the neighbours. 'And I have something for the wall.' He shook his notebook until a three-by-five card spiralled to the floor. He considered every wall and ran it through with a thumbtack over the fireplace.

Jim hand-printed in caps a quote attributed to Rimbaud, 1871:

THE POETS OF THE FUTURE WILL COME WHEN THE INFI-NITE SERVITUDE OF WOMAN WILL BE BROKEN, WHEN SHE WILL LIVE FOR HERSELF AND ... SHE WILL ALSO BE POET!

'Don't yell at me,' I said, looking at his strident letters. I wondered what the dot, dot, dot replaced. Jim's careful editing to please me.

Jim kissed my cheek. 'Let me know if you ever need paper.'

While he transcribed at the table, I sprawled my notes on the bed, internally grumbling over the relevancy of any term paper with Jim a few feet away. I was fighting the clock and losing. Shortly, Jim joined me on the bed, careful not to disturb my stacks of notes. 'Close your eyes. I'll sing you a lullaby.'

'I've got to finish this.'

'Take a little nap. I'll wake you in an hour.' He gathered my papers and relegated them to the far corner of the bed.

He still hadn't sung 'I Can't See Your Face' to me, only the one line in a car so long ago. Eager to hear Jim sing it, I closed my eyes. He touched my cheek with the back of his hand. He played with my hair. I opened my eyes. 'Close your eyes,' he urged softly. 'How does that go?' he asked. I snuggled closer. '*Close your eyes, go to sleep, little baby,*' his voice wavered. '*When you wake, you shall have all the pretty little horses. Dapples and greys,*' he la-la'd a few lines. 'I think my mother, maybe my grandmother, sang that

to me when I was real little. I can't remember. Did your mother
sing to you?'

'I don't remember lullabies. She used to sing to herself, ironing.
Hymns like "I Walk Through the Valley Alone" or songs on the
radio like "It's Only a Paper Moon".'

Jim didn't know the hymn, but sang 'Paper Moon' until I slept.
He woke me. I panicked when I saw the clock. Nearly four and
time to sneak back to my friend's house.

'Calm down. You needed the sleep. I finished your paper. I'm a
wiz at footnotes. I can ibid. with the best of them.'

An afternoon I should have been in school, I was standing in a
patch of sun in the room where Jim and I spent our time. I'd
never been alone there. By summer, it would be unbearably hot
with its western windows. I brought rice paper to cover the bare
panes. I blushed, knowing Jim and I had forgotten there was an
outside world that might be looking in at us.

A Japanese friend once showed me how, as part of traditional
spring cleaning, her mother would remove the last year's rice paper
from the shoji screens and apply new paper with a rice flour paste.
How to decorate for under a dollar. I held the rice paper against the
window to see how it looked. The threads that whipped through it
glistened.

I cut one sheet of paper into little rectangles in proportion to the
window-panes. I collected anything that would hold a little water,
our unmatched cups, little bowls, the glass from the bathroom,
and lined them up in front of me on the floor. I mixed a different
watercolour in each, faithful to the most translucent colours.

I had this all laid out on the floor when Jim walked in. 'What
are we up to?'

'I thought if I could fold a piece of paper and cut it here and
there to make a snowflake in the second grade, I could fold a piece
of paper and dye it here and there to make a pseudo-stained-glass
window.'

Afterwards, he cuddled me and read his Jamaican poems. I
watched the words as he spoke them. Several were vignettes of
his restless walks, he the stranger, aching for his own American
night.

My double life was catching up with me. When Jim picked me up at lunchtime, I was so tired I fell asleep on the short drive to the room. He woke me with a kiss on my cheek. Jim had been working that morning. Around his chair were sheets torn from his notebook and crumpled. His book was open, which was unusual. He always closed his notebook. Opening it required an invitation.

'Not going well?' I asked tentatively.

'Actually, I made a lot of progress. I've been editing.' He picked up one of the wadded sheets, tossed it in the air, and hit it with the back of his hand. He juggled it a few times before he missed.

'May I read what you have?'

'Why don't we see how many places we can kiss each other first? Champagne? Have you ever had champagne? Can I send you back to school drunk?'

A problem that had never come up with our irregular rendezvous was my being indisposed. 'Jim,' I whispered, as if someone might overhear, 'I'm having my period.'

'Then a hot bath is what you need.' Jim handed me our unmatched cups, and grabbed the champagne out of the fridge. He took my hand and trotted us off to the bathroom. 'I'd have a better chance of plying you with bubble bath than champagne. Wish I'd thought of it.'

Jim stood in the tub, and offered me his hand. He stroked my right leg with his foot and poured us cups of champagne which sizzled with bubbles that popped in the air. We clanked our cups. 'To life,' Jim toasted.

I did my best not to grimace at the taste. 'I like the bubbles, but it's a little bitter.'

Jim laughed. 'Baby, this is Dom Perignon. It ain't bitter.'

'Got a thesaurus?' I snapped. 'I'll find a better word.'

'You almost sounded cranky there. You get cranky? I'll bet you have cramps. I know the cure.' He sat his cup down and caressed my neck. I closed my eyes, not having much faith in a neck rub taking care of cramps, but his hands were soothing. After a few minutes, his hand drifted between my legs.

'Jim, I'm not feeling very sexy.'

313

'You don't have to feel sexy. Just relax. Orgasms conquer cramps . . .'

'It's pretty embarrassing that you know more about women's bodies than I do.'

At the beginning of May my mother flew out. Her first news was that my dog Joey had been hit by a car. Mine since I spotted her in a cage in a pound, I'd miss her cheerful presence. I declined Jim's offer to buy me a puppy to take her place. My mother rented a furnished apartment walking distance from school. My dad was going to follow later.

She and I said nothing of the painful separation she caused between Jim and me. Knowing she had acted out of love, not malice, made it possible to get on with things, but our relationship had changed. We agreed we should invite Jim up for dinner.

Jim called me for the third time for details. 'Want me to shave?' he asked.

'I told her you look like a buffalo hunter, but you're the same sweet soul.'

'Sweet soul? Sweet soul? Do I have a wrong number? This is Jim Morrison.'

Jim gave my mother flowers and a hug, both of which were meant for me and a last-minute thought for her. Jim gave me a wink and a kiss on my cheek. Nervous about how my mother would take his change in appearance, Jim played with his beard and kept checking to see if his shirt were tucked in. Nervous about the wisdom in wowing Jim with my cooking, I spent more time planning the dinner than I had on that last term paper. Jim had been miffed by the B it received. I wanted my cooking to fare better.

I opted for something spicy. I put out chips and salsa made without the hated cilantro I'd watched Jim pick out of restaurant salsa, claiming it was so nasty even caterpillars wouldn't eat it. I had hopes that Jim would engage my mother in conversation in the connected living-room while I constructed cheese enchiladas, but he leaned against the counter where I was working, munching chips and talking with my mother, who sat at the kitchen table. They split a beer, which seemed friendly enough.

My mother asked Jim who his favourite poets were. He skipped

314

Rimbaud and Ginsberg, and tried out Walt Whitman, whom Jim had never mentioned, though Whitman was as outrageously bold in his time as Ginsberg was in the fifties, and quoted something from *Leaves of Grass* to prove he didn't deserve the suspicious look I had given him.

After food, conversation slowed. Dishes never lingered on my mother's table. She was likely to whisk away your plate as soon as you lifted your last forkful. She washed dishes while Jim and I dried. She asked Jim to recite some of his poetry. He was, after all, to her, a graduate from UCLA who aspired to be a poet.

What I could see of Jim's face blushed. 'Sure. Let's see,' he said, closing his eyes, but still drying the plate in his hands. He spoke the first line of 'Horse Latitudes' in a raspy whisper, as if confiding a secret. When he said the word 'Consent' he opened his eyes. The poem finished with a wave of his hand over the ocean, his eyes intent on mine.

He recited 'I Am Troubled'. He let a few seconds elapse before he smiled and spoke several of his beautiful morning songs, ending with the one he had given me in Maine which had grown from five lines to six.

'Excuse me,' my mother said, drying her hands. 'I'm dumbfounded. I saw the little poem you had written for Lin a couple Christmases ago and knew you had a way with words, but somehow you don't expect people you know to be so talented.' She asked, 'You're going to do something with this, aren't you?'

Jim asked me to go brush my teeth. 'For about fifteen minutes,' he added. They talked, but neither would tell me the content of their conversation. Jim was invited to stay and slept on the couch. Or at least lay on it. He was up at five with my mother. He made us scrabbled eggs and English muffins, buttered and toasted under the broiler.

School was out! My mother and I rode the Greyhound to San Jose, where my sister had settled. We checked into a downtown motel near her. Jim appeared, nearly on our heels, with a blooming African violet as a house-warming gift.

'I remembered your beautiful plants in your house in Stockton,' he said so earnestly my mother was brought to tears. Setting the potted plant in the middle of the Formica and chrome dinette immediately made it home.

The realization struck after Jim had gone in search of his own digs, why I was so willing to spend hours sculpting ice polar bears or dyeing bits of paper that would fade in the sun. Everything was impermanent and there was peace in going into something knowing that, rather than being surprised by loss.

The next morning, I babbled my discovery to a freshly wakened Jim at his motel door. Jim choose his motel, not by location or luxury, but by its neon. A female neon diver was his dream come true. As I was rattling about art and life, he was glancing over my shoulder at the unlit sign.

I taunted, 'I thought you told me that you stopped looking when you found me.'

He hauled me into his room, asking, 'Will you be my dream sequence?'

The next time Jim called from Los Angeles he repeated the question. Jim explained he was really going to make a movie with friends from UCLA. He'd had a dream about my brother Bill and created a script about that hitchhiker who was the past they were both compelled to pick up. The one they knew would kill them. 'I want to recreate our erotic swim on film.'

'Not with me. I'm no actress,' I said.

Jim pouted, persuaded, and promised if I flunked a screen test, he wouldn't push. I gave in knowing the movie was on hold until somebody could afford film for the camera.

New friends who lived in a cabin in the luscious Santa Cruz mountains asked if I might house-sit for them, care for their pets and tend their garden. When I relayed my lucky housefall, Jim flew up. I met him at the airport in shades as dark as his. I had to keep lifting them enough to see my way. I wore a to-the-ankle skirt that looked like a stormy sky with a dark blue shirt tied at what waist I had. He made me twirl in my skirt and insisted on a public kiss, then let me drive.

Slumped down in the seat with his knees up on the glove compartment, Jim stabbed at the buttons on the Blaupunkt. 'Music! Music!' he demanded at the commercials on every station.

When the Stones finally sang out, he sang along. We merged on to Highway 17 heading west. We had to span the width of San Jose before Los Gatos was on our right. I looped through the way Jim liked me to – because Neal Cassady had lived there, and Kerouac had visited there. That they hated the place didn't seem to matter. Then we drove up to the little town of Saratoga. There, we headed west again and through the narrow and winding Highway 9.

Welcome to redwoods, to hairpin turns, and to vistas in blue atmospheric perspective! I was doing my best to drive more boldly than I felt, taking to heart Jim's first driving advice to use centrifugal force and not the brakes.

'Wanna slow down?' he asked, his hand gripping the handle over the glove compartment, provided for anxious passengers.

'Driving is like dancing,' I explained, 'to the car radio.' My parents let me use the second car, a black Volkswagen bug with snappy red interior, the reverse of Jim's Mustang he'd had to shoot after an accident.

Jim borrowed my journal, skipping pages to claim one. He lowered the radio volume to hear what was in his head. Between downshifting, I helped him fight the wind whipping the pages.

My friends' directions instructed a left after the biker bar. Their cabin was on a dirt road off a one-lane semi-paved road. Like most of the little places hidden away in the mountains, it was originally a summer vacation getaway. The only heat was the fireplace, the bathroom a recent addition. The hydrangeas were heavy with blossoms, green going blue. The big orange cat lurked on the roof.

Jim leaped out of the car and ran over to hug a redwood. He danced back to the car to help with a couple bags of supplies. The lock on the door was a puzzle box. There was no key, you had to pull out carved pieces of wood in a set order to release the door.

Jim played with the amazing lock while I carried in the groceries and jammed everything in the already stocked refrigerator. I joined Jim on the porch. He returned my diary closed so I had to search for his new song. Rare to have a title from the beginning: 'Hwy 9' followed by two lines of driving suggestions.

'You taught me to drive,' I said, my feathers ruffled. 'And you left the *u* out of *your*.'

He inserted the *u* and added a couple lines. 'I'd ask you not to sulk, but you're so darn cute.' He fancied I pouted as well as Shirley Temple.

Jim fed the cat. I fed the rabbit. In the garden, Jim gently eased the surplus seedlings from the ground the length of the row before he washed his hands in the cool hose water and returned to the step. When I finished my row, I rinsed my hands and watched Jim in the sun, stretched across the steps, a contented cat. He produced Kafka's *The Trial* from a pocket and read. When I walked by, he brushed my thigh with his fingers, but did not look up from the book.

'It's a beautiful little book,' he said, looking down at the steps, 'but don't try to fix me.'

Jim was moody and silent the remainder of the afternoon and through a barely touched dinner. He settled on the pleasantly lumpy green sofa to write. Having unpacked his own, he didn't even need my journal. For the first time in our time together, I went to bed alone.

In the wee hours, he slipped into bed for physical comfort. In the morning, I woke with Jim's arms around me in sleep, his face nestled in my hair. I tried to find sleep again, but the birds were awake. And the trees! They rustled against each other and the roof. When I edged from under him, Jim settled back to sleep without opening his eyes. I pulled on a sweater and jeans to survive the walk to the bathroom. Rain was threatening. The air in the house was still and damp.

My friends' coaching for fire building was a list impaled on a nail. Jim emerged from the bedroom wrapped in the quilt. We lay together on the sofa, my head against his chest, Jim rubbing my back under my sweater.

'I wrote a fan letter last night to Maya Angelou,' Jim said.

I asked, 'May I read it?'

'I'm not moving, but it's over on the table in my notebook.'

I left the warmth of Jim and the fire long enough to fetch the notebook. Jim turned a few pages and held the notebook open for me. The page was covered with writing, top to bottom and edge to edge, bursting through margins. But almost all of it had been scribbled over with frantic circles. All that remained readable was, 'Dear Miss Angelou,' near the top, and one sentence,

'Thank you for giving a voice to all of us who haven't yet found ours.' He signed, James Douglas Morrison, his whole name, his poet's name.

'I guess I'll make a neater copy,' was all he said before he returned to the beginning of the notebook to read me his night's poems.

We played in the woods all day, me pointing out poison oak to Jim a dozen times. He watched the orange salamanders in a nearby brook and jumped when he came upon a garter snake lazing on a sunny rock. When night fell, we hiked out to the highway so Jim could have a cold beer.

Even though I wasn't imbibing in more than Jim and an occasional dance, I was carded and ousted. Jim wanted to argue with the bartender and a biker wanted to join a fight on either side, but I managed to yank him out to the comparative safety of the road. We walked by the cabins for rent which were that dreadful pseudoredwood colour by day and grim grey by night, and up the narrow road to my friends' cabin.

'Like to get a place of my own up here,' Jim said wistfully.

Jim followed the list to make a good fire and created an impromptu bed before it, but grabbed his notebook instead of me. He opened it to his song page, tapping his pencil against it, but not adding anything. Soon, he set his writing aside in my favour. Jim asked that I rub his shoulders, which gave me a good view of his notebook. The song had become Roadhouse Blues/Hwy 9.'

'*Ashen?*' I asked.

'You,' Jim answered.

I rubbed. I couldn't keep silent. 'You see me grey?'

'Ashen is white,' he corrected me.

'But in romance novels, I always thought when the damsel went ashen, she was a sort of sickly grey.'

'Look it up,' he advised. Then added with a smile, 'If I'm wrong, I'm not changing the song.'

I was stubborn enough to leave the warmth of the fire and Jim to look the word up in a dictionary. Naturally, Jim was right. 'Like Moby Dick,' I sighed from across the room.

He bestowed one of those winning smiles. 'You are quite often as much of a challenge, but the image in my head was your skin as white as rose petals.' Why he gave me white roses on my birthdays. While I was feeling flattered, Jim added, 'Now, of course, I will always see that damn whale.'

19

---·•◦•·---

Cars Hiss By My Window

'Well, gosh, baby,' Jim said with suitable pathos. 'What are we going to do?' We were hungry and I'd informed him my standby burritos were a food of the past, having just discovered tortillas were made with lard.

In reply, I guided him to a drive-in on San Carlos, a street that connected the old and new sections of San Jose. Like any drive-in eatery in appearance, this place served these sumptuous things called falafels. I refused to let Jim participate in the ordering.

'Look, they are deep-fried and have hot sauce,' I told him. 'Go sit down.'

Jim claimed a picnic table nearly on the sidewalk, the major essence of the place being traffic exhaust. Jim predictably considered that great ambience. When I handed Jim his meal in a pita, he picked the tomato and cucumber garnish off before tasting my offering. He smiled and hummed approval at his first spicy bite, then studied the little fried ball he had bitten into. 'It's green,' he complained. 'I don't eat green food.' But he ate anyway, not to be polite, but because he liked the exotic Middle Eastern flavours.

'Garbonzo beans,' I informed him when he was nearly finished.

He stuck out his tongue at me. I couldn't begin to tell him

321

the pleasure of the mundane with him. While I was trying to find a grand way to say it, Jim said, 'Nice just hanging out with you.'

By mid-July, Jim was hanging out on the cover of *Rolling Stone*. I looked at a copy, knowing Jim would disapprove, but wanted to see the pictures. The one on the cover was a year and a half old, not the bearded Jim. Drawn to the article by Jerry Hopkins, I read a paragraph before I forced myself to keep my word not to read Jim's interviews, and returned the paper to its stack. On the way out of the bookstore, I bought it. Just for the pictures. Inside, there was the best picture I'd ever seen of Jim, making a face into the camera.

When my father arrived from Maine, my parents and I had moved into a furnished apartment across from the shopping mall where my mother worked. The living-room was decorated in Danish modern knock-offs.

I was delving into the article at the rickety kitchen table, when Jim called and I immediately confessed my crime. When we hung up, I made myself toss the *Rolling Stone* into the dumpster out behind the apartment to keep myself honest, then wished I'd saved that photo of him.

A few days later, I made my first pilgrimage to San Francisco since my return to California. Cutting through San Francisco's Union Square, trying to avoid an ardent mime, I heard a man call, 'Ginger!' Bill Graham broke through the crowd, his New York stride sending the mime scurrying. Strange to see him out of his *Bill Graham Presents* context! He could not, I realized, spend all of his time saying, 'Ladies and Gentleman . . . From Los Angeles, California, The Doors!'

When he reached me, I held out my hand and he pulled me in for a hug as if we knew each other. I hadn't seen him since the insult side-stage in San Jose over a year before, nor spoken with him since he asked if I knew about Jim's drinking problem. 'Is Jim with you?'

'No. On my own.'

'Great!' he said. 'Can I buy you lunch?'

No excuse leapt to mind, so we angled up Sutter. I had to skip every few yards to catch up with his brisk pace. Bill held open the door of a corner diner. We slid into a booth. Although it had the trappings of a burger joint, the menu was Chinese.

The plate in front of me wasn't what I thought I'd ordered. There were long black strips across the top. I lifted one inexpertly with chopsticks for a closer view. 'Is it an eel?' I asked secretively.

Bill laughed. 'It's a Chinese mushroom.'

I felt relieved, and after several failed attempts to manoeuvre chop-sticks, switched to a fork so my food wouldn't get any colder than it already was. Bill pushed his food around without trying it. I couldn't tell if he hadn't gotten what he expected or was preoccupied. Finally, he clarified. 'Did you read the article about Jim in *Rolling Stone*?

'Part of it. I was on the first page when Jim called and asked me not to read it.'

'Why?' he asked bluntly.

'He never wanted me to read interviews. I haven't since we met.' I immediately regretted confiding that. 'He plays games.'

Tight-lipped and staring directly at me, Bill Graham said, 'You mean, he lies.'

I sighed and looked away. 'Plays games *is* more accurate. He feels he's honest in his work, but that publicity and the whole media thing is a separate career.'

His presence was so intense, I felt compelled to look at the man across from me again. When our eyes locked, he said bitterly, 'Jim told me his parents were dead. He had tears in his eyes and couldn't say more than that. I was an orphan. I believed we had that common sense of loss. Jim is quite the consummate actor.'

Despite Graham's anger, I felt no need to apologize for Jim. 'He wasn't acting, Mr Graham.'

'The interview makes it plain his parents are living. Is that a lie, then?'

The little bowl of tea was too hot to drink. I wanted to tell him about my thinking Jim's parents were dead, too, and the anxious call I made to him, but knew it would only confuse things, not make him understand Jim. 'No,' I said.

'One or the other has to be,' he said.

I tried to explain without explaining. 'The facts and the truth aren't always the same thing.'

'Sounds like you've spent too much time with Jim,' he said sharply. 'I was a Jewish boy in Nazi Germany. I lost my mother. My sister barely survived Spandau. I don't find Jim's *game* amusing.'

My hand went across the table to touch his. The gesture made us both feel awkward. 'He once told me, in a way that was meant to sound light, that he was an orphan in his soul,' I said. 'It wasn't funny.'

'Could you be more direct?' His stare was direct enough.

'No. He told me, though, that he had that loss in common with you. He feels the same bond you do.'

Bill Graham sat across from me, not eating, not drinking the tea, lost in thought. Then he talked about his life in Europe, the real name he missed, a child's driven march through France, during which he never asked what happened to the boy who was beside him the day before and nowhere in sight that day. 'I just kept walking . . . I'm sorry,' he said when the waiter interrupted him with the check. 'You're too easy to talk to.'

'I'm just young,' I said and beat him to the check.

'I invited you,' he tried to insist, but it pleased me to pay for the meal. At the door, we didn't really say goodbye, but wandered in opposite directions. I had planned to go to the Fillmore that night, but chose instead to walk from museum to museum until I was so tired I sat in the Museum of Modern Art and cried over the fragility and endurance of children. I hoped when I was Jim's age, when I was Bill Graham's age, I wouldn't carry my childhood as heavily as they carried theirs.

Jim buzzed up from LA. We gorged so many wild blackberries in Santa Cruz, we broke out in raging hives. He rushed to the ocean and threw me in. Then fished me out. The dip did wonders to save our bodies and sanity.

The next I heard from Jim, he had come up with enough cash to buy a reel of film. The screen test, regrettably, was on. He was so anxious to get started, he fronted an airline ticket. I pretended I was off to Stockton for a few days. My dad drove me to the bus station. I hitchhiked to the airport. Jim met me at the Los Angeles airport with, 'Could we get married at one of the old missions?'

As far as I knew, Jim was a lapsed Protestant, possibly Presbyterian, but not a lapsed Catholic. 'Out of the question,' I told him. 'I can't bear what the missions did to Native Americans.'

Rather than get angry, Jim put his arm around me for a verse of 'Wild Child'. Well, maybe that was his idea of anger. Then it occurred to me that in 'The End' the King's Highway was the El Camino Real. Fourth-grade history of California. The mission trail.

'Oh,' I said, enlightened at LA International. 'The El Camino.'

Jim chuckled his way into downtown Los Angeles. He leapt from the car near The Doors' office, leaving the door open. Planning a mad dash to snag the camera and a quick getaway, he left the keys swinging in the ignition. I fidgeted in that latest of Jim's rental cars, something in marine blue, at least. After a warm fifteen minutes, I collected all the scraps of paper under foot and under seats, cast-off poem shards, into one neat pile, wondered if the black bobby pin I clipped them together with came with the car or with a dark-haired companion of Jim's, and centred them lovingly on the dash for Jim's approval. Then I relocated myself to the stripe of shade across the nose of the car.

'Ginger!'

Like a friendly yellow dog, Brandon de Wilde loped across the street and planted himself on the hood next to me. His golden hair was longer. His moustache more confident. A Super 8 hung from his left hand. 'This is so weird,' he exclaimed, 'I woke up thinking about you. I called that Florida number after you moved and the woman who answered the phone said you were in Maine. And you're here!'

'Temporarily,' I told him, wondering what his morning thoughts of me were.

'How long are you going to be here? Would you like to spend the day together? We could go to the beach. Have dinner and see a movie later. Go to a party.'

His day was fuller than my year's calendar. 'Oh, that sounds very nice, Brandon, but I have plans. And,' I said impishly, 'as I recall, you have a wife.'

He grinned. He seemed to have given up on contact lenses and simply settled on attractive gold-rimmed glasses. 'I'm no longer with wife. Are your plans still with Jim Morrison?'

'Still.'

'So . . .' Brandon dragged the word out, 'he's your exception to dating married men.'

I stared at him. 'Who in the world told you Jim was married?'

'His wife,' Brandon said softly to soften the blow.

I pretended surprise. 'Who might she be?'

'Pam. The redhead.' He reached out and tugged at my hair. 'The other redhead.'

'Pamela is many things to Jim, but his wife isn't one of them.' I'd like to have tugged at his golden hair, but didn't dare. I sat on my hands to keep from touching him.

'Honey,' Brandon whispered, 'maybe Jim's not being honest with you.'

On cue, Jim made his entrance with a serious-looking camera. Brandon whipped up his Super 8 and pointed it at Jim.

Jim hefted his camera. 'Mine's bigger than yours,' he said, enjoying the double entendre as he brushed passed Brandon to heave the camera into the back seat. Considerably lighter, Jim proceeded to misbehave for Brandon's camera. He danced across the parking-lot like an escapee from *West Side Story*, took a running leap from bumper to dented trunk to rooftop where he was a convincing whirling dervish until he slid down the windshield, grabbing me for a breathless kiss.

'Could you do that again, Jimbo?' Brandon asked, echoing some patronizing director he must have known. 'The light wasn't right.'

Jim repeated the kiss obediently and perfectly.

'I meant the dance,' Brandon said.

'I know.' Jim rolled his eyes. They shook hands. 'Haven't seen you in a while. I'm going to do a screen test of Ginger.'

'You want to be an actress?' Brandon asked with disbelief.

'Nope,' I shook my head, feeling like a horse neighing. I tried not to giggle, which I felt would only underscore that impression. 'But Jim insists I prove to him I can't act. He's promised to burn the film when I have satisfied him I am, for the most part, honest.

Speaking of honesty,' I turned from focus on Brandon to Jim, 'Jim, you married?'

Brandon took a step back as if he were afraid Jim's answer might be to punch one of us. 'Not yet. I can't get the right girl to give the right answer.'

I smiled at Brandon's very visible relief. His thoughts played across his face the way Jim's did, something necessary for an actor and dangerous for a man.

'I'm sorry. Pam told me you were married. She introduced herself as Pamela Morrison.'

Jim shrugged. 'If it makes her happy to say that, I don't care.' He chuckled and mumbled, 'Really, it pisses me off.'

Jim ducked into the car, picked up the bobby-pinned bundle and shoved it unlovingly into the glove compartment. Might not ever become another *Soft Parade*. He wasn't exactly invited, but nobody had said goodbye to him, so Brandon stepped over Jim's camera and settled in the back seat. I was going to make my reluctant début in front of an actor who could act since he was four years old.

Jim declined Brandon's offers of pot and acid on behalf of both of us, in between singing at the top of his lungs along with the radio, giving no quarter for commercials. Brandon, silent in the back seat, seemed happy to be along on an adventure.

Jim drove us to a wooded spot with hot white rocks. He lugged the heavy camera down an embankment which ended in a pool. Jim waded around its edge to a wider bank and waited there for Brandon and me, as if we were slower siblings out for a hike.

When we reached Jim, he lowered the camera on to my shoulder to give me a feel for it. I swayed slightly with the unexpected weight. 'Now I know how Atlas felt,' I said with difficulty.

Jim snorted and collapsed in the dirt in laughter. Never know what's going to nab that man. Brandon looked perplexed and asked, 'Is this a private joke, or can anyone laugh?'

Jim pointed helplessly at the camera. 'That's it!' he roared, still pointing. 'That's filmmaking.'

'Atlas,' I made a stab at filling in a baffled Brandon, 'carried the world on his shoulders.'

Brandon beamed, obviously recalling the image and seeing our resemblance, 'Oh, yeah! My education wasn't very traditional. A lot of what you say goes right over my head.'

'First of all, Brandon,' Jim got up off the ground, picking well-deserved foxtails out of his tail, then leaning on Brandon's shoulder to speak in male confidence, 'I learned early on, you can't be stoned around Ginger or you'll miss too much. I need every brain cell to keep up. And the groovy part is that after you've been with her a while, you feel high anyway.'

Jim reached into Brandon's shirt pocket and opened his little pouch so its contents caught the wind. Jim pulled the strings of the empty pouch tight and stuffed it roughly back into the pocket. Brandon's jaw dropped.

Jim reclaimed the camera and explained the scene, alternately businesslike and playful. He walked me around the boulders from which he expected my entrance. When he saw the pathway was a mine of pebbles and burrs for the required bare feet, he put down the camera and set out to remove each one. I suggested I could just take my sandals off at the water's edge.

'That's not how I see it,' he said, continuing with his vision.

Brandon found this amusing. 'No director on any movie I was ever in got on his hands and knees to clear a path for any actor.'

'Actors are like dogs,' Jim said so only I could hear, annoyed.

'I thought Hitchcock said they were cattle.' I smiled at Brandon sunning on the other side of the pond. 'So far, actors look like people to me.'

'Watch. Actors are like dogs. They are so accustomed to direction, they do what they are told, then question why.' I tugged at the elbow of Jim's sleeve, not wanting him to prove his theory on Brandon.

'Stand over there!' Jim ordered. Obediently, Brandon got to his feet and took a few steps to his left, following Jim's gesture. At least Jim's gloating was his briefly arched eyebrow, while Brandon waited, hands on hips, for his next direction.

'Relax, baby. This isn't the real thing. We'll shoot that at night and I'll cut it so everybody will think they've seen more than they have.'

'Like *Psycho*,' I said. Jim's eyes were dancing, picturing his cut.

328

'I'm not going to undress in front of him,' I whispered with a nod towards Brandon.

Jim's eyes hid nothing. I was disappointing him. I knew he was thinking what he'd first said about my diary. 'You can be shy in your life, but not in your work.' He wanted me to rise to the occasion and accept this as work. I wished his personal jealousy I'd always resented would rear up to keep me from undressing in front of another man.

'I'll go as far as my slip.'

Jim nodded and whispered, '*Just* the slip. Your ridiculous underwear goes.' He must have thought he sounded harsh, because he looked over his shoulder as he walked away and added, 'I do like that slip.'

The moment Jim lowered the camera's lens on to me, I couldn't remember how to walk. Even the memory of *right leg, left leg* deserted me. Brandon's Super-Eighting Jim's directing me only worsened my nerves. I wasn't going to act. I wasn't even going to walk. I was going to cry. I was up to my knees in the pond, unsure of how I'd gotten there.

Jim's solution was to proclaim Brandon James Wong Howe, slip out of his own clothes, and slide into the little watering hole naked. He swam a few strokes towards me. The grace he had on land increased in the water. I waded away from the rocky edge. 'Just come swim with me,' he coaxed, 'like last summer.'

Concentrating on Jim, rather than Jim behind a camera, comforted me. To react to Jim's body was natural. When I emerged from the water, my silky yellow slip had become a second skin.

Jim's jealously made a belated appearance and he yelled, 'Cut!'

I undressed and pulled on my dress behind a bush. I glanced around the leafy wall in response to a splash. Brandon had, minus either camera, joined Jim in the water. They engaged in boyish horseplay while I dried my hair in the sun. When Jim tired first and walked up out of the pool, I said, 'That's my idea of a dream sequence.'

Jim laid out his pants to laze on. I wished we were alone, especially when Brandon came out of the water. Jim was the only naked man I'd ever seen and I was doing my best not to compare this second man to him.

'Could you hand me my glasses?' he asked. 'I'm really so blind I can't find my glasses without my glasses.'

The glasses were safely in his bundle of clothes. He could have found them by feel. When Brandon could see again, he borrowed my comb. He twisted the top half of his lean body towards Jim. 'You wrote "Wild Child" for her? She's the shyest girl I've ever met.'

Jim didn't budge, eyes closed, soaking up the sun. 'It's her mind that's wild.'

We stopped at a roadside joint on the road back to Los Angeles. 'I can't believe we forgot to eat,' I said, so hungry I could have eaten the greasy menu.

'I can't believe I forgot to drink,' Jim winked and downed half a beer before looking at his menu.

'More than two and I drive,' I threatened.

'God, no! We'd wind up in Mexico!' Jim said.

Brandon laughed, 'I can't figure out if you two are like brother and sister or Romeo and Juliet.'

'That's our problem,' I said.

'Or pleasure,' Jim put in, finishing his beer and holding it up to the waitress for another.

'I felt like a voyeur filming you in that pool,' Brandon said.

'I felt like a voyeur when you got out of the pool,' I said and blushed.

The red-headed waitress caught Jim's eye. She kept thinking he looked like somebody. 'Maybe we went to high-school together,' Jim suggested helpfully.

'I went to Hollywood High,' she said. 'You can tell by how far I've come.'

'Me, too,' Jim lied. 'When did you graduate?'

'Sixty-one,' she said automatically, then wished she'd said sixty-five.

'Me, too,' Jim said.

I checked out the jukebox for something that old. I remembered all the songs Jim lined up that night in Santa Cruz. They did have Sam Cooke, but the wrong song. I lucked out with Roy Orbison's 'Running Scared', and bet a dime on it. I heard the waitress say, 'Oh, that guy could sing.'

Jim said, 'He still can. Wanna dance?'

She was a good dancer and didn't really need Jim on the floor the way I did. Jim enjoyed dancing with a woman cosying up to him because he went to Hollywood High with her, not because he was Jim Morrison.

'Dance with me,' Brandon whispered.

I liked the idea of his holding me enough to accept his hand. I learned that if I shuffled, rather than picked up my feet, I couldn't exactly step on his feet, just bump into them.

'Did you go to Hollywood High?' I asked Brandon.

'Oh, yeah. I graduated in sixty-one.' He was good at playing games. 'You?'

We dropped Brandon off on Sunset. He wanted to party and charged off, skipping and twirling to an unknown fate. Jim and I decided to hole up at his regular motel because he wanted to return the camera to the nearby office.

Less than a week later, Jim phoned to say the film was processed if I wanted to see it. 'Like a traffic accident,' I said and took the Greyhound down. We wound up at The Doors' office in a cubbyhole so small I had to sit on his lap to watch the film he and Brandon shot of me through a Moviola. The images jumped like a silent movie, which it was.

'It's in colour,' I said, stunned with disappointment. When we first talked about movies, Jim had said he didn't see why people shot in colour just because it was possible. I thought surely his own film would be in black and white.

'We plan to use this short film to get financing for a feature-length. Colour was necessary towards that end.'

'A business decision,' I said.

'Ouch! You make it sound like treason.' He rubbed my arms to warm me to the movie.

The slip, wet, left no curve of my body to the imagination. 'Oh, gosh!' I said. I'd felt shy enough looking down at myself at the pool. To look at myself on film was torture.

'Sexy,' Jim said, running the film back and forth a few times to torment me.

I tried to focus on Jim's sensual swim rather than me, but there was no doubt I was not an actress unless he meant to turn it into *Zombies from Hollywood High*. Whatever charms I liked to feel

I had as a person, were nowhere on film. I looked terrified of Jim, of the camera, of the water.

'Make an artistic decision, Jim,' I said. 'Burn it. You promised.'

Jim ignored me. He rewound the film and locked it in a desk. 'I think if we went back to the place you nearly drowned, you'd feel safe there with me, and safe in water again.'

'That's separate from my not being an actress,' I said.

'I'm more concerned about you than whether or not you want to be in my film.'

'That was Stockton,' I said, planting myself in the middle of the dark office. 'I'm not going back to Stockton.'

'We're going back to Stockton right now.' Had he forgotten we were in Los Angeles? Jim grabbed his jacket – as if anyone needed more than a T-shirt in the summer heat in that dirty town – and roared out of the office. Jim in motion was impossible to stop. If I hadn't kept up and jumped into the car, he wouldn't have missed me until Fresno.

With a mission, Jim was delighted. He hummed. He didn't even bother to turn on the radio. He sang. He sang 'Try a Little Tenderness'. He sang 'Corrina, Corrina'. Twice. I loved that on the radio when I was little. Who sang it? 'Joe Turner,' Jim said. 'Think it was the first forty-five I ever bought.' Then he settled into an hour-long version of 'Honky Tonk Women', improvising whole verses of grunts and moans. When we reached Interstate 5, he quickened the pace of his growing 'Roadhouse Blues' to suit the straightaway.

I couldn't play. I scrunched down in the seat beside him. 'I don't want to go,' I said softly, when the car fell quiet. I looked up at him. 'You don't understand.'

Jim reacted as if I'd whacked him with a sledgehammer. He jerked the car on to the shoulder. His hands were still glued to the wheel when he turned to me. 'What don't I understand?'

'I wasn't swimming.' I took a deep breath. 'I almost drowned in less than a foot of water . . . because someone held me down.'

Jim always touched me when we talked. His hand would find mine. Or he would rub my shoulder. Or brush my cheek. There was a gulf between us that my reach couldn't bridge. My feelings were so damaged, I couldn't tell which of us had created the distance.

'Some crazy high-school boy.'

We didn't speak and Jim didn't sing the rest of the long trip. Fortunately, it was late enough when we reached the Stockton city limits that we checked into a motel rather than checking out the little stream that ran near where my old house stood.

'This is the first time you've ever made me do something I didn't want to,' I said, hoping it would make him return the key and head south again.

Jim flopped on to the brown bedspread, adding the depth of his arm to the flat pillow. He watched me surveying the night come through the window. I stepped back a few inches from the musty curtains and listened to an untalented, but whole-hearted, musician play a lonesome Mexican tune on an accordion somewhere down the street.

That was missing in Florida. In New England. A stranger who played on his porch, music he may have learned from his father. The music made me feel homesick and curiously at ease about the forced return. Dirty and loud and callous, Stockton was more home than anywhere.

'You ever going to speak to me again?' Jim asked from the bed. I turned, but could no longer make him out in the shadowy room.

'I was enjoying the music,' I said in his direction.

'He's not very good,' Jim said critically.

I asked, 'Does music have to be good to be enjoyed?'

'That was the longest hour I ever spent with you,' he said with sadness, not reproach in his voice. 'My heart is breaking over here. I can't stand to have you so angry with me.'

'I'm not so angry,' I said, but I couldn't feel close to him when he was forcing me to do something I did not want to do. I lay on the edge of the bed when I was too tired to stand up. The pitiful room didn't even include a chair. But I lay on my side, turned away from him, feeling childish for not facing him when he placed a comforting hand on my hip.

'Let's get this over with,' I said, forgoing a morning shower and pulling my wrinkled dress into some sort of order before heading out the door. At the car, I said, 'I don't want to see my old house.' It belonged to someone else.

I guided him the back way which I had never taken myself. Never alone, but when a friend was over, I'd take my dog to swim in the clear brook. Two or three long steps would traverse it. The cop who had come at my mother's frantic call had only scolded me for being out of my backyard. Though I'd considered any place in walking distance my backyard, I never returned. My friend was never allowed to visit again.

Jim and I stood on the uneven banks of the little stream, a short way from the railroad crossing where my friend and I would lay out pennies to be mauled by the trains. Jim insisted I describe the incident moment by moment. 'You're really morbid,' I told him more than once, 'to want to know about this.' Every time I fell silent, he urged me on by squeezing my hand.

When I couldn't recall the boy's features, I described him as 'Lenny in a football jersey'. Jim nodded. I appreciated not having to explain that meant he was big and slow like Lenny in *Of Mice and Men* and I had feared I was one very dead puppy. My friend and the boy's friend had just looked on. My little dog barked incessantly.

After my tale, we sat by the water while Jim talked about boyhood misadventures where play took him to dangerous ground. He told the story of playing robbers in an abandoned building. He knew every timber. He remembered the discarded soda bottles, lining up the green ones as targets for rocks, finding a baseball card he meant to give his little brother but lost on the way home. The next time he ventured there he found a blue cat's-eye marble.

'I was staring at the marble when this hideous-looking hobo came at me. I ran for my life. There is that moment when you cross from play to reality that grabs you.'

'Sometimes too literally,' I said, my sense of humour returning.

The water was so clear you could make out every stone in the bottom. I looked up and Jim was staring off, talking about how a boy was at twelve, or at least how he was. He drew up into a squat, the ground's damp bleeding through.

'I think because I spent most of my life pretending, even more than most kids, that I love you so. You let me have that, but you make me take on my real self. I can play with you and I can be real with you. I brought you here because I wanted you to know you can be real with me.' He stood and reached into his pocket. 'Hold out your hand,' he said.

I cupped my hand under his. At least, I knew he was too leery of real snakes for whatever he had to be one. He dropped a marble into my hand. The blue cat's-eye. As we walked back to the car, crossing a playground that wasn't there years before, I felt the fear I'd carried like a rock in my heart lighten. He kissed my ear and took my hand.

'Told you,' he said.

I got in on the passenger side, then Jim jumped into the back seat, his knees pushing against the back of my seat, admiring the pale green paper I'd bought for the impending term. He preferred lines when he was trying to get organized. He didn't even complain about a pencil being the only writing implement between us.

I knelt on the front seat, facing him. Drumming my fingers to his hummed melody. Every once in a while, he would tap the eraser against the edge of the binder, nodding his head. Then he'd brush his hand, damp from the humidity, against his chest before moving the pencil down the page. When he reached the bottom, he eased the binder over the back seat. 'For you. Legible and all.' Just as I reached for it, he stole it back. 'Forgot the dedication.'

I could tell reading upside down as he wrote that this was a polished version of his 'Roadhouse Blues/Hwy 9'.

'Don't chew my eraser,' I teased, because he was giving the dedication more thought than the song. Continuing to read upside down as he wrote, I saw the dedication included a demand, rather than a request, to marry him. He winked and erased the small *m* in *marry* to capitalize it.

I read the song through, smiling that he thought the end being at hand belonged in a rollicking romantic song. He'd given the marble to Ginger and the song to Linda. He included a line from the song about my effect on his soul. His signature on every letter was always his initials. From the time he was a kid, he worked on perfecting his initials, but this was signed a rare, *Jim*.

'Yes,' I said, unaware myself I was at last ready for a one-word answer.

Jim leaped to grab me and hit his head on the roof of the car and fell over into my lap on the front seat. 'On the day you turn eighteen, we get married!' That seemed to be settled without further discussion. I rolled the marble around in my palm. Jim had given me a piece of his childhood.

20

Run With Me

Jim made a trip up from LA, timing his visit to come and go
while my parents were working. To please him, I made a point to
wear the turquoise and white T-shirt he had given me. The tie-dye
wasn't the worst thing about it. That it left very little about my
figure to anyone's imagination was. Jim's idea of what fitted me
and my idea of what fitted me differed by several sizes.

When he arrived, he stood in the doorway a few minutes surveying me, then Frisbeed an album at me. Caught off guard, it flew
through my hands. Jim made a little-boy-pretending-to-be-bombs
noise. 'Happy to see your fielding is off. With any luck, it broke.'
He leaned excellently against the jamb, a thumb in a loop of his
ill-fitting striped pants.

Two albums in a row he hated! The band had spent months
on *The Soft Parade*. Jim and Robby fought over the lyric in one
of Robby's songs about taking up guns. For the first time, credit
for which of them wrote the various songs was included. Jim said
the vibrations were so bad, he often recorded his vocals when the
others weren't in the studio.

Jim crossed the room in a rush and planted himself in one of the
not-quite-Danish chairs. He fidgeted trying to get comfortable.

'I know you aren't happy with the album, but even I'm beginning to like "Wild Child".' I picked up the album and opened the lid to my parents' stereo.

Jim smiled up at me. 'How much did it hurt to say that?'

'Barely a twinge,' I fibbed, focusing on the record cover. The band was a little island behind a camera on a tripod. The Jim on the cover looked little like the Jim in the room. On the cover he was slender, hair layered, face beardless. In the chair, he was in bulky clothes even in the heat, hair matted, bearded. I preferred his few extra pounds to his vomiting to keep his weight down.

'I'm deeply sorry about the album. I had such a different idea of what I wanted this to be, but at least I got the damn strings pulled off my songs. *Your songs*,' he said emphatically. 'The rest of the guys seem to want to be the Beatles when they grow up.'

We listened to the album. Jim had inserted the morning song he'd crumpled up in Maine in 'Shaman's Blues'. We laughed over 'Easy Ride'. I tried not to cringe over 'Wild Child'. *The Soft Parade* remained as I had picked up and stacked the fragments he'd strewn across the floor in Stockton. Jim's love of chance.

After the album, Jim deserted the uncomfortable chair and sat on the floor cross-legged. He pulled me down next to him. For the first time since San Francisco, he sang 'The Spy'. Not only had his voice deepened, but Jim had more patience with his phrasing. Confidence let a note hang. When his voice dropped for the last line, tears rolled down my cheeks. Jim leaned over, I thought for a kiss, but instead licked my tears.

'I think I just really sang that song for the first time,' he said between licks. 'Next album,' he promised.

Jim reached for my journal. I'd been writing while I waited. He hadn't explored it for some time. 'What's this line here about things being bad at home?' he asked.

'You know,' I shrugged. 'Seventeen.' I looked at it, surprised I had written that. I was completely open about Jim, but edited the rest of my life for him.

Jim jumped to his feet. 'You're leaving with me tonight.'

He stood in the square hallway considering the three closed doors. He pushed each open and guessed my room by the clutter. 'Just pack a couple days' clothes. I'm so sick of your shabby clothes, I'm going to buy you a new wardrobe.' The insult,

338

meant for my parents, stabbed me. Wearing the old T-shirt hadn't pleased him.

Hoisting a box of books I hadn't unpacked, he said, 'This is all you need as far as I can see.' He let out a belated grunt and the tension dissolved. He laughed hard enough to have trouble with his grasp on the box.

The front door closed and we both jumped. My father was home an hour into his shift with a fierce headache. There was no missing Jim, tall and bearded behind me. Dropped into the middle of a nightmare, I couldn't think how to react.

Jim could. 'Thanks for the books,' he said, shifting the box awkwardly under his arm. 'I'll return them soon. Gotta run.' He extended his hand to my grim-faced father with a friendly, 'I'm Jim Morrison.'

My father refused Jim's hand. Nonplussed, Jim asked me, 'See me down to the car?' I followed Jim silently. He opened the trunk of his rental and tossed the heavy box into it with a significant thump. Jim leaned on the opened car door. 'Climb in,' he said in his sleekest whisper.

My father watched from the landing. Between clenched teeth, Jim sang a Beatles' line about being able to steal, but not rob. He could be a Beatle when it suited him. I might have been able to sneak away, but couldn't climb into the car with my father looking on. I was hurt he misconstrued my reason.

I backed on to the sidewalk. 'Jim.' I thought, *you fool*. 'You told him who you are. He'll send the police after you.'

'Seventeen is pretty legal,' he said with an encouraging smile.

'You're already in trouble,' I cautioned.

'May as well get busted for something I've almost done.' He bit his lower lip. We maintained our physical separation. He was afraid to touch me. I was afraid to take the three steps to the open door. The magnolia blossoms glowed in the light from the streetlight. I turned and went up the cement stairs, heard the car door close, the engine start, a slight screech as he pulled away from the curb.

I chattered at my silent father, fetching aspirin, making an impromptu dinner. When my father turned on the televison, I believed the crisis had passed.

'What would I have caught you doing if I came home a little later?' he asked.

Nothing at all. I would have been gone. 'Nothing,' I said, giggling nervously. 'He's a friend's older brother. I promised to loan him some books a while back.' I trusted he would not compare descriptive notes with my mother. The bearded young man with amazing blue eyes who brought her African violets and recited his poetry to her was not some friend's older brother. I put the record in its sheath, grateful the picture didn't look like Jim after all.

Two beers later, my dad stood and flicked off the television he hadn't been watching anyway.

The front door slammed. I loved Jim for not leaving, but the fury in his face terrified me. At first, I thought the twisted angry look was intended for me. He covered the room in two giant steps. I made a queer sound that made Jim cock his head, but he interrupted my dad's right wrist in motion.

'Relax that fist,' Jim said calmly, 'or I'll break it.' He caught my father's answer, a left that smacked in Jim's palm. 'I don't think you want to fight with me. You're too fucking old and I'm too fucking angry.'

'Come with me,' Jim cooed softly, his hand outstretched. I was as fearful of touching him as I was when I believed he called up the wind in Golden Gate Park. He possessed a power he rarely chose to use. Even silent, Jim seemed out of control. I didn't want to be near either of the angry men.

'Come with me,' Jim insisted quietly. I followed him outside. 'Don't kill him,' I begged, afraid the door would swing open and the violence between the two of them would erupt again.

Jim lifted my chin so I could see his face. 'Honey, that was my Lizard King. My Robert Mitchum. I'm not gonna kill anyone.' He guided me towards the stairs.

Jim and I piled into the car to drive across the street to the mall. The lights hurt my eyes as if I'd emerged from a terrible darkness. I felt numb following Jim to the kiosk in the centre of the mall where my mother was the manager of a hosiery shop. I watched her face bleed from startled to pleased to troubled in a second. As vicious as he was with my father, Jim was sweet with her. She started to cry.

Customers backed off. Jim invited her to come with us if she were afraid. She refused. My feet felt cemented to the floor. Had Jim not grabbed my waist and half-carried me, I would have stayed in the brightly lit mall and not sat in his car, my hands neatly folded in my lap.

Jim did not like to drive, for example, from his motel room near The Doors' office in downtown Los Angeles to the ocean, a twenty-minute drive if the traffic played along, but he thought nothing of hauling ass four hundred miles to San Jose, making a U-turn on my behalf, and heading back to his starting point.

'Go ahead and say it,' Jim snarled at the windshield, unwilling to look at me.

'Thank you,' I whispered, knowing it scarcely covered the last fifteen minutes.

He studied me, his brow furrowed. The car veered out of the lane. He looked back at the road. 'Aren't you going to ask why the fuck I didn't do this two years ago?'

'No,' I whispered again. The thought hadn't even passed through my mind. 'No,' I repeated. 'Remember on the beach that November? You asked if I would have gone with you if you had asked.'

'But the reason I didn't ask. The reason I put you on that goddamn bus back to Stockton, wasn't that I didn't want to ask you, or I thought it would be awkward with Pamela. None of those things that should have been the point.' I waited. He approached these confessions at his own pace. 'Where the fuck is the freeway?' he asked, on the right road and needing no answer, only the time to reach the exit. The tyres against the pavement made the lulling rush that asked me to close my eyes and sleep. Jim said, 'I was afraid of your father.'

I tried to stare him into looking at me, but his eyes remained fixed to the road. 'You are so impossibly hard on yourself, Jim. You were right to be afraid of my dad.'

'I was a coward.'

'What do you think courage is?' I asked, hoping I might know myself if I kept talking. 'Being fearless? Courage is action when you are afraid.'

The truth of what I'd just said made my hands, which I struggled to keep folded, tremble uncontrollably. The façade Jim so admired was cracking. I willed him to turn on the radio. But that effort produced the same lack of result as my stare. I reached over and turned on the radio myself.

Jim's parting shot in 'Wild Child' was concluding. The song wasn't played much on the radio. Jim looked at me. 'I don't know why I'm not afraid of you,' he said, smiling, steadying one of my hands with his.

He laughed and had time to sing all of his 'Not to Touch the Earth' in person just to be sure I could still smile before the string of commercials ended and he joined in on the first line of a Stones' song. A few days' run might do us both some good.

For hours, we watched the white line, only speaking about where to gas up or if to stop for food. Jim bought a pack of cigarettes from a machine, but remembered my sensitivity to smoke and tossed the pack on the dash without opening it.

Los Angeles sprawled toward us. That spring Jim had rented a comfortable house for Pamela in Brentwood, but kept his old motel room near The Doors' office. I wanted to know if I needed to conjure up enough charm to intrude on Pamela at three in the morning or enough strength to push off the piles of groupies and books from his motel bed, but was too shy to ask.

He pulled around to a motel with a red neon sign and asked me to wait. He led me around the side away from the main building where there were cottages. The room was more pleasantly shabby than my wardrobe, but then it had a better start.

We were so tired, we fell on top of the bed to gather strength to shower, then woke just enough to sneak under the covers. Waking up beside Jim in daylight, both of us still dressed and road-weary, was as romantic as I could have dreamed.

Jim, half-awake, ordered me French toast and orange juice. Orange juice and vodka for himself. 'You know,' he whispered hoarsely, 'I never see this time of morning except with you. Nor would I want to.'

My eyes felt dry and sandy from watching the road, but otherwise I felt like singing. 'If only I could sing,' I said half-aloud while we waited for room service.

'Want to join the band?'

'Oh, no! I want to sing that song "Good Morning",' I said excitedly, 'from *Singing in the Rain*.'

'All we need is Donald O'Connor and we could flip the couch,' Jim suggested.

'No, I'm Donald O'Connor,' I explained. 'I'm the comedy relief, not the leading lady. We need Debbie Reynolds.'

'Do you suppose she's listed?'

Jim made a pretence of scanning the white pages, then dragged me out of bed and ran for the sofa in the next room. We walked it over first try, but if Jim hadn't had a firm grip on me, I would have left a cartoon cut-out of myself on the back wall. The young man who delivered our breakfast said nothing about Jim sitting on the edge of the overturned sofa, but sneered at the imp next to him, feet dangling.

When the maid arrived, she noticed the sofa with disapproval. Jim and I, guilty kids, righted it, then Jim, inspired, tried to explain to her in the Spanish that would have gotten him a whore or a goat in Ensenada how he wanted her to play Debbie Reynolds in our game. While there was a gulf between their Spanish – she actually spoke the language – there was a connection with Hollywood. She delighted in joining us and had a much better voice than I did for the song. I was really in Hollywood.

Jim left midday on an unnamed errand, something to do with The Doors, like a dirty secret, so I lounged contentedly admiring how Conrad could make as short a novel as *Heart of Darkness* very nearly as chatty as my diary, though definitely more literate, while *The Thin Man* was tuned in on the television for background music. I'd loved William Powell's screen presence since I was small. He was, one had to admit, a more charming drunk than Jim.

Bursting into the room Jim asked, 'How can you read with the TV on?' knowing full well, I could more easily do homework to the television than to music. After all, I listened to music.

Jim ripped the paperback from my grip and said brightly, 'Let's go to the beach. We both think too much. Let's promise not to have anything more than an absurd thought all afternoon.'

'The whole afternoon? Neither of us will make it. Could I ask one wee question before our pact?'

'One.' He put a finger up very close to my face, his voice was very stern.

'Why do you suppose Conrad didn't call it *The Heart of Darkness*? Do you think it was one of those things of English being a second language or an intentional decision?'

Jim didn't even need to consider. 'Every word that man wrote was intentional.'

'If the book is here, you brought it on your trip. Why are you re-reading *Heart of Darkness* now?'

'That's two questions.'

Jim rented us roller-skates at the beach, the kind with laces, not keys. At last, I got to be better at something than he was. A childhood of sidewalk practice paid off. We ate ice-cream cones and played with a stranger's beach ball in the surf until we were scorched and weary and wished some benign parent would hoist us to his shoulders and carry us back to the car.

Instead, Jim took me, still soggy, to an old Venice haunt that overwhelmed me with its Southern smell as soon as he swung open the door. There was an appealing blend of fried and smoky aromas that I'd missed since becoming a vegetarian, odours that brought back my childhood years in Tennessee in brilliant snapshots in my brain.

There wasn't much other than mashed potatoes I could eat by my rules – even the green beans were cooked with ham. Jim ordered a beer and the works. We were beginning to feel human when the irate cook appeared at the counter where we perched.

'What's wrong with our food, young lady?' The *young lady* made me feel like I was brought up before the vice-principal again.

'Take it easy. I'll eat enough for both of us. My friend doesn't eat meat.'

The black cook looked aghast. 'It's good fresh meat. You think we serve dog or something?'

Jim thought that even funnier and gave an unappreciated bark, then said lightly, 'She's vegetarian; she doesn't eat anyone's meat.'

The cook returned to her domain, twirling her finger at the side of her head denoting my craziness.

Brimming with mashed potatoes, I really would rather Jim

carried me to the car. He said something I thought I misheard. 'What was that?' I asked.

'That place. It's pretty much what "Soul Kitchen" was based on.'

'Didn't look that old,' I said.

He looked over his shoulder at it. 'I wrote that, what? Three years ago?'

'You wrote it!' I was truly stunned. I had assumed it was a Willie Dixon song. 'I thought it was an old traditional blues song that you put your sound to.'

'Thank you. Best compliment.' He hugged my mashed potatoes.

Putting an arm around my waist, he sang on the walk to the car, behind the wheel, and to his regular motel room where he could pick up a needed change of clothes. He unlocked the door and held it open, making a bridge of his arm for me to walk under. The phone rang. 'I'm only in for Elvis.'

'You're expecting a call from Elvis?' I was impressed.

He laughed, shaking his head. Feeling duly reproached for my naïveté, I lifted the receiver and felt more naïve for not knowing what to say. It didn't seem appropriate to answer a motel phone with 'Morrison residence' though it was. I said, 'Hello.'

'Oh,' a voice more nervous than mine began, 'I asked for Jim Morrison's room.'

'This is Jim Morrison's room,' I assured him. 'May I take a message?'

'Oh, well,' this wispy male voice hesitated, 'I really don't know what I want to say to him.'

'I'll write down whatever you'd like to say and be sure that Jim gets your message.' I hunted for pen and paper in the disorder.

'How very nice of you. Are you that attractive redhead?'

I giggled. 'No. I'm a less attractive redhead.'

'Oh, dear,' he fairly whispered. 'Is this awkward?'

'No.' Well, a little, but not so much as it hurt. After all, it was my turn to have time with Jim. The caller asked if I knew him. My 'Who is this?' sounded rude.

'Oh. Didn't I say? This is Andy.'

'Jim's brother?' I asked. Jim took a step back, shaking his head.

'Jim has a brother named Andy? I like that. No . . . this is Andy Warhol.'

I shook my head at Jim. 'Oh, Mr Warhol. How nice to meet you.' Jim held in a laugh with his hand and bounded out the door, keeping it open by rhythmically hitting his butt against it. 'Jim just stepped out,' I was relieved to say honestly, and a bit shaky to have a famous artist on the line.

'What is your name, dear?' Andy Warhol asked.

'Ginger.' Why did I say Ginger? Reverting under stress.

'Oh, Jim showed me a drawing he did with you. It was very . . .' If Jim quoted him correctly, Andy had called it *cosmic*. But I didn't want to start finishing Andy Warhol's sentences. 'Cosmic,' he said after a long interval, confirming Jim's accuracy. 'I'd like, I'd like to see your paintings sometime.'

Something about *the bigger they are, the nicer they are* came to mind, but I had the sense not to say it. 'Thank you, Mr Warhol, but I don't know how to paint.'

'So few artists are willing to admit that,' he said, with no sign he thought it was a funny thing to say. 'I could listen to you laugh all day,' he said sweetly.

'But you did call to speak with Jim, not a giggling teenager.' I finished his thought during his long pause, despite my efforts not to. 'Could I take a message, Mr Warhol?'

'Oh, I don't know what I wanted to say.' He thought a full minute. I didn't fill in the blanks for him. Finally, he said, 'I just wanted to hear that sexy voice of his.'

'Would you like me to tell him that?' I offered politely.

'Oh, no. No. Please don't,' he said breathlessly panic-stricken. 'Ask him to call me at my private number should he get the chance.'

Jim stepped back inside the room when I hung up the phone, which immediately began ringing. He jumped back out.

'Hello,' I answered, trying not to laugh at Jim's exaggerated antics. He had shoved his shirt in the bottom of the door to act as a doorstop, while he mimed tightrope-walking back and forth past the door-framed stage.

'Hi. This is Tim Buckley. Can I speak to Jim?'

'Tim Buckley?' I asked for Jim's benefit. Jim shook his head. 'I'm sorry. Jim just stepped out. May I take a message?'

'Yeah. Sure. I wanted to thank him for mentioning me in the *Rolling Stone* article,' he said, sounding very young. 'I mean, he just mentioned my name and my record sales picked up. I needed that. Thank him for me.'

'I will, Mr Buckley. I saw you two years ago up at Mt. Tamalpais. I went out the next day and bought your album.' I'd never done that before. I was pretty miserly with my allowance.

'Well, thank you. Nice to hear I can sell an album on my own.'

I bought his next one, too. 'You have a beautiful voice.'

'Thank you,' he said like he didn't need to be told.

'I'll give Jim your message. I'm sure he'll be pleased.' Jim re-entered the room. 'Your mentioning him in the *Rolling Stone* article made his record sales go up.' Jim smiled, but the phone rang before he could comment. For the third time, I said, 'Hello.'

'Hello, darling,' a deep voice purred. 'This is Marlene Dietrich. Jim Morrison. Put Jim Morrison on for me.'

'Marlene Dietrich?' I questioned.

Jim grabbed the receiver. Guess he would talk to someone besides Elvis.

'This is Jim.' We clunked heads when he let me share the earpiece. He put his finger to his lips to keep us both from laughing at playing grown-ups.

'How good of you to take my call, young man,' she said in the throaty voice she had in her movies. 'You have manners.'

'Occasionally,' he chuckled endearingly. 'I've been a fan of yours since *Blue Angel*.'

'And I have been a fan of yours since I heard you sing "Alabama Song". Well, to be very honest, I had to listen to it a second time. I thought you were throwing away the lyric, but then I *heard* and understood why you were casual. And, my dear, you are a beautiful man.'

'Thank you for the compliment about "Alabama".' Apparently he didn't care if she thought him beautiful.

'I also wanted to talk to you about fame. I am famous. I am a legend.'

'Yes, I know,' Jim agreed softly.

'But, you see, it is not the woman who is the legend. It is Marlene Dietrich. Do you understand what I am saying?'

'Very clearly,' Jim said.

'There is something about you that tells me you will also be a legend, but that you do not understand.' From her slur, she was possibly very drunk. 'And I thought you might learn this from me.'

I reluctantly allowed Jim sole possession of the phone for the remainder of their conversation. After the call, Jim seemed flattened rather than pleased. He dressed me in one of his many white shirts, which he tucked in for me and gave the sleeves a couple turns. He declared me 'cute'.

In the car, Jim tried to make his voice break with Marty Robbins' in 'Devil Woman', and decided he had to get the record to practise. He parked badly in front of a record store that carried older records. The boy behind the counter, for whom running the register was a summer job, had no idea who Marty Robbins was. Jim did a melody of Robbins' hits for the blank-faced kid, then spent an hour hunting. Affronted I unearthed the record in a Country bin, he gave the disinterested teenager a lecture on American music. He raced to the nearest record-player, which belonged to a friend off Sunset.

Jim spent the evening playing 'Devil Woman', which sent the friend out of the apartment, ears covered. Surprised me. I imagined everybody other than the kid in the store sang along with Marty Robbins on the radio. First Jim tried to mimic Robbins's voice, then settled into his own style of doing the song. Try as he might, he couldn't get that break in his voice.

'Maybe you have to be born in the South,' I suggested helpfully, then dissolved into giggles remembering he had been. I tried again, 'Maybe it's genetic.'

On the street, Jim settled for whistling 'Devil Woman' until we located the art supply store he had in mind. When I told him about my conversation with Andy Warhol, he insisted I produce a painting. I didn't want to paint quite as badly as he wanted his voice to break when he sang, but close. Shopping with Jim was like winning a shopping spree. Everything you touched was yours. I had to be firm to hold him down to a couple brushes, five tubes of paint – the primaries and black and white – and canvas makings.

I wanted to attempt a portrait of Jim. I said, 'After all, if you'd seen Cézanne's apples, it seems pointless to paint apples.'

Jim assented. When I described a painting of her sister reading a book by Marie Cassatt that I had seen at the Palace of the Legion of Honor in San Francisco, he bounded out of the room in search of a book to read while I painted him. *Heart of Darkness* he found inappropriate in some private way. By the time he returned, I had the canvas primed and dry enough for anything I was likely to paint. Jim stretched out on top of the unmade bed, pillows stacked behind him, backlit by the bedside lamp. He opened Mary Shelley's *Frankenstein*.

As I worked away, having some notion of what a finished painting could look like, but no idea what went underneath, Jim read aloud. I caught the grace of the hands that held the book, but faltered on the beard. When I hurrumphed over the difficulty and explained, 'You look more like Rasputin than I'd like,' Jim teased, 'I feel more like Rasputin than I'd like. Want me to shave?'

I considered it, less for my art than my face against his beard, but declined his generosity. When we became aware of time, it was way past midnight. Jim donated a handkerchief to turps to clean paint from my hands and cheek and hank of hair before we showered and tumbled into bed where he gave a last effort at that voice break of Marty Robbins. 'Maybe,' Jim considered sleepily, 'I could do better with "El Paso".'

Another whole night with Jim in bed was a gift. At least, we undressed. In the morning, I woke before Jim. In the dim room, I could see he had traded the nondescript motel painting for the one I did of him, not so good, but not nondescript. Whatever mistakes I had made in my inexpert handling of a brush, I had captured his eyes in a way the photographs that looked at me from the newsstand magazines did not.

A polite knock interrupted us; a messenger with a letter from New York. Jim handed the slender envelope to me. With a great smile, he said, 'I think it's for you.'

'I don't know anyone in New York.' I opened the envelope with

care. The letter was a recommendation to Otis, the art school
Jim wanted me to attend. The signature was Andy Warhol's. I
couldn't stop shaking. 'I guess you got around to calling his private
number.'

Jim decided a celebration was in order. Since it was my celebration and not his, he took me for an Orange Julius at a stand
that was a giant orange, then for a drive in the hills, windows down
and music blasting.

'Wanna meet Tim Buckley? He might be here,' Jim said, turning
into a drive, up to a big log cabin painted an unnatural green.
We could hear Bob Dylan. On record, darn it all. Jim gave up
on hammering on the door and walked in. I trailed behind.

We were met by incense and a girl throwing herself into Jim's
arms. He made a practised catch, then peeled her off and deposited
her gently into an empty lap on the sofa.

'Tim here?' Jim yelled.

'Yo!' answered a voice in the dark. When the man stood, I
knew he was Buckley by the wild outline of curls. He strode
so forcefully at Jim, I thought Jim was going to have to catch
him, too, but he pulled up short and settled for one of those
thumb-clasping handshakes nobody ever offered me. 'Thanks,
man, for the mention in *Rolling Stone*.'

'You're welcome. I envy you, sometimes. Doin' it on your
own.'

'Out there alone, too,' he said in the loneliest voice I'd ever
heard. 'We can talk out back. Want something?'

Tim grabbed the arm of a passing blonde and put in a beer order.
Out back was dry and unkempt, but there were wooden swings
strung from a tree limb. Acquainted with the deadly brittle live
oaks up north, Jim and I exchanged looks of mortality.

'*Widow makers*,' I said.

But Jim dropped on to the swing and kicked up. Tim offered
the empty board of the second swing, then sat when I declined.
When the blonde brought the beer, she hung around long enough
to deliver it into Jim's hand. 'I listen to "The End" over and
over.'

'Ought to check out some other songs,' Jim said, not bothering
to thank her for the compliment or the beer.

'I listen to your whole album. Over and over,' I said to Tim, catching the admiration in my voice was not unlike the blonde's.

He smiled. I'd never really met a musician I admired, discounting Robby's slicing my hand hello. I didn't know enough about music to explain why I thought his stood out, just enough to wish I'd brought a sketchbook to catch the two of them in wooden swings.

They spoke in brief snatches about work. They both loved music and hated the business. When Jim finished the beer, he pushed me on the swing for a high-kicking ride before we left.

The sun was setting and the colour was caught in the city haze. 'The sky looks like a ripe cantaloup,' I said.

'Would you like some?'

'Sky?' I asked.

Cantaloup! At an open-air market, we collected the elements of a fancy picnic to be shared in bed. Jim cut crescents of cantaloup to feed me from the blade of a pocket knife and gave me my first taste of croissants with cheese so sharp Jim claimed it bit back.

We slept early in each other's arms, then woke at midnight. 'Feel like painting the town instead of me tonight?' Jim asked.

The thought of going out on Jim's town with Jim intimidated me completely. I looked at my choice of wardrobe, neatly draped on the doorknob. Jim kneeled by the bed like he was going to say his prayers, then pulled out a box and tossed it on to the bed. I avoided it like a rattlesnake.

Jim had to do the honours. He held up a simple white dress. 'Is it close?' he asked. The dress could not have been closer to the one I'd described to him on the escalator in Weinstocks. The dress I longed for when I was fourteen was in reach.

'I thought, when I told you that story, that you couldn't understand how much something like that means to a girl. Things mean so little to you.'

He ran his hand gently through my hair. 'But you mean everything. I thought my comment about your wardrobe was pretty thoughtless. I hope this makes up a bit.'

Jim's vague errand the first day had been to engage a seamstress to make the dress. With all that had happened after his slight about my clothes, I was charmed he remembered his comment and arranged so perfect an apology.

Nobody much cared if I were underage when we dropped into a bar so Jim could give regards, drink half a beer, and move to the next. I was his little sister, whether or not he introduced me, but he never let go of my hand as if I would be lost in the dark city.

Out on the sidewalk, Jim said, 'That is what I do when you are not here. With more drinking. More swearing.'

'And more women,' I added.

His hand dropped around my shoulder. 'Now, let's do something I wouldn't do without you.'

Jim drove until I thought I recognized the area. He'd taken me there when I came to say goodbye before heading east with my family. Jim did like the view from Griffith Observatory! We gazed out at the thousands of lights in Los Angeles far below.'

'Oh, I bet you come up here to look at the city without me.'

'But I wouldn't dance,' he said, taking my hands and a slow step back. 'Have you forgotten?' he asked. 'Do I need to remind you what goes where?'

After our dance, we sat on the low wall that lined the outer drive and made up lives to go with the lights of the city.

'It's easier for me to imagine other people's lives than my own,' I said.

Jim nodded and walked the top of the wall all the way back to the car. That morning, we were slow to leave the bed, shower, and face Los Angeles. The city was hot and bright. Jim dragged me into expensive boutiques, where clerks eyed us suspiciously. I gasped at price tags and refused to try on the luscious clothes.

When we returned to the bungalow, a stack of boxes sat on the couch. Every dress I had touched, but passed by, was there. We had quite a little talk about that. Jim seemed duly chastised, but refused to return any of the beautiful garments, so I took half of them back that afternoon. Jim would have no part of it. When I planted the wad of bills beside him on the bed, he pushed them on the floor with his foot.

'I love that you wanted to give me things, but it's not what I want from you.'

He wasn't speaking to me, which felt very different from his natural silences. I poked him after five minutes. He said, 'That you don't want anything from me makes me want to make you queen of the world.'

'Ah, but I would rather serve in heaven than reign in hell.'

'I knew it was dangerous to send you Milton,' he said.

We spent the afternoon, Jim writing and me painting. Though the pose was similar, Jim looked different writing than he did reading. When I took a long bath to give him privacy and get the paint from under my nails, Jim followed me in to read poem beginnings. He placed his notebook on the back of the toilet-seat and joined me in the tub.

'I was giving you privacy.'

'I don't need privacy with you,' he said, soaping me to shave my leg. 'Point your toe,' he instructed.

'I get the feeling you like women's bodies.' He spent the night showing me just how much. By morning, our stomachs were growling. Too impatient for room service, we struck out in quest of food.

Jim and I existed in a glow for the rest of the week. He ducked calls and responsibilities to reacquaint himself with the beach. My paintings of Jim weren't greatly improving, but even Jim agreed he looked less like a mad monk. His theory was that he was happy, and himself looked less like a mad monk.

The pounding at the door was certainly not room service. The noise made me hold my breath. 'Morrison, if you don't open up, I'll have the cops here in five minutes,' a man shouted. At least, it wasn't my father's voice.

'Go into the bedroom,' Jim said, barely audibly.

I stood fast, if frightened. When Jim didn't open the door, the man did. His kick-splintered the door frame. Jim raised his right hand, like the statue of a saint. The stranger, tall, solid, craggyfaced, opened his hands to show, though armed, he didn't hold a gun. He introduced himself, flashed identification. He was a detective, private. I saw some relaxation in Jim's shoulders. I couldn't grasp the filth the man spewed at Jim.

This honourable man who had loved me enough to rescue me, wait for marriage as a high-school boy wouldn't have, bribed Andy

Warhol who knows how, was up against the lies of a man who perverted the truth into kidnapping and rape.

This beefy detective had been hired to fetch me. 'Get a move on,' he told me.

'No,' Jim turned to tell me, then back to the guy filling up the doorway. The man's size and demeanour terrified me. I saw a hesitancy in Jim's eyes, as he considered how to get on the guy's good side. I don't know how many alternatives shot through his mind before he decided on cash. 'How much not to have found us?'

'You could afford me,' the detective said in a more civil voice, 'if I didn't have a daughter. I can only imagine what's gone on here. I'm not leaving without the girl.'

I started to giggle. I recognized the shrillness as verging on hysteria, but it was also that the detective could never have begun to imagine what had transpired in that Hollywood cottage.

'Look,' Jim said, 'she's nearly eighteen. Nobody is going to make a legal fuss. Be a nice guy and leave us in peace.'

'From what I understand, this has been going on since she was fifteen. Could add up to enough counts to put you away until you're too old to mess around with little girls. You aren't going to get away with anything. I'll see to it. Come on,' he motioned to me.

'She's not going anywhere alone with you,' Jim said.

I was going, though. I could see Jim's resignation in the sudden stoop of his shoulders. I wanted to change back into the old T-shirt and jeans. The detective told me to keep talking so he'd know I wasn't skipping out the back.

'Hope is a dagger,' I said over my shoulder, trying to sound like a heroine, if you could find one, in a Raymond Chandler novel. But Jim's eyes misted. He knew it was the truest comment I had ever made about us.

21

No One Left to Scream and Shout

The night hadn't done much to dissuade August's intensity. I stared into the refrigerator, more for its cool relief than breakfast inspiration. The phone rang. I let it ring a few extra times, in case my mother hadn't given up standing beside me when I talked to Jim. I lifted the receiver to hear Jim's gravelly voice say, 'A friend of mine was murdered this weekend.'

Questions tumbled out. 'What happened? Were you there? Are you okay?'

'I just read about it in the newspaper. Looks like a cult thing. I didn't really know him that well. Jay. He gave me that Alexander the Great haircut. Jay Sebring. Good thing I didn't drop by for a trim.' He cleared his throat, rough from too little sleep and too much drink. 'I'm just whistling past the graveyard. Roman Polanski's wife was killed, too. She was pregnant. A couple other people. It could easily have been any of us.'

'Did they catch the murderer?' I asked, disbelief in even saying the word, horror anyone could kill a pregnant woman.

'No. Not a hell of a lot of information in the paper.'

'Want me to come be with you?' I whispered, already plotting an escape.

My mother came out to make morning coffee. I played my game

of half-truth and lie. I hadn't been back to Los Angeles since I was dragged back to San Jose in irons and knew there was no way to score permission. I let her think I was visiting a friend in Stockton and thought she might be letting me get away with the deception.

I intended to call him upon my arrival, but Jim met me at the gate. He'd been meeting every plane since we spoke. His whole body trembled when he kissed me. Jim had that look of at least a couple sleepless nights, as if he hadn't changed his clothes or combed his hair. I had to guess what was behind his dark glasses.

'What did you mean when you said, "It could have been any one of *us*?"' I asked as we hurried through the airport, uncomfortable with the crush of people. Any one of *them* might be the killer.

'I think these creeps were out to get celebrities. Get even for our success, somehow.'

These creeps? I half-ran to keep up with him. 'Is that what the police said?'

'It's what I feel. Let's go to bed,' he said. 'I just want to hold you.'

'Let's not go to your motel,' I said, trembling myself. There were killers on the loose in Los Angeles. I wished I'd asked Jim to come north.

Jim stopped for a short call. 'We can use a friend's place in Venice.'

'That's still Venice, California, not Venice, Italy?' His mood lightened as he got closer to the part of the ocean where he had written his first songs. He felt more at home there than in the places the songs had afforded him since.

'Nice of your friend to vacate the place for us,' I said, grateful we weren't to be company.

'I put him and his lady up at the Beverly Hills Hotel,' Jim said, then paused for a slow smile. 'Imagine, he thought he got the better deal.'

Jim knew the petite house well. The key hid in the hanging planter. He knew it fitted the top lock, not the bottom. Clean sheets were found easily, but he only tucked in the bottom sheet before dropping on to the mattress. He wanted me on his lap. I liked us eye to eye, my legs around him. As his passion exploded, I started to cry. He held me until he could ask questions between my sobs.

'It was thinking you might have died.'

'I shouldn't have said that. LA's just gotten darker.'

'You wouldn't have gone for a trim? I mean, could you have been there?'

'You know I cut my own hair,' he swept his hand through his unruly mane to suggest he was about due. 'And I really don't hang out with those people.'

Jim padded off to the bathroom, his bare feet slapping on the tile, and returned with a handful of Kleenex.

'I'm sorry,' I said. 'I'm supposed to be here to comfort you.'

'I am comforted,' he said, settling in beside me with a nearly filled notebook. He wrote, '*I know women who think they are witches,*' and thrust the book a few inches under my nose.

I wrote, '*I know men who believe themselves saints.*' I studied his line. 'Do you know witches?' Somehow, I knew he wasn't joking about my tuning him in on the radio.

'Yeah. One.'

There to ask the tough questions, I asked, 'Do you think she had something to do with the murders?' He'd said the papers were pointing the finger towards a cult.

'Oh, God, no!' he shook his head adamantly. 'She's a good witch.'

'Like Glenda.' In *The Wizard of Oz.*

'Not exactly, no. It's her religion. Know any saints?'

'No. Just came to me.' I pictured Jim's raised hand his only defence against the hulking detective, but doubted he ever thought himself saintly. Well, maybe that first night in San Francisco when he did not follow through on his bad intentions. 'We keep this up and we'll have written a Leonard Cohen song.'

'Jesus!' He flung the notebook into the air and it winged back to him. He reached over his head for the brandy on the bedside table, a gift from his friend, and fumbled for a glass.

'You don't need to drink,' I told him. 'You need to talk.'

He rested the dark bottle on his pale chest. 'But drinking is easier.'

'If you wanted to get drunk over this, you'd be hanging out with one of your drinking buddies. Asking me here means you have something you need to get off your chest.'

'Besides this?' He laughed and tipped the unopened bottle on to the bed.

'You were close with Jay?' I asked.

'No. I only saw him a few times.' He rolled over on to his stomach and dropped the bottle on to the hardwood floor, keeping it spinning with a practised finger on its lip.

I watched until he missed a spin and the bottle toppled. 'I know you are compassionate, but why are you so distraught if you did not know this man well?'

'Because I hurt him.' Jim kept his head lowered off the edge of the bed as if the bottle were fascinating. 'Jay was bisexual.' He peeked up and sideways at me. 'Know what that means?' I could figure it out. 'When he was cutting my hair, I could see his reflection behind me in the mirror. He had that look of adoration young girls have when they ask for my autograph. Like they are seeing a vision, not me, you know. Because I play with the androgyny thing, I do have guys make passes at me. If I'm in a good mood, I'll plant a big kiss on them and tell them I'm not their type. If I'm in a bad mood, I tell them to fuck off. But when Jay told me he loved me, I said the cruellest thing I could think of.' Jim shifted on to his back, his head dangling over the side of the bed, turning red.

'Which was?'

'I'm not going to repeat it over his grave. The thing is, you know, I never got to apologize. I'm never going to say the cruellest thing I can think of again.' His hand rose, then rested delicately over his heart.

'That is a good philosophy,' I said, placing my hand on his.

'And one you've always known.' Jim stared at the ceiling. 'Now can I have a drink?'

'You can have anything you want.'

Jim lifted himself on me, then scratched the side of his nose thoughtfully. 'What a dilemma! I can't decide if I want to finish our ode to Leonard Cohen or make love!'

I kissed him with enough enthusiasm to make my preference clear. The long summer day let us linger in bed and still have time

358

to walk through the pleasantly seedy neighbourhood Jim knew so well. Jim's friend's house was not one of those that overlooked the canal traversed by arched white footbridges, but he cut through that way.

Near the beach, there was a wandering troupe of actors dressed far too warm for August in Southern California. Jim didn't step back to let them pass the way the other pedestrians had. He added a line at an actor's pause and was rewarded with a tip of a hat.

'*Under Milk Wood*,' Jim explained, reciting more. 'Dylan Thomas. Ghosts talk about their lives.'

'Eerie under the circumstances,' I said.

'What would your ghost say?' he asked me.

I looked at the flat stretch of sand that ran to the ocean. 'I had a very good friend,' I said.

'I had a very good friend,' he agreed.

We lined up our footwear by the walk and followed the sand to the ocean. We played follow-the-leader along the water until Jim slipped his arm through mine. 'Let's get costumes for our ghosts and star in our own play tonight,' Jim suggested.

A little cast-off store that was a favourite of Jim's to prowl held racks of potential ghosts and stacks of bric-à-brac. We unearthed a leather-bound family album. 'There's your Great-Uncle Uriah,' Jim said, of a bearded man in a Yankee uniform, stiffly posed. Each picture was paper-framed and backed by cardboard, a single photograph for each page. We created a history for each face.

'Since it's your family album,' the owner said, 'I'll make you a special price.'

'Thanks, but we disowned them,' Jim said. He bought flimsy cotton underthings of the period for me and a Confederate jacket for himself.

We haunted his friend's cottage all night, playing out an imaginary lifetime, then wrote it out by daylight. By noon, I loosened the lacings on the slip to allow a deep breath. I sighed, 'No wonder those women were always swooning.'

'And you don't even have any whalebone. Which reminds me . . . if you're gonna be my great white whale, I'll have to come up with a whaling song.'

I thought his wink hinted he already had. 'Don't think there's been a good rock 'n' roll whaling song yet. Unless "Sloop John B" comes close enough.'

'Not nearly,' Jim said. He wore just his unreasonable grey wool Confederate jacket. The thought of wool made my skin itch. The reality made our embraces brief.

'Your jacket's all wrong if you want to be a sailor,' I scolded, wrestling the itchy coat from his sweaty shoulders.

We ventured out to retrieve the shoes we'd left behind the night before, pleasantly surprised they hadn't been appropriated. We stayed for orange juice, then Jim spotted the headline. A couple had been murdered. He read the paper on the sidewalk. Might have been the same killers, though this couple had no relationship to the celebrated.

'People get killed every day. Pretty often right here in Los Angeles. I don't know why this feels so close,' Jim said.

'Maybe it's your mood, rather than the murders, but if it's not, if there is some connection to you, you need to get out of this town.'

When Jim got back to the little borrowed house, he tore up our ghost play. Hours of work gone. 'Where is that song we started?' he asked, ploughing though the chaos of the night's game of his Confederate soldier romancing my Yankee abolitionist.

His notebook was recovered and we sat on the rugged and rickety back porch, Jim humming around to remember the music. Most of the time spent with Jim, we lived more on music than food. I was the one whose stomach would interrupt grumbling and he would see I was fed.

Venice was a haven, but we had to return to his motel room. Everybody in Los Angeles seemed to know where to find Jim. I jumped at every knock, every ring of the phone Jim ignored. When Jim had to check in at The Doors' office, I locked the door and put a chair under the doorknob. He didn't curse about having to stumble over the chair to get in. Instead, he rushed at the closet and demanded, 'Dress up!'

He shoved the perfect little white dress at me and barely gave my heart a chance to flutter at his saving the clothes I was forced to return – nice girls did not accept such gifts from men – before he was tugging at my blouse. Then he asked, 'Want to go to a concert?'

The excitement in his voice was catching. I clapped. 'Yours?'

'Hell, no! I just heard on the radio that Bill Monroe is nearby. Have you seen my little notebook?' He marked the air to define its size. Sweeping magazines off the dresser, he studied their disarray for a sign of his notebook.

Easing the notebook from where he had wedged it in a bedside stack of paperbacks, I presented it to him. He kissed me *thanks*. His hands shook as he stuck the notebook in his back pocket. That notebook would never have fitted into the tight leathers he wore the year before. He checked his reflection in the mirror. 'Should I shave? He probably wouldn't like the beard.'

'Does that matter?' I asked.

He turned to me, eyes wide, 'Do you know *who* Bill Monroe is?'

'Blue Moon of Kentucky' bubbled out from me of its own will and Jim relaxed enough to smile. I didn't realize how much of the song I knew. Music's a sneaky thing.

'I think he is the first sound I remember on the radio!' Jim explained.

'Yeah!' I agreed. 'My mother would tune him in on the kitchen radio. Makes me think of her baked beans and biscuits.'

Jim said, 'He probably wouldn't mind that at all.'

'Especially if he could taste my mother's beans and biscuits.'

I scissored Jim's beard down close to his face so he wouldn't do himself grievous harm in his excitement, then made us both nervous when I switched to the razor with a blade of unknown age. 'I've missed the beauty of your jawline,' I whispered when I kissed his smooth pink jaw.

'What should I wear?' he asked. He'd given up any concern for his wardrobe. Pamela had kept him covered.

'My feeling is a guy can't go wrong with jeans and a white shirt.'

Jim traded his T-shirt for a clean white shirt. While I buttoned and tucked, Jim looked down at me like he wasn't thinking of Bill Monroe for the first time since he burst into the room. He groaned, 'Gotta hit the road.' He hadn't strayed all that far from Bluegrass.

At the dusty little concert hall, Jim was the only man without a cowboy hat – and could have used one to hide his long hair – but once Bill Monroe starting singing and by golly, dancing, nobody gave the hatless man a thought.

'I'm Jim Morrison,' Jim said brusquely to the man who, intentionally or not, blocked the way backstage. 'I'd like to speak with Mr Monroe.'

The man stepped aside, but left the door for Jim to open. I dipped under his arm to pass through before him. A little cardboard sign that read, *Bill Monroe*, was thumb-tacked crookedly to a tan door. Jim ran his fingers through his hair and felt for the recently departed beard. He knocked sharply.

'Come on in,' a friendly voice said from the other side.

Jim wiped his wet hand on his Levi's and opened the door. 'Mr Monroe,' Jim said diffidently, 'I'm Jim Morrison.' I'd never heard Jim call anyone mister before. He used the word with respect, and not because the man seated back to a dusty make-up table was at least twenty-five years his senior.

'Have a seat,' Bill Monroe offered, still wearing the hat he had on stage, darkened with a ring of sweat he earned dancing as much as singing. His coat hung on the back of an empty chair. He lifted it to offer me the seat. 'Here you go, darlin',' he said sweetly.

I sat very erect, knees together, wishing my skirt would grow an inch and a half. Two inches. Jim stood next to me. Because it was so quiet in the hot and dirty little dressing-room, I said, 'Your music was the first Jim can remember hearing on the radio.'

'Does that make me old or popular?' Mr Monroe asked.

Jim smiled, relieved he liked this man whose music he admired.

'Want to play me a song?' Monroe winked, then looked up at Jim who hadn't taken the offered metal folding chair. 'Oh, I can tell you've got a song on you, boy.'

Jim retrieved his little notebook from his back pocket. Monroe offered up his mandolin. Jim passed off his notebook to me and accepted the instrument like a newborn baby. He admired it so deeply his face glowed, then handed it back to Mr Monroe. 'I don't play,' he said shyly.

Monroe rubbed his thighs as a prelude to standing. 'I could rustle up a guitar.'

'Wouldn't help,' Jim laughed. 'I just hear music in my head. Can't seem to get it to come out my fingers. I don't sing all that well, either.' He cleared his throat once, closed his eyes and sang 'The Spy'. At first I thought it an odd choice. No matter how deeply I loved the song, it was blues. 'Bluegrass' wasn't blues. I thought, this guy isn't going to get this, but I studied Monroe's eyes and realized that there is a crossroads where talent meets.

When he slid into the last low note, Jim opened his eyes as if from a dream, startled to have Bill Monroe actually getting to his feet in front of him. 'That's a song all right.' He touched the brim of his hat in my direction. 'I thought you were this boy's little sister until he sang that song.'

Mr Monroe reached up and turned on a small black metal fan perched like a crow on a shelf made for it. He sat back down and loosened his string tie. 'Got something else?'

With his question, I realised that he had no idea who Jim Morrison was. He wasn't listening to a young rock-star show off, but giving an unknown kid with talent some of his time. If The Doors' 'Light My Fire' had been a perfect piece of timing, Jim's talent was not. I felt love for the rightness of a world that had seemed so crazy for so long. If Jim hadn't been discovered with the band on the Sunset Strip, he would have been in this backstage closet of a room in Bakersfield or Fresno. Wherever we were.

Jim looked through the new songs in his notebook. 'This isn't polished,' he apologized before sing-reading his way through 'Roadhouse Blues/Hwy 9'. When he closed his book, he asked, 'Could I buy you a beer, Mr Monroe?'

'Buy me a cup of coffee,' Monroe said, giving Jim a predictable and welcome slap on his back.

We walked a couple blocks to an equally dusty little café. The men had coffee in tan mugs the colour of the dressing-room, the colour of the sidewalks. I had a root-beer. When no napkins arrived with our drinks, I edged Jim's handkerchief discreetly out of his pocket to dab at the sweat that was not nearly so sexy on my brow as his.

'It's not an easy road, but I'd tell you to stay with your music,' Mr Monroe said, before sipping from his cup. 'You work hard, you'll make it. Cream rises to the top.'

His breaking out the perfect cliché with the naturalness of my own mother made me smile. Jim liked his idol and I did too. I longed to suggest should he ever get to San Jose, my mother would love to have him in person in her kitchen for her baked-all-night beans and biscuits so light you had to weigh them down with molasses.

Jim must have read my thoughts. 'My friend's mother is a big fan of yours. Would it be an imposition to ask for an autograph?'

'Not at all. When we get back to the bus, I'll sign a record for you. May as well put my name on something useful. Well, now, if you'd find that useful.' He ran his fingers along the width of his hat's brim and we were up and dancing towards the door.

On the drive back to Los Angeles, Jim didn't stop singing. When he parked the car down the street from his motel he said, 'I'm going to take control of the band again.'

In celebration, we spent most of the next day in bed. When we finally faced the city, we made a quick stop at a bookstore, then Jim walked me to a very early dinner at the fanciest restaurant I'd ever been in. The huge booths were semicircles that swallowed us. The tablecloth was thick and white. I could have made a skirt from the big napkins. He poured half a glass of wine so we might toast the changing tide.

'I can't, Jim.' Since Jim could find my politics amusing, I was reluctant to tell him I was boycotting grapes, not unwilling to celebrate.

Jim smiled. 'Now, baby, I thought of that.' He lifted the half-filled glass to me. 'I'm informed. I know you'd do whatever Cesare Chavez asked. The wine is French.'

I fell into a helpless peal of giggles in Jim's willing arms while he invented the family who grew the grapes with love and harvested them with joy, based loosely on Lucille Ball's visit to Italy on *I Love Lucy*. Just as I was righting myself, a pleasant-looking man stopped by the table, 'Hi, Jim. Pa—' Stopping along the wrong redhead's name. Jim introduced him as Frank, then shooed him with his hand.

Jim drank the bottle of wine, ordered a bottle of whiskey, then changed his mind about any dinner, so we took a walk instead. He kicked a bottle-cap with pinpoint accuracy in the midst of a half-drunken sway. 'Damn it all!' he raged at the parking-lot crowded with cars and devoid of other people.

'Looked pretty good to me.' I rubbed his knotted back with my fists. 'You're even critical of your bottle-cap kicking.'

'But I can't write a sonnet to compete with Keats.' Jim frowned over his shoulder at me.

'Well, he couldn't write a song to compete with you.'

Jim smiled slowly, nodding. 'Woke up with something in my head. Music.' He hummed a little of what he had hummed that morning, dropping to the edge of the glimmering bumper of an old salmon-coloured De Soto instead of the edge of the bed. He hummed softly to himself. When he looked up, he sang to his sweet blues melody, '*I am a watcher of the skies.*' The words dropped comfortably into the rhythm.

We exchanged smiles. I scouted my purse for paper. Jim was patting his pockets, empty of notebooks, envelopes, receipts. At least, I always had a pencil. 'I wish I'd taken that bag when I bought the book.' Jim eyed my unopened *Siddhartha* hungrily.

'Jim,' I pleaded softly. 'I just spent half my week's allowance on this.' $1.25.

'Buddha wouldn't mind. Hesse neither.' He pronounced Hesse *Hessa*. Jim knew those things. I handed over the book and my pencil with a sigh.

'Can I have an autograph, too?' A male voice said behind me. I turned to see a man with a compact body, long straggly dark hair and a moustache Wyatt Earp would have envied.

'Fuck off!' Jim said casually.

Jim's rudeness startled me. Approached before, he'd grant the request and chat.

The man laughed. 'Can I have a drink, then?'

Jim laughed louder. 'Better watch it or people will think you have a drinking problem. Baby, this is Dennis Hopper. He was in *Rebel Without a Cause*. Knew James Dean. Dennis this is . . .'

He gave me his hand. 'Baby.'

'Only to Jim. Most people call me Lin.' I was improving. I didn't revert to Ginger in Jim's presence as I usually did.

'And I've worked since *Rebel*.' He reclaimed his hand, since I was so charmed I forgot to let go.

'*Rebel Without a Cause* just sticks with Jim because he learned to kiss watching James Dean in that movie.' I'd made Jim blush. Jim drew me a point in the air as if I intended to score when I was only nervous and attempting to say something. I tried to place this man in the movie from the fifties. He'd had to have been my age then, which made him older than Jim, because Jim had said he was twelve or thirteen when he first saw James Dean on film.

Dennis Hopper grinned. 'Maybe I should have waited for lessons from Jimmy Dean myself. Would you mind moving? I'm here to shoot the wall in this light.'

We scrambled out of his way and backed up until our elongated shadows stopped short of him. For the first time, I saw that the retreating sun cast a luminous warm light on the pale wall. A hand-painted advertisement from the forties had peeled to an abstraction. Palm tree shadows looked like distorted finger puppets. Jim and I remained very quiet as if he were shooting a movie instead of stills. Dennis turned and squinted into the dipping sun. 'It works better with you in the shot. You look like the representation of good and evil.'

I wore that same white dress and Jim was in black. 'And what does the De Soto represent?' I asked as I walked by Dennis. Jim and I repositioned ourselves on the bumper. We received a bit of direction. I looked up at Jim so I would not noticeably resemble the frightened animal caught in the headlights I did in the firstgrade picture Jim always carried in his pocket.

Jim wrote a line on the inside cover of the book and handed it to me. 'Your turn.' The pencil followed the book.

About an inch down, he'd written the line he sang earlier. We'd never played *I write a line/you write a line* with a third party. Dennis rested his chin on my shoulder to get a view of what Jim had written. My hand shook a little as I wrote in all too small and fancy script, *A wanderer on earth.*

Jim wrote quickly and returned the book to me. His new line was *Travelled the realms of gold.*

'You write so fast.' I felt cornered. By not rhyming himself, he'd backed me into coming up with a rhyme for *earth*. Three lines and the song already had an identity of its own. The only word I could think up to rhyme was *mirth*. Not much of a song word. 'Would

366

you hum the melody again?' Even if *mirth* stylistically could blend with *realms*, it didn't belong with the blues tune. 'You write so fast,' I repeated.

'I'm borrowing heavily from Keats. Of course, he was exhorting the wonders of a book . . . and I'm thinking about you.' He ran his fingers roughly through my hair.

Oh, so the *realms of gold* was my hair. Made awkward by the passion of the public touch, I pushed the book at Dennis. 'Your turn.'

Dennis retreated, shaking me off. 'I'll watch.'

'This ain't a spectator sport,' Jim said. 'Play or leave the field.'

'What are the rules?' Dennis asked with a forward step.

'You were expecting rules?' Jim laughed so hard he fell off the bumper. I wasn't in the mood to haul him back up, so he sat on the asphalt.

'What's this song about?' Dennis asked as he twirled a length of my hair around his finger. 'Love song?'

'All my songs are love songs,' Jim said. When Dennis looked as puzzled as I had when Jim first said the same to me, Jim added, 'One way or another. Want a song-writing hint?'

'Not too proud to take one if offered,' Dennis admitted.

'Don't try to think of a whole line. Go with a phrase that jumps to mind – a few words. The rest will follow.' Could have given me that bit of wisdom in two years of play.

That little hint was all it took for Dennis to think of a line. He motioned for it and Jim tossed him the book. Its trajectory was some point between Dennis and me. We both made a try for the catch and missed. Dennis bowed, granting me temporary custody. I picked up my rapidly ageing *Siddhartha*, scolded Jim with a look that forced him to bite his lower lip apologetically.

Dennis commissioned me stenographer and gave the line, '*And learned what it was worth*,' along with a friendly fluffing of my hair. Dennis played well. The three of us wound up squatting in a circle passing the bottle and book around. Every time the bottle came my way, I passed it along. Every time Dennis was handed the book, he passed it along, but spoke a line. The song was more evenly shared than the whiskey, but Jim indulged slightly more in both.

Jim jumped to his feet when he declared, 'All right! All right! All right! That's a song!' He did a celebratory dance.

'Sometimes,' I whispered to Dennis, 'I feel like Alan Bates's writer observing Zorba. I only join the dance once in a while.'

'Might live longer that way,' he whispered back.

Jim returned to grab my hand and give Dennis an over-the-shoulder wave.

Dennis yelled, 'If the song's a hit, I want credit.'

Jim nodded, but didn't look back or slow his pace. When we reached a major street that turned out to be Sunset, he asked, 'Did I tell you I learned to kiss watching James Dean kiss Natalie Wood?'

'No,' I answered, dodging a hooker reaching for Jim, saying, 'Ooh, honey!'

He didn't break his stride. 'Then how did you know?'

I survived a pang remembering his jab the year before that any sixteen-year-old on the Strip would know more about life than I did. 'From your kiss.'

Jim embraced me playfully, but kept walking so I had to hop over his boots not to fall. 'There wasn't much kissing in that movie.'

'But it was beautiful.'

Of his own youth, he said, 'The hard part was finding somebody to try a kiss out on. Wish that girl had been you!'

'You were my first kiss.' In case he'd forgotten.

'We are engaged, aren't we? I asked you and you said "yes", even if I didn't put the ring on your finger again.'

I didn't want to tell him that I thought even more of the marble he'd given me. 'You said something about getting married on my birthday.'

I'd stayed too long in Los Angeles and scurried back north. I asked Jim not to stay at his regular motel until the murders were solved. He mumbled a non-answer and compromised with daily calls to let me know he was alive and reasonably well.

Late in the month, he opened with, 'The cops showed up today to question me about Jay Sebring's murder. They found Doors albums. And found out Jay cut my hair once.'

'Well, you may as well confess.'

'I think that's what they were hoping for. To be honest, baby,

I couldn't figure out if they were trying to warn me I may be the next victim or that they might arrest me at any moment.'

'Gosh, I thought you were kidding. That's two different problems.'

'How so?'

'If you're on some crazy's hit list, you need to get out of Los Angeles. And if they think you are involved, you need an alibi. Do you know what you were doing when Jay was killed?'

'God, I don't know what I was doing yesterday. Too bad I wasn't with you. It would all be recorded in your diary.'

'Fortunately, you are an alley-cat, so you probably weren't alone.'

22

I've Been Singing the Blues
Ever Since the World Began

We rented camping gear at Mel Cotton's for a reunion with Big Sur. Initially, we were all glad to see each other, but the weather turned grim and Jim turned restless. So, we loaded up the car and headed up the coast. Just seeing the sign for Monterey got me off on my parents not letting me go to the Monterey Pop Festival when I was fifteen.

'The Doors weren't invited,' Jim said as grim as the weather.

'Probably thought you'd depress everybody.'

'I would have done my best,' Jim said with a grin. 'Who would you have come to see?'

'Otis Redding,' I said instantly.

'Too late to take you to see him, even if I had known him.' Otis Redding had died in a plane crash. I felt a wave of relief that Jim hadn't gotten into the small plane on his twenty-fourth birthday, though I worried he'd taken others without telling me.

He sidetracked me by asking, 'Who else would you have wanted to see?'

'Oh, Jimi Hendrix. Keep hearing about his blowing everybody away.'

'Yeah. You hear that,' Jim said. When we reached Monterey, Jim dived into a phone booth, as he often did there. He never told me whom he called. He returned to me stone-faced whether or not he spoke to whomever he tried to reach. This time, he used all the change we had between us, so it wasn't a local call, and came back whistling. 'Let's head up to San Francisco!'

Fine by me. Jim was hopeless at parallel parking and made me slide behind the wheel for that. He was only afraid when I was driving fast, not when I was driving precisely. We walked up the street and Jim bounded up the stairs of a purple Victorian. 'Is this Michael McClure's house?' I asked hopefully.

I knew the poet lived in San Francisco. A poet might live in a purple house.

'Nope,' Jim answered as the door opened.

'Hey,' a man said through a six-inch wedge of light. When he swung the door open, there was Jimi Hendrix dressed in a ruffled orange shirt and orange panne-velvet pants, clashing with the purple door.

Jimi looked me up and down so thoroughly, I looked down to see if I were somehow undone. He laughed. 'Come in,' he said, stepping back into the room.

Jim, as always, let me in first. The bay window provided the only light in the square living area. One sofa backed up to it, with the other at a ninety-degree angle, where Jimi had been. His guitar sat there alone. A white Stratocaster hooked up to an amplifier the size of an overnight case. On the far wall was a row of loaded bookcases, a broad table in front of them, equipped with a big reel-to-reel, a single wooden chair tucked under it. His suitcase was on the first sofa. Jimi picked it up and threw it a few feet to make room for us.

'Coffee?' he asked, heading off into another room and returning with a chrome pot and cups. He poured a little something into his cup from a silver flask. Jim nodded and put his hand over the cup designated as mine. Conversation apparently wasn't a significant part of their relationship.

Jimi lit up a cigarette and cuddled up on the other sofa next to his guitar. He kept his hands off it for a few minutes, then couldn't resist. He just held it for another five, then eased into 'Backdoor

Man', his way of saying he and Jim shared a mutual respect for Willie Dixon.

'Gonna sing?' he asked Jim.

Jim shook his head and sipped at his coffee, being audience to Jimi's performance. Since Jim wasn't singing, I focused on Jimi's long and slender fingers. His thumbs must have been twice mine. He wrapped his right over the top of the neck so it covered the top two strings. Then his rings became a bottleneck and I could close my eyes and hear that Robert Johnson record Jim had played for me. He was playing straight blues, no feedback with the little amp, which was still enough to rattle the windows when he got going.

Jimi started a wild version of 'Wild Child' to the tune of 'Wild Thing'. Couldn't pin that one on me. I did my best not to squirm when he settled down and played the song through, every word in place. I was embarrassed and gave Jim a killing side glance.

He leaned over and whispered, 'He didn't want to see me, he only said "yes" because he wanted to meet you.'

'Hey,' Jimi said. 'Want something in your coffee?' He noticed I hadn't picked up the cup and they had refills.

'She doesn't drink coffee,' Jim explained. 'She drinks tea.'

'Why didn't you say so?' Jimi was up and heading out of the room.

We tagged along after Jimi into the kitchen, which was about the size of a small walk-in closet. Instead of having clothes hung along each of the longer sides of the rectangle, along one wall was a refrigerator, a counter, the stove. Along the opposite side was a counter, a sink and a tiny breakfast bar with two stools crammed under it. Jim pulled a stool out for me to sit on. The three of us were its maximum capacity.

Jimi turned on the hot-water tap and held his long fingers under the stream until it was hot. He ferreted out a stark brown teapot and filled it with hot water. He filled a tea kettle and lit the stove. Jimi Hendrix was really going to make me tea! His long adept fingers engaged in an activity other than guitar fascinated me. Nobody was saying a word, like we were engaged in a sacrament. Jimi leaned against the counter by the stove, folded his arms across his chest, and crossed his legs at the ankle.

'When she was living in Maine,' Jim said out of the blue,

'Ginger used to play your music full blast to see if it would melt the snow.'

Jimi grinned. 'Did it?'

'Afraid not,' I said in a tiny voice. 'I guess we needed the real thing.'

'Thanks,' he smiled, accustomed to girls saying that.

'Ginger likes folk-music,' Jim said just to further embarrass me.

'Oh, yeah?' Jimi said in a tone that implied he thought about as much of folk-music as Jim did.

I looked hard at Jim. 'Yeah, it's white man's blues.' *That* was getting even.

Jim blushed, his cheeks like Santa Rosa plums. 'Well, honey,' Jim recovered nobly, 'nobody's ever gotten chills over folk-music.'

I was appalled. 'I do every time I hear Woody Guthrie's "Deportees".'

Jim was about to look cross-eyed and stick his tongue out at me.

'Yeah,' Jimi said, ganging up on Jim. 'Good song. I remember the chorus. Feed me the first line.'

Feed Jimi Hendrix the first line to a song? My mind was a blank. I looked in a panic at Jim. He smiled and hunched his shoulders. Jimi asked, 'Like Chinese?' and put loose tea in a ball, emptied the teapot, put the ball in and poured the kettle water over it slowly. He replaced the lid carefully, and returned to his crossed-arm stance. Well, the tea had to steep, didn't it?

The line suddenly came to me, and I said, '*The crops are all in and the peaches are rotting.*'

Jim spat out a laugh. 'Yeah, you know, I'm moved already.' He inspected his arms for gooseflesh.

Jimi grinned and sang the line. I had him so tied with his incredible guitar, I never gave much thought to him as a singer. A little self-conscious, he nodded to himself like he remembered the melody, closed his eyes, and began again. When he reached the chorus, '*Goodbye to my Juan, goodbye Rosalita. Adiós, mis amigos, Jesús y María. You won't have your names when you ride the big airplanes. All they will call you will be deportee,*' I looked at Jim. He was rubbing the real gooseflesh on his arms. We exchanged smiles, and listened.

At the end of the song, Jimi opened his eyes. He winked at me, reached across and tugged my hair the way Jim used to. Jimi toyed with his moustache. The three of us didn't seem to have much to say. He poured me a cup of the tea and we paraded back into the living-room.

Try as he might, Jimi couldn't keep his hands off the guitar. He avoided his own songs, and any more of Jim's, sticking with the blues until he wandered into 'All Along the Watchtower', which may have been written by Dylan, but Jimi sure made it his own. He played the intro a couple times. 'Gonna sing?' he asked Jim again.

'I don't know the words,' Jim lied. 'All Along the Watchtower' was one of his favourite songs. He sang it often.

Jimi decided not to let him off the hook and gave him the first line. A struggle of wills began between them. Jimi wasn't going to stop keying up the introduction, and Jim wasn't going to sing in front of Hendrix. I let Jim fend for himself, and concentrated on Jimi's hands. I thought I may as well learn how to play the introduction to 'All Along the Watchtower', not that I ever had even been that close to an electric guitar before.

On about the tenth take, Jim started to sing, kind of low, like he'd never sung in front of anyone before. Jimi changed his way of playing to complement Jim's voice. I wished I were wired for sound. My attention snapped to the reel-to-reel tape-recorder across the room. When Jim finished the song, I leaned to him and whispered, 'Shouldn't we be recording this?'

'No!' they said in unison.

They played and sang another hour. I excused myself to use the bathroom. Jimi stood, I thought to show me the way, then realized he was a gentleman of old-fashioned manners. He stood because I stood. When I returned, Jimi was caressing his guitar. He stood for me again.

'What's that smile for?' Jimi asked.

The smile had two explanations. I went with the second. 'The first live band I ever heard when I was ten years old or so, the guitarist . . . Dale something or something Dale . . .'

Jimi played a run of surf guitar so exactly in tune with my memory I knew he knew who I was talking about.

When he stopped, I continued, 'He held a guitar the way you do. So, the first time I ever got my hands on a guitar, I picked it up like that and the first strum, whoa! My friend's big brother called me a moron and turned the guitar over. I didn't realize that Dale held the guitar that way because he was left-handed. I just thought it was the way you were supposed to hold a guitar.'

'It is,' Jimi said, holding his guitar out to me. 'This one is right side up.'

I accepted it reluctantly, as if I might wound it. It was heavier than I expected. Jimi gave me a lesson, patient when he realized I played by rote, not genius. Holding the beautiful Fender in my arms, I couldn't imagine setting it on fire. To damage it seemed self-indulgent theatrics. I ran my thumb along the sleek edge of the guitar's neck and the image of Jim's tossing out the notebook he had filled with a night's passionate writing came to mind. I looked sideways at Jim and smiled as if I'd just gotten one of his more nebulous puns.

He gave me a questioning look and I answered, 'Throwing away the notebook and setting the guitar on fire are the same thing.'

Jim slapped his thigh. Jimi looked lost. 'What notebook?' he asked.

Jim partially explained, 'I threw out a notebook that had some pretty decent poetry in it once. She wanted to save it.'

'And he wanted to prove that he wasn't tied to it,' I explained. 'That he had more in him. I guess . . . I'm sorry. I thought that your burning your guitars was a stunt. And you burn your guitars to prove the magic isn't in them. You don't want to be tied.'

'You're fucking scary!' Jimi shouted, jumped up, and backed across the room. He retreated to the table-top and squatted there, making heavy drama of lighting a cigarette. Made me feel like a mouse. If there had been a convenient hole, I would have done some retreating myself.

'I had this guitar once,' Jimi reflected, contemplating the cigarette in his hand. 'I made this real, don't know just what to call it, *change* in how I played on it. I wasn't just fucking up blues. I was making something new. And the guitar got busted. I couldn't make that sound come out of the next guitar. I felt like I lost the only love I'd ever have. You know like *the* woman died. I thought I'd die. I still haven't found quite that sound, but I found something. I'm never going to mourn like that again. That kind of love will kill you.'

The room was still for a while. Jim automatically made this little motion of looking over his shoulder the way he so often did when he thought about Pamela Courson. Usually comfortable with silences, he broke this one abruptly. 'Can I have that line?' He sang, '*That kind of love will kill you.*'

'The music's all wrong.' Jimi jumped to the floor and ran at me fast enough I drew back and held the guitar out.

This serious business of *I write a line/you write a line* may have been way out of my league, but I was hurt not to be asked, until I was swept up with the way the two of them who had been shy about singing in front of each other fell into working out a song of their own. They were both more themselves writing than singing.

Jimi lit another cigarette. 'I'm putting together a new band in New York. Got Buddy Miles. Ever think of leaving The Doors?'

'All the time.' Jim lit his first cigarette of the day off Jimi's. Jim suspended the song by the corner of the page between his thumb and index finger. Without a word, they simultaneously used their cigarettes to ignite the page. Jim held it until it singed his fingers. My eyes stung with tears and the two of them doubled over with giggles.

'Want to get high?' Jimi asked.

'Thanks, but we need to run,' Jim said, probably for my benefit.

'Oh, let me give you a memento,' Jimi said to me. 'I'm taking up another kind of guitar. Would you like this one?'

'Oh, no, I couldn't,' I said out of politeness, wanting the guitar with all my heart.

Jimi opened a suitcase on the floor and sent the contents flying. He debated between two scarves. One was a blue paisley. The other, tangerine with a trellis. When he decided on the second one, Jim winked, knowing my preference for blue.

He wanted to autograph it. I thought that way I couldn't wear it. His pen wouldn't write on it. I provided him with a brown felt pen that at least matched the lines on the scarf. Jimi sat down and tried to hold the thin material still against his knee. 'I can usually do these drawings in a couple lines,' he said, regretting his effort to draw his Stratocaster on chiffon.

Jim kneeled to hold the fabric taut across Jimi's thigh. 'To tell you the truth, I'd rather you were holding this,' Jimi said, looking up at me, 'but you seem kind of shy.'

'It's her mind that's wild,' Jim explained to annoy me.

Jimi saw us to the door, shook Jim's hand and petted my hair before kissing the top of my head. 'Don't you tell anybody Dick Dale was an influence on me. It would ruin my reputation.'

'Why?' I asked. 'I thought that instrumental surf music was the first to make electric guitar a separate instrument, not just a louder guitar.'

'At least when you do talk,' Jimi said, 'you say something, but I'm a mean dude. I don't hang with no fucking surfers.' He winked and smiled impishly and called me back to whisper, 'After the first, I don't burn real guitars.'

On the steps, Jim put a hand on my shoulder, and whispered, too, 'You won this one, big.' I wondered what I'd won. Didn't think Jimi was going to take up surfing. At the bottom step, he recanted, 'Of course, Jimi was singing it.'

Oh, folk-music. 'I'll drag you to a Joan Baez concert. She'll give you chills, too. Thank you, Jim. It was so sweet of you to bring me here.'

'I needed you for courage. I made such an ass of myself in one of my drunken débâcles, this was meant to be an apology.'

Jim swung around a No Parking sign. He sang, 'I Get a Kick Out of You', then dropped down in front of me.

'I didn't realize Jimi lived in San Francisco. I thought he lived in England.'

'No, he lives somewhere in New York, I think. I was gonna fly you *there*, but when I got hold of Bill Graham, he said Jimi was in the Bay Area. He tracked him down for me and got Jimi to take my call.'

'You could have stayed. If you guys wanted to get stoned and all.'

'Honey, when he said *high*, he meant heroin.'

'Oh.' I didn't know what to say. 'You don't do that?'

'No. I tried opium in college. Wound up spitting blood. Decided I was allergic to opiates.'

'You mentioned that. Go to an opium den?'

'Nope. I crashed a Hollywood party. I heard that Erich von Stroheim – do you know who he was?'

I nodded. I knew he had directed silents, but really only knew him as the faithful bizarre butler in *Sunset Boulevard*.

'Anyway, I heard he was having a party. I decided to crash it. I walked right in the front door, strolled towards the noise. It turned out to be a sit-down dinner, not a big party I could disappear into. I walked to the head of the table and picked up Erich's chalice. I was pretty committed to the gesture when I smelled blood. Rumours were, he drank steer blood for virility. So, I took it down in one swallow. Got me an invitation to sit. Dessert was opium. Made me sicker than hell.'

How funny Jim even repeating the story didn't realize that the blood he spat up was what he drank, not his own. As long as it was keeping him clear of one family of drugs, I wasn't going to correct his impression.

After we'd walked a couple blocks he said, 'Let's drive down the coast instead of staying in the city. I'd like to wake up and see the ocean.'

Couldn't he wake up and see the ocean from a motel in San Francisco? Maybe he had a particular view in mind. We huddled close in the car. There was good music on the radio to which Jim was doing his *bump chunk ado wahs*. The fog gave the sky a low ceiling, but when we reached Half Moon Bay, fog was suddenly sitting on the road. The front wheel bounced off the asphalt. Jim eased the brakes. We heard the whoosh of sand. He shoved the emergency brake in.

'Fine time to find out the earth is flat,' I said.

Jim laughed. 'You wanna peek out your window and see if the world ends right here?'

I shifted my weight toward the door, and the car rocked. That was the end of the fancy patter.

'Ease back over this way. I want you out of the car before I try to back up.'

'Are you crazy?'

Jim smiled and rolled his window down in slow motion. 'Climb over me.'

'Open the door. You jump. I jump.'

'I'm the ballast for a change.' For a moment, I was warm with the realization that Jim held every little conversation we had in the same detail I did. 'As soon as you're on safe ground, I'll jump.'

'You promise?'

'Love you. Out.'

Every increment I moved, the car shifted. I held on to the roof of the car, and pulled myself through the window. My knees buckled when my feet touched ground. I got back up on wobbly legs, and reached for the door handle. Jim shifted into reverse.

'Jim, you get out of that car. Let it go! You promised.'

'I didn't promise.'

I replayed his answer in my mind. 'Do you want to die?'

The dashboard lights distorted his face, like a kid holding a flashlight under his chin to look like Boris Karloff. Jim's molten eyes looked excited. In Maine he'd said a Dante's *Inferno* version of Disneyland wouldn't be any fun because the risk wasn't real. The risk that night was real. 'If you don't come out, Jim, I'll get back in the car.'

Jim rolled the window up and locked the door. The engine growled. The rear tyres slid in the sand. I ran and stood behind the car. The brake lights went on. He rolled down his window a few inches. 'I wouldn't do this if I didn't know I could. Get out of the way.'

'The car isn't worth it. Get out.'

'This isn't the time to decide which of us is more stubborn. If my foot gets tired, I roll forward.'

I took off my pea coat and laid it under the tyre nearest the edge of the cliff. I gave my jeans to the left rear tyre. Jim whooped approval.

I backed to the edge of the pavement, shivering from fear and cold. When he reversed again, the car rocked forward slightly. I choked on my gasp. The tyres grabbed and drifted back on to the road, with a graceful little roll over the road's edge. Jim put the car in park and leaped out. He was laughing. I was terrified and angry,

380

trying to pull on my sandy jeans with stiff fingers. My hands were shaking so bad, Jim tried to help. I flailed my arm at him to keep him back.

He rested his hands on his hips, signifying how unreasonable he felt I was being. 'I wouldn't have done it if I didn't know I could make it.'

'You wouldn't have done it if you didn't know it was a risk.'

'I think we make a great team,' he said, going on about what a clever little Capricorn I was.

The pea coat was so close to the edge, I was afraid, once the emergency had passed, to retrieve it. Jim walked over and picked it up with one hand. He shook it and held it for me like a gentleman. I got back into the car and left him standing there. Jim slid behind the wheel, tossed the jacket in the back seat, and drove south, slowly, both hands on the wheel.

When we reached Santa Cruz, the fog gave way a little. At a red light, Jim reached over and ran his cool fingers down my neck. He got a room at a motel and came back to collect me. My knees were shaking so hard, Jim had to help me out of the car. 'The only vacancy is upstairs.'

I stood at the foot of the metal stairway and sighed.

'Want me to carry you?'

'How Rhett Butler of you!' I snapped.

Jim collapsed on the step, laughing. 'You're every bit as wonderful angry as when you adore me.'

I sat beside him. 'I always adore you. I'm not angry. I'm scared.'

'I wasn't drunk.'

'I know you weren't drunk. I saw what you drank today.'

'I knew I could do it,' he said, taking one of my hands in both of his. 'I wanted to win.'

'Some days with you, Jim, are a year long.'

We sat on the steps until I could take them at my own speed.

I gave a boy from my art class a lift home from school, just so I could listen to his band practise. They were trying to learn a Cream song, so I heard more Eric Clapton than the band spread out over the living-room. When I arrived home, my mother was still at work

381

and my dad sleeping, so I took the mail into my room. A letter from Maine. A letter from Stockton. A card from New York. I opened that.

The envelope was a disgusting avocado green. Inside was a card that folded out like an accordion and had *War Is Not Healthy for Children and Other Living Things* in all kinds of languages. Written in ink with a quill pen was the sentiment, '*Thank you for the beautiful afternoon.*' Jim was doing his best to apologize in fancy print. On the reverse side was a four-line poem.

When he called, I said, 'Thank you.'

'You're welcome,' Jim said cheerfully. 'What for?'

'The card you sent when you were in New York.'

'I like to think my memory lapses are fictional. I haven't been in New York since I saw you. I don't know what you're talking about.'

'The *War Is Not Healthy* card,' I said opening it up to admire again. 'Oops. It's not from you. It's from Jimi. He didn't dot the second *i*,' I said, realizing their handwriting was not all that much alike, but not all that different either. I was mortified.

'Why is Jimi writing to you?' Jim sounded a trifle put out.

'I don't know. That's why I assumed it was from you. Just a thank-you. It folds out like a long narrow poster.'

Jim was displeased. Undoubtedly enjoying a good pout, he didn't call for a bit.

'Phone,' my mom called.

When I picked it up, I heard, 'Ginger, this is Jimi.'

I was so startled, I was speechless.

'Jimi Hendrix. We met a couple weeks ago.'

'Now I remember,' I laughed. Does anyone forget meeting Jimi Hendrix? I was charmed by his belief a teenage girl just might. 'Thank you for the card. And the little poem on the back.'

'It's the beginning of a song. Want to hear it?'

There was that superb anticipation while he set up the phone. Even his tuning his guitar delighted me. Jimi sang the verse that was on the back of the card and a second. 'That's all that I've got so far.'

'It's wonderful, Jimi. Thank you for letting me in on the beginning. It's very exciting.'

'You must be used to that. Jim said he wrote all kinds of things for you, *Wild Child*. Did I get you in trouble with Jim?'

'Trouble? What do you mean?'

'He really lit into me about writing to you. I know he's got a hell of a temper.'

I was surprised that Jim had contacted Jimi. 'Jim wasn't angry. I'd call it, maybe, peeved. You see, well, I thought the card was from him. You print a bit alike. Your writing is more . . .' I thought, *feminine*, but inserted, 'Your printing is fancier.'

Jimi laughed. 'Oh, he was fucking, excuse me, pissed with me. I wouldn't want him to take it out on you, baby. If he beat you up or something because of me, I'd never forgive myself.'

'Oh, Jimi, no worry there. Jim would never hurt me. Never.'

'I've heard things . . .'

'Well, Jimi, I hear things about you, too.'

'Hey, that's what scares me. Every bad thing you've heard about me is true,' he said. Then added, 'Beware of me.'

'You are calling long distance, aren't you?'

'New York.' Jimi had a full laugh. 'If you ever want to dump that Rock God, keep me in mind.'

'Oh, my loving Jim has nothing to do with his being in The Doors. I love music, not musicians, I mean. That didn't come out right, did it? I mean, I love your music. I enjoyed meeting you, but I wouldn't go out with you because I like your music.'

'Don't think women go out with me for any other reason. Makes me want to ask you to New York for my birthday. Be cool if somebody was around just 'cuz they liked me.'

I was at a real loss. I couldn't see anything wrong with a birthday visit, so long as he didn't expect me to pop out of a cake, but Jimi had just warned me against himself. 'When's your birthday?'

'I'll be twenty-seven the twenty-seventh of next month.'

'Wow, that's cool,' I said, picking up his use of cool. As far as slang went, I was still caught on nifty, and rarely used that. 'That only happens once.' What an idiot! I couldn't think of anything to say to him. It was close enough to the Thanksgiving holidays, school wasn't the excuse it might have been.

'Take you to see the Rolling Stones,' he offered, upping the ante at my silence.

383

'Give me your address and I'll send you a birthday card,' I offered the best I could deliver. 'I make nice birthday cards.'

He gave me the address of his New York hotel with a sexy sigh. He seemed as hungry as Jim did to have an ear. I was spoiled by the natural flow of my phone conversations with Jim. Talking with Jimi was more work.

'I'm so tired. I don't sleep.'

'The lions keep you up?'

'Lions?' he asked.

'Those creative voices that roar in your ears. That's what Jim calls them.'

'Yeah. Yeah,' he sighed again.

Jimi's sighs were making a lot more progress with my steely armour than his conversation. I scolded myself. I didn't have much practice with boys. Men. It occurred to me, when Jimi started talking about his childhood in Seattle, that while boys didn't talk to me, men liked to tell me about when they were boys. Jimi told me that he used to stutter when he was young and was still pretty shy about talking and singing in front of people.

He asked if he could call me once in a while. 'Sure,' I said easily.

'You know,' he said, 'talking to you feels like calling home – without the guilt.'

23

---•◦•---

What Are They Doing
in the Hyacinth House?

The new high-school and I hated each other at first sight. It was posh and cliqueish. I was neither. The route to school crossed roads with the route to Santa Cruz and, often as not, I would turn left and wind through the mountains to the beach instead of taking the straight and narrow to class.

In November, Jim finally had to answer up to Florida for the Miami performance/disaster. Anxious before heading to Florida to be formally arrested and charged, he had been assured it would be a walk-through.

When he called from Florida, I finally thought to ask again just what he had been charged with that might add up to three years in prison. He answered, 'Oh, for being three sheets to the wind, flashing, and simulating fellatio.'

I asked what the last meant. Jim stammered with embarrassment. I've been meaning to talk to you about that. Fellatio,' he began more slowly than with most requested definitions, 'is oral sex for a man. It's like what I enjoy doing for you.'

'If they arrest you for simulating it, what do they do if you do it?' I asked. Jim's response was a five-minute laugh, punctuated by dropping coins into the pay telephone. When he composed himself, I asked who his victim was.

'Robby,' he confessed with a giggle. 'The poor guy is probably embarrassed half to death. I was paying homage to his guitar playing. Trying to distract him, too. He's got this terrific concentration. I was doing what seemed to me a very obvious guitar pun. Licking his guitar licks.'

Florida hadn't caught the beauty of the visual pun, and Jim was too pigheaded to explain it. What cost him his sense of humour was that he hadn't foreseen the Dade County police sidling up to him to tell him what they would make sure would happen to a *pretty boy* like him in prison.

Taking shallow gulps of air, in an effort not to cry, Jim whispered from that faraway phone booth, 'Do you know what they are threatening? I'd die first. Any sentence would be a death sentence.'

There was no sign from Jim for days after that call. Then, in the middle of the month, an eight-inch-square cardboard box arrived. Inside were bulbs potted in a low earthenware pot and couched in moss. There was a note in Jim's hand: 'I know the poem is dreadful, but it seemed so like you see the world. Any house we shared would be a hyacinth house.' I wasn't sure if he were making light of my tendency to lisp through the combination of *th* and *s*, or trying to tickle my appreciation of alliteration.

He included the poem he attributed to a poet named James White:

> *If thou of fortune be bereft*
> *And in thy store there be but left*
> *Two loaves, sell one and with the dole*
> *Buy hyacinths to feed thy soul*

I sent Jim a thank-you postcard and he drove all the way up from Los Angeles to knock on the door of my parents' most recent apartment with the card between his teeth. His eyes were swollen. I could smell him from a two-foot distance.

My mother was due in from work, so I didn't let Jim rest, but left a note to cover the weekend and drove us up through the town of

Saratoga. Barely into the hills beyond the town, I'd discovered a Japanese garden. There was a low Japanese-style house looking out on ponds with koi and sculpted plants. There was even a wooden gazebo draped in wisteria.

'How can you tell?' Jim asked, fingering the bare twined twigs over his head.

I picked up a long narrow fan of brown leaves from the ground and put it in his hand. He stared in wonder. 'We'll come back when it's all in bloom,' I assured him.

We sat by the pond and watched the massive orange and white fish glide slowly through the water.

'I could never be a fish,' he said.

'But you could be a dolphin,' I reminded him.

'Oh, yeah. It's not a matter of water, but intelligence.' He kissed my cheek. 'I won't go on wishing to be a dolphin if it means leaving you behind.'

'I did give the ocean a try,' I admitted. 'After that visit to Stockton, I felt so free and confident, I felt the need to try my wings . . . fins,' I corrected my metaphor.

'When was this?' he asked.

'This summer,' I took a deep confessional breath. 'The television was on where a friend and I dropped by in Los Gatos. We all lined up on the couch, self-conscious about our fascination with the moon shot. I commented that if a man could walk on the moon, a girl ought to be able to swim in the ocean. My friend's boyfriend was a surfer. He promised if I trusted him, he could get me up on his board first try. And get me back to land.'

'Jesus Christ!' Jim yelled. 'You didn't! That's crazy when you can't swim.'

His shock delighted me. For him, taking chances was so natural. 'The ride was wonderful. He kept his promise. I didn't press my luck and try again.'

'Wait until I teach you to swim. All right?' he pressed. 'All right?'

'The wet suit was uncomfortable and unflattering anyway.' And being chased by a wall of water was intimidating, but I didn't voice that observation.

Jim wanted to take me down to Los Angeles. Rick Nelson had a song popping up on the radio called 'She Belongs to Me'. Jim and I spent the first half of the trip trying to sing all the Rick Nelson songs we could think of. The first I could sing all the words to was 'Poor Little Fool', when Rick was Ricky, but Jim could sing back further.

On the second half of the drive, he filled me in on what he swore was his last fight with Pamela. Between the police threats and the fight, he told me, 'I went on a drunk.'

That was all he said for another hundred miles. Then he told me about going to Phoenix to see the Rolling Stones, but that he never got to hear a note, because he was arrested with the guy who accompanied him for harassing a stewardess, which turned out to be a federal offence. I was trying to decide if the story were an invention or the truth.

'When I harass women, usually, they think it's a compliment.'

I stuck my tongue out on behalf of all harassed stewardesses.

'Oh, don't be mad, honey. It really wasn't me. It was my friend Tom.'

The tone of his voice told me it was true. Troubled by the threats of the cops in Miami, he let someone drag him into more trouble. 'You do throw that word around,' I said. Friend. I hadn't met Tom Baker, but didn't like a single story Jim told me about him.

'I spent the night in jail,' he whined, then terrified me with the news that because of some new law aimed at skyjackers, he could face ten years in prison.

'Do yourself a favour and cross Tom off your list,' I paused, 'of leeches.'

Jim stared. I'd not said anything so pointed about his drinking pals, and it probably wasn't fair to single out one of them, but I felt I was trying to pull him up before he drifted into an uncontrollable tailspin. The box of hyacinth bulbs was asking that of me.

'I'm not worried about those charges. I am worried about Miami.'

'Jim, couldn't your lawyer make a deal? Plead you guilty as sin to being drunk, which you were, in exchange for dropping the other charges? Get off with a fine to fill their coffers.'

'I am shocked!' he said, his shock half-real, half-feigned. '*You* asking me to compromise my integrity!'

'Jim, they are threatening you because of who you are.'

'I know. But baby, you're the one who taught me the cost of not putting my body where my heart was.'

I regretted that harangue.

Los Angeles had a bright haze hanging over it. When Jim was alongside the motel where he kept a room, he saw a Porsche and swore. He pulled away, saying, 'Somebody I don't want to deal with.'

We stayed at the friend's who hadn't liked Marty Robbins. Or at least not 'Devil Woman' twenty times in a row. We waved at each other in passing.

I bathed, fed, and bedded Jim on the sofa in case his friend returned with the nerve to desire his own bed. We fitted snugly side by side in a shared blanket. We became aware that when he breathed out, I breathed in, as if there weren't room for mutual exhales.

'I've noticed,' Jim commented, 'that I feel one kind of energy when we breathe in unison and another when we alternate, but there is a connection either way. It's very sensual. And spiritual. Breathing with you.'

'In some languages,' I told him, 'breath and spirit are the same word.'

Jim wanted to find a place to rent for us. We held hands as we followed realtors through tiny Venice houses. I would have taken any one of them that offered built-in bookcases and a promise of a garden. We met men with cigars at downtown Los Angeles warehouses that Jim envisioned as combination rehearsal halls and studios, with a mattress tossed in a cosy corner. I was willing to accept anything with Jim and running water.

'It has to be perfect,' Jim insisted. 'The wedding. Where we live. Everything has to be perfect.'

Instead of pleasing me, his desire for perfection worried me. His body seemed so tightly strung, I rubbed his back.

'You're feeling the strain of a double life,' I warned. 'I felt that myself when we were together in Stockton. I was schoolgirl and girl courtesan. If you try to be rock maniac for your other friends and poet for me, you're going to crash.'

'I think I told you once, I am always either trying to be what other people want me to be, or trying not to be what other people want. With you, I'm just myself. There's no effort in that.'

Jim kissed my hair, my cheek, my lips. For Jim, that meant the subject was discussed and settled. I could have cut it open to examine, except he wasn't lying to me, but himself.

We bought ourselves wooden gliders – the kind with slots to fit them together – for a quarter. The afternoon was spent in painting them like bright exotic birds, then we found an expanse of green in a closed golf course to try them.

Jim made up a game he named 'airplane touch football', though there was playful tackling. Caught in the sprinklers, we played until we were soaked, then lay shivering in the wet grass, trying to find stars in the Los Angeles night sky.

'I could die happy this second,' Jim said.

'How about this one?' I asked, taking his hand.

'Better,' he answered.

'That's why you wait for the next second. Could be better.'

When he reached for me, I lashed him with my wet hair and took off across the broad flat stretch of grass. I could beat him in a sprint, but Jim could out-distance me, so I slowed to let him catch me when I wanted him to. He took me in hand and led me to the boulevard. We had to wring ourselves out before the cab driver allowed us in his back seat.

That night, we stayed in the hotel where Jim had taken me on the unsuccessful run in July, not in the same bungalow, but in one of the rooms which was uncomfortably musty. Jim sat up over his notebook all night, even though he'd told me he had written more than enough songs for the new album due out the beginning of the year.

Upon waking, I saw Jim sitting in a straight chair, framed by the window, his hands folded on the ledge as if engaged in matins. He rested his chin on his hands and remained unmoving for nearly an hour. Awake, he'd never been so still.

When he turned to me, I said, 'You looked as if you were praying.'

He said, 'I was, in my fashion.'

'Asking or thanking?' I asked, which covered my prayer categories.

He belly-laughed, loud in the quiet morning, contemplated for a moment, then answered, 'Thanking.'

Determined to see less trouble in Los Angeles for the next couple of months, Jim walked every street of Los Gatos proper looking for a place to rent that was close enough for me to see him without my parents stumbling on him. There were shops where he could pick up this and that and more bars than the small town or Jim needed. He rented a room in a pink house that had its own bath, but no kitchen.

Jim carried a second-hand stereo from someone's garage sale. We had one album, Jim's copy of Neil Young's *Everybody Knows This Is Nowhere*. We talked about picking up something else, but the sound suited us. Much of the time, Jim had so much music in his head, the stereo lay silent.

I discovered Jim liked to play Scrabble. He won by great margins. I would challenge words I'd never heard of, only to find they were fish that were found off the coast of Maine or in the Mediterranean. I'd lose by default. A rule we never enforced as children imposed a penalty for doubting the existence of a word, and being proven wrong by *Webster's*. In arrears, I'd give up challenging the words that miraculously tied up everything on the board. I woke in the middle of the night one night with the realization that the fun for him was when I stopped looking up his odd words, the ones that appeared logical were his invention. Invention was the only reason he bothered with Scrabble.

Even in California, the leaves had changed colour and were gathering in the street gutters. Jim and I could walk around Lake Vasonna, encountering only the ducks and geese, impatient with our never having crusts of bread to feed them.

Jim squatted by the edge of the lake. 'No honeymoon,' he said to a duck. It up-ended itself, giving Jim his tail feathers. 'I'm sorry. There's two big Doors concerts in New York a few days after your birthday.'

'Oh, so you were looking at the duck, but talking to me.' What unsettled me, other than his delivering his apology to the duck, was how often he would speak of The Doors as if they were separate from himself.

Jim laughed. 'I felt so bad. I couldn't face you.'

'You can always face me,' I said, then had a comment about my tail feathers I avoided, but Jim laughed, finishing the thought himself.

'We could get married in Mexico on your birthday, then fly to New York,' he said, holding my face to his.

'Just make sure the ceremony is in Spanish. I think I'll feel less frightened if I don't understand a word of it.'

Having just come up from a recording stint, Jim was weary. The uphill walk to the street of his rented room was slow going. When we reached the house, Jim tumbled into bed. I tumbled in beside him.

'I feel good about the album,' he said.

At one point, he had wanted to develop an album based on the cliché, *you can't judge a book by its cover*. The idea emerged from his promise to finally record 'The Spy', the first line of which was stolen from my book by Anaïs Nin, though the song had nothing to do with the content of the book. He felt it a perfect parallel joke that his image had nothing to do with his contents.

He'd written 'Been Down So Long It Looks Like Up to Me' from the title of the book by Richard Farina and 'Ship of Fools' from the title of Katherine Anne Porter's book. He'd retitled 'Roadhouse Blues/Hwy 9', 'On the Road' – naturally. And his sea chant, 'Land Ho!', 'Moby Dick'.

When he ran the idea by someone from the record company, the response he received came in two parts. First, *You Can't Judge a Book By Its Cover* was too long a title for an album. And second, a panicky, 'This doesn't mean you refuse to shave for the album cover, does it?'

Jim didn't push. 'I'm making the music I want. That's the thing.'

Then, by chance, Ray Manzerek came upon a flop house in downtown LA called Morrison Hotel. Jim said it looked like a place where Chandler's Philip Marlowe would corner a suspect, or find a body.

'I feel like I won.' Jim smiled broadly. 'That the title has nothing to do with the album is like saying you can't judge a book by its cover.'

He may have been tired of work in Los Angeles, but he grabbed his bedside tablet.

'Let's finish our Leonard Cohen song,' he said.

'Gotta keep those lions happy,' I said.

'And us,' he added.

We played with the lines until I needed to head back to my parents' apartment. Jim frowned. 'If you hadn't stubbornly refused to go back on your promise to your mother not to get married until you were eighteen, we could have gotten married this summer when . . .' he trailed off inaudibly. I couldn't tell if he were lamenting how I got to Los Angeles or how I left.

'It's been fine, Jim, except for missing you.'

'Stay tonight.' He tugged at my necklace. He tugged at my hair.

'It's amazing,' I patted his thigh, 'how many times I spend the night with girlfriends when I haven't made any friends at this school. My only friends are older and living with boyfriends who don't appreciate teenagers as overnight guests.' I shook my head before he spoke.

'I appreciate them,' he said anyway.

Jim's room had no phone, so I went out to call and returned with take-out Mexican food. When Jim recorded, he drank. When he drank, he didn't eat. He didn't complain about my not being able to bring him back a beer even if I had felt inclined. I never quite knew the etiquette of a vegetarian buying food for someone who wasn't, but Jim didn't raise a ruckus about the absence of his favourite carne asada. After dinner, we shared a sexy candlelit bath and slipped into bed

Later in the week, I stopped by on the way home from school to put a used paperback on his pillow. I knocked first just in case.

'You have a key,' he scolded.

'But you have women.'

'Oh, I'd kick them all out for you.'

'Thoughtful. I'm shy in crowds.'

'Seriously, I'd never bring a woman to a place we shared,' he said, dragging me towards the bed.

'But you expect me to share a bed with your books,' I complained. I pulled a large hard-bound book out from under me. It was a book of East Indian friezes depicting sexual postures. 'Is it an art or sex book?'

'That's a matter of taste.'

The room was lit only from a curtained window. I squinted. 'Which way is up?'

'That's . . .'

'A matter of taste,' I finished the predictable joke.

'Want to try some of the positions? You're the only woman I know supple enough for some of these.'

'Supple and willing aren't synonymous.'

'Oh, if you object,' he said with a toss of the book to the foot of the bed.

I recovered it. 'Looks like naked Indian twister.'

Jim laughed. We leafed through the volume, stopping occasionally to see if I were limber enough, collapsing in giggles. We must have looked more like a Ringling Brothers' clown tumbling act, because it hadn't occurred to either of us to try the positions naked. When I ran my insight by Jim, he started humming circus music and jumping off the bed to take bows.

When we settled in for the night, I asked without words what I'd wanted to ask since he'd called from Florida. If he'd been meaning to talk to me about fellatio, he might enjoy teaching me – just so long as I didn't exhibit the same recklessness I had with his driving lessons. When I knelt for a kiss, he pulled me up to his chest.

'Wouldn't you like more than a kiss?' I offered boldly. 'You please me so much.'

'You please me whenever we are together. But, baby, nice girls don't do oral sex for a man. It's something whores do.'

Wounded, I sat back on my heels. I crossed my arms and held my shoulders. He lay back, watching me. When his reach didn't quite meet the knee closest to him, he did not move closer so he could touch me. I released my shoulders. Jim reached for my hand and edged close enough to touch my fingertips.

I found my voice at last. 'I feel like you have one set of standards for me and another for everybody else in the world.'

Jim sighed again. 'I have one set of standards for everybody else in the world, and another for you.'

I played our lines through in my mind a few times and couldn't see the difference. I wondered if it were like a math theorem that meant something different in reverse, but I couldn't fathom how. I asked, 'What's the difference?'

'You said it like it was a bad thing. I just said it with the love I feel for you,' he said softly. Seeing me dissatisfied, he asked, 'Then why do you think *cock sucker* is an insult?'

'Well,' I revealed my innocence, 'I always thought it was a bird reference. Like yellow-bellied sap sucker.'

Jim's laugh was riotous. He drew me to him and fussed with the blankets to cover me. Several times, he started to say something, then would close his mouth and settle for a smile. We slept fitfully, taking turns accidentally waking each other. My eyes opened at first light. I dashed to the bathroom. On my return, Jim, eyes still closed, lay humming.

'My Memnon!' I whispered passionately from across the boxy room.

Jim smiled and lifted his heavy lids. Memnon? Where did that spring from? My reading was not, as Jim's, neatly filed away to be plucked at will. What knowledge I possessed was much like the chaos found under my bed. The only fact I could drag out was that Memnon was an Egyptian statue which greeted dawn with music.

'Dance for me!' he ordered, hoarse and sleepy.

Dancing with Jim was a sensual pleasure. Dancing at dawn alone with Jim looking on made me want to dive under the covers. 'Dance with me,' I taunted.

Jim sang, *'Dance with me,'* to the tune of 'Not to Touch the Earth's invitation to run, but stayed comfortably stretched out on his side in bed.

The silk shawl I'd tossed over the foot of the bed as my contribution to the room's decor beckoned. I threw it around me with what I trusted was flourish, and said to myself. 'I dance about as well as a Greek statue.' Jim chuckled, then did his best not to laugh while I danced. He lifted the covers for me to join him when my recital concluded. Isadora would not have been jealous, except of my audience.

A few days later, Jim and I pulled off a daytime burglary of my family residence. He was determined to see the family home-movies I'd joked about. There was no way to waltz the box of film and projector past my parents. My father was working nights and sleeping days, my mother the reverse. The tricky element was that the booty was stored in the closet of their bedroom.

Reason was on the side of my sneaking into the bedroom while my father slept. If caught, how much trouble could I be in for the desire to watch our home-movies? But Jim insisted he take the gamble himself. He wanted me to draw a layout of the apartment. I caught on then: he was twelve and looking for mischief.

The heist went off without a hitch. Jim hung a blanket over the curtains to further darken his room and pulled the three-drawer maple dresser, one drawer missing, away from the wall. He took great pains to centre the square of light from the projector on to the opposite wall. He threaded the projector without reading the directions.

The movies were on small, unlabelled reels. The first reel was of Moroccan soldiers mounted on horseback. Jim was enthralled for the five minutes it ran. My father took on hobbies with an obsessive perfection. His camerawork was excellent. Every five minutes, Jim ordered the lights up, rewound one film, threaded the next.

After over fifteen years of being shuttled all over the country, the colour film had taken on a wheaten glow I didn't remember as accurate. He watched the images without asking me to narrate. His eyes danced in the light of the projector as if the films were his life, not mine, though the red-headed toddler coming around the corner of the earthen house in pink panties made him turn and wink at me.

'I walked better in front of a camera at two than I do at seventeen,' I noted.

When he had spent a couple hours playing the pieces of film, he replayed the ones he had set aside in a special pile. I never knew anyone to care so much about someone else's home-movies.

The reels he chose to re-run included an Arab who took strong objection to my father's capturing him on film and chased him with a knife. Jim admired his running backwards to get the picture. He re-ran the two of my sister's birthday parties, at five and maybe ten, half a dozen times.

There was a pleasantness to the outdoor children's party in early fifties Morocco. Paper hats and coloured balloons. I was in a high chair. Stray brown and white puppies milled around, hoping for handouts.

The other was in our Tennessee living-room. Girls in crinoline slips holding their full skirts out nearly parallel to the floor. Boys with newly barbered and greased hair. Though there was no sound, there was the rhythm of rock 'n' roll. When he'd rewound the parties and reluctantly replaced them in their bright yellow Kodak boxes, I asked him why he wanted to watch that party so many times.

'I don't remember birthdays when I was little,' he said. 'I wish these were mine.'

'Maybe your parents could send you some pictures.'

Jim yanked the blanket down and the curtain rod came with it, leaving gaping holes in the wall. Jim was in the mood to fume and curse, so I borrowed a few tools from the landlord and had the rod back up in fifteen minutes.

Laughing, Jim bounced on the bed. 'You can make all the home repairs. I love your being competent.'

That was the first compliment he gave me I deserved. 'Thank you. Competent women are so rarely immortalized in song.'

'I'll work on it,' Jim promised, with a cross of his heart.

Jim and I talked on the phone more often than we had when we had less access to each other, though our conversations were often short and sweet.

'Like to see a play?' Jim asked. 'I can't reach McClure and thought you might like to check it out.'

'I love being a second thought,' I said. 'When and where?'

'San Francisco. Curtain at eight.' Jim had to call back to add, 'Tonight.'

My three best dresses were in Jim's closet in Los Angeles, so I borrowed an embroidered silk robe from my mother. I had to tell her I was attending a costume party to get out the front door in just the robe and black tights.

Jim motioned a circle in the air for me to do a turn for him. My hair was a mass of waves, not the ironed straight hair all the other long-haired girls seemed to have. Getting ready, I practically had to stand on my head to gather all my hair into a rubber band. I aimed for the effect of a picture I'd admired of Jean Shrimpton a few years before, and covered the band with a braid twisted from underneath the ponytail. The Chinese-style robe had a standing collar and three-quarter sleeves. Though it had side slits, it was long enough that Jim caught a glimpse of knee, not thigh. I bloomed with success

'Sexy,' Jim glowed. 'I love mystery.' He touched the silk at my shoulder. 'Women are always seeing how low they can cut their dresses to attract me. I'm a man, and I'll look. Even touch,' he admitted impishly. 'But I *love* mystery.'

The week before Jimi's twenty-seventh on the twenty-seventh, I dreamed birthday-card designs through my classes. Since he had talked about being a lonely kid, I decided to make him a kid's card. I loaded up a sheet of heavy paper with all the best crayon colours, blackened the whole thing, then scratched away at the surface. The magic of the process had pleased me as a child, and made my mother expert at getting crayon marks off the floor. Since he had drawn his guitar for me, I drew mine for him, wrote *It only happens once* inside, and sealed it in an envelope before second thoughts took hold.

Jim's and my nights together were candlelit when we thought to light candles, playful when Jim was energetic, but whichever mood, undeniably sensual. When Jim woke, I'd been awake for hours and was anxious to talk. 'Good-morning,' I said in good cheer.

Jim put his fingers to his lips to silence me. 'La, la, la, la, la, la, la, la, la, la, la,' he sang in his throaty morning baritone. He'd dreamed a line of a melody. All morning, Jim *la, la, la'd* the same eleven syllables. A hundred times. He sounded like a record stuck in a groove. I tensed with expectancy, listening to his coming up to the brink with that last *la*, hoping to hear the next few bars drop from the heavens. We both let out a sigh of relief when the music arrived.

He collapsed backwards on to the bed, arms flailing. 'Remember that!' he ordered.

I wasn't likely to without words, though I found the melody sweet. He disliked my description. 'Have to fix that,' he said, patting his chest. 'Pamela used to get so angry with me when I'd try to work, I couldn't write around her. She hated being shut out.'

'Oh, gosh,' I said with genuine surprise. I climbed on to his lap. 'It never occurred to me that you were shutting me out. I thought you were letting me in.'

Jim chuckled. 'Everything is a matter of perception.'

24

Until We Say Goodbye

In the early evening, right after Jim's birthday, I came in from a long walk. I was hopeless with dates, but told Jim I remembered his birthday because it was two years and a day after Pearl Harbor. He claimed that was how he remembered it, too. Restless, I'd walked all the way to Villa Montalvo, a mansion given over to the arts.

My mother looked up from the crochet in her lap to acknowledge me. I drank a glass of tap water slowly. My mother had often repeated the story of the man who had come in from mowing his lawn, downed a glass of ice water, and dropped dead on the spot. I'd never checked out the truth of the claim, but cautiously followed her instructions to drink room-temperature beverages after exertion.

I was exerted. My legs throbbed, but I still felt restless. I'd spoken with Jim on his birthday, but identified my restlessness as needing to hear his voice. Jim had been on my mind all day. I normally didn't indulge in daydreaming about him. When he was with me, he filled me completely. When he was away, I played catch-up with the rest of my life.

On his birthday, Jim called me as soon as he woke to thank me for his presents. When I bragged how far I could stretch a dollar, he dared me to see how many presents I could buy him keeping the tab under that mark. I'd found a used copy of Mark Twain's *Letters From the Earth*. There was a sign that the paperbacks were half the cover price, which would have made the price a reasonable thirty cents, but I bartered the bookseller down to a dime.

To make up for his not recalling his early birthdays, I bought Jim the smallest box of crayons, a pouch of marbles, a tiny red race car, and a pinwheel. Just as I was beginning to despair of finding something suitable for him with the remaining fifteen cents, I came upon a girl making angel sand-candles on the Santa Cruz beach. She'd collected a pile of assorted bivalves for wings. When I told her of my predicament, she even let me pick out the wings and accepted the fifteen cents as fair.

When I answered his birthday call, Jim yelled, 'Varoom!'

I interpreted that as his approval of the speedster. He read from Twain. I offered him a cake if he came up to my part of California, but he had things to do in Los Angeles. He sounded tired as if he were making an effort to talk, so I didn't hold him on the phone.

'Could I make a long-distance call?' I asked my mom. 'I'd like to call Jim in Los Angeles.'

She nodded, counting her stitches. I never called Jim from home. Trying to explain a series of two-minute calls to bars all over Los Angeles tracking him down made it seem easier to wait for his calls. I had my hand on the phone when it rang.

Jim sang 'I Can't See Your Face'. I giggled into his ear, thinking a combination of *Great minds run* and *About time!* He'd never sung the whole brief song. Throughout, his voice kept breaking. I shivered. When he sang the last line, my body went as cold as it had when I feared if he climbed into the small plane he would crash.

'Jim . . .'

'Yeah, baby. This is the call I promised I'd make. You see, I keep my promises.'

'Thank you, Jim. Thank you. Part of the promise is that I get a chance to hold on to you.'

I picked up the napkin holder from the kitchen table and launched it towards my mother in the living-room. Startled, she looked up as the napkins scattered around her. I waved her to me and scrawled on the kitchen wall, 'Jim's suicidal. Trace the call.'

The colour left her face, but she ran out the front door in her robe.

'Let me say a few things,' Jim said so softly I strained to hear. 'I love you. And I know that we were meant to be together, so we will meet next time around. Makes it all easier. I've rewritten my will. It's in my handwriting, but it's witnessed and legal. Half goes to you and half to be split between Anne and Andy. I want them to know how much I love them, even if I haven't been a good brother to them.'

He cleared his throat. His voice became businesslike. 'I added something that isn't in my previous will. I want control of all my creative work to be in your hands, even if the proceeds are split. If you have any questions, I would trust Michael McClure's judgment. I always wanted to take care of you, baby, and you'd never let me. It's not as much as I wish it were. The last year hasn't been good. Of course, I wrote a letter to you to say all the things I want to say to you and won't be able to.'

'Jim. I love you,' I said, confused. I'd been with him less than a week before. What could have gone so wrong? I needed time. 'How long did it take you to write the will?'

He laughed. 'What a strange question. About an hour.'

'If I don't hear a rip, I'm hanging up. I'm buying you a goddamn hour! Tear the will up. I want to hear it.' There was a pause. Then paper tearing. Dizzy. I took a breath. I'd forgotten to breathe. 'Where are you, Jim?'

'You know, it's interesting. You never use endearments. You always just call me Jim and it's the dearest word when you say it.'

'Are you in LA? I could fly down and we could talk in person. That would be better, wouldn't it?'

'Honey, if I tell you where I am, you would have everybody from the Boy Scouts to the National Guard at my door. I really love that Joan of Arc part of you, but now's not the time.'

I wanted somebody at his door faster than I could get there. 'Would you let me call Pamela?'

'No. I don't want to see her. Besides, I think she's out of town.'

'Ray or . . .'

'No, baby. I think they have enough tracks laid down, if they piece together some stuff left off other albums, that they can finish the album. It's a good album. That's the best I can do for them right now.'

'This isn't about the band, but your friends. If they knew you were in this much trouble, Jim, they'd want to help.'

'No,' he said flatly.

I asked. 'Jim, are you drunk?'

'Nope. Not going to find anything in the autopsy. I really needed this to be *my* decision. I'm gonna slip off a ledge. Seems the best way. I have no fear of heights.'

'Jim. I know that this trial is weighing heavily on you, but it hasn't happened yet. You have four months before it even starts. You're sentencing yourself without a trial. Even if you are convicted, there are appeals. And we could always leave the country. Really see Africa.'

Jim laughed. 'Don't make me daydream.'

'Daydream,' I pleaded.

My mother returned in tears, shaking her head. Neither the police nor the phone company would do anything. No paper in sight, I scavenged a paper bag from the cupboard, wrote down Pamela's number, The Doors' office, and the names of the other Doors, knowing they probably weren't listed, but had to try. She took the list and ran.

'I love you,' I said. My mind was blank of anything else. 'I love you.'

'I know. It's the one thing I've always been sure of. My biggest regret is that I didn't give you my name.' He laughed softly. 'I love you. Next time, huh?'

He'd kept his part of the bargain. He'd called and let me try to talk him out of killing himself. He was winding down. 'There is only *this* time. Jim.'

'No. I'm pretty sure we've always known each other.' I begged him to let me see him a last time. Jim paused. I prayed silently. *Please. Please Please.* He asked, 'Will you come alone? Promise,' he said. 'If you lie to me, I'll kill myself on the spot.'

My mother came into the kitchen shaking her head, tears fogging

402

her glasses. 'It will take me a couple hours to get to LA. I want you to stay on the phone with Mama until I get there. You can recite your poetry to her. You know how she loves it.' Jim's life was a terrible weight to thrust on her without asking. I knew she was thinking, as I was, about the loss of my brother. 'Now, where are you?'

'Honey, if I tell you where I am, a cop will be knocking on my door in ten minutes. We'll meet someplace. How about Barney's? If you're alone, I'll meet you.'

'Will you stay on the phone as long as you can? It's the only way I can come to you. Promise you will meet me, alive and well.'

'I promise. I never break my promises to you.'

Handing my mother the phone was an awful moment. I dashed to my room and pulled the bottom drawer of my dresser out and grabbed the envelope taped to its underside that held the hundred-dollar bill Jim had given me in San Francisco. I prayed for green lights and ran red ones. I parked my car and ran to the ticket counter that had the first flight to LA. I traded in the bill on which Jim had printed *FREEDOM* on a chance to save Jim's life. I wanted to believe Jim would keep this important promise, and tried to convince myself I could forgive him if he couldn't.

I tripped out of the taxi in front of Barney's Beanery in something short of two hours. I ran in and stopped dead. I looked at every man in the room twice, as if I just forgot what Jim looked like, and would recognize him if I looked hard enough. Outside, I studied every inch of both sides of the street, willing some shadow to become Jim. Just as I was going to dart back in to check the men's room, I saw Jim, huddled against a wall, I broke into a run. I slipped my arms up under his fleece-lined jacket to hold him.

'Thank you, Jim.'

His hand trembled a little as he ran his fingers through my hair. 'Let's go where we can be alone,' he said.

I tried to hail a cab, but it took Jim stepping in the street to get one. Being ignored by the string of taxis made me feel too childish to handle anything. Jim ordered the driver to the beach. We laced fingers, and rode in silence. At last he said in his sweetest voice, 'Your mother read *Leaves of Grass* to me when she ran out of things to say.'

I instantly forgave her everything for buying me time with that. Jim slumped against me for a few miles. Then he righted himself enough to pull an envelope from his jacket pocket and remove a sheaf of papers folded into thirds. His handwritten will. 'I tore the phone book,' he said to account for the sound I heard over the phone. 'I loved your willingness to pay so much for an hour of my life. Thank you, baby. I'm happy I get to read you this letter I wrote.' He separated a sheet of paper, then returned it to the envelope. 'We'll do that later.'

'Can we talk?'

'No. I don't want to talk. Besides, your being here says everything. Nobody else is here.'

'Who else did you invite?' I asked.

'I didn't invite you. You insisted. Everybody I know knows I'm in trouble. The day after my birthday, I sat in the office with friends and said I wanted to die. They let me know I couldn't split fast enough.'

I glanced up into the rear-view mirror to catch if the driver were listening. His eyes were on the road. I wondered if I could hold Jim in the moving cab if I changed the orders to a hospital. Reading my thoughts, Jim easily pulled his hand from me and shoved it into his jacket pocket.

I paid the fare. The length of beach was dark and deserted. Fog had swallowed the moon. The only illumination came from streetlights across the road. We laboured across the sand and sat side by side just above the tide line. The ocean moved Jim, and I needed its help. I watched him watching the waves. He turned to me as if he'd just remembered something important.

'I want you to have this,' he said, reaching into his other pocket.

The desolation of his gesture made me think of a line from Chandler's *Big Sleep*, 'I was as empty of life as a scarecrow's pocket.' He placed a small paperback in my hands. I could tell it was an older book, but could not read the title or make out the illustration in the moonless night. I feared it might be his beloved *On the Road*.

'This is the first book I ever bought for myself,' he said in a boastful young voice.

The volume was definitely not a children's book. The fine print was a grey blur by the night sky. I held it up in the direction of the distant lights.

'James Michener's *Tales of the South Pacific*,' Jim said. 'I was seven, I think. Second grade, anyway.'

Michener at seven? 'Precocious,' I said.

'It wasn't a literary decision,' he explained. 'It was the half-naked girl on the cover.'

As heavy as my heart felt, I smiled and repeated, trying to pull him into the normal rhythm of our conversations. 'Precocious.'

His laugh was muted, his nose stuffy from crying, but Jim laughed. And I thought, *if I can make him laugh, I can make him live*. A warm wash of pride engulfed me.

Jim faced the ocean. 'If I walked off into the ocean, you'd follow me to save me, to bring me back, without thinking of the cost to you, that you aren't a good swimmer.'

The false warmth left me. 'I hope you don't plan to test your theory.' With no moon glittering on the water like the night he pulled me into the surf in Santa Cruz, I imagined I'd stand helplessly in the sand. Stop if I couldn't reach him when the water was up to my waist. He may have been right. I might have kept changing my limit until I was beyond my depth.

Jim asked, 'Have you read Schopenhauer?'

'How about you put off this suicide thing while I do that? Take me a good long time just to figure out how to spell it close enough to find him in the card catalogue.'

He smiled. 'You don't need to read him.' He rubbed my thigh. 'Something I've tried to say before is that there is no separation between us. We are the same person.'

Schopenhauer must have philosophized on the nature of blood brothers. 'Then if you kill yourself, you'd kill me.' Even in low light, I saw a hesitation in his eyes through the tears in mine.

We sat in the cold sand for hours. When Jim gave the cue, we struggled to our feet, our bodies stiff and unresponsive. I was reminded of holding the flashlight for him to write in Big Sur. I looked up at him. He was smiling. He remembered, too. How could he step off a building and leave me the only one to remember?

We strolled to a nearby motel like lovers on a romantic outing. I hung on his arm and debated asking the woman behind the counter to call the police. Call an ambulance. But Jim had made a point of proving I could not physically hold him long enough for anyone to take over the responsibility I'd asked him to give me.

Once in the room, Jim turned on the heater. Desiring creature comforts seemed a good sign. I was anxious for good signs. That he kept his promise and called me was a good sign. That he met me at all was a good sign. That he laughed was a good sign.

While I was counting blessings, Jim sat on the edge of the bed without removing his coat, his will poking ominously out of his pocket. The wind had tangled his hair, but it was washed. He wore a fresh-from-the-cleaners white shirt with jeans. When we were off to the Bill Monroe concert, I'd so glibly assured him a guy couldn't go wrong with that combination. And he chose it as suitable wardrobe for flying off a roof.

I thought of a hundred things to say and threw them all away in favour of helping him out of his jacket. Movement seemed a chore for him, but he helped me with my coat to be polite. He dropped back down on the bed. I took his face in my hands and asked, 'Would you like me to give you a bath?'

I was afraid to leave him even to run the bath, so I dragged him along with me. I undressed both of us. I would have thrown him into the tub if I had to, but he stepped in gracefully.

'No candles,' he sighed sadly as he sat down.

I sat between his legs facing him. 'There goes romance,' I said.

'We come with romance.'

He kissed my lower lip, tugging on it gently with his teeth, drew back, then gave me a thorough kiss. I wondered how he could feel romantic and suicidal at the same time.

'No soap,' he said when he felt satisfied with the kiss.

I scouted the perimeter of the tub. 'There goes cleanliness,' I teased.

'Was that ever the point?' Jim asked, grabbing my seat to pull me up against him. He explored me, cataloguing my body's changes during the time we'd known each other.

When I started to dress, Jim asked fearfully, 'Where are you going?'

'Nowhere,' I answered.

'Then,' he said with a caress, 'don't get dressed on my account.'

The truth was I wanted to get dressed on his account. If he made a sudden mad dash for the door, he might be willing to go naked, but I needed cover. My thoughts were a maze. When he wouldn't talk or let me read the letter which I thought held all the clues needed to solve the puzzle, I held him in bed. Sometimes, I felt Jim could never be touched enough. Lying together, we fell into breathing in rhythm. To see if he would follow, I intentionally slowed my breath in a technique I'd learned in a yoga class.

After five minutes, Jim rolled on to his back laughing. He touched his temple. 'I'm high,' he said. 'Breathing with you made me high.'

He stroked my side in appreciation. Most people don't use all their capacity to breathe. The extra oxygen can make a first-timer giddy. If he could pretend to call up the wind, I could pretend to call up breath. I'd let him in on the secret another time. I wanted to believe there would be other times with Jim.

I didn't know I had slept until I opened my eyes and the clock radio on the dresser was ten minutes later than it should have been. I started, afraid my lack of vigilance had cost Jim his life. He was lying on his side beside me, watching me.

'You look like my picture of you from first grade,' he said. A wild animal caught in the headlights. I'd never been more afraid. He stroked my neck. 'You were having a nightmare. I woke you. What were you dreaming?'

The dream was me by a newly dug grave. The earth was soft. I leaned closer, thinking I saw earthworms squirm, then realized they were fingers coming up from the grave. As the hands emerged, I saw they were Jim's, beautifully shaped, the nails dirty and ragged like a boy's. With all my strength, I tried to pull him out of the mounded earth, but the dirt was so soft, his greater weight made me sink into it. I couldn't get my footing. Jim's muffled screams begged me to let go.

'I don't remember,' I lied.

'I felt guilty waking you, but didn't want you to be frightened.'

My hand felt for his heart. 'Then you have to decide you want to live.'

In the morning, Jim and I showered together, then took a taxi into downtown LA. I'd talked him into seeing a doctor. The psychiatrist Jim had chosen was someone a friend had gone to. I made the appointment for him under the pseudonym James Douglas, hoping there weren't many pictures of him circulating with his beard. He wanted to be anonymous, which seemed to mean he needed to talk about something other than the pressures of fame and the Miami trial. That could come later. His hand was sweaty in mine. While I gave his name and address at the desk, Jim sat on a small leather sofa. I hesitated, then sat down next to him.

'If I was my old self,' Jim whispered, 'I'd rip the seats up so you could sit ethically.'

I leaned over to kiss him, and missed. I kissed the bridge of his nose. 'You have a handsome nose.'

'Straight off the Serengeti,' he reminded me.

'Mr Douglas?' A tall, slightly stoop-shouldered man held out his hand to Jim. When Jim took it, the doctor patted him on the back. I saw Jim stiffen. He glanced back at me with a pleading look in his eyes. I nodded encouragingly.

The clock crawled through the fifty-minute hour. The doctor, not Jim, emerged from the inner office, gesturing me to come with two fingers like an uppity waiter.

On rubbery legs, I made it across the waiting-room. Jim slouched in a chair beside the desk. His eyes were red and swollen. There was a pile of soaked tissues wadded in his lap. I reached over and touched Jim's knee.

'I'd like to see James intensively for a couple weeks. He explained you're from out of town. Would it be possible for you to stay? Your presence is very important right now.'

I wondered briefly why Jim hadn't asked himself, then knew he had used up all his day's courage in that partial hour. As soon as the glass doors of the medical office building closed behind us, Jim put his head back and shouted, 'Jesus, save us.'

'Is a church our next stop?' I asked.

He unearthed a chuckle. 'No, huevos rancheros and a good Mexican beer.'

There was no shortage of Mexican restaurants in the area. With every physical desire Jim exhibited, I hoped he had a firmer hold on life.

'Funny thing,' Jim said suddenly, 'when I called the police and asked about the detectives that questioned me about the murders.' He meant Jay Sebring and the others that summer. They had arrested a demented ex-con named Charles Manson and conspirators he called his tribe. Jim hadn't spoken of the events since my last visit to Los Angeles. 'They claimed never to have heard of them. Maybe it was the FBI playing some game of their own. A friend from when I went to college in Florida told me he'd been questioned about me. We were just in a school play together.'

'Is that how you know all that Shakespeare?' I asked, digressing, as if we were just sitting over his favourite breakfast and chatting.

'Oh, no. I never did Shakespeare. I just read him. The soliloquies stuck with me because they're like songs.'

'You have a wonderful mind,' I smiled. With my practical outlook, I thought, let's tackle this list of wrongs that wounded you, Jim. 'How do we check out the FBI?'

'We aren't going to check out anything. Whatever's gonna happen, is gonna happen.'

'Funny, you don't look like Doris Day.'

Jim laughed and sang 'Que Sera, Sera' to the accompaniment of a Mexican band's recording of 'Via con Dios'. I complimented his ability.

'Oh, that's being in rock 'n' roll. I can tune out anything beyond myself or I'd never get through a concert. When I started singing, it drove me nuts to hear a couple arguing in the third row.'

Jim sounded more himself. He enjoyed his meal and kept his beers to two. Jim wanted to collect his mail at The Doors' office. Since he had recently been there, he may have just needed to touch base with reality. I'd never been during business hours, if they had them. I thought about tackling the first person I saw and getting him on Jim's side.

Able to read my mind, Jim warned, 'Don't say anything about last night. Or this morning. This is private.'

'Jim, I've got to do what I think is best for you.'

'You're best for me. You've gotten me help. I trust you.'

He didn't make me promise anything, I told myself. He let go of my hand as he walked into the office. A brown-haired young women with a telephone at her ear nodded to Jim as he passed. Jim had told me that one of the women in the office had helped pull together *The Lords*, a volume of thoughts on theatre he'd written in college, which he'd had self-published to maintain control. He refused to give me a copy because they had arrived printed *by Jim Morrison*, not James Douglas Morrison, as he had ordered.

A young man asked Jim how he was doing. Jim answered, 'All right.' Then the man whispered and nodded towards me hanging in the doorway. 'Out of line,' Jim said.

I felt insulted from a distance. Jim took only two letters out of a stack, asked the woman for some petty cash. She provided him with a few twenties. Jim thanked her and we left. We went by his motel, picked up his shirts, my dresses, and a dented blue car, which Jim insisted was actually his.

'Thank you for not betraying me,' Jim said softly. Would it have been to ask for their help? 'You give people second chances. I don't.'

'I don't understand, Jim. How many chances have you given the band? Or Pamela? Or your drinking buddies?'

'But I don't trust any of them. It's like, well, I forgave your mother for lying to us, but I'll never trust her again.'

I considered the woman's face I'd studied from the office doorway. Could she really have ignored a plea of help from Jim? Maybe she hadn't been there that day. Maybe Jim hadn't been as clear as he thought he had.

'What happened on your birthday, Jim?' I asked.

He coughed. I let him take his time. He wouldn't answer at all the previous night. At last, he said, 'I got drunk.'

The answer surprised me, not because it was unusual, but because from what he implied, it was so usual. I studied him in profile. His beard had filled in again since he gave in and shaved for the pictures shot for the album cover. The lopped-off hair hit his shoulders. His brow seemed swollen over his eyes in tension. I noticed he had his shirt buttoned one button off. I wondered what the psychiatrist had made of that.

'Why was it different?'

'Well, I went to a little gathering. Bill Siddons, he's our manager,' he explained, though I remembered the name. Jim had hand-picked him to replace their first manager. He liked that Bill was young and unsullied by the business. When met with resistence, Jim said he'd rather somebody who worked for him erred due to inexperience than greed. 'Bill gave me a bottle of Courvoisier.' He took a few deep breaths and struggled to say, 'Last . . . straw.'

The brandy was Jim's favourite. I could call up the smell of it as he said the name. 'Why did that hurt you? He probably thought it would please you.'

'You know. I thought he was my friend. But he's like all of them!'

I wondered if he had, with his remarkable hearing, caught a slight his friends didn't realize he could hear. 'I think you're wrong, Jim. You like this man and he likes you. It was a mistake in judgment to give you brandy when you're an alcoholic,' I stopped at the word I'd never said. Jim preferred to call himself a drunk. Drunk was more colourful. Historically, writers were drunks. 'I think your reaction came not from Bill's intention, which really was probably just to wish you a happy birthday, but from your reaching the point where you need to do something about your drinking.'

Jim turned to me. 'You make more sense than the doctor.'

He must have talked to the doctor about his drinking, which gave me a sense of relief, so I said, 'I was going to move to Los Angeles on my birthday. Why don't we just consider me moved?'

Jim's response was a gentle touch on my cheek with a whispered, 'Thank you,' and the question, 'Like to go to the movies?'

I craved sleep, but if Jim needed movies, movies won. Going to the movies took us to the house where we had our late swim before I left California. Jim had a key and let us in. Beyond the foyer was a curving staircase. There were sliding panelled doors left and right. Jim hesitated and laughed. 'I can't remember which way.'

I was intrigued he had a key to a house with which he lacked familiarity. 'Let's hope this isn't a lady and the tiger dream then,' I said and slid the right door open a few inches. I poked my head into a living-room. 'What are we looking for?'

'The theatre.'

'You mean, people have theatres in their houses?'

'We watched your home-movies on my wall in Los Gatos.'

The theatre in this house was straight ahead, left, and down. It might have been a basement in a lesser house. Halfway down the staircase there was a door to the projection room. There was a projector and a chair. The back wall contained a floor-to-ceiling rack of film canisters.

'Whose house is this?' I whispered like a trespasser.

'A friend's.' Jim leaned sideways to read the labels printed on what looked like adhesive tape.

'You wouldn't tell me when we were here before.'

'You'd disapprove and not want to watch movies with me here.' It never belonged to an actor acquaintance.

'A paramour?'

'Nope.' He pulled out a canister, then reshelved it alphabetically. Suicidal and alphabetizing films.

'Is this the house you rented for Pamela?'

'That was Brentwood. I couldn't afford this. You have to be in movies or drugs to afford this.'

Jim located the film he wanted. He opened the side of the projector and threaded the film expertly, even on a rotten night of no sleep and a long morning of soul searching. After he'd adjusted the focus, he led me to the best seat in the house. The seating was what I thought of as French provincial. The chairs were wooden with red velvet backs, seats and arm rests. Three rows of chairs, four chairs to a row.

'Where's the rest of the jury?' I asked.

Jim smiled wearily. I looked up at the screen. Oh, dear. Jim expected me to read subtitles on ten minutes' sleep. With luck, I could understand enough French to follow François Truffaut's *Four Hundred Blows*.

Jim held my hand, communicating with squeezes, his eyes never leaving the screen. During the movies we'd seen together before, he was one of those noisy people everyone else tries to glare into silence in the dark. His choice of film and his silence disturbed me. I watched him more than I watched the movie.

When he had to get up to change reels, I trailed after him. He carefully rewound the first real, but didn't shelve it. I had the notion that he was going to re-run it the way he had my sister's birthday reels. I was right. When the film ended, Jim watched it again. When he was about to show it a third time, I blocked his hand.

'Bet a swim would do you more good,' I said.

The film canisters were filed. We mounted the stairs and exited through curtainless French doors on to the backyard where Jim and I had taken our memorable moonlight swim. Jim stretched and bounced. Peeled and dove. He swam ten laps and was so spent he couldn't heave himself out of the pool. He pushed off the wall and floated half a length. Opposite the steps, he stood and walked up from the water. His eyes lifted to the roof of the house.

'You'd only sprain an ankle from there,' I said.

'A hummingbird,' he pointed. 'I was watching a hummingbird.'

I forced myself to lose sight of him long enough to get him a towel. He sighed contentedly while I rubbed him head to toe. While I still had him wrapped in the towel, I asked into his chest, 'Why do you want to die?'

'It's easier.'

He'd said something similar before. I looked at dying as a very hard thing to do, whether by choice or circumstance. 'Than what?'

'Almost anything,' he answered.

We returned to the beach motel. He carefully hung up my dresses and his shirts in the closet that was just a chrome bar in a recessed part of the wall. Jim pulled at my dress I wore. Then he backed up and looked marooned in the middle of the room.

He seemed to need to be told what to do. I suggested we shower off his chlorine. Naked, Jim was more himself. When we were finally all tangled up in bed again, Jim said, 'You look so tired, baby, close your eyes.'

'I feel like lying on top of you, so I'll know if you move,' I said frankly.

'That's fine,' he said. 'I'm softer than I used to be. Sleep well.'

The next night, Jim changed into a black shirt and pants. He said he was going to record and I had to trust he was. With all the tall structures in Los Angeles, part of me wanted to shadow him. Most of me felt the crisis had passed. He was no longer a scarecrow's pocket.

After he left, I looked at the copy of *Tales of the South Pacific* he'd given me on the beach. He wasn't that precocious. The native girl painted on the cover was back-to, facing a young naval officer in khaki. The pages were yellowed and brittle, so I didn't attempt to open it enough to read. I noticed pencil markings on the inside back cover.

The child's writing was identifiable as Jim's. He'd written with one of those thick pencils children use. Jim had been writing in books long before he asked me to sacrifice my *Siddhartha*. This wasn't a creative work but a list titled *Improv*. At seven, he couldn't spell any better that I could at my age. After a number one, he'd written, *stand strait*. He was still inclined to slouch. Beside the two was written, *be polite*. He had definitely learned his P's and Q's, but could be mannerly or a lout, depending on mood. After the three, he'd played with the period long enough to make it as big as a ladybug. There, he had written, *read*. I imagined the first two were parental suggestions, and the last his own. He was well read.

At three in the morning, Jim stumbled in drunk and beat. He dove into bed less gracefully than his dive into the pool and was out. He woke and drank a warm beer for breakfast.

Jim was wincing behind shades, so I offered to drive him to his shrink appointment. The blue car was like a jet compared to my Volkswagen biplane. The monster was too big and powerful for city streets. I was happy to get us to the medical building parking-lot unscathed.

This was our pattern for several days. The only change I demanded after the first night was that he leave his car keys with me. When we left the doctor's office for the fourth time, Jim directed me out of town on to the freeway. Merging was a breeze with all that power. The car was an investment in speed. I was beginning to enjoy myself when Jim pointed to the airport exit.

'The guys hired a keeper for me,' Jim said. 'They care enough to get me through the album, anyway.'

I glanced sideways, but made the turn-off. I wanted Jim to wait and talk when we were safely parked somewhere. But he wouldn't. He smiled when I caught his eye and cleared his throat. He'd prepared a speech and had it memorized.

'When I climb out on that ledge, you're the only one who can call me back. I need to know you'll be there. Without you, I'd be dead. The next time I ask you to marry me,' he said, gracefully cancelling our marriage plans, 'I want it to be for all the right reasons.' I was trying to let the words sink in and keep the car on the road. He guided me right up to departures. Suddenly I was leaving LA. He crumpled the three middle fingers of my right hand in his grip. Another ounce of pressure and he would have broken their bones. 'I want you to go home, graduate from high-school. We'll see each other like always.' Then he added when he lowered his sunglasses, 'I feel like I have a better hold on things than I ever had.'

PART IV: *1970*

25

Why Did You Throw the Jack of Hearts Away?

I tiptoed up to my eighteenth birthday, afraid it might explode. Since I could remember, eighteen was the line of demarcation between being a child and an adult. That had been my goal. When I was eighteen, I was going to move to Los Angeles, attend art school, and marry Jim. Like everything else regarding us, I wasn't sure how I felt about Jim calling off the marriage.

Fearlessly, Jim called on my birthday to wish me the best. He claimed to be punishing himself by vacationing in Mexico, where we were to have been married, with an old friend.

'Male or female?' I asked.

'Male. This is self-flagellation.'

Had he dulled the pain with an excess of tequila? When Jim dumped me at the airport, I watched him scoot across the seat, hug the steering wheel, and pound his forehead against his hands. He parked so long, a cop had to motion him away from the curb. Jim called that night. I elicited a promise that he would call me daily for a while.

For a guy who never wore a watch, he was punctual with the

calls intended to ease my worry. Not five minutes after I arrived home from school, the phone would ring. Jim would say a simple, 'I'm alive.'

By Christmas, he was telling me stories of adventures with his companions. He sent me a lavish present, which I returned with a note, '*None of that.*'

In retribution, he sent me jacks with a ball that looked like the pictures of the earth taken from space that didn't bounce as well as the old red ones. He included the cash-register receipt to prove he only spent forty-nine cents on the gift with a jibe, a repetition of Pamela's, 'Do you want to play jacks?'

With the joke, Jim had returned close enough to himself that I informed him he was off the hook. He no longer had to check in every day. The pun pleased him, but he continued the daily calls right up to my birthday.

Jim and I made a date for a birthday celebration, belated by the concerts at the Felt Forum in New York. We planned Chinese food, but let the evening flow. Jim flowed into a restaurant for a drink. He mumbled an introduction to an attractive blond at the bar, who I was quite sure was the guitarist from the Jefferson Airplane. Soused, he took my hand and held it while he and Jim shot the breeze.

In the street, Jim was irate, his jealousy absurd. 'Jim, if I went back in there and introduced myself, he wouldn't remember we met. Your jealousy isn't flattering.'

Not off to the best start, we walked uphill into Chinatown. He'd heard about a place on a side-street. *On a side-street* in that part of San Francisco, we would have been better off had one of us spoken Chinese, but Jim was determined. We found the place by matching the Chinese characters on a piece of paper Jim whipped out of his pocket with those on a painted sign. I wasn't sure how that would get us food.

The waiter was young and smiling. He greeted Jim with, 'My God, you're Jim Morrison!' which made us all feel better. He had caught The Doors every time they played The Fillmore or Winterland. I wished I could have claimed the same.

The menu was brief and only in Chinese. He helpfully translated. The only true vegetarian offering was steamed rice, even vegetable-dominated dishes had, he confessed, fish or chicken stock in their sauces. Rice was fine as far as I was concerned.

Jim asked, 'Could we do something about that?'

'My uncle is cooking. He's a royal pain, but I'll tell him you're newlyweds. He's a sucker for sentiment.'

Jim shrugged and winked, but took my hand under the table. 'A little irony *hors d'oeuvre*?' he asked.

While we waited for the special service, the boy pulled up a chair and chatted with Jim. He wanted to know what he was up to, with the beard and all. Jim had shaved for the concerts, but was wearing a few days' growth. 'Is it for a movie?' he asked.

'No,' Jim admitted. 'Just tired of shaving. I'm more interested in making movies than starring in them.'

'I almost didn't recognize you, but there was that picture in *Rolling Stone*. Your poetry was cool.'

'Thanks. I have a book out soon. I'll send you one.'

The two works he had self-published, *The Lords* and *The New Creatures*, were coming out in hardback in the spring. He'd given up the fight to have them published under James Douglas Morrison, but was pleased the work itself was uncensored.

Jim practically interviewed the boy about his family – how extensive was his family, when had they come to San Francisco, what part of China had they come from – then asked what he wanted out of life.

'I'd like to be an actor, but, heck, they aren't even making Charlie Chan movies any more.'

'I always thought Charlie Chan's relationship with his children was the best on screen,' I spoke for the first time. 'They made fun of his being old-fashioned and he made fun of their being hep cats, but they had real love and admiration for each other. Strange that Chan was never Chinese, though.'

'Oh, that's Hollywood,' the boy said with a laugh. 'I met Keye Luke, the actor who played Number-One Son. He's a class act.'

Jim said, 'I'll remember you if I ever get to cast anything.'

'That would be great!' the boy jumped up to fetch our orders.

The food was the best I'd ever eaten. There was no way to translate beyond a loose, *home-style vegetables*. The only way Jim intentionally ate a vegetable other than French fried potatoes was in an exotic dish. We ate until we were stuffed. The boy returned with what looked like a Chinese cupcake and the check.

'I'm sorry,' he said, scrunching up his nose. 'It's a traditional wedding treat. There's a boiled egg inside.' An acquired taste. 'Hide it in the teapot and I'll dump it later. My uncle is such a romantic.'

We walked the neighbourhood, holding hands and lingering in front of windows crowded with wares. Jim bought me a pincushion surrounded by bright silk children holding hands. When we reached my car parked back where we had started the evening, Jim extracted a book-shaped package from his jacket pocket.

'Happy birthday,' he said.

I unwrapped it quickly. I knew at once it was his treasured copy of *On the Road*. Had he given me the book a month before, I would have feared he was bestowing his treasures before he died. Giving me the book for my birthday was as close as he could come to giving me himself. I opened to the title page. Half-written/half-printed was scrawled: *To Jim, Good luck with your writing! Jack Kerouac.*

'You didn't tell me you met him!' I imagined his signed copy was a copy he'd lucked into during one of his used bookstore prowls, not personalized from Kerouac himself. I was a little hurt he'd kept the story from me.

'Haven't you ever had something that meant so much you wanted to keep it secret?'

I hugged him for the first time. 'You.'

He mussed my hair. 'I tracked him down. He was drunk enough to be in the mood to listen to me tell him how important he was to me.' Then he added, 'Spend the night with me.'

We shared a room bathed in red neon that belonged to an acquaintance of Jim's. I preferred borrowed places to rented rooms. There were always books on the shelves and cups in the sink.

Jim habitually dispensed birthday presents in three's. I had only been given one – the spontaneous pincushion wouldn't count to Jim – so, while he stared out the window, I patted his pockets from behind. He spread for the search. A pain pinched my chest that my play had reminded him of less playful searches, but when he thought I was so cold I was never going to find the little box, he guided my hand to the appropriate pocket.

The box was velvet, the kind that held jewellery. Reluctant to open it, I let it rest in my hand. Jim popped it open. What I didn't want to see, a ring. 'Jim, no,' I whispered. Even by neon, I could tell it was gold. I could barely make out two hands coming together to make a heart with a crown above. 'I can't take this, Jim.'

'It's Scottish. It's called a claddaugh. A symbol of love and honour.'

'I can't take this, Jim,' I repeated. 'It's fine we aren't getting married,' I realized the truth as I told it, 'but I don't want the ring you intended to give me.'

'It's not your wedding ring,' he explained. 'A wedding ring has to be an unbroken circle, engraved inside so it can't be hocked.'

The last comment made me smile. Jim's was a romantic nature. A gold ring could easily be sold for its weight alone. 'Jim, for someone who has no rules about anything else, you have a mile of them about marriage.'

'Because marriage means everything. To me, it represents perfection. The perfect circle. The perfect song. The perfect union.' He slipped the ring on my finger. 'This is a friendship ring,' he whispered, 'to hold my place.'

I would have preferred he had returned the silver friendship ring he'd put on my finger with the same sentiment. Though, with the claddaugh, he didn't load me on to a bus as he had with that other, but pulled me into bed. We hadn't talked about the changes we might make in our relationship. I tried to suggest if we weren't getting married, we could certainly, as my friends called it, *go all the way*.

Jim lay back against his pillow. 'We've gone where most lovers never do.'

Truthfully, our sensual play brought me a deep pleasure. Jim was as tender and careful with me as ever, the only difference was we did not talk about places to marry.

In the morning, Jim made us his best scrambled eggs and toast rescued from incineration. He only brought one fork to bed. The heater was on the fritz, and he wasn't willing to leave the comfort of blankets to scare up another. His solution was to feed me.

After a sloppy breakfast, Jim said, 'You didn't find your third present.'

I scurried around the cold room searching pockets of his discarded clothes. Making what he trusted were lascivious sounds with my every bend and reach, Jim made no secret of being enamoured of the female body, whatever his personal relationship to it. I gave up and returned to bed to torture Jim with my cold feet.

He flattened me against the mattress and screamed, 'I'll sing it! I'll sing it!' He took *On the Road* from my tote and removed a folded sheet of paper hidden in its centre. He spread the paper next to my head on the pillow. 'I don't know it by heart yet.' He rested on his elbows and sank into a song about our 'Hyacinth House'. Two lines into the song and he shook his head, 'I can't sing on my stomach.'

He made a fuss of settling into a cross-legged position. I rested the paper in the X of his lap and pulled the blanket around his shoulders. I was shivering, but not from the cold. At the Los Angeles airport, I thought I'd lost Jim's song gifts with him. 'Hyacinth House' was the melody he woke with in Los Gatos. He'd written about the creative nature of our time together. The lyric was so idiosyncratic, he obviously didn't care if anyone but the two of us understood. He asked himself why he had made the decision he had in December.

In my journal I wrote: 'Jim and I can pour our love for each other from vessel to vessel without spilling a drop.' Beneath my entry, Jim wrote: 'We have a destiny! We *know* this.'

In February, we were driving south from San Jose down Highway 101 with no particular destination in mind. Jim sunk in to one of his silences, not even wanting to listen to the radio, let alone sing. While I wanted to pin down point by point exactly what ate at him, so we could face them and cross each off one by one, I knew that wasn't Jim's way. The big monsters were his legal difficulties and his drinking. To the first end, he needed distraction. To the second, more time without pressure. I was good for both.

I began, 'Remember how I threatened to return to Los Angeles when I was eighteen so we could do a musical version of *The Razor's Edge?*'

Jim gasped. 'Should I start taking tap-dancing lessons?'

'Not just yet.' I thought about what I wanted to say. 'Maybe we could update it. A survival manual for Veterans. They come into the Peace Center and ask if I'm going to spit on them. But they come to the Center, not the government, to learn how to live with their memories and get on with life.' As lowest volunteer on the totem pole, I only handed out information pamphlets. But Vietnam Vets waylaid me in the parking-lot to talk. 'Without exception, they tell one funny story and one horror story, then head for the nearest beer.'

'You haven't made a high-falutin speech in a while,' Jim said quietly, which was enough to silence me.

Chastised for my climb on a soap box, I watched the road, swallowing tears. 'It's only that I care so much,' I said in my defence. We had a long quiet ride.

'I'll have to play the lead to get backing,' were Jim's first words after the silence. He had been thinking, not judging me. 'Would anyone believe me as a Vet?'

I gave him a sideways stare. He'd taken to living in the fatigue jacket a fan had given him. He'd once again cut his hair and his recently shaved beard was filling in again. He resembled a Vietnam Veteran more than a rock-star. Passing through Gilroy, a farming community, Jim yelled for me to stop. He leaped out and bartered for a cowboy's battered hat and pointed to a restaurant/bar across the street.

He poked his head in my window. 'Follow me in ten minutes. If I can get whoever is in there to buy me as a Vet, we'll start the screenplay this afternoon.' He walked to the door, spun on his heel, and came back to the car. Nobody was going to believe that glide cleared boot camp. 'Give me a line,' he ordered softly.

My mind buzzed. I repeated my observation about the Vets' stories. 'Give yourself some music,' I suggested. 'Play the jukebox.' I dropped coins into his hand. 'And,' I said, warming to the power of direction, 'change your walk.'

Each boot heel hit the ground with a solid click. When I guessed ten minutes had passed, I entered the restaurant side of the establishment. Jim stood in the connecting bar section, draped drunkenly over the jukebox. He played a convincing drunk. He hadn't had a drink all day. Three picks and he hung on to the bar. A redneck in a cap made a comment about dirty hippies stinking up the town.

'Got that right,' Jim sided with him. 'Hell, when I was in 'Nam,' Jim continued, drawing the redneck into a funny, rambling story about snakes in the latrine. Credence surged up on the jukebox to drown his voice. Acting, Jim merged the dark sexuality of Marlon Brando with the vulnerability of Montgomery Clift. Patsy Cline's 'Crazy' jumped right on top of 'Fortunate Son'.

Gilroy probably had no Doors on the juke. Jim hadn't sprung for a third tune. He told a story, marked by starts and stops, about his best buddy from boot camp blowing up beside him. Jim without a scratch and his buddy without a body. Larry in *The Razor's Edge* was forever changed by the loss of a friend who saved his life in the First World War. The loss in every war continued to be as great, and as impossible to detail.

Three customers, the bartender, and the waitress leaned in close, pulled in by Jim's magnet. He pushed his empty class a couple inches, and the local paid for the refill. Jim downed the beer in a gulp and eased off the stool. The waitress slipped him her phone number. As he hit the door and walked into the glare, we had a date to write a screenplay.

Jim leaned against my Volkswagen, spinning the cowboy hat. We didn't even discuss our decision, Jim reached over into the back seat for my school notebook. He turned to a fresh page and wrote, *The Razor's Edge*. We drove around, rattling off ideas until the car was nearly out of gas. Jim paid for a fill-up and a room off the highway.

'I never finished the book,' I confessed as soon as the door slammed behind us. I'd only gotten as far as Jim had read aloud to me. The whole thing, after all, was supposed to be a joke. I told myself that it didn't really matter, because I was just getting Jim's mind off the trial. A screenplay was a longer diversion than a song.

Jim detailed the book for me. There was much more to the book than I remembered from the Tyrone Power movie. By morning, we had a twenty-page outline. We were really going to write together. I'd forgotten to tell anyone excuses or lies and had to call my mother and apologize for falling asleep at a non-existent girlfriend's house, when I wanted to say, 'You see, Jim and I were writing . . .' Really writing!

My idea of a screenplay was the rapid-fire dialogue of Rosalind Russell and Cary Grant in *His Girl Friday*. Jim's was more along the lines of *cinéma-vérité*. We agreed the subject matter required something else. Every time we met, it was to write.

Our writing wasn't simply the good play it had always been. Before, our writing was our personal entertainment. The songs we wrote, other than the one we wrote with Dennis Hopper, were warm-ups for his real writing. They were races to check his timing, not win purses.

For the first time, we worked together. We wrote. We rewrote. The truth of what Jim had told me about writing rang true. During one of his discourses on the art of writing, he'd expressed the insight that, 'Writing is part inspiration and part ditch-digging. I worship the first and respect the second, but until you can do both, you are not a professional writer, just a talented amateur.'

We dug ditches until we collapsed into bed with blistered brains. Our discussions about the fictional Larry's search for answers, his search for God, became our search for God.

We met in Pacific Grove near Monterey at a beach where scuba divers gathered like mutant sea otters in their wet suits and tanks. The spot was as far as Jim wanted me to drive alone, and far enough away from Los Angeles, Jim said, 'not to pick up the city's vibes'. From the sea, we drove inland. Possibly because we struck the deal in Gilroy, Jim enjoyed pulling off the road near there and writing in my car.

Jim folded himself in the back seat with a pad on his knees. I switched to the passenger seat for added elbow room when I sat sideways to face him. There were problems in switching wars. The book took place after Larry's experiences in the First World War and the fate of the other characters depended greatly on the stock-market crash of '29. We spent an afternoon listing possible cultural undoings.

Jim laughed, scratching his head with a pencil. 'You know, my life isn't that bad compared to this.'

Re-reading a few pages of dialogue, I remarked our characters' speech patterns were too similar. Jim jerked me out of the car and into the field. He started la-la-ing and shoop-a-walla-ing at the top of his lungs. Then screeched as high-pitched as he could. Shook. Rumbled. Whispered. If I hadn't witnessed him write a melody, I might have thought him ripping drunk. An escaped mental patient. His performance was startling. He was not singing melodies, but characters.

'Now you do it,' he instructed me.

I shook my head. I may have admitted to my share of singing along with Marianne Faithfull in front of my bedroom mirror not so many years before, but I wasn't going to belt out nonsense in an open field. When we performed our private little plays and fantasies, I was myself as other creatures or in other times. Jim was asking me to be people I would never be. I would never be a soldier or a prostitute. I would never be a loving husband.

'It's like scatting to jazz. Just make noises, sounds. The words will drop in later.'

For Jim, words always dropped in. 'You know I'm not an actress,' I said.

'This is writing,' Jim insisted. 'Just make a happy sound. I know you can make a happy sound.' I giggled naturally because he was scowling at me. 'Now,' he said, 'make a happy sound as Larry.'

He guided me through the exercise until my Larry was making noises at his Isobel, the woman who loved him. My Isobel was chirping at his Gray, Isobel's husband. By the time the sun set, we were hoarse.

I accepted from the first time I heard his music that Jim was a genius, but that afternoon I collided head-on with his brilliance. He'd solved our scriptwriting problem the way he solved his songwriting problems. We hadn't produced a word that day, but all the characters from *The Razor's Edge* were lurking at our elbows, whispering in our ears.

Intermixed with these writing adventures, The Doors were touring. Jim called from whatever city they played, excited about the shows rather than shredding them. He enjoyed singing. He thanked me for revealing the secret of what he considered the magical breathing technique which increased his lung power. When audiences clamoured for more, he'd give it to them, and when they were sated, he'd call them back for just a little more. He loved feeling he and the band were The Doors anew.

My last class of the school day was in a room that faced the student parking-lot. On Fridays, I tried to be the first one off campus. Jim had broken into my car, and was lazing in the passenger seat absorbed in reading. The feat didn't make him a master criminal. When I went through a period of locking my keys in my car, I learned you only had to stick something through the side vent to push open its lock, reach in and unlock the door. The surprise was that Jim had never surprised me at Prospect High.

He couldn't resist a 'How's your *prospects*?'

Looking better than they had. The exertion of Jim's performances had made him fitter. His mood had changed his pallor. Though it had lain fallow for a couple months, Jim kept his room in Los Gatos. His only luggage was a brown paper bag with twine handles. As soon as he was in the room, he dropped it on the floor.

I'd forgotten what a barren place it was. The walls were unadorned. After I got back from Los Angeles, I'd dropped by to wash the linens. They remained stacked at the foot of the steel-framed bed. The only other furniture in the room was the maple dresser holding the stereo. Both of us were required to budge the window to let in new air.

Jim seized the bag and plopped himself on the bed. He brought out the angel candle I'd given him for his birthday and lit it. His smouldering eyes trained on me made me blush. He withdrew an album from the bag and motioned for me to come sit next to him.

'I'm in a band called The Doors. We're a pretty good band. Like to hear our first album?'

Jim and the others posed in the window of the Morrison Hotel. Jim wore a rumpled white shirt. Because Ray and Robby and John were dressed in darker clothes and behind Jim, he glowed uncomfortably in front of them, behind the window's sign reading, *Rooms from $2.50*. Nobody smiled in the photograph.

'I'll understand if you don't want to listen to it,' Jim said. When he wrote the songs, we saw each other in a different light.

The first listen to an album of Jim's was a strange experience. Jim was the only sound I heard as he wrote the songs. When he rehearsed and recorded with the others in the band, anything could happen. His voice was rich and raucous, then soft and gentle.

'The music changed some,' I said after surviving 'Roadhouse Blues'. 'And you added that *Save our city.' Right now!*

'Do you recognize it?' he asked. I shook my head. 'It was a sign I saw when we were leaving Stockton. When I was improvising with the band, I remembered it.'

As the population drifted from its centre, downtown Stockton resembled pictures in *Life* of war-torn cities. Jim soaked up its devastation. While I was in school there, he sat in bars with the drunk and punch-drunk, convinced they knew something he didn't.

Jim lifted the needle and started the album over, swaying, hands out to me. The beat was Jim's favourite dance rhythms from all over the room to no-space-between-us rocking. What Jim called 'Fully clothed sex'. He said, 'If this record doesn't make America dance again, nothing will!'

When he'd premièred the album for me, which meant we danced the whole album, I said breathlessly, 'I think I'll write a fan letter to Bill Monroe.' After meeting Monroe he was determined to reclaim the band instead of letting it drift. And he'd done it!

Jim laughed. 'That would scare the hell out of him. Knowing that he got *me* back on track.'

I reminded Jim of the concert he had done in Toronto with his teenage saviour, Bo Diddley. The ticket sales were so low, even with The Doors on the bill, that John Lennon stepped in to save the show. He, like Jim, respected the roots of rock 'n' roll, but they were a tough sell to kids my age. 'Maybe Monroe would enjoy a nod from you,' I said. 'once he knew who you were.'

Jim laughed at that. 'I'll think about writing him a fan letter myself. Until then, even I can stand to listen to this album.' He took a deep breath. 'Can you?'

'Yes,' I said softly. 'But don't ask me to talk about it yet.'

'Pamela's hot as anything because there are no songs for her on this,' he said, putting the album into the sleeve.

I was irritated he didn't lift my record by its edges and by what he'd said. 'Jim, if you really need to talk to me about Pamela, talk to me as your friend. Don't pit us against each other.'

On the fourth of May, Jim called at a yell. 'You stay out of the street!'

Stunned, I asked, 'Are you drunk, Jim? Are you all right? I'm not in the street.'

He told me to turn on the news. Four students had been gunned down on the campus of Kent State. He wasn't drunk, he was afraid for me. Afraid for the country.

During a break from the tour, he'd calmed down and asked me to arrange a meeting with one of the Vets I'd mentioned dropping by the Peace Center where I volunteered. The paranoia all around made us meet in my Volkswagen in the parking-lot of a Los Gatos supermarket at ten o'clock at night.

The Vet was stoned; Jim had a beer in his hand. Jim had wanted the Vet not to know who he was. He felt the ex-soldier would not talk to him the same way if he were known to be *that singer*. I understood, but thought that unethical. The deception wasn't the same as not wanting to embarrass my mother with the news, since Jim wanted to incorporate the man's feelings, if not specific stories, in our screenplay.

After thanking him for coming, Jim asked bluntly, 'How would you feel about my playing a Vietnam Veteran when I lied to get out of the draft?'

I'd never even considered that sore spot. The Vet locked on to Jim's directness. Even though he came to doubt the honesty of the government action, he had signed up because his father had signed up in World War II. He was as direct with Jim.

'I guess I'd have more respect for you if you'd gone to jail for what you thought was right.'

'Oh,' Jim smiled. 'I'm going to be doing that.'

Jim's trial for the charges brought in Miami was delayed until summer. Jim called the trial his Sword of Damocles. According to legend, a member of the court who doubted the hazard of being a king was forced to sit beneath a sword suspended above his head

431

to give him a feel for the dangers of being in power. Pretending to be the Lizard King, Jim faced the dangers of a true leader.

'Until Miami,' Jim had confided, 'I always thought I was obligated to make a joke of the ridiculous power I was given just because I sang a little rock 'n' roll.'

Near the end of May, Jimi Hendrix called me from the road. He spent a few minutes talking about how he never slept. He made me think of Jim's drinking to find relief from insomnia. Jimi complained of feeling sick and tired.

'Oh,' I told him, 'you have the Road Lonelies.'

'Want to do something about that?' he asked in a low and sexy whisper.

I stammered a while, then said, 'This phone call will have to do.'

'That's too bad. You could make me feel better.'

I laughed. Must be a tried and true musician's line. He sounded like Jim teasing me the one time I saw him as a Door. That I could laugh about the most embarrassing moment of my life two years later gave me hope I was growing up.

'Thank you for the birthday card. I went out and got myself some crayons!'

'Would you send me one of your drawings?'

'Sure, if you want. I was going to write back or something, but thought, you know, that Jim wouldn't like that much. The reason I'm calling is I'm going to be playing in Berkeley. Thought maybe I could leave a ticket for you if you'd like to come.'

'Oh, sure. Thank you, Jimi. Thanks. I've never seen you.'

He listened to my woes about my parents not letting me attend the Monterey Pop Festival, and my being stuck in Maine when he was first doing shows in the Bay Area.

'I'm only giving you one ticket,' he warned me. 'I don't want you bringing a date. I'd like you to come backstage between shows.'

I relayed my woes about that one backstage, or more correctly, side-stage, experience with Jim. I may have grown up a little, but I still didn't want to repeat it.

'I would have decked Graham.'

'I wouldn't have allowed that.' Allowed? I probably was idiot enough to have stepped between them. 'Anyway, Mr Graham apologized. Whenever he catches me in line at the Fillmore, he lets me in for free.'

The Jimi Hendrix concert was on May 30th at the Berkeley Community Theater. The ticket was for the second row near the centre. I'd never been that close to the stage at a concert. When I arrived, a man was in my seat. I showed my ticket to no avail. Too shy to make a fuss, I politely asked an usher to clear up the situation. He took both our tickets for study, then handed me back the wrong ticket and threatened to have me ousted if I didn't take my seat. Wasn't that called bait and switch?

'I'm Jimi Hendrix's guest,' I said.

Since Jimi had been sick, I didn't want to make a big enough fuss to involve him, and settled for the distant seat. Might have saved my hearing. My ears buzzed half the night. The concert was filmed. Could catch a close-up of Jimi in the movie.

A few days later, Jimi called to ask why I hadn't come to the show. A little idiot, I admitted I'd been duped out of the ticket. I was there, but just not where I was supposed to have been.

'Son of a bitch,' Jimi shouted. 'You should've come back and told me. That bastard wouldn't be able to sit down.'

A good spanking from Jimi Hendrix might have been justice, but I tried to remember I didn't believe in corporal punishment.

'I loved the show, Jimi.'

'Why don't you join me on the road somewhere?'

'Oh, I couldn't. I'm in school,' I said, dragging that old excuse out. I kicked myself for not being forthright. 'Honestly, I don't follow musicians around.'

Jimi was quiet so long, I nearly spoke again, but he asked, 'You wouldn't say no 'cause I'm black?'

The question startled me. I considered that possibility. 'No. I don't think so.'

'I'd say if you stopped to really think about it, it's not. Folks who are prejudiced are real defensive about it. You would have jumped right in to deny it.'

'I think probably everybody grows up prejudiced, you know. But you have a choice what you do about it.'

'You're a sweet kid,' Jimi said.

'Thanks, that's all I am, really,' I told him. 'I think Jim and I will be better off when he accepts that.'

'He does seem to think the world of you,' he said, then hesitated. 'While I have you on the line, could I ask you what that line in "Wild Child" about Africa means?'

'Oh, I was born in Morocco. The line's about Jim and me looking through my family photo album and pretending we were in Morocco together.'

'You were born in Morocco? You're the whitest person I've ever seen!' He laughed, embarrassed he had said exactly what was on his mind.

Ashen, to be precise, but I didn't want to hurl myself headlong into the explanation that might involve. 'Well, it was where my mother happened to be.'

'I went to Morocco last summer,' he said.

Someone should have warned him about the swelter of Moroccan summers. He'd expected good drugs and sexy women, but instead had been trailed by mysterious men everywhere he went. Jimi was lonely enough to talk a long while about his trip to Morocco. I listened eagerly, regretting that we hadn't the sort of connection I had with Jim that would let me travel along with him over the telephone.

Jim asked me to my senior prom. I told him it would be like being such a wallflower I had to have my big brother take me. He suggested that he would have been considered a terrific first prize by most high-school girls. *Win a Date With Jim Morrison.* Moot. He was conveniently on tour.

Jim had launched the tour with an optimism honestly founded on the rock he felt *Morrison Hotel* was, but every critic that wasn't positive, every audience that didn't respond, every offhand remark chipped away at his belief. By the end of the tour he was as low as he was high at its start. Although he provided reasonable explanations of his mood shift, I was unconvinced by their tidiness. I could have drawn a graph of Jim's peaks and valleys since I'd known him. Grand Tetons.

'Jim,' I asked over the phone, 'you don't have to answer this. What you and your doctor talk about is personal, but has he talked to you about manic depression?'

Jim made a sucking sound, like his tongue was pushed up against the back of his teeth as he took a deep breath. 'No,' he said at last. That was the end of that.

School was over. I couldn't leave it behind fast enough. I didn't even bother to pick up my diploma. My parents didn't give me anything for graduation. My sister gave me a portable typewriter.

Jim gave me a bound notebook and a less traditional sensual message. I stretched out on the bed, bursting with the freedom of graduation summer and too languid from Jim's hands to more than smile.

'The difference between your relationships with other women and me,' I said in a moment of inspiration, 'is that they drive you away with demands and possessiveness, and you leave me because sirens call.'

Jim, lounging beside me, sat bolt upright. The best way to reach Jim was a mythological allusion. In mythology, sirens lured sailors with tempting songs to crash their ships upon rocks. I was a safe harbour, but drink and danger lured Jim.

I loved writing until we couldn't think straight, then falling into bed with him. Jim called my writing, 'Spare, like Jean Harlow in a silk dress.' I made him write the compliment out for me, knowing how much he thought of Harlow in silk.

We allowed our relationship to float along. When asked, one night over the phone I honestly told him I didn't know what I wanted from other men. How could I consider someone else with Jim there? Our undefined relationship confused me.

After our discussion, Jim abruptly cancelled a visit. He called from New York, kitten-like from a bout with pneumonia. 'At your age,' I scolded, 'you shouldn't need someone to tell you to button up your overcoat.' The need for an overcoat in June being doubtful, but my way of asking him to take better care of himself.

'But I do,' he said softly, humming the song that inspired my advice, then headed off to Paris to scout locations for what he had begun to call *our film*. Sirens called.

435

26

If They Say I Never Loved You

The second week of August, Jim was in Miami, tethered between jury selection and prosecution. He'd already telephoned a few times. No matter how many times or ways I offered to go join him for support, he begged me to stay away.

He had said, 'You make me feel too open and vulnerable. I'd never maintain the charade with you in court.' Then suddenly, Jim called and cried, 'I need you. Could you come right away?'

On the first plane. When I arrived in Miami, Jim was plastered against the hotel edifice, reading a newspaper. He smiled and nodded appreciatively at my near run at him. When I reached him, he whispered, 'Walk ahead of me to the elevator,' which made every paranoid bone in my body vibrate. No one but the hotel staff stirred at that hour. I stood in the back of the elevator. He waited until the elevator doors closed to take my hand.

'No rooms on my floor,' he apologized.

I knew Jim's friend slash bodyguard slash baby-sitter, Babe, was in close proximity, but was disappointed not to be in Jim's room. Jim looked down at me, humming and smiling.

I asked, 'Are you being followed?'

He shrugged and said, 'I wanted to watch you walk.' He hummed.

The doors opened. Jim hesitated, then straightened his shoulders before striding confidently to a door and unlocking it. Once inside, he folded the partial newspaper into thirds the way paperboys used to before the rags got so big so that it held itself closed.

'Did you have a paper route?'

Jim didn't seem to hear. 'Hold me,' he whispered, his smile gone.

I wrapped my arms around him. 'Is the trial going badly?'

Rather than answer, he played with my hair. Abruptly, he asked, 'Do you still want children?'

I was startled by the subject we hadn't discussed for more than a year, but answered, 'Yes.'

He followed with, 'But you want to be an artist?'

'I don't find them mutually exclusive. I have to be an artist, or the lions would devour me, but I could hang my pictures on the fridge next to the kids' drawings.'

Jim rocked back on a heel, considering what I'd said. 'You could be famous. You'd be giving up fame.'

I smiled and poked him gently. 'You don't make fame look very appealing. Doing the work is important.'

He smiled again. Wearing an embroidered jacket that he needed more in the too-cool air-conditioning of the hotel than in pre-dawn Miami, he looked handsome. At last, I thought lightly in the midst of the heavy atmosphere, he's buying his own clothes again.

Jim returned to the subject of children. 'You remember when we talked about children in Maine? I said, "Imagine a mother who makes snow bears," and you said, "Imagine a father who believes in them?"' I remembered. 'That part of me would be a great father,' he said quietly, then more quietly, 'But that's not enough.'

'No, but Jim, that's not all you have to give.' I held his waist, wanting to shake his shoulders. 'You were the only person to tell me I could do anything. And made me believe it. Do you know how that changed my life? If you can give that to me, you could give it to your children.'

'Thank you. Sometimes, I think you are the only person who sees any good in me.'

Jim pulled away and crossed to hold the curtain back from

the long window. Looking out, he said, 'This should be our anniversary. We would have been married seven months. Do you hate me for that?'

Why did he want to go over this pain at seven months, when he didn't at six? 'No. I understood what you said then, that you needed me to be there for you. Is that why I'm here?'

'I'm not suicidal. I'm, I don't know. Confused. Lonely. The hardest thing I ever did was to tell you to leave Los Angeles last December. It broke my heart. I had you and I let you go. I wrote a song about it no one will ever hear.'

From the sound of it, not even me. I thought 'Hyacinth House' was enough. We weren't going to marry. We weren't going to have a family but we were going to be boon writing companions. His chin dropped against his chest. He said so I could barely make out the words, 'The psychiatrist told me to.'

I was so shocked and angry, I took an involuntary step back.

When he spoke again, Jim's voice was very young. 'Not *not* to write the song,' he explained as if I might not understand, 'He told me to let you go. He told me I was too dependent on you, a teenager. And that . . . I was killing you.'

I was vehement, 'How dare he! That's not true!' Someone else had again made a decision that should have been ours. The well-meaning psychiatrist ended our wedding plans after only a few hours with Jim. 'Why do we keep making the same mistakes?' I asked us both in disbelief.

Jim didn't answer, but said softly, 'I'm guilty.'

'Of trying to kill me or shooting your mouth off on stage?'

Jim pulled the curtain over to block out the approaching sun. I blinked to adjust to the lower level of light. Jim boosted himself on to the dresser rather than sit in the chair.

'Friends tell me that Pamela's living on heroin. I told her I won't take her calls until she's straight. And she's never straight. I'd hoped this store would give her confidence and independence. Instead, it's pretty well wiped me out financially. My Beloved Albatross,' he said gently. Jim had financially backed a boutique Pamela wanted. Clearing his throat, he said as gently, 'I just found out I have another friend in trouble. A friend from New York. Someone I had an affair with. Someone I shouldn't have gotten involved with . . .

I can't . . . or heaven help me, won't help her.' Jim looked straight into my eyes for the first time. 'Honestly, I believe it's *can't*. Not able. I'm guilty,' he confessed again, eyes on the narrow triangle of sky where the curtain hadn't quite closed. 'I feel I'm guilty of crimes that will go unpunished. And I'll be punished for crimes I didn't commit.'

'I think you need to lay off Kafka and whiskey,' I said, trying to take in all he'd said. He flashed a great grin which briefly lit his eyes. 'Do you want me to go to LA and talk with Pamela? Or help this other friend who's in trouble?'

'Come over here,' he beckoned.

He leaned his arms on my shoulders and laced his fingers behind my neck. A familiar pose. I played with the braided ties of his jacket that ended with little tassels.

'What can I do?' I asked.

'I nearly told her on the phone why I am not who she thinks I am.'

'Pamela or this other friend?' I asked. He didn't seem to want to identify her.

'My friend.'

'Are you still having an affair?' I don't know why I felt compelled to ask when I never had before.

'I'm having several affairs. I do fuck around a smaller circle. I'm sorry. That's only true as far as it goes. I thought my affair with this woman was over. I think it is. We never saw much of each other. We haven't seen each other for a couple months. I don't know. I asked you here not knowing myself it was to ask you to handle this for me.'

'Tell me about your friend.' I had never asked about any of his myriad of women. They never seemed important to me, but this woman seemed important to Jim.

'I met her right after your mother said you wanted me to leave you alone. She interviewed me in New York. She was bright. I wasn't in any shape to get involved with anyone, and really thought too much of her to make her a one-night stand. I needed someone I could talk to, though I found her intelligence is a little . . .' he searched for a word, 'brittle.'

'Well, Jim, isn't everyone's compared to yours?'

440

He disagreed. 'No. I find Michael McClure's flexible. And yours is . . .'

'Silly putty?'

He laughed and shook a scolding finger at me. 'I figured out who you really are,' he said. 'You're the love child of Dorothy Parker and Albert Schweitzer.'

I giggled, wishing it were true. Dorothy Parker, the smart alec I most admired, taught the men at the infamous round table at the Algonquin a thing or two. 'I suppose you have proof.'

'Do you know that Schweitzer won the Nobel Prize the year you were born?'

'Undoubtedly inspired by my entrance into the world! But ole Dot was too old and dotty to have borne anything but short literary pieces by then.'

Jim laughed. 'You'd kick me if I called you a short literary piece . . . at the end of her career.'

He hadn't come up with a good Coda Queen joke in a long time. 'Or take a bow.'

Jim smiled, anxious to switch from talk to kissing. 'Golden. Burning,' Jim murmured, playing with my hair. I would have thought him drunk, but there was no alcohol on his breath or in his kisses.

'Not altogether wise to be doing acid during the trial,' I said.

'Oh, I'm not high.' He asked, flaring my hair out like wings, 'Are you an angel?'

I smiled and said, 'We're not supposed to tell.'

'You give yourself away!' he accused playfully. 'Ever since I met you – three years and three weeks ago!' he stopped to exclaim. Men were supposed to be lax regarding the significant dates in a relationship. 'Whenever I've had an important decision to make, I'd ask myself, "What would Ginger do?" And I know what I should do, but am rarely strong enough to do the right thing.'

'Me, too,' I said, then asked as if it were a riddle he could answer, 'What's the difference between a pedestal and a hangman's trap-door?'

He twisted a strand of my hair around his finger in thought. 'Could we cuddle a bit?' Jim asked, his voice wispy and far away. 'I have to get upstairs before I'm missed.'

I slipped his jacket off his shoulders and helped him tug his arms free. 'I like your jacket,' I said, giving it a try. The sleeves fell to my fingertips.

'Got it in Mexico,' he said. I wondered if that were on the weddingless trip he had made. 'It makes me feel like Zapata. I need all the help I can get in court.'

'It's not going well?' I repeated the question he wouldn't answer earlier and carefully deposited the jacket on the back of a chair.

'It's a sham. Nothing's happened yet. It's draining to feel so helpless. Let's not talk about it.' I unbuttoned his white cotton shirt and pulled its tails out of his black Levi's. As he jumped off the dresser, he said, 'Thank you for coming.'

We held each other in the huge island of a bed for an hour, then Jim, restless, ran a bath. The first sign that he had been in the room before my arrival was a dozen white roses sprawled in the bathroom sink, and a cluster of candles by the tub.

I stood in the doorway. 'How sweet of you, Jim,' I said,

'An anniversary present. He pressed a crumpled piece of paper into my hand.

A morning song! A smattering of lines about our lying together. The way we fit. We hadn't indulged in that pleasure enough that summer. He tossed one rose after another into the bathtub. My throat was too light to let me say what I wanted to.

'Thank you, Jim. I've missed you.'

He'd mailed a cheery postcard from Paris and a completely illegible letter with an equally illegible postmark which might have been Tangiers, both of which I received after he was back in Los Angeles. We met a few times to consolidate pages of the screenplay.

' "Roadhouse Blues" is on the radio a lot. It's the kind of music I like to drive to.'

Jim laughed at my liking to drive to his scolding me for how I drove. 'Well, baby, it's your melody.' I thanked him for the gift. 'No. I mean it's *your* melody.' He sang, '*Ridin' in the country . . .*' As I recognized the line, he mirrored the shock on my face. 'Count your syllables like a good girl.'

So pleased I could pop, I sang it to myself to be sure. The single line was all I could invent on demand when Jim had taken me for a ride for my sixteenth birthday.

'When one-line songs become the rage,' I said self-consciously, 'I'll be a hit.'

'Well, maybe not a hit,' he comforted me with a bear hug. '"Roadhouse Blues" didn't do that well on the charts.'

I re-read the poem on the crumpled paper. I looked up at Jim's troubled face. I nearly choked on, 'I love you.'

'What's that?' he said with a fresh grin. 'Four times you've told me you love me? *When* I'm convicted,' he said sombrely, not *if*, 'would you run with me?'

'Yes,' I said without hesitation, hurt he hadn't counted my 'I love you's' correctly. I sang a bit of 'Not to Touch the Earth', ta-dah-ing through the guitar part of Robby's I envied.

He smiled. 'We could really go to Morocco, the land of your birth.' He always added the *land of your birth* in a respectful voice, as if a kingdom awaited me there. 'I loved those pictures in your album. The home-movies. I dream of living in one of those flat-topped houses. We could sleep on the roof under the stars. Like when I lived in Venice. We could write a novel together.'

'We could,' I stepped into the tub, 'do that anyway.'

Jim lowered himself into the water behind me, and held me against his chest. 'Are you in love with anyone else?'

'No.'

'Do you go out on dates?'

'No. I occasionally hang out with a couple friends from high-school. But nobody else recognizes quotes from Dickens. Or dances on their knees. You've spoiled me.'

'Guys have to ask you out,' Jim prodded.

'Do they? Okay, I went out with a draft counsellor, but all we had in common was hate for the war and being vegetarians.' We'd eaten at the falafel place I liked to take Jim. 'I expected him to be sweet and gentle, but he was an octopus.'

Jim laughed. 'Did you slap his face?'

'No. I told him I didn't like being manhandled, and he tried to make me feel silly and young by asking me if I had ever dated a *real* man before. I felt like saying, "Only Jim Morrison and Jimi Hendrix, you know, *gentlemen* like that."'

'You've been seeing Jimi?'

I burst into giggles behind my hands. 'Oh, no. Guess I said that wrong.'

'When did you last see him?'

'Must have been the end of May. In Berkeley.'

'What did you do?'

'Well, he played guitar on stage. And I sat in the audience.' I didn't tell him about Jimi asking me to the show, or being tricked out of the second row. On the scale of injustices, it didn't rank very high.

'That it?' Jim's hands rested on my shoulders. He massaged my neck with his thumbs.

'*That* was wonderful. The perfect symbiotic relationship.'

'What about Hawaii?' he asked, withdrawing his hands.

'Hawaii?' I was puzzled.

'I heard Jimi went to Hawaii with a woman named Ginger.'

'Was I sleepwalking?' Jim wasn't very amused. 'Jimi did call up and ask if I wanted to go. He was doing a couple shows. On Maui. And in Honolulu. He said he'd teach me to play guitar, but even I didn't believe that. I told him the only one I knew who lived in Honolulu was Charlie Chan, but since he was fictional, he would be tough to visit.' Jim laughed. I said, 'You see, Jimi didn't laugh, so I didn't go to Hawaii.'

'I ache for you,' he said into my hair. 'After what you said about wanting to get on with your life, I tried to stay away.'

I turned to face him with a fierce splash. 'I didn't say that.'

'On the phone. The beginning of summer. You said my being in your life confused you.'

Not the same thing at all, Jim. When other people weren't interfering in our lives, we interfered ourselves. We talked, then drifted for a long while, Jim's arms loose around me, and mine resting along his legs.

He tightened his hold. 'Don't let me kill you,' he said softly. 'Go back to California.'

'You can't kill me.'

'Honey, I'm not going to off myself. I have people watching me all the time. Somebody's probably beating the palmettos for me now.' He kissed the top of my head. 'How do you love me?'

'*Let me count the ways.*'

444

'Will you love me better after death?'

I regretted my glib answer. 'I'll hate you. As much as I can love, I can hate.'

'That's enough to scare me into a long life.'

Jim lifted me with him as he stood in the tub. We prolonged the visit with slow towelling, but he had to sneak back into the rest of his life. Midday, Jim made a sleepy call to promise an escape as soon as Babe was asleep. I had to laugh over his sneaking around instead of me. He had the idea that if the FBI found out about our friendship, I'd be in danger. It didn't much matter if the grizzly were my father or Hoover.

I hid from Hoover and the intense sun under a straw hat. A cab took me to a Cuban restaurant Jim recommended. I was early for dinner, but the owner sweeping out front invited me to wait inside with a tall glass of ice tea with lime. I thought a lot of an owner who sang as he swept up and let fair-haired girls lounge in the cool shade of his establishment.

When he brought me a menu, I only recognized foods that were also in Mexican dishes. I explained I was a vegetarian on a budget. He offered to choose for me. The peacefulness of the place made the intensity with Jim unreal.

To while away the long afternoon and evening, I walked the neighbourhood. By the time I got back to the hotel, I was tired enough to sleep. I woke to Jim's humming what he had begun in the elevator. 'Do do do do do do do,' over the whisper of his undressing. He crept up from the foot of the bed singing:

> *Now the wild fires are burning*
> *In the dusky hour*

A forced absence had made his heart grow fonder of Los Angeles. Every summer, the hills of Southern California were fated to flame by nature or man. 'Nice beat,' I said.

He hovered over me. He said, 'You ran to me with it.'

My laugh rose and fell in the darkness. 'You're speaking in that rhythm.'

'So are you.' He sang, '*You're speaking in that rhythm.*'

'You can speak in that cadence until it drives you crazy.'

'*Until it drives you crazy,*' Jim sang playfully. 'Voices in rhythm. Bodies in rhythm.' Jim danced on his knees beside me, making slow circles with his hips.

Stretching to turn on the bedside lamp for a better view, I said, 'Out of rhyme, though. Hour and liar don't quite rhyme.'

'They don't?' he asked with a laugh. 'Nice of you to let my English slide. *Our hearts are bright with fire,*' he sang, then shook off the line. He pulled me up to him. 'I don't dance in bed with anyone else.' We knelt in each other's arms. 'I still have that dress. The one with the tiny pearls that make,' Jim paused to trace the pattern on my shoulder, 'I've forgotten the name of the flowers again.'

'Wisteria.'

'I kept it for you.' I didn't know how to respond. Meant to be a wedding dress, it didn't belong in my closet. Jim asked, 'Do you know what I've been trying to say?'

I whispered softly into his chest, 'Not since I arrived.'

He laughed wickedly. 'I love you.' He ran kisses down my spine. 'When I've straightened my life out, will you be my Natasha?'

'You know, Audrey Hepburn was in the movie. You're right. They lost the book.'

I looked over my shoulder. Jim nodded at my ducking his question. 'You still don't love me the way I love you, and it's still all right with me.'

When he raised himself to meet me, I kissed him hungrily. I said, 'We do have the most beautiful common ground.'

He lay back again. I kissed his thighs. His penis shifted. I kissed its tip. Jim pulled me up to his lips.

'You don't have to do that,' he said.

'I don't have to be here.' If I could be one place, why not the other?

'No,' he said sternly. I wondered which of us had more growing up to do.

We talked about his court situation in Miami, and how before he left Los Angeles Pamela threatened to sue him back into her life. 'She says if I don't come back, she'll lie away what remains of my reputation.'

He was quiet for a few minutes, contemplating his financial ruin.

'Aw, shit!' he yelled, hitting his forehead with his fist. 'I forgot to take care of the rights to *The Razor's Edge*! You haven't told anyone, have you? If word leaks out, the price will be out of my range.'

I laughed. 'There was a time when you lived on oranges, Jim.'

'Might be better for me if I did that again. Live the artist's life. All I hear is how I've let down all these people whose income depends on me. I'd hate to count the bodies. And I'm just a writer.'

In the same pose he wrote about in the poem he'd given me, Jim was nestled against the curve of my spine when we fell asleep. Dawn was just seeping into the room, when Jim woke with a shudder. 'Nightmare?' I asked.

'My friend is arriving from New York. We'll get drunk and argue.' Reality.

'How about you don't drink. Don't argue.'

'We could not drink, but we'd still argue.' He arranged my hair over my shoulders. 'Will you talk to this woman for me?'

'Give me the boundaries of what you want to say.'

'Tell her everything,' he said in a secretive voice. 'I nearly told her once. We were talking about our families. I hinted a bit and she asked a very direct question about what it was like for me at home. I nearly answered it, but I wasn't sure I knew her well enough to trust her.'

My turn to be direct. 'You seem to be telling me that this woman is having your baby. I thought that wasn't very likely.'

'It's not. Not very likely at all. Maybe it's wishful thinking. I know you were open to adopting children, but I wanted . . . I hate being impotent.'

I giggled. 'You mean *infertile*. The other, you definitely aren't.'

Jim flushed at his slip. 'Freud might have been right about a few things after all.'

'I think . . .' Jim nudged me to continue. 'I think, both for this woman and yourself, you should see a doctor. Maybe the doctor who told you that you had a low sperm count was mistaken. Or the test was faulty. You shouldn't make a decision that will effect three lives without knowing the facts.'

Jim nodded and fell silent.

447

'Are you going to tell me this woman's room number, or do I just knock on doors until a smart-mouthed redhead answers?'

'Ah, that would work.' Jim chuckled. 'I do seem to have this weakness for that particular combination. Do you know how rare it is?' He wrote her room number on a pad. 'Don't contact her until I've spoken to her.'

Waiting was not what I did best. I finished the novel I'd brought for the red-eye. I listened to my transistor radio until the batteries died in the middle of Donovan singing 'Riki Tiki Tavi'.

Jim let himself in and leaned against the door as if he'd outrun a pack of wild dogs. 'I've changed my mind. I don't want you to do this. Thanks for coming, for agreeing to speak for me, but I can't trust her. She's threatened to sue me. I guess my first instincts were right.' He immediately added, 'Do you want someone to take you to the airport?'

Dismissed. He'd never passed responsibility for me off on anyone else. 'Are you sure you want to be alone? I could pick up a temporary job to be here during the trial.'

'With you here, I can't pull off being Zapata,' he said. When he came closer, I noticed his eyes were red from crying. 'Would you do me an incredible favour?'

'Besides leaving?' I asked. My playing with his tassels would have become an annoying habit if I stayed much longer. 'Name it.'

'Call Pamela. I'm trying to be so strong, but I want to know how she is.'

When I arrived at the San Jose airport, I dialled the number he gave me for Pamela at the first pay phone I saw. If I waited until I got back to my parents', I'd lose courage. I let the phone ring seven times. Then another seven. Pamela's sleepy voice said, 'Hello.'

I asked, 'Pamela?' even though I recognized her voice.

'Ginger?' she asked. At least we knew who we were. Dutifully, I asked how she was. 'Not so hot,' she said softly.

'Jim was worried. He asked me to call.'

Her voice perked up, 'Jim was worried?'

'He heard that . . .' I trailed off, unsure of how to repeat what Jim had told me without hurting her.

'I OD'd. Good!' she said with childish defiance. *Good?* 'Son of a bitch!'

'Would you like me to come lend a hand for a while?' I found myself childishly crossing my fingers in hopes she wouldn't ask.

'Oh, that's real nice of you, but I'm staying with a friend. I'm surprised that Jim knew this number. Did he want you to find out if I was fucking around?'

'No,' I could answer honestly. 'He was concerned about your health.'

Pamela was disappointed. 'I don't know why I want him to be jealous. Our relationship hasn't been physical for a year or more. It was kind of you to call.'

'I like you,' Pamela said so sweetly I felt guilty for being angry with her. 'Even before we met. Jim's always nicer after he's been with you. Wish more of it could rub off.' She paused after insulting him. 'How's Jim?'

I couldn't think how to describe him for a moment. 'Tense. Tired.'

'He's making such a big deal out of this nonsense. You'd think they were going to hang him.'

I hesitated. 'I think he feels like they are.'

'Jim likes to be melodramatic,' she said with an exaggerated sigh.

I ignored this joust at Jim. He hadn't told her about the threats from the police and it wasn't up to me to enlighten her. Maybe Jim felt she couldn't handle the truth.

'Well, if you need me, I'm here,' I told her. 'Do you have my number?'

'Yes. I think about calling you sometimes. That would be strange, wouldn't it? If we were friends?' Fortunately, she didn't allow time for an answer. 'We were at this party and they were going around the room asking, "Who would you want to be stranded on a desert island with?" Jim said, "Ginger." Everybody laughed, picturing Jim watching *Gilligan's Island*. I didn't laugh, because I knew he was talking about you. If he could only be with one woman, he'd choose you, not me.'

'I wouldn't overlook the possibility of the bimbo myself.'

'See how nice you are?' Pamela said too brightly. She took in a sharp breath. 'Did Jim tell you what he thought the difference between us was?'

Thankfully not. 'I really feel uncomfortable about this, Pam.'

'Maybe you can explain it to me. You're so smart. He said that the difference between us is that, let me get this straight, I would do anything to keep him and that you'd do anything to save him. And the thing is, it practically destroyed him when you called off the wedding.'

Jim's chivalry shouldn't have surprised me. I looked out at the people passing, arriving and departing, and felt incredibly touched by the new knowledge, and pained by the reason he sent me away that December.

As the trial progressed, Jim called not to talk about it. We spoke of the script. The Doors had scraped through obtaining the court's permission to perform at the Isle of Wight Festival off the coast of England. Jim asked me what he should wear, as if he'd forgotten how to appear on stage.

'Oh,' I said. 'Show them your Zapata.'

Jim didn't want to talk about his performance. An outdoor event on no sleep wouldn't have pleased Jim anyway, but he was most disappointed he had to sing earlier material and not *Morrison Hotel*. 'Then again,' he sighed, 'rockin' through "Roadhouse Blues" might have killed me.'

The trial dragged into September. Jim had testified for a couple days. He'd called to tell me about the experience. When he repeated segments of his testimony, the words didn't even sound like Jim.

Then the phone woke me. I said a sleepy 'Hello' into the receiver.

'Darlin', it's Jim. Did I wake you?'

'Yeah. Nice way to wake up, though not so nice as in person.'

'Wish I could be there. I hate to hit you with this first thing, but wanted you to hear it from me.'

I snapped awake. 'What's happened? Did the verdict come in?'

'No. No. I'm real sorry. It's Jimi Hendrix,' Jim's voice was dreamy. He was on acid. 'Jimi's dead.'

'Oh, no, Jim.'

'There aren't many details so far. I didn't want you to hear it on the radio first. The report I heard said that he OD'd on sleeping pills . . . The ultimate cure for insomnia,' he spat out, then apologized, 'I'm sorry.'

450

We held the phone connection in silence for a few minutes, then he said, 'I was just thinking about the chills I got when he sang that Woody Guthrie song. I didn't see him very often, but he always hummed a little of that song, always asked after you. His last words to me were, "How's your Ginger?" Are you gonna be all right?'

I felt a wave of anger and loss. 'Not for a while.'

27

Motel Money Murder Madness

A couple days after Jimi's death, Jim's jury reached a muddled guilty verdict. From the beginning, Jim felt fated. He was resigned, grateful he wasn't hauled off to jail, but released on appeal. I believed in justice and was sure if, when he had taken the stand, he had told the story of the Miami performance as he had relayed it to me, the jury would have seen him as a man and not a rock-star.

In the end, Jim said bleakly, 'Law and justice aren't the same thing,' then true to his adoration of a good play on words, added, 'I was hoisted on my own canard.'

I'd been strangling the receiver. With his bull's-eye of a joke, I became a helpless pile of giggles. Jim was right. The false image he had created to amuse and protect his true self had done him in. Nothing he said on the stand would have made any difference.

When I stopped laughing enough to hear him, Jim said, 'Let's cast this film.'

When in a positive mood, Jim would take hold of a day and shake every last minute out of it. When depressed, he'd lose hours in drink. He could be editing his poetry, drafting a screenplay, and wrapping up an album, and say, 'I need to get busy.' But with Jimi's death and his conviction, Jim was even more certain the end was near.

Though he in no way fitted the physical characteristics of Isobel's huge husband, Gray, stalled in life by business losses resulting in a nervous breakdown, I asked, 'How about Brandon de Wilde?'

'How about him?' Jim asked back. 'You want him. You call him.'

The line went dead. I stared at the phone. Jim's jealousy. Jim rang again with Brandon's number, but no apology.

He said, 'Ask him if he can keep a secret. Tell him he'll be lucky to get lunch. It's all for glory.'

An hour later, I dredged up the courage to call Brandon. He bubbled with alacrity. 'He wants me in his movie? Hey, great. I'd do anything with that maniac genius. Where do I sign? By the way, what's the part?'

I wanted Brandon to understand why he didn't have a shot at the lead, but not being exactly professional, wandered off telling him about a scene where Larry uses a Greek coin to help Gray control his headache. The neat part was that in the book the coin depicts Alexander the Great who happened to be a historical figure Jim admired enough to suggest his hair be cut like a bust he saw. It created the image Jim grew to regret, and the man who cut his hair so perfectly was Jay Sebring who was killed with Sharon Tate.

When I came up for air, Brandon said, 'Just so I get to work with Jim. Hell, just so I get to work.'

Jim admitted he was pleased I'd gotten Brandon on the team. My wanting Janis Joplin to play the tragic Sophie set off a long discussion. In the original movie, the actress who played the part won an Oscar. I stuck by wanting her to be a blues singer, rather than a prostitute. And I wanted Janis. Unfortunately, she and Jim were oil and water. Their meetings had been hellacious. He didn't hang up, but also didn't produce her phone number.

My checking Pamela for him while he was in Miami had set a dangerous precedent. When he returned to California, Jim had walked in on her with a man. Drugs. He left, then fell to worrying.

The year before, he had given me hell for calling an ambulance when I discovered Tim Buckley comatose, insisting it was his choice. *Let him go.* His feeling for Pamela, however convoluted, ran deep. He didn't want anyone in Los Angeles to know of his concern. He asked if I would make the trip to see if she were alive.

Jim gave me the address of the apartment they shared off and on, located on Norton Avenue. I'd never been there. Upstairs. I rang the bell. I knocked. Jim had me concerned enough I was ready to use the key he'd given me when the door opened a crack.

'What do you want?' a European voice asked.

'I want to see Pamela.'

'Another time.'

I put my sandalled foot on the threshold. 'Now,' I said firmly as if I were wearing combat boots. From the streak of light that fell across his face, I could have sworn the man's eyes were each a different colour. The glimpse made me uneasy, as if I'd walked into a werewolf movie.

He stepped aside enough to let me brush past him. He remained at the door and left me to find Pamela. She was so pale against the floral pillows of the bed, I feared her dead. I felt for a pulse. No expert, it took me longer than I thought it should to find it. After I called her name several times without result, I sat with a bounce on the bed, hoping that would wake her. Then I took her narrow shoulders in my hands and shook her.

'Why don't you leave her alone?' the man asked from the bedroom doorway. He wasn't that big, but big enough to fill the exit. Ice on the back of her neck brought Pamela around enough that I could tell Jim she wasn't dead.

Startled when she recognized me, Pamela pleaded, 'Don't tell Jim about Jean. He's in the country illegally.' She didn't even remember Jim had seen them together.

My next assignment was more welcome. I was to contact Janis Joplin. She wouldn't take Jim's calls. He said he couldn't stand another concussion anyway. She had a history of hitting him over the head with any convenient bottle. Jim provided me with her room number at the Landmark Hotel where she was staying while recording her latest album. When I couldn't get a message through to her, and Jim didn't want me to wait until she returned to San Francisco, I drove down to LA.

Even in my lucky white dress, the desk clerk wouldn't let me past him, so I lay in wait outside the hotel. When I spotted her, I momentarily lost confidence, and squeaked, 'Miss Joplin . . .'

She had a throaty laugh. She peered at me over purple shades and said, 'Good God, I'm Janis. Hello, honey.'

Despite the voice, in a sleeveless black top and jeans, she looked fragile on the city street. The sunglasses, even at night, and all the bangles and beads were talismans to ward off evil spirits.

'Jim Morrison asked me to speak to you,' I said.

Janis rolled some spit around her mouth and sent it flying. Jim did say they hadn't hit it off, his exception in Capricorn chemistry. She lit a cigarette. 'Sorry, kid. What does Jim want?'

I explained. As I talked, she hissed curses about how the *bastards of the music business* treated her because she was a woman. An arty movie might shake them up. She marvelled that a *dear little thing* like me was working with Jim.

She stroked my hair and said, 'I've seen you before.'

'At a bookstore in San Francisco a couple years ago.'

'I remember your hair,' she said. She puffed her hair up. 'Trade you.'

Though I was careful not to tell her the script was based on *The Razor's Edge*, since Jim was having difficulty securing rights, she was well read, and guessed. 'Bet it was your idea to make Sophie a blues singer and not a whore.' After promising not to say anything until Jim gave her the word, she said, 'If I'm over the title,' she made an extravagant rainbow gesture in the air, 'it's a deal.' Then she added, with a goodbye peck on the cheek, 'Tell Jim he's welcome in my bed any time he brings you.'

When I told Jim about the proposition, he asked, 'Don't suppose?'

Curious as I was, I answered, 'Don't suppose.'

The next time Jim invited me down to Los Angeles was for the sole purpose of writing a line for him. He thought I believed such enticements. Jim had rented a place to get away from all the places he was likely to be found.

Two trees stood as sentinels at the walkway to the bungalow. To the left loomed a mature magnolia, heavy with its waxy leaves, and to the right a young jacaranda, bouncing in the evening breeze.

Jim nabbed my wicker carry-all to hurry me into the courtyard. He opened the heavy wooden door without having to unlock it.

Since Miami, our time together was all work. On the way from the airport, he decided we had developed a pleasure deficit and writing could wait. Afterwards, Jim conked right out. Deserted, I stood on the mattress and stared down at him for a different viewpoint. When he woke, he fluttered his eyes a few times in bewilderment.

'I think we shoot the album cover from here,' I teased, making a lens of my hands to check out the possibility.

Once awake, Jim sat naked and cross-legged in the middle of the bed, prepared for work. Only half of the bottom sheet remained on the mattress after our greeting. The sheet became a white sky on which he arranged clouds of paper scraps.

'You're the great alliterator,' he began.

'That's alliteratrix,' I interrupted, kneeling behind him for a better view of the pieces of paper strewn everywhere.

Jim rolled his eyes in appreciation. 'I have this line that isn't right.' He plucked a scrap of a road map and handed it to me.

'I hope somebody isn't lost in Ventura,' I said, after squinting to identify the map in what light a dimming ceiling bulb contributed. The line was about moods.

'Eight syllables that rhyme with sadness. This rhythm,' he said, slapping his thigh.

The band may not have let him play harmonica on 'Little Red Rooster' – his harmonica wasn't *that* bad – but he played thigh very well. I counted out the syllables on my fingers. '*Motel. Money.*' The perfect word came to me. 'On the plane down, I was looking through a magazine someone had left behind. It was from last year.'

Jim shivered. 'Shit. Don't do that.' Not since the previous summer had he mentioned Jay Sebring by name. Even when Charles Manson and members of his *family* were arrested he referred only to *the murders.* 'We could earn our fortunes in a mind-reading act.'

I wrote *Murder*, which we seemed to have agreed upon, then, *Madness*. I handed the four words back to him. A free trip to Los Angeles for five minutes' work.

He let out a hysterically mad laugh, then went on sanely, 'I thought I'd try to pull these together and make a neat copy. Neatness impresses the band. When I show up with neat lyrics they think I'm on top of things. They get so nervous when I show up with these, ah, scraps.'

'Flashes of genius,' I corrected.

Jim fell back against me. A human domino, I fell awkwardly against the pillow. 'Wonder where I could scare up a camera,' Jim mused, looking up at me. 'Maybe if you stood over me like before and shot down. I'm gonna go get a camera.' He was off the bed, pulling on a pair of overalls and his friendly god-awful Frye boots. 'Coming?' he asked halfway out the door.

My dress was on in a wink, then I hesitated, suddenly feeling less like those scraps were airy clouds than cubs a mother bear like me should protect with her life. 'What if the maid comes and thinks they're trash?'

'Maids don't come this time of night. I'll hang a Do Not Disturb sign to ward off aberrant housekeepers.' He waved for me to hurry. 'Come on! Come on!'

I hovered. 'We could take them with us.'

Jim was impatient with my practicality. 'I don't want to disturb the composition. Pretend for an evening you are a Sagittarius and not a Capricorn. Be reckless! Spontaneous!'

I tried to comfort myself by seeing how much of the song I could remember should sleepwalking maids descend or floods flash, but running down the few stairs and across the courtyard, I was only pretending. Jim held the car door open for me, jumping up and down, anxious to be on the road. He'd rented another American monster car. I'd been afraid to ask, 'Where was *Old Blue*?' Jim called his car *Blue Lady*, but it wasn't a very feminine car. Quite possibly, he had run into so many palm trees, agencies would only rent him cars they hoped stood an equal chance against a tree trunk.

Jim disliked driving the city. If there had been any possibility of my reaching the pedals, he would have tossed me the keys. I loved driving with him, never knowing exactly where I was as he swung from neoned boulevards to dark side-streets, where we dodged parked cars, and wondered whether the tense shadows were dogs or coyotes.

We stopped in front of apartments stacked against the hill like building blocks. Jim took the wooden steps two at a time and pounded on a middle door without catching his breath. A sleepy voice grumbled from inside. He opened the door to a grinning Jim, who asked, 'Can I borrow your camera?'

'Are you drunk?'

'Can I borrow your camera?'

'Are you drunk?'

I giggled, and said '*déjà vu*' as if it were a sneeze.

Jim turned and lifted an eyebrow. 'Bless you.' He grabbed the wooden railing that edged the road and jumped on to it. He teetered a few seconds, facing the black canyon below, then casually walked the sixteen-foot length of rail. He squatted on the rail across from the doorway.

'Trust me with your camera?' he asked, having proven his sobriety.

'Hell, no!' Jim's barely wakened friend led us into his apartment without turning on a light. 'I think this proves one of us is crazy.'

As Jim drove us back out of the hills, I punched the buttons on the radio a dozen times, then gave in to a commercial with a catchy tune.

'No Doors on the radio,' he said flatly, then yelled, 'Gotta do it!'

Jim turned the radio up full volume. Martha and the Vandellas came on singing 'Dancing in the Street'. Jim grabbed my hand and yanked me out of the car into the middle of the road. He had to boogie.

After the dance, he heaved himself up on the front fender, and said, 'The only thing wrong with that song is that it is too damn short!'

Jim didn't want to pose while I took pictures. He wanted me to record what he was doing naturally. He found it possible to be himself with my balancing on the headboard, whirring through two rolls of film.

'Jim?' I asked, hating to interrupt his word gathering.

He leaned his head back. He asked, 'Is my head blocking my head?' I got it. That was sexual. When I finished the last roll, Jim unloaded the film. He said, 'We should do an exhibit of your photographs. Those you took in Big Sur. These. Let everybody see what they didn't in Miami. I like the idea that I could be plastered in full view all over gallery walls and that is art, but in a rock 'n' roll context, it's criminal.'

Later, we crawled back into bed, he with my copy of Nancy Milford's biography of Zelda Fitzgerald, F. Scott's wife. Jim showed no mercy in pilfering a book that captured his interest. Since he had my reading material, I opened my journal. After only a few minutes, Jim lay with the book on his face.

'Want me to turn out the light?' I offered softly.

He peeked out from under the book. 'Don't you dare stop writing! The sound is putting me to sleep.'

My writing didn't proceed as surely when I knew Jim was counting on being lulled by my pencil. Obligated to continue this pencil-and-paper lullaby, I wrote about the day until I was sure Jim was asleep.

The next day, while Jim was out, I thumbed through to a fresh page. I was surprised by Jim's handwriting, noticeably darker than mine because of the pressure he used. On a poem I'd written before the trip, he had crossed out words he felt unnecessary and written in ones he preferred. I wasn't much of a poet, but his deft hand had greatly improved my effort. At the bottom I'd signed with my usual flowery *LA*. Before my initials, Jim had written *Little* and after them *Woman*. A Jim-joke in print. When I turned the page, he'd printed a parade of *LA. LA. LA. LA. LA.* across the bottom, as if he couldn't stop rolling.

When he returned with a six-pack of beer, he questioned my giggling. Seeing my journal open in my lap, he understood. 'I never could resist a double meaning. Just don't tell anyone I started the song in Miami.'

He sang a bit of what had become 'LA Woman'.

Burning hair. 'Good metaphor,' I said, though I missed the *dusky hour.*

'Suits both of my LA's,' he said. He saw my reddish-blonde hair as being on fire when he was on acid. The hills around Los Angeles were covered with easily ignitable dry wheat-coloured grass in the summer. Jim added, 'There is this Zen thing about living every moment as if your hair were on fire.'

'Sounds a bit intense for Zen, but I guess it's that razor's edge you're always shredding your boots on.'

Jim stuck his tongue out at me and rambled excitedly about starting filming. For the most part, the book took place in Chicago and France. To save money, Jim was using Los Angeles as the American locale. He wanted to roll like his LA's across a page.

'If Rothchild weren't producing her album, I'd shoot Janis recording.' Jim had intentionally annoyed Paul Rothchild into quitting as producer for the new album. After a taste of control on *Morrison Hotel*, he wanted more. He considered. 'Maybe I could shoot some background footage around the city.'

Ever practical, I asked, 'Wouldn't it save money to have the screenplay as tight as possible before starting?'

'That insight just made you the youngest film producer in Hollywood.'

Janis Joplin died over that weekend in early October from an overdose of heroin. Jim and Janis arranged only one clandestine meeting concerning the film. Always before when they had met, Jim said they had been '*Rock and roll brats trying to out-asshole each other*', but with a project to discuss, Jim said sadly, 'We realized we probably would have been those two outcasts eating lunch together under the bleachers in high-school.'

The next day, Pamela took off to Paris with her male companion.

'I don't give a fuck who she fucks,' Jim screamed over the phone, loud enough to prove he probably did, 'but that prick is going to kill her. I'm sure it was his stuff that killed Janis.' The man Pamela called her Count, Jim called her pusher.

Jim calmed down enough to invite me for a visit. We sat over the breakfast he made and served at the ornate walnut table that came with the place. Jim enmeshed in domestic duty was charming. He set out the blue Fiesta plates he'd rescued from the Stockton efficiency. Napkins forgotten, he lined up the silverware all on the right side of the plate. As part of the setting, he arranged a steno pad and pen to their right.

He was repairing songs in between bites of pancake. Jim could make pancakes all the same size, a talent I fancied. I tried to live up to his writer's compliment that being with me was like being alone, which meant I didn't compete for his attention while he wrote. He was rewriting 'Hyacinth House' and curiosity was needling me.

When he looked up from his tablet he swallowed his mouthful of cold pancake and asked if I wanted to hear how the song was progressing. He hadn't sung 'Hyacinth House' to me since my birthday. While I admired his ability to even sing that combination of words, when I had to slow way down to even say them, his latest version included a verse that disturbed me. I wasn't sure how to approach him about the changes.

'Jim,' I began and stopped.

He head was down, and he looked up at me, one of his most endearing natural poses that caused me to hesitate to object to anything. He added an encouraging nod.

'Don't put "Hyacinth House" on the album, Jim,' I pleaded.

Unruffled, Jim said, 'You haven't made that poignant a request since "Wild Child". What's wrong with saying I want to live a creative life with you?'

'Nothing. I'd be proud to serve the . . .' I hesitated, editing out the tempting *pride* that sprung to mind. Too cute. 'Lions.'

'Now, I expected you to say *proud to feed the pride*.'

I giggled, embarrassed I'd nearly said that awful line. 'I rejected that. I love your writing something about our creative . . .'

'Connection,' he finished for me. 'But . . .'

'This verse about wanting someone who doesn't need you . . .'

'I thought you'd like that. In my rush to get something together for your birthday, I forgot I promised to write about the pleasures of a competent woman.'

'But I've needed you. You've been there when I most needed you. My father hasn't touched me since you scared him. You saved my life, Jim.' We didn't talk about those things.

'But you don't cling to me.'

'The public goodbye will hurt Pamela.'

'Pamela won't get the song.'

'That makes it meaner.'

All too soon, Pamela was back from Paris. His New York

friend appeared for an unexpected visit. Jim was upset that the two women had commiserated about him.

'Well, Jim,' I said, 'it was bound to happen. It was probably only restraint on both their parts that kept it from happening sooner.' I had to add, 'You sound drunk.'

'I've been drunk for a week. It was the only way I could get through it.' Jim felt the woman had been unkind. He admitted, 'When my doctor told me there wasn't a chance in hell I could be the father of her baby, I paid for the abortion, but couldn't see her through it.'

'I'm sure it was a terrible experience for her to go through alone. You could have been there for her as a friend.'

'Do you think I'm a heel, too?' Jim asked defensively.

'The important thing is, Jim, you feel like a heel.'

Jim was quiet on his end. 'I know I confront people when I shouldn't, and avoid them when I shouldn't. I can't seem to get it straight. I thought I was being a gentleman. She thought I was being a coward. I tried to give her a nice goodbye. And I didn't say the cruellest thing. That's the best I can say for myself.'

'Maybe it's just awkward now. You need to decide what will make you feel better about the situation, not rake through the past. You told me in Miami that the reason you became friends was because you needed someone to talk with when, well, when things fell apart for us.'

'Yeah, but one person can't replace another. Nobody else understands I am an artist first and a man second. It wasn't like I made a conscious decision to be that way. You accept it. You've always accepted the real me.'

Jim had an identifiable knock. Two raps. A pause. Then three. He had watched my father leave for work before using it. I opened the door. Rather than looking up at Jim, I found him sprawled on the doorstep. My five foot two was mostly muscle, but I couldn't lift him when he couldn't even give himself a little boost. My mother, despite her fragility, provided just enough oomph to help me drag him to his feet.

Then he released a collection of papers. When I let go of him to grab for them, he slumped back to the ground. I chased the papers in the wind. Jim wasn't going to blow away. I folded them in half and stuck the whole batch in the waist of my jeans.

My mother and I made a better team getting Jim to his feet a second time. Hanging between us, Jim found enough footing to make it to the bathroom before he vomited. My mother took a step back. 'I'll handle this, thanks,' I told her. Jim had drenched the room. The second go-round was bloody. I held his face with one hand.

He looked up from his toilet-side seat and mumbled a pathetic, 'Sorry.'

I wiped his face with a washcloth to see if he were bleeding from his nose or mouth. 'You aren't spitting up blood. Your nose is bleeding.'

'Figures,' he said.

The bathroom stank so badly, I helped him through to my bathroom. When I had him undressed and in the square stand-up shower, I realized he wasn't going to remain on his feet without more help from me. I climbed in with him and held him against the wall until his own legs held him.

Cleaned up, Jim looked forlorn on my flowered comforter. I handed him the work shirt I used for an artist's smock and fetched a pair of my father's boxers.

When his nose started to bleed again, he leaned back. I packed his nose with cotton and pinched his nostrils.

'Don't lean back. The blood going down your throat will only make it sore.'

He mumbled, 'Do you moonlight as a corner man?'

'Pays better than baby-sitting.'

'Not if you baby-sat me.'

If he could make jokes and breathe through his mouth at the same time, he was well enough to let me scrub down the bathroom and run his clothes out to the laundry room. The bathroom was going to be a floor-to-ceiling job. While I was occupied with Jim, my mother had taken on the chore.

'When Jim feels a little better,' she said gently, 'I'll make him waffles.' She was a believer in starches settling upset stomachs.

When I returned to Jim, he was sitting at the card-table I'd commandeered as a drawing-table. He had opened the shoe box in which I stored my friends' letters, filed by name and date, and was reading an illustrated note my Maine friend Brian had sent after Woodstock over a year earlier.

'Snoop,' I said to announce myself.

'He draws well,' Jim commented, refolding the brown-ink drawing Brian sent from his sketchbook.

'And he made it to Woodstock. That was better than you or I did.'

'August in upstate New York! Bah! Told them they'd be singing in the mud.' He gave the box a shove. 'Don't you keep my letters?'

'Not in plain sight. That might work in 'The Purloined Letter', but yours are too numerous and too . . .'

'Erotic,' he completed their description. He enjoyed making love on paper almost as much as in person. 'Where are they?'

'My box spring.'

Jim chucked softly. 'That's one way I can sleep with you.'

'How are you feeling, besides curious?'

He teetered in the chair. 'Like an idiot. I'm sorry. Is your mother upset?'

'No, she wants to make you waffles to settle your tummy.'

He smiled. I handed him the items I'd removed from his pockets before washing his clothes and the worse-for-wear poems. He lined up the thirty-five-millimetre film canister, his American Express card, and the photo of me at six, then shuffled the pages of poetry into the order he desired.

'Did you read them?' he asked. When I shook my head, he said, 'I'd like you to go through them and tell me which ones are good.'

'Does that ploy usually work? You know which of your poems are good and which aren't. Boost someone else's ego.'

Jim rubbed his face and laughed. 'Caught. I should know better with you. The thing is, I really do respect your opinion.'

'In my opinion, your nose is bleeding because you are doing too much cocaine.'

'Caught.' He tossed the film container at me. 'Want to dole it out to me?'

I took it. To give him a bit at a time seemed safer, but that seemed like pouring him a drink. 'If you leave this with me, I'll flush it.'

He didn't ask for it back. While he read samples of my friends' letters, I sat on the floor and read his poems. They were ones he had been working on for over a year. A few lines went back even further. Jim constructed poetry like an album. The poems were like related songs. These began with an invocation of the spirit of 1965 which he considered the beginning of his adult writing.

When his clothes were dry, he opted to keep on my work shirt, but did trade my father's boxers for his own jeans. He dutifully ate my mother's waffles. Her pecan and peach waffles were delectable, but Jim provided a real test to her theory of what set on a drunk's queasy stomach.

She adjusted the net over her curlers as if it had just occurred to her she had been readying for bed when Jim arrived. Jim sat in the corner of the kitchen, his back against the wall like any good gambler, and read poetry from the crumpled sheets we gathered. He had the discretion to omit the one entitled 'Ode to My Cock', keeping his long-ago promise not to mention his cock in front of my mother.

There was a poem entitled 'A Wake', not 'Awake', a Finnegan joke for me. Finnegan was not dead, just dreaming. But let's not miss the party. The poet had awakened me in many ways.

My mother made up the couch for him, the way she did when I was home from school sick, a sheet halved to make a bottom and top sheet and a spare blanket. The invitation was to expire first thing in the morning. Jim needed to be up and out before my father came home from his graveyard shift. Jim was sleeping so soundly, I hated waking him.

Yawning, he sauntered into the kitchen and helped himself to a beer from the refrigerator. 'You're not giving me this. I'm stealing it.'

In gratitude for my mother's hospitality, Jim sent her an auto-graphed copy of *The Lords and the New Creatures*. Proud to know a published poet, she sat in her straight-backed wooden rocker and read it from cover to cover.

'There aren't any poems about you in here,' she said. 'What I find interesting, from what I've heard of his new poetry, Jim is

466

becoming more gentle as he gets older. Most men become more
. . . harsh.'

That night, Jim called to ask if I would see him through as I had
in Maine. He couldn't say the words, *I want to stop drinking*. For
privacy, he changed motels. That week Jim was like the tide. He'd
come crashing in on me, then rush out with friends. He'd say he
was going to work on *LA Woman* and return drunk.

'How many times can you do this?' he asked.

'As many times as it takes,' I assured him. I wanted him to know
it was all right if he didn't pull it off that time. 'It's important you
try. Like picking up a pen when you don't feel like it.'

Jim made a fresh start. Three days later, he was heaving and
shaking, and testy. I gave promised sponge baths. We walked
off his jitters with frequent stops to rest. He bought a book he
wanted me to read to him that night. I read until I was hoarse
while Jim tossed and turned and would have preferred a drink to
help him sleep.

The next day, feeling buoyed by eking through a rough couple
days and a near-endless night, he placed a few calls, went out with
a few friends, and returned at two in the morning high on cocaine.
A sexual tornado for twenty minutes, Jim wanted to dance and
cavort. Then he fell as low as he had been all week.

Jim needed a drink desperately. 'I'm not going to do it behind
your back,' he said. We both dressed and hiked to the nearest liquor
store. He bought a bottle of expensive wine. He made himself stop
at two glasses. Close to sleep, he asked for reassurance, 'As many
times as it takes?'

He woke with a foul headache and the decision he couldn't
finish the album and quit drinking at the same time. 'Maybe I'll
make it my New Year's resolution,' he sighed.

Knowing the territory around his birthday was a minefield, I was
surprised when he called, pleased he had recorded the collection of
poems he'd shown me. He was looking forward to a Dallas concert
where he intended to première 'LA Woman'. That appearance
made for an upbeat call, too.

Particularly pleased with what he called 'a beautifully ragged
performance' in which he had improvised a little. Knowing his
questioning my being a *lost angel* burned, he wanted to hear

how *dark witness* sounded. 'You said that was what you were. A camera, but the truth is, baby, I still believe what I said then. You are the rain that lifts me.'

Then he called from New Orleans. The first thing he said in a slur was, 'I lost myself on stage. The beads from Big Sur broke.' Then he added in the weariest voice, 'I'll never get on stage again.'

He had people in the room he wanted to get back to and I wanted him to hold on to be sure he wasn't planning any ledge-walking. If I misjudged his voice, I thought I'd read headlines about a rock-star who slipped off the roof of a hotel in New Orleans.

I dreamed again of pulling Jim from his grave. A few days later, he made another suicide call to me. He said, 'I'm not afraid of death,' as if he were talking about the weather. 'But I want to choose my own time . . . and means.'

I flew to Los Angeles for the first time unannounced. I took a taxi to the little bungalow, praying he was there. The door was wide open. Jim's face was tucked into the crook of his arm. White and lifeless against the polished walnut, he looked like spilled milk, held to its human shape by surface tension, not bone, muscle and flesh.

'Jim?' I asked.

His head rose slowly. The unmistakable agony on his face gripped my heart. I expected an anguished plea, but he said, 'I want to go to the bank.'

Jim let me clean him up enough to face the short trip. He wanted to show me papers he had squirrelled away in a safety deposit box. When he signed the card to gain entrance, I didn't think it looked much like his signature, in the way he didn't look much like himself. His appearance couldn't have changed overnight, but his face looked puffy and undefined. There were wiry grey hairs among his silky brown ones. When he caught my look, he said, 'Don't look so worried. Men in my family turn grey early.'

The whole process of entry into the safety deposit box was like a modern ritual; two keys to unlock the little door where the box was hidden, then a personal escort down a narrow hallway. We were left alone in a small room with divided cells like confessionals. Each had a flat surface for the box and a chair.

The first thing Jim showed me was a letter from the desk of J. Edgar Hoover.

I looked up at Jim. 'You two pen-pals?'

'Not the way we are,' he smiled wanly.

I gasped in the airless room. I read the letter through twice in disbelief. When Jim told me he never called me from his own phone and used cash for our visits because he was afraid of the FBI tracking him to me, I chalked it up to surplus paranoia surrounding his trials and cocaine.

'Is this real?' I asked of the letter in my hands.

Jim nodded. He studied the letter himself. The letter was brief and to the point: a demand for Jim to remove himself from public life.

'Isn't this illegal?' I asked. 'I mean, he's not asking for money, but it seems like blackmail.'

'The mistake he makes is thinking he has leverage. If anything would have shut me up, it was the threats I had from the cops.'

'Why does he care about you?' Why was Hoover so interested in a rock singer?

'He probably has an old picture of me and thinks I'm pretty cute. Other than that, he seems to think I have the power to move the masses. Like if I told kids to kill their parents and take over the government, they'd say, "Right on, Jim!"'

'Well, you wouldn't say that.'

'That logic seems to escape them.'

He pulled out his latest will. Handwritten, not trusting anyone again. Witnessed. 'See, I made the changes you told me to. I left everything divided between my brother and sister, except the control of my creative work. I left that to you. You're the only one I trust.'

'You left Pamela out completely this time. You guys have a fight?'

'Endlessly. She's threatening to sue me.'

'She was threatening to sue you this summer. That's not new.'

'But it's more real. She's the icing, really. I just can't be dragged through court again.'

I invited a practical thought into the room. 'Jim, you can hand that problem over to a lawyer. I don't think you even have to be there for a civil suit. Last year . . .'

'Now, don't say the cruellest thing you can think of,' he chastised me gently.

He removed the emerald ring from the safety deposit box, put it on my finger and held it there, saying, 'This is yours.'

We locked up the box and got some food into Jim.

'I've written love songs,' he said after devouring a carton of Szechuan. 'I started to know what real love was when you told me that you'd never pour a drink for me, but you'd pick me up off the floor as many times as it took. I've been thinking a lot about the rain in *African Queen* lifting the boat out of the reeds.' Jim waited to be sure I had the same picture he did, then said, 'That's what love is. Love lifts you. Everything else is something else. Maybe it's passion or duty. Romance or obsession. I'm not saying those things are good or bad, but real love,' he paused to smile, 'real love lifts you.'

PART V: *1971*

28

My World on You Depends

Jim met me in San Francisco for my birthday celebration. I wore the stormy-sky skirt Jim admired. First thing, Jim ran into a florist to buy me two dozen white rose buds, then reclaimed four. 'Nineteen and one to grow on,' he explained as he bit the head off one and spat it at a passing pretty girl. She reacted with first revulsion at being spat at, then surprise at the rose. Jim dispensed the spit-gifts as we ambled down the street.

He turned into one of those strip joints in North Beach and I dug my heels in the sidewalk. The sign directed *No One Under 21 Allowed*, though I told Jim I would have reworded it, *No One With Any Taste Allowed*. Jim pulled me. I was a mule.

He insisted, 'Your birthday present is in here!'

I couldn't imagine and changed from mule to curious cat. The place wasn't open. Dark. Chairs up-ended on tables. The two-piece band was playing two different songs. The drummer brushed his way through a Frank Sinatra hit, while the piano player whipped out a little boogie. Jim looked down at my hand he held, not able to look me in the face.

'I'm the singer with the band,' he whispered.

When the beads and he fell apart on stage the month before in New Orleans, he announced he was never going to climb on stage

473

again. This birthday present was his getting back on the horse that threw him, something Jim proved good at doing. Nervous and shy, he greeted the musicians with, 'Hey, man, how's it going?'

After he had a couple successful shows in New York at the Felt Forum a year before, Jim wondered if he could get on stage without the band. He rehearsed with a blues guitarist and auditioned as James Douglas at a coffee-house in Stockton called *Beauty and the Beast*. Since he never brought the incident up, I thought he didn't get the job without his name. A second try at a solo. That he was dressed for a performance explained Jim's new black threads.

After he lifted me on to a stool to watch, he arranged one for himself behind the microphone. The sound check consisted of each of the three tapping their microphones a few times. When I saw Jim on stage before, he made love to the microphone. He wound himself around it. He couldn't get close enough.

That day he sat back on the stool, back straight, his hands rubbing his thighs. He and the microphone kept a safe distance. He belted out 'Crawling King Snake' without mercy. His singing was a raw shock. Then slid right into 'One Bourbon, One Scotch, One Beer'. Jim's voice was so raspy, how was he recording *LA Woman*?

Singing with his eyes closed, Jim relaxed a little. Despite the last song, he took a sip of water and told me that the beads that meant so much to him had caught in his shirt in New Orleans. When he came back to earth, he was stunned that they were an intact rope. 'Like a newly hatched snake,' he said, producing the strand from his pants' pocket.

'Now, for your little present,' he teased.

Jim sat back on the stool. He leaned into the mike like they were becoming friends and sang the last song we'd written together, which had the chorus, '*That was never true . . . Baby, they lied to you.*' The song sounded a little pale next to John Lee Hooker's, but Jim had never performed one of our collaborations. I was sailing. What a birthday present!

On the way out into the glare, Jim said, 'That's all you get, because the birthday card I made was suitable for framing.' Jim had made me a birthday card. To let me know Jimi Hendrix had shown him the card I had made for his twenty-seventh birthday, he had used the same method of scratching through black crayon scribbled over colours. Jim had created a self-portrait and scratched out lyrics from 'Riders on the Storm' as a border. He dug into his coat pocket. 'Except for this,' he said, rocketing a box to the heavens.

I caught the carved wooden box just before it was splintered on the sidewalk.

'Your fielding is improving,' Jim said.

'Not enough to count on.' The box was fragrant, intricately carved, with mother-of-pearl inlays. 'It's beautiful. Thank you, Jim. The day we met, you were wearing a shirt with mother-of-pearl buttons.'

Jim smiled and winked. The detail was why he had chosen the box. 'I know you love boxes, but the present is still inside.'

'Things in small boxes make me nervous.'

'You can't say it doesn't fit us. I won't listen,' he argued even before I opened it.

The diamond he had given me the first Christmas, which he had bought with his first royalty check because it reminded him of the moonlight on the water in Santa Cruz, lay mounted in an Art Deco setting.

'Give this to me in September. When you get back from Paris.'

He insisted I try it on. Perfect. We were right in front of City Lights Books. He bought me a book of poetry-stuck both the ring and the book in his pocket so I didn't have either, and asked me to tell him the story of the carved box, to save his life like Scheherazade. I told him I thought Scheherazade told stories to save her own life. Jim rolled his eyes and ordered me not to be so *persnickety*, which was another old-fashioned word I'd picked up from my mother.

In late February, we agreed, as we had so many times, to meet in Pacific Grove. Except Jim had those plans to fly to Paris. I saw him, huddled against the constant ocean breeze that stunted the cypress, the same time he heard the roar of my Volkswagen. In his baggy khaki jacket, he resembled a Vet turned philosophy professor. Jim jumped into the car while it still rolled, and planted a kiss.

My suggestion was, 'Let's go to a motel so we can hold each other while we talk.'

'No,' he said firmly. 'The way I feel, we'd do more than talk.'

'Great!' I said with all the enthusiasm I felt. I kissed his grin. Jim was so good to kiss. I said, trying out aggressiveness, 'I want to make love with you.'

Jim caressed my hair for a few blocks' drive. 'Me, too, but if we make love I won't go to Paris. And I have to go.'

'Yeah, I know,' I said reluctantly. And hated it. 'I love you for wanting to end things decently with Pam, and selfishly want our time to begin now.'

Much had happened in a couple months' span. Jim had ground out *LA Woman* with the last of his creative strength. When he played me the raw tapes, I thought the album was the best work he had done, even on his see-saw of cocaine and whiskey.

Pamela had returned from Paris angry and unhappy, alternately wanting to begin afresh with Jim and drag every mean thing she could think to say about him through the courts. They found a balance I viewed as precarious as the one he had with coke and booze. He'd give her six months to help her get off heroin, a settlement to give her a start, and she would sign an agreement not to sue. I had a hundred misgivings, but he said, 'I need to do this to be the man I want to be.' I loved him too much to ask him to be less.

After Janis's death, Jim shelved the script. Neither of us wanted to think about replacing her, and I was sure Jim didn't have the energy to see a film through. What had begun as a game to divert him from his problems would have become another problem. I discovered in my diary, where I had written about my motivation for starting the project, Jim had written, *Sly*. I asked how long he knew; he said when he read my diary while I was sleeping during the visit he had written the *Little . . . LA . . . Woman* joke.

We followed the coast we knew well. I steered the car off the asphalt into sand, stopping short of the ice plants that bordered the cliff. We hiked down to the beach. The wind took the six-gore skirt of my long dress like a sail. We walked, holding cold hands, unable to talk. We'd look at each other and choke up.

Finally, he repeated himself about the six months promised Pam to get her on her feet. 'I owe her that,' he said.

She thinks she can keep you, I thought. *It's a trick.*

'I'm divided enough,' he said bitterly. 'Pam . . . the jail thing.' He pulled himself up short, though we had another hundred feet before the beach ended in a pile of rough rocks. 'I have to go.'

At first, I wanted to protest he'd just arrived, but realized he meant he had to go to Paris, not leave the beach. 'I'm not arguing with you, Jim. You're arguing with yourself.'

He said, 'Yeah, I know. I'm doing what my head says to do. My heart says to stay with you.' I barely listened to the full goodbye speech he prepared.

Though he didn't have a set departure date for Paris – he wanted to wake up one day and get on a plane, not dread it – we knew it would be soon. Any day. On the deserted beach, I looked up at him, his face obscured by his beard and windblown hair.

'You told me once to listen to my heart. And I didn't. And I've regretted it,' I said, arguing my case, though I promised myself not to. When he leaned down to put his forehead to mine, his hand bracing the back of my neck, I whispered, 'I've made a big mistake. I've fallen in love with you.'

He said sadly, 'We've loved each other since San Francisco.'

I wanted to explain how my love had changed. I loved him then as a stranger who was a kindred spirit. I'd grown into my feelings for him. I loved him newly as a woman loves a man she wants to spend her life with. I batted back tears as we retraced our steps.

Jim stopped and kissed me gently. 'You're the only one I've never regretted. Not once. Not for a moment.'

When I touched his chest, I felt a book in his upper left pocket. He carried the paperback of Hemingway's *A Moveable Feast* I'd given him as a bon voyage gift. The book was Hemingway's look at Paris in the twenties. Jim, more than likely, had read it, but in the way we give others what we want ourselves, I'd given him what I desired. When I grew up, I not only wanted to travel, but time travel.

His lower pockets were also heavy with paperbacks. If there were only hardback books in the world when Jim had come into it, he would have had to become the publishing genius who saw the wonder of a book in a pocket for his own survival.

In one pocket was Lillian Hellman's memoir, *An Unfinished Woman*, in the other a collection of plays from the 1950s, which included a play by Hellman, *The Autumn Garden*.

'Ahah!' I declared. 'Did you choose the play because you liked the author, or the other way around?' I was so clever.

'Neither. I bought the book of plays for Edward Albee's play. Hers just happened to be in it.'

'Never assume,' I said. Especially with Jim Morrison.

The included Edward Albee piece was a one-act play called *The Zoo Story*. Jim stood on the beach and read it to me. He read it to me again. 'This is where I'm going.'

'To the zoo?' I teased, because the play was a puzzlement. Allowing for the distraction of the sound of the ocean and my committing every gesture and cast of eye Jim made to memory, I didn't understand the play.

'I was thinking I might use the time in Paris to write some one-act plays. At this point, movies are so far beyond me financially, I want to work on something I can do in the street if I have to. I want to be the writer I am. There is my poetry. I have that novel kicking around in my head. I still hear music. There is no end to the work,' he finally stopped for a breath. 'I love that knowledge, but I'd like to see something through on my own without compromise. And when I saw this book, the scene reminded me of the games we play. As if those were the rehearsals, and this is the answer.'

He stuck the yellow volume back into his pocket and invited me, with an opening line, to play out one of our imaginary lives. He joshed about what I'd do with the husband and six kids I'd have by the time he was ready to settle down. I pretended to be my own child, begging, 'Uncle Jim, sing one of those songs you made famous in the music halls.'

Jim grinned, slowed his step. 'Oh, it's been so long, Jimmy . . .' My heart tugged at his boyhood name he refused to allow anyone to use, and my prince of a husband who let me name my son after my first love. 'Even I can't remember,' he continued, looking skyward, and shaking his head. 'Something about a fire.'

I tried to join in the game. You are this and I am that. I pictured Jim and me while my *husband*, ably portrayed by Brandon de Wilde, ploughed the back forty, but I couldn't play. I wanted the dream of Jim and me together too much.

Back in the car, I asked, 'Can I ask a big favour?'

He glanced at his crotch and smiled. 'Now, we talked about that.'

'Not that big,' I laughed. 'Sing me a song.'

Jim smiled, pleased. 'You've never asked me before.' I never had to. 'Let's cuddle in the back seat. I want to hold you.' From the first, Jim enjoyed a good cuddle.

In the confines of the back seat of a Volkswagen, even strangers had to cuddle. I rested against his chest, his arms around me. He hummed. 'My voice is a little rough,' he apologized. His breath sounded ragged. Jim started singing Van Morrison's *Crazy Love*, thoughtfully changing all the *shes* to *yous*. I pulled away to see his face, expecting a glint in his eyes and a grin emerging from his beard, but his eyes were closed.

When he finished his sincere cover of the song, he kissed my hair. His hair was a tangled mess from the wind. His cheeks ruddy.

'You're in worse shape than I thought.' I patted his chest. 'That's the other Morrison.'

'Is it?' Jim asked. 'I meant to write that for you. I've been busy.' He'd completed an album of his own. 'You know Van?'

'Never met the man,' I said. We'd seen him in concert once, but I'd refused to be taken backstage.

'See that you don't. You're obviously his kind of woman.'

Jim had hitched a ride up the coast, but I argued him into letting me drive him back to Los Angeles to give us more time. In Santa Barbara, Jim whispered, 'Give me a bath.'

We checked into a cosy little place. 'Let's unpack our notebooks and move in.'

I ached too much to answer. Jim lifted me. Angel light. On the bed, Jim was content to fold himself between my thighs, kissing me with such delicacy, building to that rhythm in his head that my body tuned in. He gave me a gentle orgasm, then backed off. He kissed thighs and feet, massaging my toes, making me giggle.

'You taste so sweet,' he said, but wouldn't let me reciprocate.

He pulled me on to my knees. 'Let's make love,' I begged.

'This is,' he said.

We *had* pulled off the highway for a last bath! We held hands in the bright bathroom. I wanted to look at him, but sat between his legs, leaning against him. We were so quiet, matching our breathing in and out, that I could feel us both near tears. Jim splashed wildly, breaking the silence and our rhythm. He groaned, 'Riders on the

Storm' flat and out of tune. We laughed. He laced his fingers across my stomach, let them ease down.

'What do you have?' he asked.

I wasn't sure what he meant, considering the direction of his caresses. 'You,' I answered.

'I mean,' he explained, 'what do you have inside that makes me feel so at peace?'

'I don't think it's me, Jim. It's me with you. The combination.'

He asked me to wash him. I soaped every inch of him, the ins and outs. I ended, sitting in his lap, my hands on his shoulders. Jim had a preference for my being his lap ever since those Indian friezes. He was energized and I was frantic. We rinsed under a shower. He sang 'Riders on the Storm', froggy and laughing.

'I feel like I'm already on my way back to you,' he said, taking the force of the shower full in the face.

'If you feel that way, couldn't we . . . make love to celebrate?'

'No, baby. I know once we make love, it's *once-and-forever*,' Jim said, careful to use my description of marriage. 'When I get home.'

We didn't rush out of the room, but lay in bed a while, talking about nothing. Reminiscing. I brought the promised drawings from Big Sur he wanted to take to Paris to write poems for. He wrote one there sitting on the bed. He studied the nudes of himself.

'My body has changed,' he sighed, lifting one that was only torso, like a remnant of a Greek statue.

'Everything changes,' I said.

'You don't find me unattractive?' he asked.

'I find you attractive, body and mind.'

He set aside one of the two of us drawn from my view in the mirror in a motel room. 'My butt crack is wrong,' he said, the plain-talking art critic. His criticism was accurate. The drawing was not. He was generously going to let me keep the worst of the lot. Afraid he had hurt my feelings he noted, 'The toes are beautiful.'

Looking at the drawings made us remember an all-night painting session in Los Angeles that began with one of Jim's lectures on writing. I had been sitting in one of the bungalow's two chairs, hugging my knees, reading *Zelda* while Jim wrote.

He said, 'The girl sat in a blue chair.'

'That your poem?' I asked.

480

'Could be. Any kid can write that line. It's what comes before and after it that would make it art.' A writing lesson in itself.

'Or how you wrote it down,' I suggested. Uncoiling enough to reach a sketchbook, I wrote the line out divided differently. I tried the words running single file down the page, then by twos, with a lonesome chair spelled out in one corner by itself.

Jim joined in and, before long, my watercolours were in use and Jim was searching for the exact words in the newspaper to cut out and arrange like a ransom note. By morning, we had filled every page of my sketchbook with variations of *The Girl Sat in a Blue Chair*. Jim wouldn't take a shower because he wanted to keep the paint on his hands so people would think he was a painter.

'They say that's how Van Gogh went mad,' I scolded, but he only heard that as encouragement. Jim wanted to call galleries, convinced they'd want to hang our art.

But we hadn't got around to that. We'd let months slip away. Jim was leaving for Paris. We were running out of time together. He pulled me over to him and asked, 'Is it too much to ask that you wait six months for me?' As he directed me to move so he might memorize me as well, drawing his finger along my body, he repeated, 'Wait for me. Wait for me.'

Back on the road, Jim slouched, knees against the glove box, punching the radio buttons, drinking a little. At the Ventura sign, he pointed, 'Look, we found Ventura without the map,' glancing up at me to see if I remembered part of 'LA Woman' began on a corner of a map,' then he asked if I had Bill Graham's phone number in case of emergency.

'I had a nice talk with Bill about you. So Bill knows we are . . . whatever we are.' Jim's laugh felt warm as he reached over to massage my neck. 'He knows all I know.'

He lamented, briefly, the end of The Doors. I said, not just to soothe him, but believing it, 'You just graduated from The Doors, like you did from high-school and college – except The Doors were a better learning experience. You can always go back for reunions.'

Jim smiled. 'Yeah, when they hate me less.'

'You've all been in a pressure cooker. You need to make music at your own pace.'

'Yeah,' The rarely monosyllabic Jim stared at the road.

'And you need to learn to talk to each other. You've taken your silent families to the band. We talk.'

He sunk lower in his seat. 'Apples and oranges.'

'Pip and pith.'

Jim chuckled and went back to pushing the radio buttons. He settled back to sing along with 'Itchy Coo Park'. He didn't miss a word! At the end of the song we looked sideways at each other and burst into laughter.

'Radio waves are insidious! No wonder Hoover's scared shitless!' Jim said. After all, he had kids screaming they wanted the world!' He added quietly, seriously, 'J. Edgar wants my ass in more ways than one.'

When we reached Los Angeles, Jim said, 'Just let me out on the Strip like I was a hitchhiker.'

I couldn't believe how soon we were idling on the Sunset, pulled over, but not parked. Jim had one hand on the door handle, ready to spring out. He expected something bright of me, before he darted out of my life for six months. I was the court jester in danger of being beheaded for not entertaining the king.

'*It was the best of times. It was the worst of times,*' I quoted.

That pleased him. He smiled. 'With you, it was only the best,' he said, then caressed my cheek. Thinking the response too pat, he said, 'It may have been in bits and pieces, but I gave you the best of me.'

There was a final kiss. He ducked out of the car and swung the door closed. His palm hit the roof as an all-clear to pull into traffic. Jim became a small figure in the rear view mirror, haloed in red neon, his right hand raised, not quite to his shoulder. I circled the block for another memory of him, but he was gone. When I pulled off the Sunset Strip, I thought how much like his self-portrait Jim appeared in that last look I had of him.

Jim sent a postcard from Los Angeles before he even took off for Paris. He wrote he'd taken a last look at me, too. I felt cheated that he had seen me, but I had missed him on the crowded sidewalk. Ten days later, I received a note from Paris. A few hurried lines questioning what in the world he was doing, closing with the postscript that nobody laughed at his impression of Gene Kelly as *An American in Paris* when he became bored touring the Louvre.

482

Bored at the Louvre? There were two more letters that, to my disappointment, included no poems. One page each saying he was lonely and tired and not finding the time he counted on to write.

Jim disapproved of my giving up college for a year to lend my ailing mother a hand. With Jim gone and friends breezing in and out over the spring holiday, I needed to nail down a regular job or go nuts in the solitude.

That accomplished, I was attempting to catch a little sleep before my new swing-shift job. I hustled out of bed to answer the insistent ring of the telephone. My mother reached the phone just before me. I made a dramatic turn back to my bedroom, determined to invest in earplugs, when she held the receiver out to me.

A faraway voice asked, 'Watcha readin'?'

'James, James, Morrison, Morrison!' I began, then couldn't remember the nursery rhyme. 'How does your garden grow?'

He chuckled. 'You have a way with a misquote,' he said, then hesitated. 'It's a dust bowl. I'm walking Montmatre singing Woody Guthrie songs.'

We both could see Jimi Hendrix singing 'Deportees' for us in San Francisco. 'Sounds pretty desperate. The writing isn't going well?' I asked. He'd hinted at writer's block in his brief letters.

'Not going at all. I thought talking to you might help. This is a bigger strain than I expected,' Jim admitted. 'Pamela is having this fantasy about our getting back together. She seems to have confused the public image we've had for some time with the reality of this trip. If she introduces herself as Mrs Morrison one more time, she's going to have to slap me out of hysterics!'

Jim realized he was on a tirade and laughed, then paused to explain that he had given a stranger an excessive *pourboire*, French for tip, to use his phone in privacy. He'd warned me before he left, he was on a shoestring and there would be no calls. Delighted by the sound of his voice, I had to make myself pay attention to what he was saying.

'What makes dealing with Pamela worse is that I can't write worth shit. I keep telling people about this novel I'm working on. Don't remember what the hell I've told them, but it sure isn't on paper. September seems awfully far away.'

I ignored his complaining. I couldn't do anything about Pamela or the calendar, so I went to the crux, where I could help. 'So, Jim, tell me about this novel you are writing.'

He snorted. 'Knew there was a reason I called you. It's about a guy on trial. I'm trying to be honest, fictionally. But I sit with paper in front of me, and I can't write a goddamn sentence. Did I ever write anything? I can't remember what I sounded like.'

'If you can fucking talk you can fucking write!' I said as forcefully as I could.

'Whoa, I am a bad influence on you! Never heard you swear before. You still blush every time *I* say fuck – which is half the fun of saying it.'

I believed I'd let out a good goddamn and the occasional hell in his company. If not the F-word. I laughed. 'Did I use it right?'

'Not real creative, but effective. Swell first attempt. Made you sound real pissed at me.'

'I'm sorry, I can't stand it when you are so hard on yourself. This is a big change in your life. Trying to end things with Pamela, the band, and LA. Give yourself some time.'

'You are so sweet. You apologize for telling me I can write. I wish I felt it. I was hoping . . . I was wondering . . . if you would help me with this book.'

'Want me to hold the flashlight?' I offered.

'That was a good night,' Jim said. There were two of them, but I didn't correct him. Too obsessive about details. 'I'd sell a chunk of my soul for another one like it. But, no. I was hoping I could talk you into holding the pen.'

'Ah, Jim. Things *are* dry. Anything I can do, you know that, but the one time I tried to write like you, you emphatically told me it sucked.'

'Did I? Why didn't you slap me?'

It was on paper. 'I'm non-violent . . . and you were right.' You were in Hawaii and I was in Maine. The logistics were impossible.

'I was thinking that if you could rough out a chapter, I wouldn't be looking at blank pages.'

'You have such an American rhythm, maybe you are out of sync with Paris.' I thought a moment, fearing the cost of transatlantic thought. 'Go listen to some blues. Come out singing your novel.'

The silence was so long on his end, I started to ask if he were still there. 'Most loving advice nobody's ever given me. You always find a way for me.'

Jim's next letter implied the writing was rolling; the next, a false start. Then he wrote a postcard claiming at least he was writing a poem about the blues. I stood at the mailbox laughing. On the very day I received the postcard, Jim made a second call.

He started out with, 'Guess who I met today at a sidewalk café?'

His voice was so bright, I answered, 'Anaïs Nin.'

She had been my introduction to Paris through her diaries, and I would ever be grateful to her for inspiring Jim to write 'The Spy'.

'Who else but you would answer that?'

'Henry Miller!'

'And you are *so* close.' Jim chuckled. Did it matter so much that he was way off in Paris when we could talk? 'I was having a glass of wine, writing a never-ending letter to you, and eavesdropping every time I heard an English word, when I heard, "In the early days with Otto . . ." I look up and there is a woman in her sixties, dramatic eyes, hair pulled back, and I stand up and say, forgetting I am interrupting her mid-sentence, "Excuse me, are you Anaïs Nin?" slaughtering her name the way I always do, and she says, "No."'

'Damn it!' I said, an involuntarily reflex.

'Don't swear, dear,' Jim scolded. 'She knows Anaïs. And she is a psychoanalyst who studied with Otto Rank – the very woman you told me to find, and I have refused to find! Her name is Deirdre. That's why I'm here, isn't it? We talked all afternoon about being well and creative. And I have an appointment to talk with her tomorrow.'

Otto Rank was the analyst Anaïs fancied who was convinced that creativity and sanity could co-exist. There was a part of Jim that balked at operating within a normal sphere for fear of losing his creative edge. Jim had written that first Christmas poem about coming to me for one thing, and leaving with another. He was finding the same was true of Paris. He had gone to help Pamela and found help for himself.

'Oh, Jim!' I screamed with childish delight.

'Was that a scream? I feel the exhaustion lifting already.'

When he hung up, I dug out the signed *On the Road* Jim had

given me from its hiding-place with his love letters. I cut airmail paper to fit its measurements and shuffled them into the book. I included a note as if I were Kerouac, '*Use my voice until you find your own.*' No matter what else was going on in his life, Jim needed to be writing. I knew the basic truth he had taught me and he had forgotten: TO WRITE, WRITE.

When Jim received the book he called to cry in gratitude, then read from a Western for ten minutes. 'I bought it off an American college kid. Louis L'Amour. It's called *Reilly's Luck*.'

'Guess this means I can safely assume you're homesick.'

'Yeah, talk American to me, baby,' Jim said, his voice soft and sexy.

'I'd like to hear what you've written,' I said, hoping I was encouraging and not backing him up against a wall.

He read from a long poem he had teased about in his postcard. A man in Paris reflects on America. The expatriate has a love/hate relationship with his own heartbeat of a country. His reading commenced, as he frequently began what he called dry readings, Dry Water – no music, with his voice soft and uncertain. His voice grew deeper and louder as the reading progressed. The new poem was angry.

After he read it, he asked, 'Would you call that a whole poem?'

'Can you afford to read it again?' The long, long distance made me anxious, but Jim didn't need a false shoring up.

'Can I afford not to?' he asked. 'You tell me the truth.' He read the poem again.

'Whole,' I said.

'That's with a *W*, right?' he asked, but hung up, laughing, without waiting for an answer. The poem had enough pussy, cunt, and whore references to deserve the question.

A photograph in my family album had entranced Jim. Taken at the beach in Casablanca, it pictured my brother seated with my sister between his legs, and me, a baby blob in a sun-hat, between my sister's. Not an unusual shot of all the kids in a family squinting into the sun, but Jim loved it. When Jim went to Morocco, he sent me a postcard with stick figures lined up as we three children had been in lieu of a written message.

I had made a notebook for him from leftover rice paper we used to cover the windows in Stockton. In a book on traditional Oriental crafts, he discovered that the Orient had discovered dyeing paper as we had long before me. I was heartbroken my idea was not original, but Jim reveled in proof that there was a cosmic consciousness. He returned the notebook filled with short poems he had written in Morocco. To my delight, he had incorporated a bit of my dream poem he had corrected in my diary.

A long letter followed in which he detailed an opera, more *Porgy and Bess* than *Madame Butterfly*, he was hearing in his head. For the first time, he didn't mind that lions were stealing his sleep. He wrote about searching for a tutor to teach him the wonders of musical composition, because, he admitted, he misunderstood what a downbeat was and had explained it to me wrong. Whatever his misinterpretation, he enabled me to fingersnap him through the bluesy 'Spy' for my first slow dance. He added a *P.S.* that he was quite certain that *Coda* was just what he thought. I finished him.

Thirty days hath September, April, June . . . Yes! It was the last day of June. Jim's calls were infrequent, but long. The thirtieth of June, his voice was so tired, I wanted to send him my exuberance over the wire.

'I woke up with a song in my head about the dream you described in your last letter,' he said. 'That line *I dreamed we met in Guadalajara* just stuck with me.'

Jim loved other people's dreams. He'd ask strangers in movie lines, 'What did you dream last night?' When I woke up, he'd ask, 'What did you dream?'

I asked, 'What in the world rhymes with Guadalajara?'

He laughed wearily. 'I cheated and split the line.' He paused. 'I have something difficult to tell you.'

My heart stopped. He didn't sound depressed. I asked, 'Is this a goodbye call?'

'Hell, no! It's a hello call,' he took a deep breath. 'Pamela and I had our last fight. She made confetti of all my recent work. She's never destroyed my writing before. I told her that ends my obligation to her.'

A hello call! 'I'm sorry about your work, Jim. When things calm down, I'm sure you can recreate it. I remember a lot of what you read to me.'

'With my new writing and my feelings for you, I feel as if I'm emerging from a chrysalis.'

New writing. 'Looking for a safe place for your wings to dry?' I asked, happily offering my new place. At long last, I had a real sanctuary to offer.

His answer was a breathless, 'How deeply I love you!' He talked on, but that was enough to give me chills. 'I was running that last visit through my head. You said you were *in* love with me, not that you loved me. I was concentrating on the speech I made, so it didn't soak in. I was wrong to do this. Pamela's crazy.'

Jim wanted to fly back to Morocco to pick up something for me he saw on his trip there. I only wanted him to fly back to me. He delineated a careful plan. We were to meet in Mexico City, rent a car, drive to Guadalajara. 'It's about time our dreams came true,' he said, then he added, 'After a settlement with Pamela, I'm gonna be broke.'

'My $3.51 an hour will keep us under a roof and in paper,' I bragged. My last job only paid $1.70, so my pockets were jingling. My obligations were running down, too. I was finally moving into my own apartment that weekend. I told him about the apartment's wooden balcony where he could drag out a mattress and stare at what stars San Jose had to offer. 'What timing for American rebels to declare their independence!' The weekend would be the 4th of July holiday.

'Nice start,' he said.

'Continuing,' I corrected gently.

'Time to live with my best friend, the person I love most,' he said casually.

'You're that for me, too. It's the way people must feel who have family homes, places they return to. They see their front porch and know they're home. Toys in the attic. Bicycle in the basement,' I said. 'You're like that for me. I see you – and I'm home.'

'Rather be your front porch than anything.' To say the words made his voice tight with emotion.

Jim gathered his strength by telling me he had made a tape in a studio of his three new songs to send to the other Doors as a peace offering. Having given another stranger a roll of French paper for the use his phone, Jim took the time to sing the songs. I wrote down the lyrics on the newspaper that was spread out on the table. In case Pamela got her hands on them, I told myself, I'll have copies to present him at the airport. The songs were so beautiful, they made me cry.

My reaction drove him to say, 'Guess I should stop apologizing for the music in my head.'

He promised me credit for the 'I Dreamed We Met in Guadalajara' song. He apparently didn't get 'Watcher of the Skies' by the band since it wasn't on *LA Woman.*

'I like this,' I told him. 'I do no work and get credit.' Then I felt shy, his proving my letters were naturally better than when I tried to write poetry.

'You remember telling me you'd pick me up off the floor as many times as it takes?' Hesitantly, he asked, 'Do you still feel that way?'

When he said he felt too tired for one more fight with Pamela, I asked that he go straight to the Paris airport. I felt selfish, but also decided it was time that I was selfish – or at least time I was honest about not trusting Pamela. That she had inspired 'Five to One' with her screaming, 'You'll get yours, you son of a bitch, and I'll get mine,' didn't imbue me with confidence, even if Jim thought she was all bluff and bluster.

'I owe her a decent goodbye,' he said, making me wish I hadn't spoken of my admiration for his desire to end his relationship decently. 'A few days won't matter.'

Neither of us willing to break the connection, we went over the plan to meet in Mexico the next week, savouring every detail. If his appeal fell through, we could live in Mexico. We would make love under the palm trees. He made love to me verbally. He still wanted my help with his novel. He could talk and I'd take it all down, so he wouldn't stare at blank pages. That our passion so naturally included writing pleased us both. Part of what drew us to each other was that creativity was not separate from life.

'We're going to get ink all over the sheets!' he declared victoriously.

'I heard "Riders on the Storm" on the car radio,' I told him. 'I teared up and had to pull over.'

'It's about us, you know,' he said.

Singing in the tub aside, I thought it was about the band. 'I thought it was about the band. Us. Anyone in the struggle.'

'Yeah,' he agreed. 'But I wrote it for you. My world does depend on your being in it. Not just 'cause you've saved my life; you've given me life. Don't know how you can seem like the earth to me when you're the most spiritual person I've ever known. Our life will never end.' When he realized he was quoting himself, the way pieces of conversation worked their way into his songs, he laughed softly, 'Still laying songs at your feet.'

Becoming aware I was continuing to write down what he said as if everything he said was song, I lifted my pencil. 'Not where your songs belong.'

He laughed a merry laugh. 'Yeah,' he said. 'I love you, darlin'. See you soon!'

Stephen Stills' new song, 'Change Partners', came on the kitchen radio. I turned it way up so Jim could hear some good American music. I relished Stephen's timing.

'I love you, Jim,' I said, more easily than ever before.

'Exquisite passion.' A message he had whispered to me and I was shy about whispering in return.

'Exquisite passion,' I said.

'I'm going to have to take a *long* walk,' he said, laughing full out as he hung up the phone.

29

❖

When the Music's Over

I buzzed around the apartment senselessly. The walls had to have shrunk. They couldn't hold me. Sure to have been a road hazard without a head on my shoulders, I half-ran, to the mall to buy notebooks. If I were going to meet Jim in Mexico, I needed more paper than wardrobe.

I bought six tablets in a crisp white with green lines. How could Jim write a novel on those steno pads he'd taken to using? I picked out a bound notebook for his private thoughts and a handful of pens. I bought a ream of typing paper. Neither of us were great typists, but we'd get his novel off to the publisher between us. And by Christmas, I decided. I counted the months on my fingers like syllables to a song line. Jim had told me that he never counted syllables, that he made his lyrics fit the music. The pause in 'Roadhouse Blues' was a wink at me to prove he could no matter what it took. I'd coax him fit in a novel in the music of half a year.

The bright one-bedroom apartment I'd rented for myself would easily accommodate two. Except in the kitchen. The kitchen was so small, it had to be evacuated to open the oven door, but there was a window over the sink for daydreaming while doing the dishes.

At my parents' apartment, I packed books, clothes, art supplies,

and my meagre record collection. That accomplished in an afternoon flurry, I bought a map of Mexico. I had my hair trimmed.
Jim would notice every missing inch. You'd think it was his hair
the way he doted on it, but it still reached my waist. I dressed in
my grubby clothes for work, sorting mail in the bowels of the post
office. As I was about to leave, the thought crystallized that I had
no passport. Did I need a passport for Mexico?'

The phone rang. A heavy French accent asked for me and
declared, 'Your party is on the line.'

Jim never called person to person. Jim never called at that hour. I
was still trying to count hours backward – forward? – to Paris when
I asked, 'Jim?'

'Baby's dead,' Pamela Courson's voice said, then silence.

My first thought was, *She killed him!* They had one of their
insanely dramatic fights and he had backed off the curb into a
French taxi. He had missed his step roof-walking to prove he
was sober.

'What happened?' I asked, twitching like electricity had been
shot through my body.

'He OD'd,' she said.

'That's not possible,' I argued.

'He'd been drinking, just a few drinks the evening before and
when we got to our flat, we had an argument. Just a tiff,' she
assured me. 'He caught me sniffing and he did some heroin,
too . . .'

I interrupted, 'You mean cocaine?'

'He thought it was . . .' she said quickly. 'And he got sick and
wanted to take a bath because he felt hot.'

That didn't sound much like Jim. If he were hot, he'd take a
shower. Even if Paris flats didn't have showers, Jim would never
have bathed alone.

She went on, 'I went out . . . when I saw he wasn't in bed, I
went to check on him. He was still in the bathtub. I told him to
get his shrivelled ass to bed, but he was asleep. I couldn't wake
him. I couldn't lift him out of the tub.'

When she paused for a breath, I jumped in, 'What did the
doctor say?'

'There wasn't one.'

I panicked. Jim could still be alive. Hadn't I thought her dead when I couldn't rouse her in Los Angeles? 'How do you know he's dead?' I asked, near hysteria. I snapped orders at her. 'Go to him. Pull the plug. Get in the tub. Resuscitate him!'

'Oh,' she cried. 'I did that. I called the fire department. They said he was dead. They said there was nothing I could have done. He was gone.'

Jim was gone.

'Could you think of a story?' she asked in a little girl voice. She complimented my intelligence. 'I don't want people to think he died like Jimi and Janis. I want him to be remembered as a writer, like Hemingway.'

Not quite like Hemingway, I thought. Hemingway shot himself. 'Five to One'. I was angry for her not knowing that. And for being there instead of me. How could she stand by and wait for the fire department to arrive? Why hadn't she done something? Anything. I tried to breathe. I tried to be more generous. She thought of Hemingway because Jim had taken his present, *A Moveable Feast*, with him. She could be looking at the book lying nearby while she talked.

'He was so depressed,' Pamela sighed, 'I'm afraid he killed himself.'

I weighed her feelings of responsibility for a few seconds before I told her the truth. I knew from my brother's death, the heaviness of the guilt of a loved one's suicide outweighed what jealousy she might feel that Jim and I had so recently been in touch.

'I spoke to him Wednesday, Pam. He wasn't suicidal,' I said. 'You know, I've pulled him off some emotional ledges and I can read his voice as well as what he says.'

I ended the truth there. No point in wounding her with his plans to meet me in Guadalajara. That was between Jim and me. She must feel as awkward, lost, and disbelieving as I did. She needed to hear the voice of someone else who loved Jim.

'Do you have someone in Paris to help you through this?' I asked.

Relieved she said she was in good hands, I stood shaking and boneless, upright only because I was leaning against the wall.

'Jim recently told me,' she said, 'that he trusted you more than

493

anyone else on earth.' She promised to send me some things she knew I had given Jim, then asked, 'Will you support me if I can get a doctor to say Jim died of natural causes?'

Suddenly? At twenty-seven? I didn't believe my agreeing would bear much weight. 'What doctor would do that?' I asked bluntly, too shocked to couch it more politely.

'I thought I might pay someone,' she suggested, but was concerned about money and went on at length about her straits. I counted that as her being in shock. I was.

I hated myself for feeling that her compliment about Jim's trust of me had been a down payment for my silence. Not knowing if it were the moral thing to do, I said softly, 'Just so you don't say it was suicide.'

Dead was dead.

Pamela was adamant about not wanting an autopsy. She insisted fans would carry away pieces of Jim's body. When I couldn't listen to grisly detail any longer, I cut her off by recommending she call someone to come stay with her.

'I'll go home and do that,' she said and hung up.

Where was she? Jim! His peyote vision of a death pool seeped into my mind. My legs gave up. I slumped to the floor. My mother came out of her room, saw me on the kitchen floor, the phone screaming like a siren in my hand.

She asked, 'What's wrong?'

An echo from a canyon, I heard my voice say, 'My friend Jim's dead.'

And she asked, 'The poet?'

30

And I Know

In the week following Pamela's call, I was a hollow reed. Wind blew through me. My father and a friend from high-school had used the station-wagon to move me into my new apartment. I hadn't even directed their efforts and dragged the mattresses and the dresser around after they left. I hadn't cried about Jim.

My five-day-old telephone rang for the first time. I lifted the white receiver to my ear and said a suspicious, 'Hello?'

'Hello, this is Bill Graham. Is this Ginger?'

'Yes, hello,' I said with more warmth.

My mother had given him my phone number. My older sister had cautioned her I was grown up and on my own and to let me call her, so my mother hadn't used the number herself.

Mr Graham growled, 'I wanted to express my sympathies about Jim.'

I thanked him, despite the growl.

'How are you doing?' he asked.

Jim and I coveted our privacy, but I hadn't realized how alone I felt until that moment when someone who knew Jim cared about my feelings. With his death, I discovered how much of my life belonged to Jim. I wasn't sure if I felt more like an orphan or a widow.

'I don't quite believe it. I just talked to him last week.'

He hesitated. 'I don't know if anyone has been in touch with you, but Jim was buried in Paris yesterday. There was a lot of us who would have liked to have paid our respects. I was wondering if you would like to go to Paris. I know it's hard to come up with travel expenses on short notice. I'd be happy to pay your way. I know how much you and Jim meant to each other.'

His whisking me through his entrance to hear bands for free more than made up for our less than cherished meeting, but to take me to Paris to say goodbye to Jim was the kind of generosity I only expected of Jim.

'Thank you, Mr Graham,' I said, then after consideration, added, 'I would have hijacked a plane to get to Jim if he needed me, but I can't stand by his grave.'

Jim was buried. He'd spoken of wanting his ashes scattered from LA to north of San Francisco. How lonely he would be in Paris, heartbroken never to return to nature. He'd love to have been a piece of the desert, Big Sur, the Santa Cruz mountains, and north to Point Reyes, Ano Nuevo, where he said he had spent that perfect day with Bill Graham. Jim didn't belong in Paris dead any more than he did alive.

'I understand, honey,' Graham's voice was smoother than I'd ever heard it. 'You must be feeling pretty raw now. Let me give you my number and if you ever need anything, or ever want that trip – next week, a year from now, five years – no time limit, you call me.'

'Thank you. You're very kind.' The number Mr Graham offered sounded different from the one Jim had given me, so I dashed it off.

'You sure you're okay? If you need a loan or anything . . .'

I smiled, thinking of Jim willing to live on my pittance an hour. 'Oh, no. Thanks. I have a job. It's so thoughtful and generous of you, though. Thank you.' All I could think was *Thank you. Thank you*. We hung up, awkwardly, without goodbyes.

Fifteen minutes later, the phone rang again. 'This is Bill,' he began. 'I was wondering if things were left unsaid between you and Jim. This was so sudden.'

Summer was settling in for its long stay in California, but I forgot to ask Jim about the weather in Paris. Had it been hot in Paris the early morning of his death? Pamela phoned at 6 a.m. if they didn't keep daylight savings there. She had said he was hot. Drugs or the weather. *That was never true . . . Baby, they lied to you!* Jim's voice rang in my mind.

I wanted to tell someone how Jim felt the last time he called. 'Jim said he felt he was emerging from a cocoon and needed a place to dry his wings,' I continued. Jim had said *chrysalis*, but I wasn't certain of the pronunciation even though I had Jim's echo in my head. 'We've been that place for each other. We were going to meet in Mexico. I just keep feeling I should go to Mexico. Like he'd be waiting there.'

There was a sigh on Bill's end. 'What were you going to do in Mexico?'

I laughed. Our plans would sound ridiculous to anyone but Jim and me. 'I wrote to him about dreaming we met in Guadalajara. He thought it was time to make my dreams come true. He thought it would be a good place to start.'

Bill Graham and I were both fast talkers, but we weren't doing well on either end. We paused for our own thoughts about Jim before speaking of him.

'I Dreamed We Met in Guadalajara'. Jim had said that Robby could cut loose and play Spanish guitar to his heart's content. Though he saw The Doors as a white blues band, he couldn't escape California's other cultural influences. I was still running Jim's song through my mind when Graham's voice eclipsed the memory.

'I don't know if this will comfort you or break your heart, but Jim came to see me before he went to Paris. He asked me,' Mr Graham cleared his throat like Jim did when he struggled for words. He hesitated, and I waited. At last, he said, 'To be the best man at your wedding.' His voice broke. 'I'm holding your wedding rings.'

He went on, 'I don't think he ever explained a song to me in the years I've known him . . . always said, "That's for me to know and you to find out," or "Yeah, yeah," to anything I suggested, but he told me that "Riders on the Storm" was about the two of you and that the lines, *The world on you depends, Our life will never end*, were his proposal.' His voice cracked, 'He said it was better than his first one.'

When Bill's voice broke again, I broke, too. I tried unsuccessfully to make a coherent apology. Bill made a soothing sound in my ear. After I had been crying a long time, I said, 'I should let you go. You're so busy.'

Graham's usually gruff voice softened completely. He said, 'I have nothing more important to do than this.'

Entrusted with them for months, Bill Graham insisted on delivering the rings into my hands. I invited him down from San Francisco for lunch. Between my being vegetarian and his being Jewish – and not sure if he kept kosher, or exactly what it meant if he did – I wound up with what would have suited a ladies' luncheon.

I recognized the tilt of the hat as Bill Graham's through the amber glass in the top half of my blue door. Even in the heat of summer, he wore a snap-brim hat. For some reason, when I imagined Bill Graham, I pictured the satirist Mort Saul, so I was a little surprised as the real man's features fell into place. He gathered me into a warm hug, I thought so we wouldn't have to look into each other's reddened eyes.

Right away, too soon, he handed me a dark blue velvet box. I held it without opening it. We ate sporadically, trying to talk about anything but why he was sitting over homemade brioche stuffed with scrambled eggs and fruit salad at the card-table that had been my art space in my old bedroom.

'I'm sorry about the food. Jim made the best scrambled eggs, so I thought of scrambled eggs,' I explained, detailing his secret.

Bill Graham smiled. 'I never thought of Jim cooking.'

'That's funny. I was always a little startled myself when he did something practical.'

'There was something about the way he moved. His grace. I liked watching him. If that doesn't sound too strange coming from a man.'

My eyes kept drifting to the midnight-blue box. Bill Graham lifted my face to look at his. He said, 'It might be easier if you looked at them while I'm here.'

I intended only to take a peek, but the box sprung wide open. I jumped. The rings, side by side, were plain wide gold bands. Jim's didn't look much bigger than mine.

'They're engraved.'

Jim's wedding-ring rules. They only counted if they were perfect circles, engraved so you couldn't hock them. I lifted mine. Tears blurred the inscription inside the band. I looked at Bill Graham for help. He shook his head when I held it out to him. He didn't have to read the engraved words.

He told me, besides our initials, 'They say, *Our Life Will Never End.*'

Jim had said that in our last call, the one we didn't know would be our last. 'Jim believed we'd always known each other. He believed we were old souls.' *If you are right about reincarnation, Jim, hurry back into my life.*

Graham said, 'Jim said he had the worst time with the German jeweller, who kept saying, "It should be *love.*" That's when Jim called me. He had me call the jeweller to tell him in German that Jim was not crazy. I told Jim I could lie as well as the next guy.'

We both laughed as we left the table. Bill Graham held me, and kissed the top of my head. I closed the box. I wouldn't try the ring that day.

'I'm sorry Jim didn't get further in his short life. Seems like he's saying the same thing way back in "Horse Latitudes",' Graham said. 'He told me he wrote that when he was in high-school.'

'Oh, no,' I disagreed softly. 'They are very different songs. The imagery is similar, the storm, but they say very different things about life. In "Horse Latitudes", he's giving up, lost without a trace. In "Riders", he's not alone. He does not give his consent. He worked very deliberately on that.'

'Jim and I only had two long personal conversations. One was about our childhoods. The other was about you.' Graham wandered out on to the wooden balcony. He leaned on the railing. I smiled. The first thing I checked, knowing Jim's propensity for leaning, was the strength of the rail. 'What we had in common was acceptance, I'd guess you'd call it, of the inevitability of loss. We had a level of unspoken understanding I rarely feel with anyone, particularly younger, who didn't know the holocaust. Maybe he had his own. But the thing of it is, neither one of us could really love a hundred per cent. We hold back to protect ourselves. He said the exception was his love for you.'

'Thank you,' I said. Jim and I may never have defined our love, but we both trusted it was always there. 'Every once in a while, Jim would stare off and ask what that place was you took him that had the elephant seals. I'd tell him and he'd say, "That was a real fine day."'

'Yeah, I think that day meant a lot to both of us.' Graham went back into the living-room. I didn't want him to leave. 'I came here, in part, because I wanted to answer questions for you, but I feel like you can answer some questions for me.'

'Why don't we let Jim answer your questions? I have four years of letters.'

One of the pleasures of packing was to pry loose the staples in the box spring and move Jim's letters to a more accessible box of their own. Their bulk surprised my guest.

'Jim sent me a note once,' he said. 'I can't remember what it said. I remember laughing. I think it surprised me that he had a sense of humour. His songs are so serious.'

I told him about Jim's making me read *Finnegans Wake* as a hint that the first album sang in a circle. '"The End" is not the end, because you "Break on Through to the Other Side". The information produced a wide smile on Bill Graham's face.

We sat on the floor to explore the box. Graham read a few random letters. 'I feel like I'm intruding.'

'You were invited. I need to have you see them, more than you need to see them.'

'Jim's handwriting is very . . . boyish.'

I nodded. 'Once, on a lark, Jim and I had our handwriting analysed. This woman examined Jim's writing, which I always saw as open and young. She said he was a dark spirit because all his words ended with a downstroke and thought he'd come to a bad end because all his words did. I asked if he couldn't try to change his handwriting, and he laughed at my being so superstitious.'

The woman looked at my tiny script with curls and swirls folding back on themselves and told me I was *a keeper of secrets*. I resented the sharpness of the truth. I kept family secrets, Jim's secrets, suddenly Pamela's.

'All these songs he shared with you,' he held the mass of

song-filled letters, 'but I never saw you at The Doors' performances at the Fillmore or Winterland.'

'Early on, I just couldn't seem to get to a show. It became a private joke – that I was probably the only teenage girl in California who hadn't seen The Doors. The only time I did see them was accidentally. The day, um, we met.'

He looked nearly boyish himself. 'I still feel like a heel.'

'Well, you made up for it. That was a part of Jim's life he didn't want to subject me to. And I didn't want to subject me to. If it had been important for me to be there, I would have been. He started to think that anyone who wanted to hang out backstage wasn't a real friend.

'He loved to sing in the car. He liked to sing his own songs less. Except when he was writing. He did a show just for me at the band shell in Golden Gate Park because he was disappointed in the show at the fairgrounds.'

'I used to get so mad when he showed up drunk.' Graham shook his head.

'Part of that was shyness. He couldn't get up in front of all those people without a buzz. And, I think, Jim was such a perfectionist, drinking was an excuse why the performance was never perfect.'

'I guess nobody heard him sing much lately.'

'For my birthday. In January. Jim surprised me with a performance at a strip club, of all places. He didn't strip. He sang.'

I related the day from the spat rosebuds to the diamond ring. When I returned to the room with Bill Graham, I realized I'd been taken back to being with Jim so vividly, I'd forgotten I was telling the man much more than he was interested in hearing. I apologized.

'Oh, don't. I could picture Jim. It was like having more time with him than I ever got.' Then Bill Graham, the practical man, asked, 'Where's the diamond?'

He went to the door by inches. We'd stop and tell a story. Jim had bopped him in the head playing with a microphone stand and had brought him a hand-painted pith helmet for an apology and protection. So, I had to tell him about Jim wanting to keep the paint on his hands after we painted all night so

501

people would think he was a painter, a better thing to be than a rock-star.

In the open doorway, Bill Graham bent down for a startlingly passionate kiss. 'Just thought you needed to get that over with. Another man's kiss.'

The following day, a long narrow roll arrived from Paris. I wanted to tear it open if it were the last thing Jim sent me, but didn't want to see it at all if it came from Pamela. The poster unrolled into a two-and-a-half-by-three-foot close-up of a lion's face. A note torn from the corner of the thin brown paper the gift was wrapped in, was in Jim's biggest scrawl: *LA, What are you doing to please the lions . . . this day? Love, JM.* The postmark was faint, but I thought it read the first of July. The day after we talked, he'd sent a house-warming gift. He was ready to stare the lion down.

Pamela called wanting my new address. She had a box of Jim's things to send me. Our conversation was very polite and tense on both sides.

'Of course, I'm including the friendship ring you shared. Do you know how much that meant to Jim?' she asked. I couldn't tell if she was trying to be kind or hurt me. 'Jim put it on just before he died.'

A minute before? An hour? After we talked on June 30th? Before he took a bath? I could so easily imagine Jim spotting the lion poster and conning some French clerk into wrapping it, then stealing a corner of the paper for a note, but I could not picture Jim climbing into a bathtub to die.

My own voice was screaming in my head, 'Is Jim really dead? Is Jim really dead?' Over and over so there was no room for Pamela's voice at all. I had to ask. I felt no great snap as I would have imagined if Jim were no longer out there in the world somewhere. So, I asked aloud over whatever she was saying, 'Is Jim really dead?'

Silence on her end. Did I shock her or did she have to think about it? I thought, crazily, that maybe he was only hurt, or worse, brain-damaged. The longer the silence, the more I hoped there was hope. 'He's really dead,' she said at last, sobbing. 'I was there.'

'What happened?' I asked.

'Another time,' she answered. While both of us cried, she repeated that Jim was wearing the friendship ring when he died. When he left for Paris, the ring we had shared since our first goodbye was too small for him to wear on his ring finger. It had always been a compromise size, snug on him and loose on me. I imagined Jim beardless – he told me he shaved before he got on the plane – and a few pounds lighter. She said, 'I tried to call you to see if you wanted it buried with him, but your line was busy.' Was I talking with Bill Graham about the other rings? No, his was the first call and he had said Jim had been buried. She was lying.

I asked Bill Graham's question. 'Where's the diamond ring?'

'Oh,' she said carelessly. 'I'll pay you back. I had to pawn it for cash. Everything cost so much more than I expected. I'm his sole heir, so I can pay you back.'

If she thought a diamond that Jim thought of as moonlight on the ocean that he bought with his first big royalty check was the same as cash, I thought cruelly, let her be surprised when she was made aware of Jim's handwritten will that replaced the one he had written after my mother split us up in the winter of '69.

The anticipated box did not arrive; instead, Pamela telephoned to say she was at the San Jose airport. She had flown in on a whim. I was so afraid she'd disappear on me, I flew out of bed and into yesterday's dress. I ran a brush through my hair between shifting gears in my Volkswagen.

I was afraid I wouldn't recognize her, but she still looked more like my sister than my sister. Pamela Courson appeared tiny and translucent outside the low terminal building. She climbed in and asked me to park. When I pulled into a parking space, she threw the box she carried into the back and inched way down in the seat. She had to stretch to put her knees on the glove compartment.

'This is how he likes to sit and read while you drive,' Pamela said, speaking of Jim as though he lived. Looking up, batting her tear-soaked lashes, she added, 'He told me that. Can you imagine? He thought it wouldn't make me jealous!'

Jim was discreet, but when he told the truth, he was always aware of the repercussions. I wished she would call Jim by his name, not treat him as a secret between us. Pamela removed a

503

small envelope from her purse, ripped open a corner, and Jim's and my silver friendship ring fell into my hand.

What hurt me most was that in our years of trading the ring back and forth, for the first time the piece of silver was a cold circle in my palm. I slipped in on my finger.

'My life is in your hands,' Pamela said dramatically. For a moment, I worried I had inherited Jim's Beloved Albatross. She brushed the long fringe of bangs from her eyes and gazed directly into mine. Her hands trembled. Her cheeks trembled. Her nose was less perfect than I remembered it. 'I killed Jim,' she said quietly.

I automatically enclosed her cold little hand in mine. 'We all feel we had a part in his death.' I felt if I had been there, I could have saved him. If I had asked, he never would have gone. Why had I believed in holding him with an open hand? The cliché was a stone in my heart. Pamela had told me that Jim said the difference between us was that I would have done anything to save him, and she would have done anything to keep him. I would have asked him not to go to Paris had I only sensed danger. I'd read my misgivings as selfishness. 'We all are carrying guilt.'

Pamela shook her head. 'He told me the Thursday before he died that he was leaving.' The day after we spoke. 'On Monday, he was going to make arrangements for a settlement. He was gonna find someone to see me through. He was so quiet. I told everyone how depressed he was, but he was just . . . decided. He went out Friday night and came back late. I was out of it. He'd just missed my friend . . . There was a mound of my friend's heroin on the table. He asked if it was cocaine. I said, "Yeah."'

Jim asked and she lied to him. I withdrew my hand from her, fearing I would snap her delicate fingers. She twisted her own fingers roughly enough to bruise them. She said, 'As soon as he inhaled it, he grabbed his chest and fell on one knee.'

I bit my lip. The rusty taste of blood dribbled into my mouth. For the first time, I felt hate. Had I a dagger, I would have plunged it into her on reflex. 'Get out of my car.'

Pamela looked stunned by my anger, her eyes big. 'I did try to get help. When I got back with my friend, Jim was dead.'

'You left him to die alone?' That was a deeper betrayal than letting him take the wrong drug. 'Why didn't you call an ambulance right away?'

'Jim understood.'

When did he have the chance to understand? His loyalty to her killed him.

'Did he tell you that?' I asked angrily. 'Could he talk?' I asked in tears.

'He fell forward,' she said matter-of-factly. 'Like on his face.' Pamela yanked open the door handle and yelled, 'You want the truth?' I got out of the car so we were staring at each other over its curved roof. 'The son of a bitch said your name. I could have killed him!'

'You did,' I said softly.

'I didn't mean to! I didn't know he'd die! Are you going to call the police?'

My head was a hazy maze. 'Could I have Jim's *On the Road* back?'

She was mystified. 'What? What? My life is at stake and you want a book?'

'Is it in the box?' I asked.

She said, 'I left all that junk behind. I think I tore it up.' When she tore up Jim's novel, she made confetti of Kerouac. Jim had started his novel within Jack's. For the half-hour wait for the plane to Los Angeles, Pamela begged me not to turn her in. She couldn't see that the only evidence I had was a confession she could simply deny making.

Not until I took a break at work did I calm down enough to remember the box in the back seat of my car. In the parking-lot, I examined the box, not taped for mailing, but the flaps folded to hold it closed. On top was the white shirt I'd embroidered with lizards for Jim's twenty-fourth birthday. Beneath it, lay a pair of black leathers he wore with it – a woman's thoughtfulness in making an outfit for Jim at a particular moment in time.

There were paperbacks Jim had taken to Paris, but not the nudes of Jim. Not the screenplay. There was a green steno pad filled with phone numbers and doodles, lines from songs from several years' work. It was a looking-back notebook, not looking ahead. I laughed out loud over a page of *LA's*, wondering which

505

of his ladies he had on his mind. I was never jealous of Los Angeles. I only wondered what Jim saw in her.

At the bottom were a shoebox and drawings of mine Jim had on his wall, the bookcase and Jim's boots, and the sketchbook that was to have been my tiny portfolio for Otis. Inside the shoebox, torn into pieces no bigger than half an inch each, were my letters to Jim. When Jim had said Pamela made confetti of his work, he had not exaggerated. That was confetti.

I dumped the shoebox's contents in a trash can on my way into work. A drifting envelope caught my eye. Curious why one was spared, I rescued it. I sat on the back dock of the post office out of the line of flying mail sacks.

The envelope had no dramatic *In the event of my death* on it. Addressed to me at my parents' address and with a US stamp, it was an unmailed letter from who knew when. Inside was the gridded paper used in pads of unlined stationary. Out of paper, Jim had written a poem on it. Every birthday since we met, Jim had given me a poem or song. I thought he had forgotten, but he'd only forgotten to drop it in the mail. Pamela's letting me have the last birthday poem let me feel less an avenging angel, and more the bewildered teenager I was.

After a sleepless week I felt what I had the first night. Jim's instinct would have been to protect Pamela as he always had. I cared more about what Jim would have wanted than the law. Jim distrusted the law. The law hadn't protected us as children. The law had tried to destroy him. Jim had said justice and the law were not the same thing.

I placed a call to the number Bill Graham had given me and was surprised he answered his own phone. I had never reached Jim on a first dial and had assumed the same was true of all busy men. He repeated his, 'Hello!'

I considered hanging up, but said, 'Mr Graham, this is Ginger. The reason I'm calling . . .' What was the reason I was calling? 'Someone told me something disturbing about Jim's death,' I began, knowing I was being too vague, and disturbing barely met the requirements of describing what Pamela had confessed. 'I don't know whether to tell what I know, or keep silent. I feel Jim would want me to . . .'

'Keep the confidence?' he asked. 'You've always done that. Go with your instinct. Every time. Go with your instinct.'

'You sound like Jim,' I whispered.

'Want to tell me what you know? If it would help to tell someone, I can keep a confidence, too.'

I was never so tempted. Jim had said Bill Graham was the only man he trusted. 'I'd like to, but feel like I'd just be trying to pass on a responsibility that's mine.'

'Maybe you bear too much responsibility for someone so young. Let me be there for you since Jim can't.'

I thanked him, feeling Jim had left me a real legacy, someone I could trust.

A man, not the one with the European accent, answered the phone at Pamela's number, but she took my call. Without preliminaries I said, 'I feel that Jim would want to protect you.'

She sighed, 'Oh, I'm so glad you understand that. Jim is always doing what he thinks is best for me.'

'My condition is that you tell me exactly what happened.' Each time she told the story, she came closer to the truth. 'Don't try to protect yourself. You told me you were telling people Jim was depressed. Like you were planning this. That you were going to kill Jim and say he committed suicide.' I meant to ask every question I had.

'No. No. I just didn't want people to know Jim was leaving me. It was a horrible accident. I told you. Truly. Except, well. We didn't go out. He went out alone. He'd had a bottle of wine. He said he wasn't going to drink hard stuff any more. How many times did he say that? He was an alcoholic. He would have died from that eventually.'

'His doctor told him his liver was in fine shape. Jim certainly had more time with his drinking, and time to do something about it, than you gave him.'

'Jim said you were so nice,' she said bitterly. 'I always thought you were, too. You aren't being very nice.'

'Don't expect me to be nice, Pam. I've never hated anyone before. Whatever I do is for Jim, not you. What was the bathtub story?'

'Well, you see, I ran out and called my friend Jean de Breiteuil. I knew he'd help.'

'Why didn't you call from your apartment? Why didn't you call a doctor? How many times did Jim call a doctor for you?' I asked in a voice more bitter than hers.

'I know. I know. I wasn't thinking straight. I was high. I can't speak French. And . . . and I was afraid they'd trace the call to me.'

Truth, at last. 'You were alone with Jim? This Jean didn't force anything on Jim?'

'Jim and I were alone. You can ask Marianne Faithfull. When I called Jean, she was with him.'

'Why didn't Jean call an ambulance? Sounds like he could speak French.'

'Jean said if we involved a doctor or the cops that we could be charged with murder because he had supplied the heroin and I was there when Jim took it.'

'Why didn't you tell him it was heroin?'

'Well, he was so mad about my still using it. I didn't want him to be mad at me.'

I was scribbling everything we said on the phone pad. 'You would rather he died?'

'No. No, I honestly didn't know that would happen. Cross my heart.'

And hope to die. 'Was Jim alive when you got back to the flat?'

'No. I swear.'

'Why this lie about Jim dying in a bathtub?'

'I knew you didn't believe that. It seemed peaceful. That he sort of drifted away.'

I didn't like the hard and flat sound of my own voice. 'Instead of dying in pain.'

'Do you think he was in pain?'

'Pamela, you said he grabbed his chest.'

'I don't like to think about that. Jean figured out that if we put Jim in a hot bathtub, it would change the time of death, so he could get out of Paris. He was going to take Marianne to Morocco. And I could say I woke up and found Jim in the morning.'

I was distracted for a moment, by Jim's soft voice in my head saying, *the land of your birth*. 'Jim thought your friend Jean was responsible for Janis Joplin's death. Sounds so similar. He cuts out both times. You left LA right after Janis died.'

'That was a coincidence.'

I wondered. The night we met, Jim anointed me his lie detector. Four years later, I was Pamela's. If I believed she planned to kill Jim, not his love for her, nor his hate for the legal system would have kept me from calling the authorities. I went against my instincts and did what Jim would have. I let Pamela deal with her own conscience. I handed her over to karma, wishing I could have handed the decision over to Bill Graham.

In September, friends charged off to their colleges. I stayed with my night-shift job out of apathy. When I broke loose at seven in the morning, I often disappeared into the Santa Cruz mountains. I stopped at my apartment for forgotten hiking boots, and found Brandon de Wilde sitting on the top step. I hadn't spoken to him since the film project was set aside. There seemed so much to say when Jim died that I said nothing at all.

'This must be our annual meeting,' I said, bounding up the cement steps. He stood to give me a hug. 'How in the world did you find me?'

From his jacket pocket, Brandon extracted a blue envelope like the ones Jim had sent me from March to June. A repeated *Par Avion* made a red stripe across its width. The return address was mine in Jim's tidiest printing. The letter was addressed to Brandon. I wiped my tears with the back of my hand to clear my vision.

The postmark was Paris, the fifth of July. This was why Pamela couldn't keep her story straight. This was why I felt no great snap. This was why. He was biding time in Morocco. Mexico.

'It does say the fifth!' My heart hammered. 'Jim's alive!'

'Oh, no, honey. No,' Brandon's soft voice ripped through me. 'He wrote it the day before he died. It must not have been picked up until that Monday.' Brandon held my arm. I was shaking so badly, I couldn't get the letter out of the envelope. He took it gently from my hands and helped me up the two remaining steps. 'Jim sent the letter to a friend. He had no idea of its importance. I only picked up the letter last night. As soon as I read it, I jumped in my bus. I was waiting for you to wake up.'

'I'm sorry. I work nights,' I said, feeling the need to explain why

I was coming in instead of going out at that early hour. 'It pays a little more.'

Brandon stooped to take the keys from my limp fingers, afraid to let go of me while he unlocked the door. He fetched a glass of water and held it to my lips and brought the only other chair around next to mine. He laid the letter between us on the unfinished pine table I'd bought a few days before.

'Give me a minute,' I said, my stare fixed to Jim's using what had been my brand-new address as his. The mutual friend was David Crosby. The envelope was addressed to Brandon in care of David. For Jim to write a letter to Brandon seemed odd. I had pushed for Jim to include him in the scrapped film. Although he respected Brandon's talent, he was jealous about my innocent crush on him. 'Jim liked to give me presents in threes. This is the third message I've had since he died.'

Brandon straightened. My saying that had made him uncomfortable when it had comforted me to tell him.

'Would you like me to read it to you?' Brandon asked, taking the envelope.

'Please,' I said, though I let go of it reluctantly.

Brandon adjusted his glasses. I took the letter back and flattened it against the table to look at the neat printing Jim used for finished songs. Six words in his cursive could fill a line. This was the same neat printing he used on the envelope; neatly printed words, crammed up against each other. He had signed his name with the usual flourish, though with *Jim Morrison*, rather than his more usual *JMorrison*. I ran my finger along his name, then nodded for Brandon to begin. 'It's dated the second of July and starts out:

Dear Brandon,

Don't faint! Did you faint? Now get up off the floor and pay attention. I have a proposition for you. Would you be willing to trade some acting lessons for music lessons? I'm assuming you are as broke as I am, and it occurred to me we may as well do this exchange on stage and get paid for it.

Brandon interrupted his reading to say, 'I was struck by the energy in his writing. All the gossip I heard was that he was on a downward spiral. And you can tell from this, that wasn't true.' *Baby, they lied to you.*

I've been going over the screenplay that Ginger and I were working on when Janis died. There are some compelling moments that I'd hate never to be seen. I thought we could rework the bar scene into a two-character play. I'm going to go hard at it tonight, so that when I see her next week, Ginger can whip the dialogue into shape over a lemonade. Tonight, I bid adieu to wine.

'And that's another thing,' Brandon interrupted again. Jim called me Ginger, that pathetic old horse. 'There's a lot of talk about Jim not caring about his drinking problem. He just ran out of time. Pamela said he drank himself to death.'

'Pamela is lying.' The tone of my voice sounded cruel, so I added to what Jim wrote, 'Jim read a play by Albee that got him thinking about writing plays himself.'

She thinks we are going to spend a couple days in Guadalajara. I have in mind a couple of weeks. I'm trying to plan this so we can get married on the anniversary of the day we met, because I'm a romantic fool. I don't know what it makes *us* that I'm so sure Ginger will be cool about spending our honeymoon writing – except you can always tell which of us slept on which side of the bed because she writes in pencil and I write in ink. Sheets do tell!

I laughed. I'd been so hard a minute before, Brandon must have believed me demented. The sleeping dream I dreamed about Guadalajara didn't include writing, but our reality would have demanded it. 'That's so Jim,' I told him. 'No matter what we started out doing, we always wound up writing.'

'I think that makes you very lucky,' Brandon said, wiping my wet cheeks with the cuff of his shirt.

After Mexico, I thought we could stop in LA to lay this on you. I'm moving up north. Ginger has a place in San Jose, but she's been trying to run away to San Francisco since '67, so I think I'll pack her bags for her. I forgot to ask her if she signed a lease, but I bet I could break it without half trying.

I'll call Bill Graham tomorrow and charm him into letting us use one of his venues for a preview. I have some new music that nobody owns but me. I want to score the play like a film. I thought I'd use a jukebox. Ginger can tell you where that inspiration originates.'

Brandon paused again, waiting for the juke story. I told him about Jim's buying the hat off the cowboy on the main street of Gilroy. I ran the scene through my head, the movie we never made – Jim trading in his glide for a march, Credence and Patsy on the jukebox. For a moment, Jim was there between us.

I remember you were struggling with some songs. Maybe I can smooth out your songs and you can smooth out my acting. If you would be amenable to a three-way split, I'll have my lawyer draft something up. Give Jesse a wild hug for me.

Jim Morrison

Jesse was Brandon's young son. Jim had coloured with him on the floor of his motel room. Brandon patiently let me copy the letter into my slender new journal. His bringing me the letter made him the kind of friend I meant to keep in my life.

The February after Jim's death, Anaïs Nin lectured at the De Saisset Gallery on the campus of the University of Santa Clara. I presented her with a copy of The Doors' *Morrison Hotel* album, nervously explaining that her novel had inspired 'The Spy'. She invited me to send her a few pages from my journal.

I asked, 'How do you know I kept a diary?'

Anaïs answered, 'If I'd known Jim Morrison, even if I didn't normally keep a diary, I would have kept a diary!'

Jim would have been tickled she knew who he was. After reading the excepts I mailed, Anaïs telephoned from Los Angeles to tell me she thought Jim was my Henry Miller and offered to work with me on the two novellas I admitted to starting. One was about my brother, Bill, and the other about Jim – novellas-à-clef that

I envisioned fitting together like a clam shell. What held the two men together was Jim's unfinished film *HWY* which he based on a dream he had about my brother who had died before Jim and I met.

When I told Jim I admired Brontë's *Jane Eyre*, and regretted I was not so brave in my own life, Jim had said, 'Neither was Brontë. She was brave in her work and you will be, too.' So, at twenty I wrote two brave little books on the tablets I'd bought for Jim to write his novel, and tried to be brave when Anaïs and I went to lunch at Henry Miller's in Big Sur. She'd imposed on their years of friendship to get him to read my novellas and he was grumpy. When he hadn't said a word about my writing all through lunch, she finally asked him outright, which was not Anaïs's way.

'If she needs me to tell her she's good,' Miller barked, 'she's not the writer I think she is.'

He went through my manuscripts page by page, marking all my laboured typing up with big *T*'s and *F*'s. At the end, there were more *T*'s. 'Don't look like I swatted you,' he said. 'My first novel was the reverse. True and false. I don't have a clue about the truth of your story, just what's true to art.'

Soon after, my apartment was burgled. Though the television and stereo were piled by the front door, nothing seemed missing. Weeks later, when I lifted the box where I stored Jim's things on the top shelf of my bedroom closet, it flew weightlessly over my head. All those treasures I had packed away – the letters and notebooks, wedding rings, and albums were gone. All that remained were those things of Jim's mixed in with mine – books I hadn't returned, a poem on an envelope I kept meaning to put away, the friendship ring I always wore.

They were only things. Jim wouldn't have cared, but I felt the loss of Jim all over again. Threatened by the theft, I withdrew my novellas and Anaïs Nin abruptly withdrew her friendship. I turned to art, which I thought would hurt less.

Brandon de Wilde died mid-June when his VW bus was sheared by a semi in Colorado. Acting in a road company of *Butterflies Are Free*, he joked he just had to take his glasses off to play a blind man.

Bill Graham came to a few minor art exhibits I had in the Bay Area. Though we never spoke of him, Graham always brought a single white rose, as Jim might have. At the last show, he looked at the room with sculpted glass and metal envelopes and laughed. Everyone else who came to the show asked, 'Why envelopes?' I concocted a spiel on the history of the letter in art, but Bill Graham knew how personal they were. The small copper ones were love letters, the brass five-by-sevens his songs and poems. I'd enlisted a friend's father, by profession a guitar maker, to shoot three holes through one of them which he pulled off with the accuracy of a hit man.

Years later, Graham tracked me down in Arizona despite a marriage and half a dozen moves through three states. The answering machine kindly filtered calls while I was laid up with an undiagnosed illness. When I heard the voice out of the past ask for Ginger, I felt a rush of warmth.

'Mr Graham,' I said, 'what a wonderful surprise!'

He laughed that I still called him Mr and asked, 'Isn't it time you called me Bill?

I gave Bill a lame try. He asked how I was, a question I'd grown to loathe. I answered with what I told everyone, 'I've been side-swiped by the Pontiac of life. I need bodywork and can't get out of second gear.'

I preferred a laugh to questions I couldn't answer. Confined to bed, my joints so stiff I could barely move, I'd taken to dreaming up Hitchcockian plots in my head to keep my brain cells from running to the cliff like lemmings. As soon as I could hold a pencil, I thought I might write one down. Not that I ever stopped writing, I just let art take precedence when the truth became so hard to write.

The reason he had looked me up after so many years was to ask me to participate in a panel being created to collect background for *The Doors* movie he was working on with Oliver Stone. Refusing him was difficult. I'd never even read any of the books written about Jim.

I told him honestly, 'I still can't even listen to Jim's music.'

Bill Graham, who could probably have sold anyone anything, didn't try to sell me. Instead he asked, 'Who are you listening to?'

He always asked that, the way Jim asked, 'Whatcha readin'?' I had a good ear. When he would pull me out of line or mob in front of the old Fillmore or Winterland, I would stand at Mr Graham's elbow, shy when he introduced me to bands I didn't want to meet, just hear. I liked to think I was the one who told him that Carlos Santana would cross cultural boundaries, but I suppose everyone who heard Carlos at the Fillmore had said the same.

'Chris Isaak,' I answered, without fudging. His music was playing while we talked. I may have bought Chris's first album because he was Nick's little brother, but kept buying them because he was good. He incorporated all the sounds I remembered from Stockton into something of his own. Listening to Chris was like tuning in the closest thing I had to a home town.

Bill Graham was silent on his end, so I started to explain who Chris Isaak was. With my penchant for detail that amused Graham, I wandered all the way back to following his brother down the high-school corridor because of Nick's captivating voice.

He laughed. 'I didn't know that, but I know Chris.' Bill told me he had been deeply depressed about the whole music scene, gone out walking alone, and turned into a little club off Castro drawn by the music. Chris was playing. 'I listened to both sets,' his voice brightening as he remembered. 'When I went back into the street, I wanted to grab somebody and yell, "Music is alive again in San Francisco!"'

We traded stories for the first time since he'd brought me the rings. He offered to replace them. When I was feeling better he wanted to take me to Paris. He said, 'I'll drag you if I have to. I think you need to say goodbye to Jim so you can get his music back.'

I promised to send him the diary I kept from the days with Jim, telling him he could use the stories – the way Jim spoke, so much of it was *he said, then I said.* Bill returned it by messenger with a note: '*Put this in a vault and write your own book.*'

Time dashed away. Still doing my homework to the strains of television, I was taking a stab at a screenplay with MTV as company, when I heard Bill Graham's helicopter had crashed north of San Francisco. The world seemed less without Bill Graham in it. His sudden death brought me back to his telling me to write the book. Paris was never the way to get Jim's music back.

* * *

Music broke through the static on my car radio. The Doors' 'LA Woman' strained for attention as a scrawny coyote broke across the road. For nearly twenty years, my hand automatically reached up to change stations when I heard The Doors' definitive drumbeat, organ, guitar, or Jim's voice. But, distracted by the coyote, I let the music play.

'If he makes it,' I made the sort of bargain I hadn't made since I was fifteen, 'I'll write the book about Jim.'

The odds were against the coyote. That section of Shea Boulevard was a busy four-lane road on the outskirts of Scottsdale, Arizona, where the desert still fought civilization. When the coyote made it safely to sage and cholla, I idled at the stop sign listening to the song for the first time since Jim died. I pictured Jim sneaking into bed singing me the song's first lyrics that didn't quite rhyme. That better have been a real coyote and not a trickster spirit.

1

Index

TO PREVAIL

AN AMERICAN STRATEGY FOR THE
CAMPAIGN AGAINST TERRORISM